VCs

OF THE FIRST WORLD WAR

THE
NAVAL VCs

STEPHEN SNELLING

The
History
Press

First published 2002
This new edition first published 2013

The History Press
The Mill, Brimscombe Port
Stroud, Gloucestershire, GL5 2QG
www.thehistorypress.co.uk

British Library Cataloguing in Publication Data.
A catalogue record for this book is available from the British Library.

ISBN 978 0 7524 8733 5

Typesetting and origination by The History Press
Printed in Great Britain

VCs
OF THE FIRST WORLD WAR

THE
NAVAL VCs

CONTENTS

ACKNOWLEDGEMENTS

This book owes much to a great many people in many countries who have given assistance and support over rather more years than I care or dare to remember. From relatives of the recipients to fellow researchers, librarians to museum archivists, they have all made sacrifices towards a venture which at times has threatened to take over my life.

My debt of gratitude to them is immense and can never be adequately settled. However, I hope that they may feel that this book, so long in gestation and preparation, will go some way towards repaying the faith and trust they have shown me during the course of the project.

Many of them feature at the end of the book in the list of private sources which have been instrumental in my being able to shed new light on the lives of the men featured in this volume. To those I have not included, I offer my sincere apologies, but to name each and every one of them would have required another chapter. However, I cannot let even this brief acknowledgement pass without mention of the following: Gerald Gliddon, who talked me into three books when even one seemed a tall order; Jonathan Falconer, commissioning editor at Sutton Publishing, whose tolerance and understanding over a prolonged period is worthy of a medal in itself; Frank Gordon, friend and fellow journalist who has wielded a judicious pen through this and my previous two books without a word of complaint; Nigel Steel, of the Imperial War Museum, who never seems to tire of my appeals for help and guidance; William Spencer, at the Public Record Office, who helped me chart a course through the Admiralty archives and pointed me in the direction of a wealth of untapped treasures; John Mulholland, Kenneth Williams and Alan Jordan of the Victoria Cross Research Group, who have been unstinting in their support and practical assistance.

My greatest thanks, however, are reserved, as ever, for my wife Sandra, the single most important person in my life without whom this book would probably have remained no more than a half-finished manuscript gathering dust in a dark corner of the loft. Throughout a project spanning three books and half our married lives, she has been my inspiration, my soul-mate and my greatest source of encouragement. No medal yet exists that could possibly do justice to her sacrifice. Instead, I offer only my undying love.

PREFACE TO THE 2013 EDITION

Since the original edition of *The Naval VCs* appeared in 2002, there has been a surge of interest in all things appertaining to the First World War that is only likely to grow with the centenary anniversaries and commemorations just around the corner. The public's deep engagement with a catastrophic conflict that continues to cast long shadows has been marked by a rash of new books and documentaries. They range from the academic to the populist, from studies of grand strategy to deeply personal missions of remembrance. Among the myriad titles offering fresh perspectives on the 'war to end all wars' have been several devoted to Victoria Cross recipients and the actions in which their acts of valour were recognised. More biographies have made it into the public domain, and more family papers have surfaced in public archives to shine new light on some of the men who deserve to be counted among the bravest of the brave.

I am once again grateful, therefore, to The History Press and, in particular, Jo de Vries, the general history head of publishing, for giving me the opportunity to revise and expand my earlier work. Jo's support, allied to the great assistance of editor Paul Baillie-Lane, during this and previous volumes in the series has allowed me to add significantly to a number of the remarkable stories covered here.

An assortment of previously unpublished and little-known eyewitness accounts offers graphic new insights into some of the most celebrated naval encounters of the First World War, from Henry Ritchie's dramatic escape from the bullet-torn 'Abode of Peace' to Barry Bingham's last moments aboard the gallant *Nestor*, and from Rowley Bourke's daring rescue effort at Ostend to Edward Unwin's matchless heroism on the bloodstained shore of Cape Helles. I am thankful to all the archives, libraries and families who have allowed me to access the countless diaries and letters that have so enriched this new edition. In particular, I would like to place on record my appreciation to Alistair Petrie for permission to make use of his late father's recollections of his participation in the second attempt to block Ostend harbour in May 1918 and to Michael Lowrey, an acknowledged authority on German U-boat operations, for generously passing to me copies of war diary records relating to submarine encounters with the Lowestoft armed smacks *Nelson* and *Ethel & Millie* and the Q-ship *Stock Force*. The revelations contained in some of these accounts have allowed me not simply to revise my original account but also to significantly rewrite them, thus ensuring that a few more hoary old myths are exploded and, hopefully, consigned to the waste bin of history.

As ever, however, my greatest debt is owed to my wife, Sandra, who has continued to make sacrifices in support of a grand obsession, which, I am afraid to say, shows no sign of ending.

Stephen Snelling
Thorpe St Andrew
June 2013

PREFACE

I believe it was the late Margaret Pratt who coined the phrase 'The Aristocracy of the Brave'. It was to have been the title of a book about the Victoria Cross, which she spent years assiduously researching but sadly did not live to write. In so far as it ranks the holders of the country's highest honour at the summit of martial valour, it is both apt and gloriously evocative, conjuring images of a worldly Valhalla. Personally, though, I prefer the description proffered by the Prince of Wales, the future King Edward VIII, during his address to the assembled ranks of recipients gathered at the grand VC reunion dinner staged at the House of Lords in 1929. In his speech, he referred to 'the most democratic and at the same time the most exclusive of all orders of chivalry – the most enviable Order of the Victoria Cross'. This, to me, is the essence of a distinction that transcends class and rank, age and reputation, and serves to honour the virtues of leadership, selflessness and undaunted valour.

Such principles and qualities are manifest in the rich diversity of award-winners from the Senior Service during the First World War. The Royal Navy and its associated branches produced in Jack Cornwell and Frederick Parslow the conflict's youngest and oldest recipients of the Victoria Cross. It also produced heroes of all ranks, from seaman to captain, and from every strata of society. Furthermore, the awards bear testament to the resourcefulness and adaptability of the service's officers and men. During the First World War, naval servicemen were awarded VCs for feats of outstanding bravery on land and in the air as well as at sea. And, for the first time, the country's highest honour was given for acts of daring performed by a new maritime branch: the Submarine Service. Indeed, the variety of vessels in which Crosses were earned was never greater. They ranged from battleships to a humble sailing smack and included cruisers, destroyers, motor-launches, river-boats, converted colliers, a steam drifter and even a horse transport.

In all, forty-eight VCs were awarded to the men of the Royal Navy, Royal Naval Reserve, Royal Naval Volunteer Reserve, Royal Naval Air Service, Royal Naval Division, Royal Marine Light Infantry and Royal Marine Artillery – a relatively small number compared to the hundreds won by soldiers. This reflects not only the limited opportunities for acts of individual daring but also the high standards and sometimes parsimonious attitudes prevalent in the higher echelons of the service. This book tells the stories of the forty-two recipients whose awards resulted from naval operations as opposed to those won by aviators (R.A.J. Warneford and R.B. Davies) and by seamen and marines fighting in what were effectively army operations (W.R. Parker, F.W. Lumsden, D.M.W. Beak and G. Prowse). These have been covered by other books in this series.

A breakdown of these forty-two awards reveals that twenty-three went to regulars (including two wartime volunteers), nine to RNR men, five to the RNVR, two to the Merchant Navy (though both men were given ante-dated RNR commissions), two to the RMLI and one to the RMA. In all, thirty-two were gained by officers – an unusually high proportion, perhaps reflecting the greater degree of responsibility and influence that ships' officers and particularly captains have in any given action.

The engagements in which the VCs were earned were widely spread in theatres as far apart as the Atlantic and Mesopotamia, East Africa and the North Sea, and reflect the multiplicity of roles performed by the Senior Service as well as the changing pattern of naval warfare. A conflict that was, in part, a consequence of the tensions arising from an arms race conducted in the shipyards of Britain and Germany, where huge battleships were built by the score, produced barely a handful of fleet actions. As a result, only five VCs were awarded for 'big ship' actions (two of which went to destroyer captains), four of them in a single day's fighting at Jutland, and a figure matched by volunteers from the Grand Fleet engaged at Zeebrugge. This contrasts sharply with the fourteen VCs earned in either combating or waging submarine warfare, a figure which rises to twenty-five, and more than half the total, if you count also the eleven Crosses given for the operations aimed at denying enemy submarines access to the sea via the Belgian ports of Zeebrugge and Ostend. Of these, no fewer than eight went to officers and men manning Special Service vessels, better known as Q-ships – for the most part converted colliers carrying concealed guns. It was a mode of warfare which required cool heads, brave hearts and calculating leaders willing to risk self-destruction in their attempts to trap enemy submarines.

The navy's greatest Q-ship exponent was Gordon Campbell, an officer whose career was going nowhere fast until his transfer to decoy work. In the course of the next two years, he sank three submarines, lost two ships with a third badly damaged, and earned the VC and three DSOs to make him the most highly decorated naval hero of the war. For Campbell, courage appeared to be instinctive, almost an extension of duty. In this, he was little different from a host of naval officers who earned the highest award: men like Eric Robinson, one of Roger Keyes's 'thrusters' in the Dardanelles; Edward Unwin, who risked his life time and time again on the shores of Cape Helles; the submariner Martin Nasmith; William Loftus Jones, who fought on though his leg had been shattered; and Victor Crutchley, whose great courage was displayed in three ships in a single night. But there were other kinds of heroism performed by men who viewed war as something of an adventure. George Drewry, one of the young midshipmen heroes of V Beach, was one such. So, too, were George Samson and Rowland Bourke, the latter a young English-born Canadian whose eyesight was so poor that the Army had rejected him as unfit for service. He was not the only unlikely recipient of the VC. Geoffrey Drummond, a frail-looking motor-launch captain, described himself as a 'professional invalid' before the war, yet showed remarkable endurance and enormous courage in rescuing the crew of a blockship at Ostend despite wounds so serious he almost bled to death.

What unites each of them is a rare defiance, an unwavering bravery against the odds, whether battling through a maze of minefields, underwater nets, patrol boats and shore batteries to reach the Sea of Marmora or taking on an enemy battleship in a tiny steam drifter. It is often said that acts of courage in triumphant engagements are more readily recognised than those in failures, but the opposite seems to be true of the navy, at least as far as the First World War was concerned. Of the forty-two VC actions examined here only eight could be said to have ended in triumph, while perhaps eleven more may be regarded as partial successes. Victory or failure, every one of them represented triumphs of the human spirit.

In precisely a third of these cases that triumph was achieved at the cost of the recipients' lives, beginning with William Williams, the first posthumous naval award in the history of the decoration, and including Charles Cowley, who survived the action only to be murdered by his Turkish captors. Among those who did not live to receive the honours their courage so richly merited were Frederick Parslow and Tom Crisp, whose sons were also participants in the actions in which their fathers were killed. Parslow's gallantry in command of the *Anglo-Californian*, a horse transport, was significant for another reason: it helped bring about a change in the VC Warrant, making members of the Mercantile Marine eligible for the highest award.

To each of the forty-two men covered in this book, the Victoria Cross represented a passport to fame. For some this was short-lived and extended little further than their own locality. For others, it lasted a lifetime and beyond, as in the case of Norman Holbrook, the first submariner VC who had the distinction of having a town in Australia named after him. As celebrity goes, however, this was as nothing compared with the adulation bordering on mass hysteria which followed the posthumous award of the VC to the 16-year-old boy seaman, Jack Cornwell. The most famous of all naval VCs of the First World War, and possibly of any war, he provided a war-weary nation with an inspiring symbol of sacrifice and devotion to duty that one can only pray will never be required again.

I hope that this book will go some way to ensuring that his courageous example, along with all the other lesser-known heroes from Henry Ritchie to Harold Auten, will not be forgotten.

H.P. RITCHIE

Dar-es-Salaam, 28 November 1914

The *Helmuth* trailed a white wake through shimmering waters freckled with coral reefs. Ahead, the channel twisted past palm-fringed creeks as it meandered towards the harbour of Dar-es-Salaam, the Kaiser's 'Abode of Peace'. The war was almost four months old, yet it seemed part of another world. Everything about the white-washed colonial port, capital of Germany's East African empire, seemed calm. To the crew of the small armed tug, Dar-es-Salaam on the morning of 28 November 1914 represented a tropical idyll at odds with the conflict in which they were engaged. Petty Officer Thomas Clark would never forget the beguiling beauty of that African scene:

> Before us lay the wide sweep of the white pebbly beach fringed with waving palms above the top of which could be seen the houses of the town. Here and there massed clusters of red and purple bougainvillaea added splashes of colour to their gleaming white exteriors. The sun beat down from a torrid sky, blue as turquoise ... The houses on the shores, with their green shutters and shady verandahs, appeared utterly deserted ...

To Surgeon Ernest Holtom, the town's verandahs appeared 'cool and inviting'.

A young midshipman aboard one of the ships anchored in the bay was so struck by the apparently 'harmless' scene that he found himself recoiling at the prospect of being a participant in its ruination. 'It was rather an awful thought that we might have to shatter and destroy those quiet-looking houses in which lived women, and worst of all

– children,' he confessed. 'War is a ghastly thing, and it seems so wantonly stupid ... '

It was to avoid such a catastrophe that Dr Heinrich Schnee, Governor of German East Africa, had sought to keep the colony out of the war. He had even entered into a local agreement with the British, under which the port's neutrality was recognised in return for granting the Royal Navy rights to inspect shipping trapped in the harbour. But his unauthorised pact was repudiated by the colony's military commander and ignored by the captain of the light cruiser *Konigsberg*, which had slipped out of Dar-es-Salaam shortly before the declaration of war.

The first blow was struck by the *Konigsberg* on 20 September. In a surprise attack on Zanzibar, she reduced the elderly cruiser *Pegasus* to a smoking hulk. Six weeks later, Lieutenant-Colonel Paul von Lettow-Vorbeck dented British prestige still further when he routed a bungled amphibious assault on Tanga. Not until November did the British have good news to cheer, with the discovery of the *Konigsberg* in her jungle lair, deep inside the Rufigi delta, almost 100 miles south of Dar-es-Salaam.

Thus far, the 'Abode of Peace', ostensibly a demilitarised zone since Schnee's pledge, had been largely untouched by the conflict. However, Admiral Herbert King-Hall, C.-in-C. Cape of Good Hope, had grown increasingly concerned about the ships trapped there: the 5000-ton steamer *Konig*, the 6000-ton *Feldmarschall*, the *Tabora*, an 8000-ton liner apparently converted into a hospital ship, and a small steamer bearing the Kaiser's name. A floating dock had been sunk in the main channel, but it was unclear how much of an obstacle it was. Fearing that any one of the vessels could run supplies through to the *Konigsberg* or be used to block British ports further along the coast, the admiral decided to revisit Dar-es-Salaam. Plans were made to venture into the harbour to inspect and immobilise the merchantmen under cover of the *Goliath*, an out-moded and newly arrived battleship, and HMS *Fox*, a light cruiser. Though modest in scale, the operation was to have far-reaching repercussions and would result in the award of the first naval Victoria Cross of the war.

Heading the naval demolition parties was Commander Henry Ritchie. At 38, he was *Goliath*'s second most senior officer and had been given the independent though temporary command of the small cable ship *Duplex* which had been recently converted into an armed auxiliary. Although painfully slow, she was thought more than adequate for inshore operations. She was to be accompanied by the *Helmuth*, a former German tug boasting a 3-pounder gun, two machine-guns and an eventful war record. Seized in Zanzibar at the war's outset, she had already survived the *Konigsberg*'s attack and endured the ignominy of Tanga.

By 6 a.m. on 28 November she was back in familiar waters off Makatumbe island.

A German deputation came aboard the *Fox* under a white flag of truce and Captain F.W. Caulfeild, senior naval officer, explained his mission. He told the German party that the local agreement had not been ratified by the British government and that steps were to be taken to ensure the 'disablement' of the various ships as well as rendering useless or commandeering 'any small craft and floating stores that might be made use of against us'. Caulfeild made it plain that the *Tabora* would be treated as a prize of war and not as a hospital ship, although he stressed that any demolition operations would only be carried out with the approval of a British medical officer who would be sent aboard. Any opposition, he warned, would be met with the 'strongest measures'. The interview ended on a curious note. 'The acting Governor, to my surprise,' commented Caulfeild, 'asked me whether our boats would carry on their operations under the white flag to which I returned an answer in the negative.'

The operation finally got under way around 10 a.m. But by then the plan had already miscarried. First the *Duplex* had broken down and then the *Goliath*'s picket boat had blundered on to a reef. Forced to transfer his command to the *Helmuth*, Cdr Ritchie led off towards the harbour, his demolition party divided between the tug and *Goliath*'s following steam pinnace. White flags were seen near East Ferry Point and the scene was peaceful. Rounding Ras-Makabe Point, *Helmuth* swept past the *Tabora*, Red Cross flags fluttering at her mast, and made for the *Konig* and *Feldmarschall*, further along the creek. Both vessels were boarded, charges placed and the crews, mainly Lascars, taken off and placed under guard in lifeboats. Fifteen minutes before the first charge was due to be fired, they were interrupted by the sudden appearance of a launch drawing alongside the *Konig*. Aboard her was the Port Captain. A bizarre 'consultation' followed, in which the German official insisted on observing their inspection while a perplexed Ritchie reminded him that they were at war. Eventually, having learned what they were about, the German official departed, leaving Ritchie to continue his mission.

About this time, *Goliath*'s steam pinnace arrived with the other half of the demolition party, led by Lieutenant-Commander John Paterson. Leaving them to finish the task, Ritchie boarded the *Helmuth* and, with a pulling boat, went on down the creek, only to run aground. Eventually, having transferred stores to the other boat, *Helmuth* wriggled clear and Ritchie returned to the two steamers. Paterson's party were placing the final charge on the *Feldmarschall*, so Ritchie transferred to the steam pinnace and made another run down to the

Kaiser Wilhelm II. There, while charges were being fixed, he made a disturbing discovery: scattered on the upper deck were several clips of Mauser bullets, including some with their points sawn off. 'The ship was nearly ready for service, the ship's boats were on shore,' wrote Ritchie. 'It was decidedly suspicious, the crew had evidently gone to take up arms. I seized the ship's papers and also any German charts I could find.' He was not, however, to be deflected.

Leaving the steamer, Ritchie's party set about destroying a floating crane, a lighter loaded with pumping machinery, and three water tanks. Finally, as added protection against any mischief, they gathered together five lighters, lashing one each side of the pinnace and taking the remainder in tow, before slowly returning along the shallow waterway towards the inner harbour. Passing the *Konig* and *Feldmarschall*, they saw no sign of life. The *Helmuth*, its mission apparently complete, had gone, and *Goliath*'s pinnace, labouring under the strain of the attached lighters, was barely able to make 2 knots as she followed the twisting creek towards the sea.

At that moment, the 'Abode of Peace' erupted with bursts of fire from both sides of the harbour entrance. The shooting was directed at the *Fox*'s steam cutter, which had been inspecting the sunken dock. Caulfeild, who was aboard, wrote: 'Bullets were raining over and into the boat and through and against the thin iron plates rigged on either side of the boiler and around the coxswain.' Two seamen fell, but the coxswain, although twice wounded, steered out of harm's way. Then, as they neared the *Fox*, another explosion of firing came from the harbour's mouth. The target this time was the *Helmuth*. Towing two lifeboats filled with prisoners, she seemed to Caulfeild to be the 'centre of a hail of rifle, maxim, pom-pom (or small field gun) fire'. Lieut C.J. Charlewood, who was aboard the *Helmuth*, later recalled the shattering fusillade as the 'whistle and crack of bullets' combined with the 'deafening hiss of escaping steam':

> Our first casualty was the helmsman [he wrote], who collapsed with a bullet wound in his neck. With great courage and promptitude two seamen got him out of the wheelhouse and dragged him to a place of comparative safety. The naval officer in command seized the wheel, but was struck on the hand in less than a minute. Then I took over and, by great good fortune, managed unscathed to coax the tug through that inferno.

So numerous were the holes peppering her hull and funnel that when they were eventually plugged, she resembled 'a porcupine'. Charlewood could scarcely believe his luck. He wrote: 'I have never understood how we missed running aground in the narrow entrance or avoided colliding with the sunken drydock, for I think we passed on the un-surveyed side of this.' In all, five men, including her commander, had been wounded, and there were two further casualties among the prisoners in the lifeboats. They included the chief engineer of the *Konig*, who, when asked where he had been hit, replied with some venom, 'The bloody bomm!'

With *Helmuth*'s escape, attention then shifted to the fate of Ritchie's boat. 'We realised that the pinnace could hardly survive such heavy fire as *Helmuth* had experienced,' wrote Charlewood, 'but we were confident that the Commander would not surrender without a fight.' Worryingly, as *Goliath* and *Fox* rained destruction on the Governor's palace and the buildings lining the seafront, there was no sign of the small craft. We last encountered her, screened by steel lighters, making for the harbour entrance. Nearing the *Tabora*, Ritchie slipped three lighters he was towing in order to gain speed. As he did so, he suddenly noticed a small boat shoving off from *Tabora*. Aboard was Surgeon Holtom, who had been put aboard *Tabora* to check her credentials as a hospital ship, and a native crew. But just as Ritchie diverted to pick him up, heavy fire broke out from both sides of the creek. The commander was now faced with a dilemma. 'I could not get alongside of Surgeon Holtom owing to the difficulty of steering, and the boat swinging round on its own axis,' he later explained. 'Surgeon Holtom could not get alongside ... as the crew insisted in paddling for the "*Taborah*" [*sic*].' So, instead, he took the difficult decision to ignore him and press on 'with the object of drawing all the fire on the steam pinnace'.

In this, he was entirely successful. The small boat was peppered by pom-pom, machine-gun and rifle fire. Indeed, the range was so short and the pinnace's speed so slow it was impossible to miss. Sub-Lieutenant Lionel Lloyd fell dangerously wounded. Then two seamen were hit. All around was a scene of confusion, as the deafening roar of the Royal Navy's retaliatory bombardment mingled with the rattle of gunfire. To PO Clark, the pinnace's coxswain, 'it seemed that a veritable hornets' nest lay hidden behind the waving coconut trees'. Far from silencing the German guns, the shelling merely provoked a fiercer response. 'Bullets whistled overhead,' wrote Clark. 'Some rattled against the iron plates which had been rigged for the protection of the boilers and myself by the wheel amidships. Others shattered the woodwork of the lighters.'

The bullet-swept vessel forged on through a hail of fire that fortunately contrived to miss her vitals. The sea drew near, but rounding Ras-Makabe Point, she became the target for every weapon that could bear, including a 2-inch field gun. Clark recorded:

Cdr Ritchie sat calmly in the boat alongside myself through it all until a piece of shell struck his arm and he doubled up with a groan. The rest of the crew … and the demolition party were sheltering in the lighters. The next minute I was hit … and my place had to be taken by Able Seaman Upton. Then Upton was hit, and I, my wound temporarily dressed, went back to my old post. It was now clear that only by means of skilful handling would the little pinnace negotiate the most difficult part of the channel which lay ahead, and Cdr Ritchie, although he had been wounded several times since he was struck by the first piece of shell and was suffering great pain, scrambled towards the wheel and himself took charge of the steering operations. Meanwhile, I was trying to get our machine-gun, which had jammed, to work again …

The pinnace was a shambles. Most of the crew lay wounded and she was still drawing a fearful fire. Yet Ritchie, with Clark's help, succeeded in bringing her beyond East Ferry Point, where, in grim irony, white flags still flew. But as they neared the harbour's mouth, Ritchie was hit again, this time through the leg, and he sank to the deck, having brought his little boat through the worst of the fire. Leading Seaman Wilcox immediately took the helm, but the drama was not yet over. 'Owing to not knowing the direction to take we ran aground twice and nearly a third time,' wrote Gunner J. Egan. 'The third time it was decided to get the wounded into [the] steam pinnace from the lighters and slip lighters and ship's boat, which was accordingly done.'

Four distress rockets were fired, and Capt. Caulfeild, who had abandoned all hope of Ritchie's safe return, brought down covering fire. Two cutters, one from *Goliath* and the other from *Fox*, went to the pinnace's aid, but before they arrived she floated clear, cast off the remaining lighters and shaped for *Goliath*. When she bumped alongside, Ritchie and Clark were lying on the deck 'simply smothered in blood and barely conscious'. Hoisted aboard, his face 'absolutely white', Ritchie was immediately taken below where he was found to have wounds in both arms, his left leg and left thigh. It was around 5.30 p.m., and the desperate escape from the 'jaws of death' was finally over.

The balance sheet revealed three vessels disabled, a variety of harbour installations destroyed and thirty-five men captured at a cost of one man killed, fourteen wounded and twelve missing. It later transpired that the latter, who included Surgeon Holtom, Lt Cdr Paterson and most of his demolition party, were prisoners. Paterson's men were victims of a misunderstanding between Ritchie and *Helmuth*'s captain. Each thought the other was to have picked them up, with the result that neither did.

Two days later, the Royal Navy returned to Dar-es-Salaam in vengeful mood. After a morning's wait without reply to their flag of truce, *Goliath* and *Fox* began a systematic bombardment of the port that left fires raging along the seafront. The action served no military purpose and conspired only to stiffen resistance. Hardly had they departed than a war of words began; the British accused the Germans of abusing the white flag and the Germans claimed the British had broken their agreement by sending more than one vessel into the harbour. Even then, they claimed that Captain Friedrich von Kornatzki had only opened fire after the crews of the *Konig* and the *Feldmarschall* had been 'kidnapped'. It emerged that only two days before the operation, Schnee had sanctioned resistance to any attack.

Amid recriminations on both sides, one thing was certain. The men who ran the gauntlet of fire out of Dar-es-Salaam had shown incredible courage. Of nine gallantry awards granted, three went to the men in *Goliath*'s steam pinnace. Able Seaman George Upton, later lost when *Goliath* was torpedoed in the Dardanelles, was awarded the Distinguished Service Medal, but Vice-Admiral R.H. Peirse, C.-in-C. East Indies, writing on 9 January 1915, selected three men for special distinction: Leading Seaman Thomas Gallagher, coxswain of the *Fox*'s steam cutter, PO Clark, the pinnace's coxswain, and Cdr Ritchie, who had 'stuck to his post' until 'incapacitated' by his eighth wound. Clark and Gallagher were both recommended for Conspicuous Gallantry Medals while Ritchie was put in for a Distinguished Service Order. Both CGMs were granted, but Ritchie's award was upgraded, although by whom is not clear, to a Victoria Cross, which was gazetted on 10 April 1915.

Henry Peel Ritchie, the first naval VC of the war (but the second to be gazetted), was born at 1 Melville Gardens, Edinburgh, on 29 January 1876, the son of Dr Robert Peel Ritchie and Mary (née Anderson). He attended George Watson's Boys' College in Edinburgh (1883–85), where he distinguished himself at football, fencing and boxing, and Blair College before joining HMS *Britannia* as a cadet on 15 January 1890.

Ritchie was serving as a midshipman aboard the battleship HMS *Camperdown* when she was involved in a disastrous collision with HMS *Victoria* during fleet manoeuvres off the Syrian coast in June 1893. *Victoria* sank with the loss of 358 lives, including the commander-in-chief of the Mediterranean Fleet, Vice-Admiral Sir George Tryon, but the damaged *Camperdown* survived to reach Malta.

Qualifying as a gunnery officer, Ritchie earned high praise while serving on the *San Paulo* for a brave attempt to save a drowning seaman. Promoted lieutenant on 30 June 1896, he later served as a junior staff officer at Sheerness Gunnery School; he went on to become Army and Navy lightweight boxing champion in 1900 and was runner-up the following year.

On 31 March 1902 he married Christiana (Chrissie) Lilian Jardine, the only daughter of James Aikman, a wine merchant, at St Cuthbert's Church, Edinburgh. They had two daughters.

Ritchie was appointed to the *Goliath* on 14 March 1911, and by the end of the year had been promoted commander. Following the outbreak of war, he served as second-in-command, operating in the Channel as part of the 4th Battle Squadron, before being ordered to East Africa, arriving in the autumn of 1914.

Following the bloody action on 28 November, Cdr Ritchie spent six weeks in hospital at Zanzibar, before being sent back to England where he made a rapid recovery. By 13 February doctors at Plymouth Hospital were reporting his wounds as healed, with the only obvious sign of his ordeal being a deformed right thumb! Ironically, the injuries he sustained at Dar-es-Salaam almost certainly saved his life. For had he not been hospitalised, he would almost certainly have been aboard the *Goliath* on 12–13 May 1915, when she was attacked and sunk by a Turkish destroyer with the loss of more than two-thirds of her crew. Instead, Ritchie returned to duty in the same month that the *Goliath* met her end.

Cdr Ritchie received his Victoria Cross from King George V at Buckingham Palace on 25 November 1916, almost two years to the day after his East African exploit. Promoted acting captain, he retired the following year and was promoted captain on the retired list after the armistice.

A taciturn man with a sharp temper, he was a forbidding figure to many junior officers who saw him as something of a martinet, though such views were by no means universally held. A midshipman who served with him aboard *Goliath* wrote: 'Ritchie had the reputation for being very strict, but I always found him most fair.'

He retired to Edinburgh, living at Craig Royston House, Davidson's Mains, until shortly before his sudden death on 9 December 1958, at the age of 82. His body was cremated at Warriston after a funeral service in the Cloister Chapel. Almost half a century on, no memorial tablet is thought to exist to commemorate the hero of the 'Abode of Peace'.

N.D. HOLBROOK

Sari Sighlar Bay, The Dardanelles,
13 December 1914

Tension had given way to relief, but the backwash of excitement had barely subsided as the high-spirited commander of HM Submarine *B11* tried to put into words the most extraordinary few hours of his life. Norman Holbrook and his crew were the toast of the navy's Mediterranean Detached Squadron for a feat unparalleled in war: the destruction of an enemy battleship in one of the most heavily defended waterways in the world. In an exuberant letter to his parents, the 26-year-old submariner told of being showered with congratulations for his 'stunt' and signed off with a mixture of modesty and ebullience: 'Wasn't it a bit of luck? All I can say is, lay on McDuff, I am ready for the next ...'

The reaction of some of his crew was more subdued. Leading Seaman Wilfrid 'Fred' Mortimer was merely grateful to be alive. 'Honestly speaking,' he confided, 'there was not a man expected to see daylight again when we went below on the Sunday morning to dive ... It was a 9 hours' wonder, expecting to be blown up any minute.'

On the face of it, *B11* was an unlikely contender for a place of honour in submarine history. Built in 1906, she measured 140ft, carried only four torpedoes and was driven by a sixteen-cylinder petrol engine which gave her a maximum surface speed of 12 knots and a top speed submerged of about 6 knots – but even that could be attained only fitfully owing to the constraints of her limited battery power. Conditions on board were primitive. There were no dividing bulkheads. The seating and bedding were portable and ventilation for the crew's quarters was non-existent so that the air reeked of slops and stale sweat laced with petrol. 'Sometimes,' observed Admiral Sir William Jameson in his book on submariner VCs, 'the fumes caused a form of drunkenness. It was a little like living inside the bonnet of a motor car.' Certainly there was almost as little space. Even a crew of two officers and thirteen ratings was sufficient to make her seem overcrowded. When war broke out, *B11* was already effectively obsolete. Yet she was still, by virtue of a new battery, the best-equipped of three B-class boats that slipped into Tenedos on 6 September 1914.

Turkey was still at peace and the little fleet's role was to keep a watch on the Dardanelles, one of Europe's most sensitive waterways, 15 miles distant. In particular, they were to guard against a breakout by the battlecruiser *Goeben* and the light cruiser *Breslau*, which had eluded the combined might of the Allied Mediterranean fleets to reach Constantinople. For a time, *B9*, *B10* and *B11*, under the overall command of Lieutenant-Commander George Pownall, were the only submarines in a fleet dominated by the French. Their work was dull and wearisome. Throughout October, they patrolled the mouth of the Dardanelles from dawn to dusk, two days on and one day off. It was a routine that continued after 5 November when the stand-off turned into a war.

Their burden was eased by the arrival of two French submarines, and a spirit of friendly rivalry was quickly formed as the two allies competed for the 'honour' of making the first raid into the lower Dardanelles. The idea of such an operation was said to have come from the French, who were the first to go beyond Sedd el Bahr. But that feat was soon dwarfed by Holbrook's chase of a torpedo-boat 4 miles into the mouth of the Dardanelles. The next step was to strike right through the Straits and attack enemy shipping around Chanak, where a sliver of water separated Europe from Asia Minor.

The operation presented an immense challenge. Naval historian W.G. Carr compared it to attempting to 'cross the Sahara in a 1909 Ford'. The narrow corridor was covered by a rash of forts and coastal batteries and there were reports of five lines of mines spread across the fairway, though their location was not known. Patrolled by day, the waters were lit at night by a cordon of searchlights. And to add to the problems, nothing was known about the strength or the direction of the current at varying depths. All that Pownall knew for certain was that the surface current was fast – 4 knots through the Narrows and 2–3 knots from the Narrows to Kum Kale – and that for a submerged B-class submarine to make any headway it would have to run at close on its highest speed, placing enormous strain on its batteries. There was, as Captain C.P.R. Coode, Pownall's immediate commander, acknowledged, only one choice among the British boats: *B11* with its brand new battery.

As senior officer, Pownall was originally chosen to lead the attempt, but this was thought unfair on Holbrook, who was equally keen to make the first try. He later recalled:

> Well, of course, I was young and foolish in those days and I said, 'Oh yes, I'll have a crack at it. Certainly, I'd like to.' But, of course, it was the daftest thing I've ever done, because a B-boat could never possibly get there. She hadn't got the battery power. It was against the tide. Our underwater speed, I believe they say in the books it was eight knots, well, I've never known a B-boat do much more than six. And if you were going to do six knots under water, it would last for about half an hour with any luck …

Preparations for the operation began in earnest on 3 December. Engineers started work, fitting a 'jumping wire' and improvising makeshift guards around the submarine's bow cap and hydroplanes to prevent mine moorings fouling the boat. By the second week of December the job was complete. A trial run against a simulated mine mooring was carried out and deemed a success. No amount of testing, however, could disguise the risky nature of the enterprise. Leading Seaman Mortimer, *B11*'s helmsman, noted that 'nearly all made out their wills and gave cash to their chums in the other two submarines to forward it on to their parents'.

There was one final addition, not to the boat but to the list of crewmen. Shortly before leaving Tenedos, *B11*'s small complement was boosted by the arrival of Petty Officer William Milsom. A member of the submarine detachment's spare crew, he had volunteered specially for the mission. Milsom was an extremely experienced hand, but came with a reputation for drunkenness. One such binge had just cost him three good conduct badges. However, Pownall was convinced his virtues outweighed his vices, even though it meant adding to the congestion aboard the submarine. He later wrote: 'His qualifications as a Petty Officer have always been excellent except in the matter of sobriety.'

By 12 December everything was ready. At 3 a.m. the next morning, *B11* cast off. The sea was calm, the night still, and she was quickly consumed by the darkness. As far as Holbrook and everyone else in *B11* was concerned, they were venturing into the unknown against targets only vaguely realised.

When the idea of penetrating the Dardanelles was mooted, the *Goeben* had been the glittering prize. But her reported location at Constantinople rendered an attack on her impracticable. Sights having been lowered to the waters around Chanak, attention then turned to the *Lily Rickmers*, a Turkish vessel said to be used as a floating headquarters for German staff officers. Failing that, Holbrook was instructed to attack 'any other hostile vessel as opportunity might offer'. First, though, he had to negotiate the Lower Straits.

By 4.15 a.m. *B11* was within 3 miles of the Dardanelles. Searchlights swept back and forth across the entrance and Holbrook waited for about forty-five minutes until shortly before dawn when the lights were turned off. Then, trimming down, with little more than the conning tower showing above the surface, he approached to within a mile of Cape Helles. Twenty minutes later, having noted various landmarks and believing there to be enough light to see through the periscope, he ordered *B11* down to 25ft. The shore was just visible, but no sooner had the boat begun to make way than it was jolted by a strange vibration running through the hull, which caused the periscope to shake. Holbrook slowed the engines, but still the sound remained. There was no option but to surface. Clambering on to the conning tower, he surveyed the boat and discovered that part of the bow guard had sheered off, leaving a twisted claw of metal. To continue was out of the question, but Holbrook was not prepared to abandon the mission. With the sky lightening and the risk of being sighted growing with every minute, he ordered two men to dismantle the bow guard – thought to be essential to their safe passage through the minefields. After an anxious few minutes, the guard fell away and *B11* disappeared once more beneath the waves.

Holbrook had worked out his own plan: he intended to hug the steep northern shore where the water ran deep and the current, he hoped, would be less turbulent. 'Being a fisherman, I knew where the slack water would be, so I kept right in, close to the shore,' he later said. To check his course, he surfaced every forty-five minutes, taking care to ensure his periscope was up for no more than a few seconds. Progress against the current was painfully slow, hardly more than 2 knots in places, but that was as nothing compared with the difficulties encountered when *B11* reached the point where the salt water of the Mediterranean mingled with the fresh water flowing from the Marmora. Holbrook later wrote:

> As soon as I got inside the Dardanelles she took full dive helm &
> 300 on two to keep her down at 60ft. Often she came up as far as
> 40ft & then went down again without altering the speed or helm.

> When I wished to bring her up I had to give her full rise helm &
> speed up to 500 on two & even then I sometimes remained at
> 20ft for a quarter of an hour or more, before she would come up
> the remaining five feet to see …

The difficulty in controlling the boat placed a severe strain on the men
manning the primitive hand-operated hydroplanes. And it was at this
point that Holbrook had reason to be thankful for the last-minute addition of PO Milsom to his crew, as he was able to relieve his coxswain
and take over working the important after-hydroplanes.

As *B11* gamely struggled on, breakfast was taken in relays. Holbrook
found time to consume half a cold lobster, given to him as a leaving present by a French submariner. By 8.30 a.m. *B11* was close to the entrance
to the Suan Dere River, which Holbrook took as his cue to dive to 80ft
to begin the perilous passage beneath the Kephez minefield. For the
next hour they travelled blind, oblivious of the whereabouts of the five
lines of mines and uncertain even of the distance covered. Taking as a
rough guide the revolutions of the propeller shaft, Holbrook judged
that they had probably passed Kephez Point. Waiting ten minutes to be
sure, he brought *B11* to periscope depth.

It was 9.40 a.m. The sun was dancing on the water. A mile away on
the Asiatic shore was the shimmering spectacle of Chanak. Holbrook
had miscalculated. He was further on than he had anticipated. As the
periscope swept round to starboard, he recognised the sweeping outline
of Sari Sighlar Bay, occupied by a 'large two-funnelled vessel', painted
grey and flying the Turkish ensign aft and another flag that he did not
recognise from its jackstaff. Momentarily surprised, Holbrook was
heard to exclaim: 'Good God, we are nearly on top of a big ship.'

Only a matter of weeks before the *Messudieh* had flown the flag
of Vice-Admiral Arthur Limpus, head of the British mission to
Constantinople. Now, the forty-year-old, 9,120-ton battleship stood
guard, at German behest and against Turkish advice, over the Narrows.
An obsolete floating fort, she was armed with twelve 6-inch guns and
twenty-eight small quick-firers. To Holbrook, she seemed 'a pity to
miss'. As *B11* altered course towards the grey bulk, the crew settled
into their action stations. LS Mortimer described what followed:

> Not knowing who she [the *Messudieh*] was he gave the order
> 'Take her down 60ft, make the tube ready, speed up on the motor,
> 400 on'. He bring [*sic*] her to 15ft then gave me the necessary
> order to get our Bow in shape to fire. Not many seconds elapsed
> when the order fire was given. At that moment hard to starboard

the helm, take her down to 80ft and a few anxious minutes elapsed and we heard such a crash but did not know whether the torpedo had struck her or the shore. So we brought her to 15ft again and the Captain said, 'We've done it'. You should have heard the cheer. She was sinking by the stern and they were planting shot and shell all around us but could not hit our Perescope [sic]. So we dived again, but with difficulty, so all spare hands, baring [sic] people on special duty aft, rushed forward and she went down but was on the bottom and stopped there longer than we wanted her to; was expecting to see a rock come through her at any moment …

In his official report, Holbrook stated:

I was able to see track of torpedo going straight for ship, but the submarine dipped before torpedo hit … Immediately after the explosion the boat came up sufficiently to put the periscope above water, the vessel was then on my starbd beam and opened fire from a number of guns. The boat then dipped and when I got her up again … I had the vessel on my port bow and she appeared to me to be settling down by the stern; no more guns were fired.

Torpedoed from about 800yd, *Messudieh* rolled over in just seven minutes, her ruptured side showing above the shallow water. Remarkably, given the speed of her demise, only thirty-seven men died from a crew of nearly 700. Many of the survivors were released through holes cut in the exposed hull. Their fate, however, was of less immediate concern to Holbrook than the plight of his own craft.

As *B11* dived again, her compass, in Holbrook's words, 'chucked its hand in'. According to Mortimer, the glass simply fogged over 'owing to the boat sweating'. Whatever the cause, Holbrook was mortified. Mortimer heard his captain shout: 'If you cannot read the Compass we are done.' Holbrook himself told his parents: 'All I knew was that I was in the middle of the minefield [and] hadn't the faintest notion in what direction I was pointing.'

At that moment *B11* grounded hard, stern first, at 38ft. Putting the helm hard a-port, Holbrook ordered full speed and the boat scraped clear. By then, he had lost all sense of direction. 'I was a bit flabbergasted,' he later admitted. Rising to periscope depth, he discovered they were hemmed in by land on all sides. Judging, as best he could, the way out, he took *B11* down again 'and continued to hit the bottom for ten minutes when luckily I got into deep water'. To his parents, he explained:

I had to come up twice more in the minefield to find out where I was and each time I was practically running ashore, but finally managed to get the boat more or less pointing for the open, the man at the wheel steering by a dirty mark on the compass which was all he could see ...

Twenty minutes later a sea horizon appeared on the port side. 'We made for it,' Holbrook recorded, 'and were more or less swept out of the Straits.' A Turkish torpedo-boat gave chase, but B11 escaped unscathed. Finally, at 2.10 p.m., Holbrook ordered the main ballast blown and the small submarine rose to the surface 2 miles outside the entrance to the Dardanelles. It was not a moment too soon. Although Holbrook reported that 'the foulness of the air was not noticeable' while under water, Mortimer insisted that the gasses from the batteries had left the majority of the crew 'as sick as dogs'. All told, Holbrook reckoned that B11 had been submerged for a total of nine hours, a record for a B-boat.

Everyone at Tenedos was full of praise for the submariners. In Pownall's estimation, Holbrook had displayed 'judgement', 'skill' and 'coolness', not simply in disposing of the Messudieh but in successfully 'extricating his boat from a difficult situation'. Even the enemy were impressed. Talking to the American vice-consul a few days later, Vice-Admiral Merten, senior German naval officer in the Dardanelles, described the attack as 'a mighty clever piece of work'. At a light-hearted ceremony aboard HMS Indefatigable, flagship of the Mediterranean Squadron, fellow submariners presented an amused Holbrook with an over-sized Iron Cross made from cardboard. Vice-Admiral Sackville Carden, however, went one better. On Christmas Eve, he recommended that Holbrook be awarded the Victoria Cross and his crew suitably rewarded for their part in a 'most gallant' service.

The awards, including a DSO for Holbrook's second-in-command, Lieutenant Sidney Winn, and DSMs for the crew, were granted with unusual alacrity, those to the officers being gazetted two days before Carden's formal recommendation. Seven members of the crew were also put forward for early promotion, although Milsom would have to wait six months and prove his good behaviour before being rated chief petty officer.

Holbrook was taken aback by his honour. Writing to Commodore Roger Keyes, then Head of the Submarine Service, shortly after the raid, he admitted: 'I feel that the great distinction conferred upon me is too much for the small service I have rendered, as the Messudiyeh [sic] was a very old ship & not much of a loss to the Turks.'

True though this was, it rather missed the point. Holbrook's remarkable achievement transcended mere collateral damage. The men of the antiquated *B11* had proved beyond question that while the difficulties in navigating the Straits under water were immense, they could be overcome with skill, daring and a hefty slice of luck. And where they led, others would soon follow.

Norman Douglas Holbrook was born in Southsea on 9 July 1888, the fourth son in a family of six boys and four girls to Colonel, later Sir, Arthur Richard Holbrook and Amelia Mary (née Parks). Colonel Holbrook was proprietor of the *Portsmouth Times*, founder of the *Southern Daily Mail* and the Hilsea-based Holbrook Printers, a deputy lord lieutenant and later MP, who managed to combine business, civic and political duties with a keen interest in military matters.

In all, five of the Holbrook boys were to serve in the war, three in the army and two in the navy, earning between them a VC, DSO, MC and CBE. Not to be outdone, their father, a former officer in the Volunteers and a commanding officer of the 6th (Portsmouth) Battalion, the Hampshire Regiment, commanded Royal Army Service Corps' units in the Salisbury Plain training area throughout the war, for which he was knighted.

Norman Holbrook attended Portsmouth Grammar School, where despite modest academic ability, he succeeded in passing the entrance examination to HMS *Britannia*. As a midshipman he served in the battleships *Revenge* and *Jupiter* (1905–06) and then in the cruiser *Monmouth*. Promoted sub-lieutenant in 1908 and lieutenant the following year, he reported to HMS *Mercury* for submarine training on 4 January 1910. Having gained experience in A, B and C-class submarines, he did a spell in the *Bonaventure*, the Home Fleet's submarine depot ship, before gaining his first command, the *A13*, on 19 March 1913. His progress continued with his posting to HMS *Egmont* in Malta on 30 December, to take command of the *B11*, in which he was destined to make history.

Following his spectacular success, which brought him the embarrassing nickname 'Five Rows of Mines' Holbrook, the larger, more powerful E-boats came to the fore and the crews of the B-boats found themselves increasingly relegated to more mundane duties. However, Holbrook's spell in the Dardanelles and Eastern Mediterranean was not without further incident.

On 18 April 1915 he led one of the attempts to destroy the wreck of the *E15* which had run aground near Kephez Point. Defeated by the morning mist which blotted out the wreck, he returned with his battery almost exhausted. The following month *B11* was ordered south to patrol the entrance to the Gulf of Smyrna, from where it was feared German or Austrian submarines might strike against Allied shipping supporting operations at Gallipoli. On 17 May Holbrook made the first sighting of an enemy submarine in the region, but was himself spotted before he could carry out an attack.

More unorthodox work followed. In August, in company with another B-boat, *B11* was dispatched from Mudros to Alexandria to patrol the Egyptian coast to deter Turkish gun-runners seeking to incite rebellion among the Senussi tribesmen. On 16 August the two boats were anchored 700yd off Cape Lukka. The crew saw on the shore a party of Arabs under a flag of truce, accompanied by what looked like a group of European officers. As senior officer, Holbrook set off in a small boat towards the shore. His attempts to parley with them, however, served only to arouse his suspicions and he turned back. As he neared the *B11*, they opened fire, sinking his boat and leaving him to swim the last few yards. Moments later, the submarines withdrew at speed, their casings and bridge screens peppered by bullets, with one man dead and three wounded, one of whom was Holbrook. The victor of Sari Sighlar Bay was lucky to be alive, as he acknowledged in a letter written to his mother from Alexandria on 18 August:

> A bullet after hitting the conning tower lid caught me on the nose and made a very clean hole in one side, the big part came out thru [*sic*] the nostril and four little bits remained behind. I was X-rayed this morning and they didn't advise removing them as they would have to make such a mess of my face. I can't tell you anything about the episode bar how I got off whole I don't know. They played the dirty with the white flag …

The incident, however, did little to dampen his spirits. After three days in hospital, he was able to enjoy Alexandria's many attractions. 'This is a great spot and such a change to Malta,' he wrote. 'You see an occasional pretty girl, in fact, I have met two or three rippers and have been having an 'ell of a time, took one out to tea this afternoon in spite of a bandaged nose and black eye.' The following month Holbrook returned to England to recuperate. His command of *B11* was over, but not forgotten. On 5 October he attended Buckingham Palace to receive his VC. More honours and awards followed. In July 1916 a Navy prize court awarded the *B11*'s crew £3,500, of which Holbrook's share was £601 10s 2d! The French made him a Knight of the Legion of Honour (gazetted 7 April 1916). But the most extraordinary of all distinctions came courtesy of the patriotic inhabitants of a small town deep in the

Australian outback, who voted in the summer of 1915 to change the name of their town from Germanton to Holbrook 'in memory of the valiant deeds done ... in the Dardanelles'.

Holbrook continued to serve in submarines throughout most of the war. His first boat after returning to England was the new *F3*, which, on completion in July 1916, he took to Harwich. Five months later he transferred to *V4*, before taking command of the new mine-laying submarine *E41*, in which he carried out a particularly daring mission in July 1917. Having mined a channel close to one of the enemy's bases in the Heligoland Bight, he deliberately attacked an auxiliary vessel in an attempt to lure a posse of patrol boats on to his mines. Unfortunately, just when it seemed his ruse would work, they gave up the chase and returned to port. Holbrook was mentioned in despatches.

Despite almost three years of relentless submarine service, he continued to display considerable boldness. Reports refer to his 'zealous' behaviour and 'very keen' example, although one senior officer thought him 'above himself'.

In January 1918, by then a lieutenant-commander, he left *E41* to take up his last submarine appointment as commanding officer of the *J2*, one of the new fleet submarines, more than twice the length and over four times heavier than his first and most famous wartime command. Strangely, given his long experience of undersea warfare, he had begun to suffer severe bouts of seasickness, and it was on account of this that he sought and was granted a return to general duties. On 31 August he joined as second-in-command the *Glory IV*, formerly the Russian cruiser *Askold*, serving in North Russian waters. Subsequently he oversaw her decommissioning the following year.

He married a widow, Viva Dixon, daughter of Frederick Woodin, on 21 June 1919, and they had one son, who was killed in action towards the end of the fighting in Italy during the Second World War.

Holbrook retired from the navy in 1920 and was promoted commander on the retired list in 1928. Shortly afterwards, he and his family moved into Four Acres, Kingston Hall, a mock-Tudor mansion they had built in Surrey. During the Second World War the house, with its eighteen bedrooms, served as a base for the American High Command and for a short while was home to the Dutch royal family. By then, Holbrook was back in uniform, as an officer in the Admiralty Trade Division, interviewing survivors of ships lost to enemy action.

Throughout war and peace, Holbrook maintained close links with the family printing firm, serving as chairman for a number of years, but his prime interest was farming. Leaving Surrey, he settled at Stedham Mill, near Midhurst in West Sussex, where he had a 300-acre mixed arable and dairy farm. His wife died in 1952 and the following year he married Gundula Felder of Innsbruck. They led a full and hectic life together and Holbrook remained active until well into his 80s.

He died on 3 July 1976, six days short of his 88th birthday, while watering his garden at Stedham. The navy's first submariner VC was buried in St James's churchyard, Midhurst, with a small outline of the Cross carved at the top of his headstone.

Holbrook's daring achievement has not been forgotten. In 1983 a road in Portsmouth was named in his honour, while the over-sized cardboard Iron Cross he received after sinking the *Messudieh* was given to the RN Submarine Museum. But the most enduring and extraordinary tribute was provided by the small Australian town that began life as Ten Mile Creek and became known as Germanton before emerging as Holbrook. Over the years this small outback farming community has established a Cdr Holbrook Memorial Park, complete with scale model of the *B11*, opened a submarine museum and raised a statue in honour of the man whose exploits inspired their change of name. Holbrook himself was deeply touched by their efforts. He visited the town three times, in 1956, when he and his wife were given a special reception, in 1969 and in 1976, shortly before his death. Six years later his widow Gundula returned to present his medals to the town.

Since then, Holbrook has become a shrine to the submarine service. In 1986 the Royal Australian Navy's Submarine Squadron was granted the freedom of the Shire. And the unlikely ties between a landlocked town 300 miles from the nearest ocean and the navy was further cemented when the local council bought the decommissioned Australian submarine *Otway* as a permanent memorial to its maritime heritage. The ambitious project was supported by a $100,000 donation by Gundula Holbrook who, at the age of 92, made her fifth journey to the town in June 1997 to officially dedicate the 90m-long monument during a weekend of celebrations attended by 400 current and ex-submariners and almost the entire population of Holbrook Shire.

Dubbed the town's 'fairy godmother', Gundula Holbrook maintained that she was merely repaying the great honour done to her husband. 'He thought the world of this town,' she once remarked and, as Holbrook toasted the arrival of its own submarine, she reflected:

It is very rare for a place to be named after someone who was still alive at the time. My husband was extremely proud when he heard that the town had changed its name to Holbrook. He was always very modest but I think he was very touched and surprised to get such an honour.

E.G. ROBINSON

Nr Yeni Shehr, The Dardanelles, 26 February 1915

Events moved rapidly in the wake of Holbrook's audacious coup. Within a month British strategy in the Dardanelles, influenced by Russian defeats in the Caucasus, had moved from the defensive to the offensive. In an attempt to relieve the pressure on her ally, Britain agreed to act. Since Kitchener was unwilling to spare troops for the operation, it was, initially, an entirely naval venture. Churchill, who had lobbied for a strike towards Constantinople almost from the outset of Turkey's entry into the war, favoured a precipitate charge by pre-dreadnought battleships through the Narrows, arguing that the risk of heavy losses was outweighed by the potential results. However, Vice-Admiral Sackville Carden, commanding the ships blockading the Dardanelles, was more cautious. Deferring to the man on the spot, Churchill gave his backing to a plan for 'extended operations with [a] large number of ships' which involved the systematic reduction of the Turkish fortifications prior to a full-scale naval assault. That plan was put into action on 19 February 1915 with the first, and largely ineffectual, bombardment of the outer forts at the entrance to the Straits. After a week's delay, forced by bad weather, the assault was resumed with a strike against the intermediate forts, which culminated in a small-scale, commando-style action that brought to prominence a young naval officer whose exploits during the campaign were to become the stuff of legend.

Lieutenant-Commander Eric 'Kipper' Robinson was torpedo officer of the *Vengeance*, an elderly battleship flying the flag of Sir John de Robeck, and carrying in it Carden's belligerent chief-of-staff, Cdre (later Lord) Roger Keyes. Aged 32 and a veteran of the fighting in China, where he had been wounded at the turn of the century, Robinson was soon to acquire a reputation for bravery which was to mark him out as 'the foremost of Keyes's thrusters'.

Returning from the foray on 26 February, de Robeck decided to complete the destruction of the Orkanieh battery, between Kum Kale and Yeni Shehr on the Asiatic shore, which had been the target for the first day's bombardment. Handing Robinson the task, he gave him a fifty-strong force of seamen to act as demolition party with the same number of marines as a covering force. They landed unopposed at 2.30 p.m. and advanced along the line of the Mendere river. They passed a cemetery and descended into a horseshoe-shaped depression where they came under heavy fire from snipers and a large force approaching from the direction of Yeni Shehr. A salvo from one of the ships anchored offshore temporarily quietened the Turks moving up, but the landing parties were still under fire.

At this juncture Robinson would have been justified in abandoning his mission. The way back to the coast was threatened and the ground ahead hotly contested by an unknown number of enemy troops. But he decided to press on. Dodging the snipers, he led his party towards a slight rise, known as Achilles Mound, beyond which lay the main battery. Officers aboard *Vengeance* saw them stop half-way up the slope and take cover from renewed fire coming from Yeni Shehr. All that is, except for one man, in a white uniform, who was seen to scramble up the hill and disappear into what looked like a crater. Moments later, he emerged, his calm, unhurried descent followed by a loud explosion.

The lone figure was Eric Robinson. Anxious not to expose his men unnecessarily to the enemy fire, he had left Midshipman John Woolley in charge while he advanced into the gun position which, as luck would have it, was unoccupied. There, he fixed gun-cotton charges to two guns and detonated them with a slow fuse that allowed him just enough time to escape. Then, making the most of the effect of a protective bombardment by the ships stationed offshore, he led a small party into the main battery and succeeded in destroying one of the 9.4-inch guns.

All of this was viewed with a mixture of awe and anxiety by de Robeck and his staff. To Bertram Smith, captain of *Vengeance*, Robinson appeared to be 'strolling around ... under heavy rifle fire ... like a sparrow enjoying a bath from a garden hose'. Even as the seamen and marines were making their way back to the boats, Smith and de Robeck 'were happily arranging our recommend [*sic*] for his VC'. But their optimism was quickly dented by a signal from the raiders, stating that they were held up by Turks in a large domed tomb.

The control could see the tomb [wrote Smith] and I could just distinguish its top ... It was invisible at the guns, but I was able to note its whereabouts in the treetops, and went down to let off a 6-inch lyddite. The range was short and the range-finder laid it exactly, so the first round sent the tomb and fragments of its inmates, both ancient and modern, flying heavenwards. Using the burst as a starting point there was no difficulty in taking the guns on to any other target to get our people clear.

Extricating themselves with only a handful of casualties, Robinson's party made it back to the waiting ships, where their action was already being counted a success. Later, the Official Historian would credit them with the destruction of two anti-aircraft guns on Achilles Mound and the last remaining 9.4-inch gun in the Orkanieh battery. However, in citing Robinson for a VC for his part in what he called 'a very pretty little fight', Keyes made reference only to his 'most gallant act in pushing in alone [*sic*] into Fort IV [Orkanieh] and destroying a 9.4-inch gun, which he found loaded and undamaged'. Either way, there was no disputing the degree of courage shown in the face of considerable odds. To Keyes's recommendation, Carden added the note: 'This was a specially brave act, giving most valuable practical results.'

Robinson's contribution to the naval campaign had only just begun. As bombardment of the forts gave way to mine clearance operations, he showed himself to be as dauntless at sea as he was on land. During March he made four sorties into the minefields, always under heavy fire, in command of a converted trawler. His cool leadership was most marked on the night of 13/14 March when he carried out his task despite his boat being hit no fewer than eighty-four times.

His actions, worthy of reward in their own right, were merely appended to the original recommendation for his VC which was eventually gazetted on 16 August. But by then, his exploits within the first month of the campaign had been spectacularly eclipsed by a daring mission worthy of a Bar to his hard-earned Cross.

Eric Gascoigne Robinson was born on 16 May 1882 at 1 Diamond Terrace, Greenwich, the son of John Lovell Robinson MA, Chaplain of the Royal Naval College, and Louisa Aveline (née Gascoigne). He was educated at St John's, Leatherhead, and The Limes, Greenwich, before joining *Britannia* as a cadet on 15 January 1897. He joined the *Victory* as a midshipman on 15 May 1898, and had a spell in the battleship *Majestic* before being posted to *Endymion* on 8 June 1899. It was while serving in her that the young midshipman first saw action in China, as a member of Admiral Seymour's expedition sent to relieve the besieged legations in Peking. His boyish enthusiasm for the fray was reflected in a letter home. 'How nice I shall look with a medal!' he wrote. 'I have not fired a shot yet, but live in hopes.' He did not have long to wait. At a place called Lang-fang, he was with a naval detachment that beat off a heavy attack, during which he had a narrow escape. 'I felt a sudden shock in my helmet,' he wrote, 'and found that a bullet had gone through just above my ear ... and just after another grazed my right arm.' Later, on 27 June 1900, while attacking an arsenal near Tien-tsin, he was shot through the left arm. Robinson ended the campaign with his first medal, a mention in despatches and tales of 'countless narrow shaves'.

Promoted sub-lieutenant shortly after leaving *Endymion* in October 1901, Robinson was made lieutenant two years later and after service in a Yangtse gunboat and a spell at *Vernon* he qualified as a torpedo specialist in 1907. In 1910 he was promoted lieutenant-commander and posted to the submarine depot ship *Thames* in the Home Fleet. Service in *Blenheim* and *Amethyst* followed, punctuated by further spells at *Vernon*.

In 1913 he married Edith Gladys (née Cordeux) and they had two sons, one of whom was killed in action during the Second World War, and a daughter. That same year was notable also for another narrow escape when a train in which he was travelling was involved in a collision, which left him unconscious but, thankfully, not seriously injured. Serving in *Amethyst* again at the outbreak of war, Robinson was appointed torpedo officer in *Vengeance* on 20 September 1914, and sailed with her to the Dardanelles where he was to earn everlasting fame.

By April 1915, with a VC already on the way, Robinson's reputation for daring was such that he was the automatic choice to lead a naval 'forlorn hope' attempt to destroy the submarine *E15* which had run aground in Kephez Bay under the guns of Fort Dardanus. Battleships, destroyers and submarines had all failed to deny the Turks their propaganda coup. So Robinson was handed the job and given two torpedo-carrying steam picket boats, manned by volunteer crews from *Majestic* and *Triumph*, to carry out a mission his colleagues considered tantamount to committing suicide. One friend, Lieutenant-Commander Charles Brodie, was so concerned 'at the thought of him being sacrificed so unnecessarily' that he appealed to de Robeck to cancel or, at least, postpone the operation. But the attack went in as planned on the night of 18/19 April. Braving a storm of fire, the two picket boats pressed home their attacks. The *Triumph*'s boat, with Robinson aboard, was coned by no fewer than eight searchlights. Barely able to see, Robinson nevertheless got within 300yd of the stranded submarine before attempting a 'blind shot' which narrowly missed. At that moment, the *Majestic*'s boat, which was following up, in Robinson's words 'caught a lucky glimpse of the submarine quite clearly as a searchlight beam flicked over it'. Forging on, they fired both their torpedoes at 200–300yd range, 'the second one securing a hit just before the conning tower'. Moments later, the picket boat was rocked by a direct hit and began to settle. Despite being bracketed by shells, Robinson went to its aid, circling the stricken boat four times until every man was taken off. He later estimated that the Turks had fired well over 300 rounds during the attack, and a further 190 at the sinking boat after they departed. The results fully justified the risk. Years later the German diver Ernest Roschmann, who was engaged in trying to salvage the *E15*, confirmed the success of the mission and added: 'I have never in the course of the war seen an attack carried out with such pluck and fearlessness.'

In commending the three officers who accompanied Robinson in this hazardous enterprise, Capt. Smith of the *Vengeance* stressed that 'the greatest merit is due to Lt Cdr Robinson himself for the success which attended the operation – organised and directed by him – which enhanced the high reputation for coolness, resource and gallantry which he has already gained from his previous work in connection with creeping operations and demolition work'. In an astonishing omission, however, Robinson was the only man among the two boats' crews not to receive a decoration for the attack on *E15*. Instead, he had to be content with promotion to commander, back-dated to 20 April.

Later, after the invasion of Gallipoli, Keyes appointed the 'gallant and stout-hearted' Robinson as Naval Transport Officer at Anzac Beach, before transferring him to Suvla Bay, where he was wounded 'badly … not dangerously' on 7 August, a day after the landings. It marked the end of his involvement in the campaign. Having recovered from his wound, he was presented with his VC by King George V at Buckingham Palace on 5 October.

After a spell of leave, Robinson was appointed to command the monitor *M21* based at Port Said in December 1915. For the next twenty months, he was engaged in supporting army operations along the coasts of Egypt and Palestine, earning in the process the Order of the Nile, 4th Class (*London Gazette*, 6 December 1916), and a further mention in despatches. Robinson returned to Britain in August 1917, and in the following January Roger Keyes, who had never forgotten his bravery in the Dardanelles, unsuccessfully tried to recruit him for the impending operations against Zeebrugge and Ostend. A period of relative inactivity ended in June 1918, when he was appointed to Osea Island for training in coastal motor boats. The following year that training was put to good use when Cdr Robinson helped wrest control of the Caspian Sea from the Bolsheviks. In an echo of his Dardanelles adventures, he led his boats into the enemy-held Fort Alexandrovsk, sank a barge and so cowed the defenders that they hoisted the white flag. In recognition of his actions during the war of intervention, Robinson was made an officer of the Order of the British Empire (*LG*, 11 November 1919) and awarded the Russian Order of St Anne, second class with swords (*LG*, 13 July 1920).

Following a spell in the *Iron Duke*, Robinson was promoted captain and sent on the senior officers' war course. For the next twelve years, he held a variety of both shore-based and sea-going appointments, including two spells in command of destroyer flotillas, at *Defiance* (the Torpedo School at Devonport), at the Artificers' Training Establishment at *Fisgard*, Torpoint, and in the cruiser *Berwick* on the China Station, during which he was awarded the Japanese Order of the Sacred Treasure, 3rd class (*LG*, February 1929). He served as Captain of Devonport Dockyard from 1932 until 1933 when he was promoted Rear Admiral on the Retired List. Recalled at the outbreak of the Second World War, he served as a convoy commodore until ill health brought about his second retirement in 1942, his work being recognised by a Norwegian award, King Haakon VII's Freedom Cross.

Settling at the White House, Langrish, near Petersfield in Hampshire, Robinson played a full part in community affairs, representing the village on Petersfield Rural District Council, and serving as a churchwarden and member of the parochial church council. The hero of so many desperate actions died peacefully in Haslar Naval Hospital on 20 August 1965, and was buried in the churchyard of St John the Evangelist, Langrish. An altar frontal inside the church commemorated his gallant services, but it was not until thirty-three years later that a memorial headstone was placed over his grave. At a dedication ceremony attended by more than a hundred ex-servicemen, naval officers and two grandchildren, 'Kipper' Robinson was honoured again. Paying tribute to the boldest of Keyes's 'thrusters', Admiral Sir Derek Reffell declared: 'The admiral was a hero, but more importantly he was a naval man from the finest mould. Now at last we can accord him the dignity he deserves.'

E. Unwin,
W.C. Williams,
G.L. Drewry,
G. McK. Samson,
W. St A. Malleson and
A.W. St C. Tisdall

V Beach, Cape Helles, 25 April 1915

The waiting was almost over and Lieutenant-Commander Josiah Wedgwood, radical politician and part-time sailor, could hardly contain his excitement. Days of arduous preparation had given way to keen anticipation for his small party of machine-gunners, last-minute recruits to one of the navy's most unorthodox missions. The next few hours would mark the fulfilment of their ambition to play a leading role in a military operation fraught with hazard yet intoxicating in its glorious potential. On the eve of the attempt to land an expeditionary force on the defended shores of Gallipoli, Wedgwood wrote to his mother:

> The Captain is going to run this ship ashore so that troops can disembark, dry-shod, and our guns, mounted on this ship, will cover the landing. It is just exactly the job I should have liked to get ... The Captain calls this ship the Wooden Horse of Troy, for it looks like a collier gone wrong, and from it will spring men in thousands armed to the teeth ...

The 'Captain' to whom Wedgwood referred was Edward Unwin and the ship was the *River Clyde*. Together they would provide the single most enduring image of the campaign, though sadly it was one more reminiscent of squandered heroism and diabolical slaughter than of military glory. The tragedy of it all was that the scheme, imaginative in its conception and daring in its execution, was designed to save lives.

In the weeks following the navy's failure to force the Dardanelles, the Turks had been busily strengthening their defences to meet the anticipated invasion. At the same time British commanders had been racking their brains to find ways of overcoming the obstacles placed in their path, particularly at Cape Helles, designated V Beach, the most critical and potentially difficult of all the landing zones. Everyone acknowledged the importance of speed and the need to give as much protection as possible to the troops during the critical run-in to the beach, but until Unwin's intervention none could see a way to achieve either objective.

At 51, Unwin, a brusque, forceful officer recalled from retirement at the outbreak of war, was a man of great resourcefulness and considerable powers of persuasion. His idea was to fit out a collier and run her on to the beach, with a steam hopper and three lighters providing a makeshift jetty across which her cargo of 2,000 troops, mainly Royal Dublin and Munster Fusiliers, would dash ashore, thus doubling at a stroke the first wave of troops who were to be towed and then rowed in aboard open boats. With the enthusiastic backing of Rear Admiral R.E. Wemyss, the plan was adopted and Unwin was charged with the task of carrying it out. The ship he selected was the *River Clyde*, a 4000-ton, 10-year-old collier, a product of the Clydeside shipyards. Most recently she had been employed in shipping mules from North Africa. Conversion work began on 12 April. Four doorways, called sallyports, were cut on both sides of the ship's hull, with a wooden gangway leading from the rearmost towards the bows. There they sloped down to meet the stern of the flat-bottomed steam hopper *Argyll*, which was to be towed in by the *River Clyde* and then released shortly before beaching to form the vital shore link. If, however, the distance proved too great, any of the three specially decked lighters towed by the collier could be used to bridge the gap. As a further means of covering the landing, Unwin accepted the offer of volunteers from Wedgwood's RNAS armoured car squadron who, desperate for employment, agreed to man machine-guns mounted in sandbagged casemates and on the armour-plated bridge. To crew his new and unconventional command, Unwin looked first to *River Clyde*'s own crew, telling them 'they would never get such a chance again'. But his offer fell on deaf ears. While willing to help prepare the ship, her captain told him: 'I don't think you can expect us to be there when the bricks begin to fly.' So Unwin turned to his own ship, HMS *Hussar*, a torpedo-boat operating as a fleet communications yacht, where he had no difficulty finding 'plenty of volunteers'. From those wishing to accompany him, he selected six deckhands, six stokers, six men to tend the lighters, a warrant engineer and ship's carpenter. To these were added some petty officers and a leading seaman, which brought the total to twenty-three. Unwin chose well. Of his small ship's company, no fewer than four would earn Victoria Crosses.

As his Number One, Unwin took with him Midshipman George Drewry, a pre-war Merchant Navy officer who looked even younger than his 20 years. Drewry's job was to take charge of the steam hopper, assisted by Seaman George Samson, a young Scot with a love of adventure. Together with a volunteer crew of six Greek seamen, Drewry and Samson clambered aboard the hopper at 5 a.m. on 25 April 1915, with the mist-shrouded shore just 2 miles away. As they closed Cape Helles, the covering bombardment thundered over them. Turkish reaction, by comparison, was muted, leading some to suppose they might even land unopposed. But such optimism was quickly dashed. Drewry later wrote:

> Shells began to fall round us thick but did not hit us. We were half a mile from the beach and we were told not yet, so we took a turn round two ships. At last, we had the signal at 6am and in we dashed, Unwin on the bridge and I at the helm of the hopper ...
>
> At 6.10 the ship struck, very easily she brought up, and I shot ahead and grounded on her port bow. Then the fun began, picket boats towed lifeboats full of soldiers inshore and slipped them as the water shoaled and they rowed the rest of the way, the soldiers jumped out as the boats beached and they died, almost all of them wiped out with the boats' crews ...

The landing was met by a hurricane of fire, and almost immediately things went awry. The *River Clyde* grounded further out than expected, while the hopper, her Greek crew panicking at the vital moment, veered off course and ran aground in the wrong place to become a 'death trap'. A horrified Unwin looked on helpless as his plan miscarried. The lighters that were to form the 'bridge' to shore had shot ahead of the *River Clyde*, and Drewry and Samson were desperately trying to haul them into position by hand. Realising, however, that the task was an impossible one, Unwin took matters into his own hands. 'Seeing what an awful fiasco had occurred,' he wrote, 'I dashed over the side ...' Helped by a pinnace, he managed to push them under his ship's bow toward a spit of rocks. Suddenly, with the sea being lashed by machine-gun fire, he realised he was not alone. Chest deep in water alongside him was Leading Seaman William Williams, a Boer War veteran and a late addition to *River Clyde*'s volunteer company.

On the eve of the landing, Unwin had told Williams to stay close by him, and despite the storm of fire, the stout-hearted Welshman had taken him at his word. Following his captain into the sea, he half swam, half waded through water whipped by fire to assist in dragging the lighters against the current toward the shore. 'We got them connected to the bows and then proceeded to connect to the beach,' wrote Unwin, 'but we had nothing to secure to, so we had to hold on to the rope ourselves. And when we had got the lighters near enough to the shore, I sung out to the troops to come out ...'

With Unwin and Williams hanging on to the painter of the nearest lighter to the beach, two companies of Munsters immediately dashed from the ship's sallyports to be swept away by a storm of fire. Only a handful lived to reach the shore, leaving the rocky spit strewn with dead and wounded. With nothing but their strength and courage to sustain them, Unwin and Williams clung to the lighters in a widening sea of blood:

> For an hour we held on [wrote Unwin] and, thinking I could be more use elsewhere I asked Williams if he could hang on without me, but he said he was nearly done and couldn't. Just then a 6-inch shell fell alongside us ... Williams said to me, 'what ever is that?' I told him and almost immediately I heard a thud and looked round and Williams said, 'a shell has hit me'. I caught hold of him and, as I couldn't let him drown, I tried to get him on to the lighter ...

In attempting to do so, Unwin let go his grip on the rope, and the lighters drifted apart. Carrying the body of his loyal helper in his arms, he waded across to the nearest lighter and was met by Drewry and another man, who together helped haul the wounded seaman aboard. But it was too late. Williams was dead before he reached the *River Clyde*.

Since grounding, Drewry had hardly had a moment's rest. When Unwin took charge of positioning the lighters, he ordered Samson to take cover aboard the hopper while he braved the enemy fire to wade ashore. On the way he picked up a wounded soldier, who was shot again and killed in his arms. Having reached the beach, he ran towards the spit, stripped off his jacket and hat and threw away his revolver, before joining his captain and Williams in the water. After pulling for a few minutes, he climbed on to the lighters, no easy feat at the best of times, let alone under heavy fire, and helped lower the ship's brows on to the nearest lighter. Ordered by Unwin to fetch more rope, he returned from the *River Clyde* to find the 'bridge' broken and Unwin carrying the dying Williams back. The whole assault was in danger of grinding to a halt, but Drewry refused to give in:

> I got a rope from the lighter to the spit and then with difficulty I hauled the Capt onto the lighter, he was nearly done and I was alone. He went inboard and the doctor had rather a job with him. All the time shells were falling all round us and into the ship one hitting the casing of one boiler but doing no further damage. Several men were killed in No. 4 hold. I stayed on the lighters and tried to keep the men going ashore but it was murder and soon the first lighter was covered with dead and wounded and the spit was awful, the sea round it for some yards was red. When they got ashore they were little better off for they were picked off many of them before they could dig themselves in ...

With no sign of movement from the *River Clyde*, Drewry dashed back to find Unwin, almost unconscious from his prolonged immersion, being rubbed down. He murmured something about the third lighter which sent Drewry scurrying back into the tornado of fire and down on to the lighter, where he was soon joined by Lieutenant Tony Morse, in charge of a thirty-eight-strong party from the battleship *Cornwallis*. Morse was responsible for taking the third tow of troops to the shore. Amid the chaos and carnage, the lighter was given a helpful shove by a picket boat which carried it as far as the hopper, where Samson was still sheltering. Drewry wrote:

> Just as we hit the hopper a piece of shrapnel hit me on the head knocking me down for a second or two and covering me with blood. However, we made the lighter fast to the hopper and then I went below ... and a Tommy put my scarf round my head and I went up again ...

In an attempt to make a connection with the other lighters which had drifted with the current, Drewry swam out with a rope. But it was too short. Stuck in the middle, he saw a midshipman aboard one of the lighters and called for a line. The youngster was 18-year-old Wilfrid Malleson, one of the *Cornwallis* party which had gone along the starboard side of the *River Clyde*. He had already had at least one narrow escape when a midshipman beside him was hit and fatally wounded while getting on to the lighter. There he lay, face down, sheltering from the fire:

> Nothing very much was possible as bullets were whistling over our heads and the lighters were all isolated and swaying backwards and forwards on account of the current. After about an hour of inaction, during which time occupants of the lighter sustained about one casualty every ten minutes, I observed a lighter on the starboard side, manned by Lieut Morse and Mid Drewry, being pushed from behind by our 2nd picket boat ...

From his prone position, he saw the lighter pushed into place between his own boat and the hopper, and watched Drewry's futile effort to reach the other lighters. Hearing Drewry's call, he searched for a rope, but the only one was that which had originally held the lighter to the spit. To haul it in meant standing up totally exposed to the furious fire. But this is exactly what he did, with a soldier paying it out until they managed to get it across. Malleson wrote:

> I was a bit done, so Lt Morse made it fast. The new lighter had by now drifted to forward of the hopper. I therefore swam to the hopper and managed to get a rope from it and started to tow one end back. However, [the] rope was too short, and feeling exhausted, I scrambled aboard the lighter again. Lt Morse told me to get a dry change so I crawled into the *River Clyde* where I remained till evening.

Once more the troops charged out only to be defeated by the murderous machine-gun fire. Again the assault was halted. But Unwin refused to be beaten. Ignoring the ship's doctor's protests, he clambered down onto the lighters, which by then were smothered with the dead and dying, and made his way across to the hopper 'to see if I could do any good'. Drewry, watching from the *River Clyde*, saw him 'standing ... in white clothes' exposed to the storm of fire, making good one of the lines. Unwin recalled being helped by a boy and an old merchant seaman who looked as though he was at least 70, and though they succeeded, he doubted if their efforts were any use. 'I don't think it was ever used,' he wrote. The hopper, which had become a magnet for enemy fire, was a shambles of troops, many of them wounded, who had been turned back from the beach. Among them was Brig. Gen. H.E. Napier, commanding 88th Brigade, who had been mortally wounded as he leapt onto the boat, followed by his brigade major, Captain J.H.D. Costeker. Unwin recalled Costeker calling him to 'lie down' as he was drawing more fire on them:

> This I did for a bit. Then he gave a yell and said, "they've got me". I believe he was shot through the stomach. A bullet then hit a stanchion alongside me and spluttered over my face and neck. And, as I was doing no good there and I couldn't see a live man, I ran up the inclined staging, in through the foremost port.

Later, he discovered that the man helping him back inside *River Clyde* was shot through the lungs, though he hadn't realised it at the time. Back on board, he told Lt Col Hubert Carrington-Smith that 'it was no good trying to land any more men as it was certain death crossing the lighters'. Moments later, Carrington-Smith fell dead with a bullet through the mouth. For a while, Unwin remained on the upper bridge, together with the expedition's senior staff officers, Lt Col Weir de Lancy Williams and Lt Col Charles Doughty-Wylie, 'staring at the beach' strewn with British dead:

> Not a Turk did I ever see [he wrote]. I thought I saw one once and took a rifle and fired ... and an old vulture flew out of the tree ... I saw a party of 6 men leave the beach and clamber over the ridge evidently with the intention of trying to cut the wire. They got 10 yards, 5 fell down shot instantly and one ran back and jumped over the heads of the men lying under the ridge. One of those shot turned imploringly round towards us and rolled about but eventually was still ... I felt a brute in not going to his assistance.

Such sights combined with the constant cries of the wounded lying helpless on the spit of rocks became too much to bear, and at about 2 p.m., Unwin, apparently 'maddened by the failure of his landing plan', was ready to intervene again. This time, his intention was not to help men get ashore but to rescue those lying injured and trapped within sight of the *River Clyde*. And so, for the third time that day, he braved a storm of fire:

> I got a boat under the starboard quarter as far from the enemy as I could get and, taking a spare coil of rope with me, I got some hands to pay out a rope fast to the stern of the pinnace I was in and paddled and punted her into the beach, eventually grounding alongside the wounded. They were all soaking wet and very

heavy but I cut off their accoutrements with their bayonets or knives and carried two or three into the pinnace. But as her side was rather high out of the water I'm afraid they were not too gingerly put on board, but still they were very grateful. I could not pick up any more so I got on my hands and knees and they got on my back and I crawled along to the pinnace. Four more I managed like this and then I found a man in his trousers only alongside me ...

This was Petty Officer John Russell, one of Wedgwood's machine-gunners. Seeing Unwin struggling to save the wounded, he had swum out to help him. Together, they managed to carry one man to the pinnace, and then Russell fell, shot through the stomach. Using his own shirt as a bandage, Unwin staunched the bleeding before lifting him into the boat with the other wounded. By then, the strain was beginning to tell. 'I was again beginning to feel a bit dicky,' Unwin understatedly noted. And having struggled aboard the craft, he called out to some men on the *River Clyde* to haul them back. On the way across, he noticed somebody in the water, standing alongside the pinnace. He asked why he was returning, to which Unwin candidly replied, 'Because I could do no more'. Not until much later did he discover that the man posing the question was Sub-Lieutenant Arthur Tisdall.

The 24-year-old Cambridge scholar was the only officer of the Royal Naval Division aboard the *River Clyde*. His unit, 13 Platoon, D Company, Anson Battalion, had been attached to the ship as a carrying party. For hours, they had been cooped up in No. 4 hold, during which time they had lost three men to a shell burst. Finally, he had decided to go 'topside', where he was confronted by the full horror of the failed landing. Listening to the cries of the wounded, he was heard to say, 'I can't stand it. I'm going over.' Shortly afterward, Wedgwood saw him heading for the beach in a lifeboat with two other men. From eyewitness reports, it is clear that from that point on Tisdall became the prime mover in the rescue effort begun by Unwin. With *River Clyde*'s captain on the brink of collapse, he took charge, making at least four and possibly five journeys to and from the spit. He was variously helped by Petty Officer Mechanic Geoffrey Rumming, another of Wedgwood's party, and Petty Officer William Perring and Leading Seamen Fred Curtiss, James Malia and James Parkinson from his own platoon.

PO Rumming, who at the time had no idea as to the sub-lieutenant's identity, was one of three who helped Tisdall bring off seven men during two journeys. He reported:

Beyond getting a few bullet holes in the boat above the water-line, the first trip was quite successful. On the second trip Sub-Lt Tisdall and myself clambered over a spit of rock, to get the men lying higher up. We got shot at, lay down for a time. As we were lifting the last wounded man into the boat I got hit again in the back.

We had taken the boat a little further ashore, and when we went to push off again, we found her grounded. When we did eventually succeed in getting off Lt Tisdall and myself were unable to climb into the boat and so we hung on to the side as the two men, keeping as low as possible, rowed us back to the *River Clyde*.

Unfortunately, on the way back Lt Tisdall got some wooden splinters off the boat driven into his wrist by a bullet ...

Others among Tisdall's party had narrow escapes. LS Malia had an oar broken in his hands by a bullet, while a bullet passed through Parkinson's cap without hitting him. By the time Parkinson had completed his second trip, the lifeboat was leaking so badly that one of the wounded was found to have drowned:

We were then called back by one of the ship's officers who stated that it was sheer madness to go on, and if we did not return on board and under cover, anything we did would not be recognised. And if we did carry on we should probably be dead men because the Turks had by now got a machine-gun trained on us ...

According to Parkinson, they had no alternative but to obey orders and so, grasping holes in the side of the *River Clyde*, they finally pulled themselves aboard. Tisdall had been toiling in the water and on the spit for more than an hour. For others, however, the ordeal went on. Among the many acts of selfless heroism at V Beach, none was of longer duration than those performed by Seaman George Samson. As Drewry's assistant aboard the steam hopper, he was under fire from the beginning of the landing to well into the evening.

Urged to take cover by his young officer, Samson had spent most of the day doing the reverse, helping to connect the 'bridge' of lighters and ferrying wounded back from the beach. In all, he reckoned he was 'about 30 times off and on the hopper', during which he managed to pick up fifteen wounded men, bringing them back to the *Argyll*, where they remained until darkness when he was able to get them on board the *River Clyde*. Samson later recalled:

In this work Cdr Unwin and Mid Drewry worked most gallantly. Every moment they were risking their lives, and really it was nothing short of a miracle that they were not hit. As long as I live I shall treasure memories of the bravery of these men; they hurried hither and thither, giving a hand when needed, just as if they were aboard the *Hussar* in peace-time. As for myself I cannot say that I felt quite as cool as I may have looked. I am not a very excitable sort when there is serious trouble about. It takes a good deal to disturb me, but I can say without hesitation that this was the 'goods' for excitement. During these first hours ... I had many narrow escapes just the same, of course, as my companions ... Bullets were whizzing about our heads every few minutes, and we were soon aware of the fact that machine-guns were in operation ... Men were falling down like ninepins quite near us, and perhaps it was only the thought that we must give them a helping hand that made us forget our own danger ...

At one point Samson, having just carried a wounded soldier back to the hopper, was forced to lie flat on the deck while bullets peppered the vessel:

This time I began to think that any moment would be my last. Indeed, it became so hot that I finally decided to make a bold bid for safety. I began to roll over towards the side of the little vessel. There was no rail, and that fact was very much in my favour, for I was able to keep low down all the time. Bullets were flying all about the deck; once again I seemed to bear a charmed life ... When I reached the side of the hopper I gave myself a big lurch, and fell into the sea. The sea was extremely choppy but ... I was a good swimmer, and I did not find the slightest difficulty in getting back to the ship.

Samson's luck ran out the following day around 1.30 p.m. With the beach-head almost secured and Turkish resistance beginning to crack, he was hit in the left shoulder and left side of his body by a burst of machine-gun fire that bowled him over. Dragging himself to his feet, he was hit again. Surgeons treating him later counted seventeen separate wounds and one later wrote, 'he was in great agony ... and whether he lived or died I knew he had won the VC'.

The young Scot did survive and did, indeed, receive his richly deserved Victoria Cross, one of six granted to the Navy on 16 August 1915, in recognition of the valour displayed during the landing at V Beach.

They included the service's first posthumous VC to Leading Seaman William Williams and awards to two midshipmen, George Drewry and Wilfrid Malleson, whose survival bordered on the miraculous. There was also a VC for Sub-Lieutenant Arthur Tisdall, though his honour would not be announced until 31 March 1916, by which time he had been dead almost eleven months. Of all the VCs, however, none was more widely welcomed than that awarded to Edward Unwin. Faced with disaster, he had scaled peaks of heroism few imagined possible – so much so, in fact, that the army commander was inundated with recommendations. Commodore Roger Keyes wrote: 'The general told me at least half a dozen dirty scraps of paper reached him from comparatively junior officers which bore testimony to Unwin's devoted heroism, some written in the heat of action by officers who did not survive it.'

For his part, Unwin, writing sometime later, insisted he had only done what he 'had to do', with the word 'had' underlined. Despite the heavy loss of life, he remained convinced that the plan to use the *River Clyde* as a makeshift landing craft was a sound one, if not entirely without error:

> Speaking after the event [he wrote], I think we should have run an hour before dawn, or possibly two hours, then we could have got all the troops ashore before the enemy could distinguish our exit. What I do claim is that the old '*River Clyde*' saved hundreds of lives that would have inevitably been lost had the troops she carried landed, or tried to land, in boats ...

As the originator of the 'wreck ship' plan, Edward Unwin ranks among the most important figures of the Dardanelles campaign. In a matter of weeks, he rose from relative obscurity to play the central role in the drama of the main landing.

He was born on 17 March 1864 at Forest Lodge, Fawley, in Hampshire, son of Edward Wilberforce Unwin and Henrietta Jane (née Carnac). After attending private schools in Cheltenham, Malvern Wells and Clavering, he joined the Merchant Navy training ship *Conway*, aged 14. A tempestuous two years, during which he was once punished with twenty-four strokes of the birch, did not blight his career. He spent fifteen years as a Merchant Navy officer, first with the firm Donald Currie and then with P&O, before transferring to the Royal Navy as a lieutenant on 31 October 1895.

Two years later he married Evelyn Agnes Carew, a general's daughter, and shortly after took part in the punitive expedition against Benin, in West Africa, which resulted in his baptism of fire and his first campaign medal. Following a spell in HMS *Thunderer*, Unwin saw active service in the Boer War and in 1903 was made lieutenant-commander. He retired six years later as a commander, but was recalled shortly before the outbreak of war. Appointed fleet coaling officer on Admiral Jellicoe's staff, Unwin was given command of *Hussar* in February 1915.

Following a brief spell in Egypt, he returned to England to recuperate from his tremendous exertions during the landing on V Beach. Back in Mudros, he was given command of the cruiser *Endymion*, but no sooner had he taken up his new appointment than he was handed a key role in the August operations designed to open a new front at Suvla Bay. Responsible again for getting the troops safely ashore, he took charge of a fleet of specially designed motor-lighters, assisted once more by his faithful number one of V Beach days, Midshipman Drewry. The night landing, if not the subsequent advance, proved a great success. In a letter to his wife written on 20 August, he described his experiences:

It was a lovely dark night. I was in a picket boat so that I could dance about from lighter to lighter. When we were about 200 yards from the beach they began firing, but only very ragged stuff. I don't believe 20 men were hit, certainly none near me. Everything went off without a hitch ...

For three days and nights he toiled to bring men and supplies ashore, serving first as beachmaster and then as naval transport officer, for which he was awarded the Victoria Cross. From his beach-side burrow, where he was living like 'a rabbit', he admitted to his wife: 'I can't help feeling somewhat elated ... I've had a heap of nice messages. The V.A. (vice-admiral) told me no officer had ever had more recommendations ...' As ever, Unwin continued to lead by example. An army officer serving with him noted:

Cdr Unwin ... stands over 6ft and is broad in proportion, with the typical clean-shaven face of a sailor, and with a voice that roars orders through a megaphone, causing those who are ordered to jump about a good deal quicker on their jobs than they probably would do otherwise.

Reputedly the last man to leave Suvla when it was evacuated in December, Unwin ended his Gallipoli career the way he began it, with an act of selfless gallantry, rescuing a soldier who fell overboard while being shipped out to the waiting transports. Recommended for a Royal Humane Society Medal, Unwin was also commended by Admiral Wemyss for his services throughout the campaign: 'His conduct during the intervening time [25 April–20 December] has been such as to call for the admiration and respect of all with whom he has been brought in contact and I would respectfully ask that his acting rank of Captain may be confirmed.'

For his part in the evacuation, Unwin, who received his VC from King George V at Buckingham Palace on 15 January 1916, was made a Companion of the Order of St Michael and St George (*LG*, 14 March 1916). The rest of his war service was dull by comparison. Command of the light cruiser *Amethyst* on the South-East America Station was followed by Staff duties as Principal Naval Transport Officer, firstly in Egypt and then in the Eastern Mediterranean. Honours and promotion, however, continued to come his way, including the Order of the Nile, 3rd Class (*LG*, 17 March 1919), Companion of the Order of the Bath (*LG*, 27 May 1919) and the French Legion of Honour (*LG*, 12 December 1919). Also in 1919 he was made commodore. He retired for a second time in 1920 with the rank of captain, his seniority back-dated to 11 November 1918 in recognition of his distinguished war record.

In the years after the war, Unwin maintained close ties with fellow veterans of the Gallipoli campaign. He was a regular at the 29th Division's annual memorial service in Kent and remained a fierce critic of those he held responsible for the defeat at Gallipoli. 'If the campaign had been properly managed,' he once declared, 'Constantinople would have been taken ... A few more guns and we could have got there.'

An accomplished yachtsman with a passion also for tennis and croquet, he led an active retirement, combining sporting pursuits with civic duties. He lived in Cheltenham before moving to the family seat, Wootton Lodge, Ashbourne, in Derbyshire. From 1929 to 1939 Unwin was deputy lieutenant of Staffordshire and, until 1936, when he moved to Hindhead in Surrey, president of the Ellastone branch of the British Legion.

Edward Unwin collapsed and died on 19 April 1950, while on his way to have his customary early morning shave in Grayshott. He was buried in St Luke's churchyard, Grayshott, six days later, exactly thirty-five years after the disastrous landing which was his own finest hour.

According to Cdr Unwin, LS William Charles Williams 'was the man above all others who deserved the VC at the landing'. He was born on 15 September 1880 at Stanton Lacy in Shropshire, the son of William Williams, a gardener, and his wife Elizabeth. One of a large brood that included six sisters and, after his father's second marriage, a number of stepbrothers and stepsisters, William was still a youngster when his father uprooted the family to Chepstow to take a job with Pillinger's Nurseries.

Educated at Chepstow Grammar School, he enlisted for Boy's Service in the Royal Navy on 17 December 1895. Three years later, aged 18, he signed on for twelve years. His papers described him as 5ft 8½in tall, fair-skinned, with black hair and grey eyes. His baptism of fire came during the Boer War, when he was a member of Percy Scott's Naval Brigade, formed from the crew of HMS *Terrible* and sent to help relieve Ladysmith. By April 1900 Williams was in China, helping to defeat the Boxer rising. His services in both campaigns brought him commendations for gallantry, and reports on his character throughout his career were consistently marked 'very good'. From his first ship, *Lion*, he spent most of his time at sea in battleships, including spells in *Inflexible*, *Majestic*, *Furious*, *Hampshire* and *Renown*.

His regular service ended a day short of his 30th birthday. Able Seaman Williams joined the Royal Fleet Special Reserve on 19 September 1910. Returning to the Welsh borders, he lived with a married sister at 12 Victoria Crescent, Newport, and was employed by Messrs Lysaghts Orb Works, before joining the Monmouthshire Constabulary. Police service took him to St Mellions and Tredegar, but the lure of the sea proved too strong. By August 1914 he was back at sea, serving in the Merchant Navy.

Recalled for active service on 28 August, Williams joined HMS *Hussar* on 22 September. His family had not seen him for a year and had no inkling about his role in the Gallipoli landings. His last letter home before his death had merely been a request for his family to send on his pension and service documents. Williams was, in fact, a late addition to the *River Clyde*'s crew. By then a leading seaman, he made a special plea to Unwin to be allowed to join his team. Unwin later recalled: 'I told him I was full up and that I did not want any more petty officers, to which he replied, "I'll chuck my hook [relinquish his rating] if you will let me come", and I did, to his cost but everlasting glory.'

Williams's father received his son's Cross from King George V at Buckingham Palace on 16 November 1916. Memorials to the navy's first posthumous Victoria Cross recipient were unveiled in his home town of Chepstow on 8 January 1922. They consisted of a gun from a German submarine, presented to the town in his honour and unveiled by his sister, Mrs Frances Smith, and a painting by Charles Dixon of the V Beach landing. Purchased by public subscription, this was unveiled in St Mary's parish church by Capt. Unwin. Both memorials survive to this day, though the gun now stands nearer the town's principal war memorial as a result of redevelopment work.

Williams's medals – the VC, Queen's South Africa Medal with clasps for Relief of Ladysmith and Tugela Heights and China Medal 1900 – were auctioned at Dix, Noonan, Webb on 18 June 1997 and now form part of the Lord Ashcroft VC Collection displayed at the Imperial War Museum. The whereabouts of his 1914–15 Star, British War Medal and Victory Medal are not known.

William Williams was buried at sea and is commemorated on the Portsmouth Naval Memorial. The most fitting epitaph was provided by his former captain and fellow VC winner Edward Unwin, who called him 'the bravest sailor I ever knew'.

Among many letters received by George Drewry's parents after the landings was one from the *River Clyde*'s doctor, R. Burrowes Kelly,

in which he marvelled at their son's survival and applauded his courage. 'His absolute contempt of death, love of duty and modesty were proverbial amongst us all,' he wrote. 'You must indeed be proud of this splendid fellow and that he will be spared for many years to gladden your hearts is my one wish.' Tragically, his wish was to be unfulfilled.

George Leslie Drewry was born at 58 Claremont Road, Forest Gate, Essex, on 3 November 1894, third of four sons to Thomas Drewry and Mary (née Kendall), who both originally came from Lincolnshire. Thomas Drewry was works manager for the P&O Steam Navigation Company and George attended Merchant Taylors School, Blackheath, prior to joining the Merchant Navy as a 14-year-old apprentice in 1909.

Accident-prone as a youngster, he was to be the victim of numerous mishaps throughout his short life. Even before going to sea, he had survived being run over by a car and narrowly escaped death when he and his brother Ralph fell into a bog while playing in Wanstead Park. By the time their cries for help were heard, they had sunk up to their necks. The catalogue of calamities continued at sea. While training aboard the sailing boat *Indian Empire*, he fell from the mast into the sea, only to be saved by the gallant efforts of the vessel's mate. During another voyage in 1912 his ship was wrecked on the uninhabited Hermit Island as it rounded Cape Horn, leaving him and his crewmates to survive for two weeks on a diet of roots and shellfish before being rescued.

Shortly after his return to England he joined the P&O Line, serving as fourth officer in a mail steamer on the Australia, China and Japan routes. In July 1913, while still a P&O officer, he joined the RNR as a midshipman. Called up on 3 August 1914, while his ship, *Isis*, was at Port Said, he was appointed first to HMS *Egmont*, guardship at Malta, and then to *Hussar*, the fleet's communications ship. A largely uneventful few months ended in April 1915 when he was chosen by Unwin to help prepare the *River Clyde* for the Gallipoli landings. According to Burrowes Kelly, Drewry was 'devoted' to Unwin. He was certainly desperate to join the expedition, and in a letter to his father noted with pride how they had painted the collier's starboard side 'P&O colour'.

Despite his head injury, Drewry worked long into the evening of that memorable day at Cape Helles. His last task was to take wounded men from the hopper and lighters and place them in a trawler alongside the *River Clyde*. It was 'an awful job'. He wrote: 'They had not been dressed at all and some of the poor devils were in an awful state, I never knew blood smelt so strong before.' Three days later, while visiting a ruined village near the beach, he fainted at the sight of so many dead bodies. 'Never afterwards would he photograph anywhere near Sedd el Bahr,' noted Burrowes Kelly.

By the time newspapers fêted the young midshipman, Drewry was employed with Unwin again in the landings at Suvla Bay. The contrast with V Beach could not have been greater. He found it 'uncanny' that the troops could be disembarked with hardly any Turkish reaction. 'I thought of Helles,' he wrote, 'and then wondered if we had landed by mistake at Lemnos [the British base] or if we were ambushed and the Maxims were just going to clear the beach of living in one sweep.'

For five days during August he toiled to bring men and supplies ashore, once going under heavy fire during a run-in to Anzac Cove. 'I had no cover,' he wrote, 'and felt most funky.' Drewry rejoined *Hussar* on 11 August, having been barred from remaining with Unwin by an order preventing midshipmen from going ashore without being inoculated.

Promoted acting lieutenant in September 1916, Drewry was appointed to the battleship *Conqueror*. Shortly afterwards he was given leave to receive his Cross from the king at Buckingham Palace on 22 November. As the first RNR officer to achieve the distinction, he was given a Sword of Honour by the Imperial Merchant Service Guild.

By the summer of 1918 the hero of V Beach had his own command, HMT *William Jackson*, a decoy trawler. It was while serving in her that he suffered his final misfortune. On the evening of 2 August, while berthed at Scapa Flow in the Orkneys, he was struck by a block that fell from a derrick, fracturing his skull and breaking his left arm. This time there was no escape for the boy who had cheated death so many times in peace and war. George Drewry succumbed to his injuries the next day. A tragic accident had accomplished what countless enemy machine-gunners and marksmen had failed to do on that blood-drenched day at Cape Helles.

Fellow officers from the Northern Patrol commissioned a memorial window to him in All Saints' Church, Forest Gate, and his VC was later displayed at his old school alongside a painting of the *River Clyde*, before being presented to the Imperial War Museum, together with his sword. George Drewry's body was brought home for burial in the City of London Cemetery, Manor Park.

As one of the youngest VC recipients, he had been fêted by the press. Yet despite all the adulation, his family detected no change in him. 'He said he was only doing his duty and had never expected the VC,' recalled Ralph Drewry. 'When I showed him all the newspaper cuttings about him that we had kept he told me to put them in the toilet.'

'I am of a roving disposition. I can't settle anywhere very long,' said George Samson, the only Scot among the six V Beach VCs. It was a comment borne out by a life of adventure that might have been torn straight from the pages of the *Boys' Own* magazine.

George McKenzie Samson was born on 7 January 1889 at Carnoustie in Fife, Scotland, the second son of David Samson, a shoemaker, and Helen (née Lawson). One of nine children, he grew up at 63 Dundee Street, Carnoustie, and was an irregular pupil at the public school, where his classmates included Charles Alfred Jarvis, who was to earn a Victoria Cross at Mons. An habitual truant, Samson was forever getting into scrapes.

His first job was working on an uncle's farm near Arbroath, where he drove a milk cart for seven months. Bored by what he called his 'stale' life, he tried to run away to sea as a cabin boy in a sailing schooner, but was rejected as being too young. His chance came when, aged 17, he was engaged by a Forfarshire dealer to take thirty prize bulls to Buenos Aires. Having fulfilled his contract, he ventured inland and found work on a cattle ranch as a cowboy. After a year in the Argentine, he returned home and enlisted in the army, joining the King's Own Scottish Borderers. He completed his basic training, 'which stood me in good stead', but bought himself out a year later.

Answering once more the call of the sea, he signed on at Dundee to go whaling off the coast of Greenland, after which he sailed and travelled widely. 'I think,' he later observed, 'I can claim to have touched nearly every country in the world – certainly most places to which British ships sail – as the hymn goes, "From Greenland's icy mountains to India's coral strand".' In about 1910, while serving in the Merchant Navy, he joined the Royal Naval Reserve.

In 1912, seeking a 'new start', he worked his passage from Leith to the Turkish port of Smyrna, where he was employed for six months in a gas works. Growing restless once again, he volunteered to work as a fireman on one of the company's railway locomotives operating between Smyrna and Adana. 'This life suited me excellently,' he later recalled, 'and even better so when, after becoming acquainted with the line, I was promoted to the position of driver. I was the youngest driver in the service, and I think it was my nerve and confidence which got me on.'

Having progressed to mail train driver when war was declared in 1914, he immediately quit his post, packed a suitcase and took passage to Port Said where he unsuccessfully tried to join one of the warships. Reaching Malta in early August he was taken on and sent to HMS *Hussar*, then in the process of being fitted out as a communications ship.

Following Turkey's entry into the war, *Hussar* was sent as part of the Mediterranean Squadron to patrol the entrance to the Dardanelles and guard against any attempted breakout by the former German cruisers *Goeben* and *Breslau*. The work was monotonous, with winter storms posing a far greater threat to life and limb than the enemy. In a letter home, written in early 1915, Samson commented:

> We are having awful weather here, and the ship has been trying to stand on her head for the last fortnight, but has not managed it yet. The cold is far worse than the Germans, the only differ-ence being that you can feel the cold and not see it, and see the Germans not feel them. We are all very anxious to have another go at them and get it finished.

The arrival of Rear Admiral Rosslyn Wemyss as Governor of Lemnos, responsible for establishing a base at Mudros, provided Samson with a temporary diversion. As one of the few members of the fleet able to speak Greek and Turkish, he frequently found himself called upon to act as the admiral's interpreter. Indeed, it was his linguistic skills more than his ability as a seaman which earned him a place among the party selected by Cdr Unwin. He had not been present when the initial call for volunteers went out, and feared that his job as interpreter would keep him out of the fight. Unhappy at the prospect of inaction, he went to see Unwin, who defused the situation by saying: 'Who's to talk to the Greeks in the hopper if you don't come? None of us can speak Greek!' An interview with Wemyss followed, in which the admiral agreed to him taking part, though with the warning: 'Don't forget that you are not going on a picnic. There are 18 [*sic*] of my men going on the steamer and if any one of them returns alive I shall congratulate myself.'

Samson was one of the fortunate ones, although few among those treating the injuries he sustained the day after the landings gave him much chance of surviving. Evacuated by hospital ship, he spent three months in Port Said undergoing treatment before being shipped home. After four days in Haslar Naval Hospital, he was declared fit to return to Carnoustie, even though surgeons had only managed to extract four of the seventeen bullets from his body. He was recuperating in Aboyne when news reached his family that he had been awarded the VC.

The following day he returned to a civic reception, being greeted at a specially decorated railway station by the provost and an array of town councillors together with the Burgh band. A procession through the town followed with crowds cheering every foot of the way. It was a scene to be oft repeated. In the coming weeks Samson drew crowds wherever he went, a fact quickly exploited by recruiting officers.

On 5 October, shortly after his life story had been serialised in the press, he went to Buckingham Palace to receive his Cross. Promoted chief petty officer, he was a guest at the 110th anniversary celebrations marking Nelson's victory at Trafalgar. Half a century later his home town would honour his memory by naming a street after him, but at the time they settled for giving him a smoker's cabinet and a solid silver rose bowl. A more unexpected gift was the white feather given to him while he was travelling out of uniform!

George Samson married Charlotte Glass, a farmer's daughter, at the Huntly Arms Hotel, Aboyne, on 31 December 1915, and they were to have two sons and a daughter. His wounds, however, continued to cause him problems and in June 1916 he was given a year's sick leave. He returned to Aboyne, where his wife was living, and was described in one account as 'bright and cheery'. A year on his health was scarcely improved and he was officially discharged from the navy, and he took up 'a Government appointment' in Aberdeen. He still harboured hopes of being passed fit for further service, but as the war continued Samson spent prolonged spells in a variety of hospitals. And it was while on the sick list at Invergordon that he was presented with the Medaille Militaire (*LG*, 28 August 1918), presumably in belated recognition by the French of his actions at Cape Helles. Restless as ever, despite his painful injuries, he tried in vain to volunteer for service in North Russia in the spring of 1919, arriving at the recruiting office in Dundee in full chief petty officer's uniform with his VC and Medaille Militaire ribbons adorning his breast.

Unable to settle, he eventually found his way back into the Merchant Navy, sailing out of Dundee as quartermaster aboard the new Caledon-built oil tanker *Dosina* in February 1922. His last letter home was written nearly a year later from the Gulf of Mexico. In it, he complained of feeling ill and said that if they encountered another ship he was to be transferred and sent home. Shortly afterwards, he was put aboard the SS *Strombus* and taken to Bermuda. But it was too late. Comatose when he arrived, he succumbed to double pneumonia in St George's Hospital on 23 February 1923, never having regained consciousness.

George Samson, farm-hand, cowboy, train driver and seaman, was buried with full honours in the island's military cemetery, a corner of a foreign field that was a peculiarly apt last resting place for one of the most restless of all VC recipients. Ninety years on, his medals have found a home at the Imperial War Museum, forming part of an impressive array of awards to fellow V Beach heroes Unwin, Malleson and Williams, having been acquired at auction by Lord Ashcroft for the princely sum of £210,000.

Much was made in the British press of the great gallantry displayed by so many young midshipmen, boys too young to vote but willing to die for 'King and Country'. Typical of the banner headlines was one in the *Daily Express* on 17 August 1915, which ran: 'Middies Answer the Query: Is Britain Decadent?' The youngest of the six V Beach VCs was 18 years and 5 months old. His name was Wilfrid St Aubyn Malleson.

He was born on 17 September 1896 at Kirkee, in India, the eldest son of Major General Wilfrid Malleson (later Sir Wilfrid, KCIE, CB), a distinguished Indian Army officer. Wilfrid was brought to England by his grandmother to attend prep school at Edgeborough, near Guildford, and it became his second home, with holidays being spent either with relatives or with the headmaster and his wife. Progressing to Marlborough in 1908, he joined the Royal Naval College, Dartmouth, four years later and was appointed a midshipman in the battleship *Cornwallis* three days before the outbreak of war. Having taken part in the bombardment of the Turkish shore defences in early 1915, *Cornwallis* was assigned to cover the landings at S Beach, Cape Helles, on 25 April. Malleson was among a group of officers and men formed into a beach party to carry reinforcements and stores on to V Beach after a landing had been effected. So great, however, was the enemy resistance that the third tow, in which Malleson was a member, became embroiled in the struggle to gain the merest of toe-holds.

The only one of the six VC recipients to escape without physical injury, Malleson spent six days toiling on the beach, unloading water and ammunition and helping to guide units of the French army ashore. The strain of that work, coming so soon after his ordeal during the assault, took a heavy toll. He was evacuated to Bighi Hospital in Malta suffering from rheumatic fever which his brother Rupert, then a 15-year-old 'snottie' in the *Lord Nelson*, attributed to his 'long immersion and physical exhaustion off V Beach'. After recovering, he was promoted acting sub-lieutenant on 15 May 1916, and joined his brother in *Lord Nelson* six months later, his rank being confirmed on 30 December. He was the last of the V Beach VCs to receive his award, attending a Buckingham Palace investiture on 2 January 1918.

Three months earlier Malleson had embarked on what was to become a long association with the submarine service. Promoted lieutenant on 30 March, he joined the depot ship *Lucia*, under the command of Martin Nasmith VC, on 5 November and was in her when the war ended. Peace-time service in the submarines *L7* and *L19* followed, before he gained his first command, *H50*, in 1923. A two-year 'big ship' spell was then followed by command of *L69* in 1927.

That same year he married Cecil Mary Collinson at St Mark's, in St Marylebone, London, and they had one daughter. Malleson was based at the time in Gosport and they settled near Plymouth.

After a spell on the staff at Devonport, Malleson, by then in his mid-30s, was posted to the cruiser *Berwick* on the China Station. With a slightly hooked nose, he had the look of a pirate. One of his contemporaries, Commander J.P. Macintyre, recalled: 'He was known as "Mad Malleson"; that is not meant to be pejorative mad, but a chap who is a bit unpredictable. He was fiercely forgetful, abnormally so.'

Advancement in the peace-time navy was slow. By the outbreak of the Second World War Malleson was a commander serving at Devonport. He joined the Retired List in 1941 only to be recalled and appointed Assistant Captain of Malta Dockyard. He remained on the island throughout the rest of the war, being joined in 1945 by his family. Promoted Captain of the Dockyard and later King's Harbour Master, he served on Malta until finally retiring in 1948 as a captain.

Still in his early 50s, Malleson settled briefly in Lifton, Devon, before moving to Washaway, near Bodmin in Cornwall, and then on to Galloway, where he ran a hotel in the first of a number of attempts to establish a second career. Returning to Cornwall, he and his wife spent ten years managing a caravan park near St Austell. In the early 1960s they retired and moved to St Clement, near Truro. Malleson spent his last twelve years here, in a bungalow he had built on a plot of land that included an orchard.

A notable village character, Malleson, who had taken to wearing a monocle, was active in the community, serving as chairman of the parish hall committee and chairman of the local sea cadets, but few knew of his distinguished war record. A painting of his exploit at Cape Helles was hidden away from public view and he declined all invitations to join the Victoria Cross and George Cross Association. According to his brother Hugh, himself a retired naval commander, Malleson's modesty was 'very real'. Hugh added:

> He reckoned that he and his companions trying to replace the landing barges at V Beach ... were available for any odd jobs, and this was an emergency. Of course, he was frightened, as were the others, but like truly modest men, he seemed to prefer keeping his reflections on the action to himself.
>
> The hours spent in the water, trying to get the lighters back into position, under heavy fire was one thing, but the visible execution of hundreds of our soldiers before slipping into the water might well have un-nerved others. On this subject, therefore, Wilfrid's reluctance to talk or join in celebrations about VCs was initiated by his illness at Bighi Hospital and prolonged by the curious.

Captain Malleson, last of the heroic band of V Beach VCs, died on 21 July 1975, aged 78. His body was cremated, and in keeping with his wishes, his ashes were scattered at sea off Falmouth by his old colleague Commander Macintyre. His medals, originally presented to Edgeborough School, were later acquired by Lord Ashcroft and are displayed at the Imperial War Museum.

The only one of the six VCs earned at the Cape Helles landing not gazetted on 16 August 1915, the award to Arthur Tisdall might not have been made at all but for the persistence of his parents in pressing their son's case.

Arthur Walderne St Clair Tisdall, the first member of the Royal Naval Division to receive the country's highest award for valour, was born on 21 July 1890 in Bombay, India, the second son of the Revd Dr William St Clair Tisdall, an expert on comparative Eastern religions who was running the Church Missionary Society's Mohammedan Mission, and his wife Marian (née Gray).

Following a brief stay in England, the Tisdall family embarked in 1892 for Persia, where Dr Tisdall took up a new appointment, heading the CMS Persia-Baghdad Mission. Arthur, nicknamed 'Pog', was educated by an English governess and his father. A gifted child, he could speak Latin by the age of 10. When the family returned to England in 1900 he went to Bedford School. His scholarly progress to Trinity College, Cambridge, was paved with prizes. A popular figure with an infectious sense of humour, 'Wally' Tisdall, as he became known, matched academic achievement with sporting prowess and some slightly eccentric behaviour – he once walked from Bedford to Cambridge at night. Over 6ft tall, powerfully built, his broad forehead crowned by a mop of dark brown wavy hair, he was a man of enormous potential.

At Cambridge he rowed for his college and amassed a collection of prizes, culminating in a Double First BA Honours degree and the award of the Chancellor's Gold Medal for Classics. Among his enthusiasms were the growth of socialism, women's suffrage, economics and literature. While at university, Tisdall developed a passion for writing poetry. Noted for his comic verse and nonsense rhymes, he showed in his poems the first stirrings of an unfulfilled talent. For a while he considered becoming a writer, but eventually opted for a more orthodox career as a civil servant. In 1913 he passed the combined Indian and Home Civil Service examination and took up a post in London. The higher echelons of Whitehall beckoned. Then came the war.

When the RNVR was mobilised in August 1914, Tisdall, who had enlisted three months earlier, cut short a camping holiday to join his unit as an able seaman. His only previous military experience had been in the ranks of the OTC at Bedford and Cambridge, but after training at Walmer Tisdall went with the Royal Naval Division to Belgium to help defend Antwerp. Although only a rating, he acted as interpreter to the local Belgian commandant. His first experience of war made a deep impression. In a letter home, he wrote: 'The burning city of Antwerp is a terrible but magnificent sight against the blackness of the night, and lights up the whole country round. The sight of the poor women and children driven from their homes makes one's blood boil. It's horrid to feel so useless.'

Unable to save the city from the Germans, over a thousand men from the division marched into internment in Holland. Tisdall was among those who escaped. Back in England he was commissioned sub-lieutenant in the Anson Battalion, back-dated to 1 October. Posted eventually to Blandford Camp, Dorset, where the division underwent reconstruction, Tisdall spent a dismal winter training before news arrived in February 1915 that they were to be posted overseas. 'We have been promised a six-week or two-month campaign, probably fairly exciting,' he wrote. After an inspection by Churchill, the division left their quarters on 27 February bound for Bristol, the first stop on a journey that would carry them to the Dardanelles. By March they were on the island of Lemnos, full of optimism for a campaign that had taken on the aura of a latter-day crusade. On 9 March Tisdall wrote:

> Life is so pleasant here and there's something to look forward to; to turn the Turks out of Constantinople, etc., would be a thing well worth doing, and give me a feeling I had really done one satisfactory piece of work. Here one really feels that we are fighting on the side of civilisation.

The division was shipped to Egypt while preparations continued, before returning to Lemnos where Tisdall was informed of his platoon's role aboard the *River Clyde*. Of the landings, and his part in it, he left no record. His diaries were never found and his last undated postcard home was sent on 7 May. By then, he was already dead.

Following the landings, Tisdall's platoon had carried out the supply duties that they were originally tasked with. On 27 April Tisdall had written: 'Have been under fire ... all day spent in burying soldiers. Some of my men killed. We are all happy and fit. Plenty of hard work and enemy shells, and a smell of dead men ...' His courageous leadership, so evident on the first day, was plain for all to see. Once, when a shell burst near a French gun team, injuring a horse and panicking the crew, he calmly went out, got the horse to its feet and made the gunners return. For five days the Anson Battalion, including Tisdall's platoon, helped to bolster the newly arrived French, while preparations were made for an advance on Achi Baba. The Second Battle of Krithia began and ended on 6 May with little progress made and many casualties sustained in the process. Among them was Arthur Tisdall. Leading his men into an abandoned Turkish trench, they were heavily bombarded and, while sheltering there, he was shot by a sniper. Mortally wounded in the chest, he died without regaining consciousness. 'He was one of England's bravest men,' wrote one man from his platoon. 'All his men cried when he went because all the boys thought the world of him.'

He was buried close to where he fell on 7 May, the news reaching his father in Deal, where he was vicar of St George's, three days later.

A memorial service was held on 13 May, and an engraved tablet was later placed in the church. But Tisdall's actions would almost certainly have gone unrecognised had it not been for his parents' determined lobbying. Lt Cdr Wedgwood, who recommended two of his own men for VCs for their part in the rescue work (both received CGMs), had mentioned 'Lieut Tidsdale's [*sic*] gallant exploit' in a letter to Churchill two days after the landings. But, while many had witnessed his acts of selflessness, none had officially reported them, because of what Wedgwood called his 'anomalous position' as senior officer of a detached platoon. In the weeks after his death his parents received many letters from officers and men, describing their son's heroism. And when his name was not mentioned among those honoured for the V Beach landings, they started asking questions: first of Edward Unwin, who by then had been awarded his VC, and then of more senior officers. Eventually, in late 1915, after letters had appeared in *The Times*, Major General A. Paris (GOC, RN Division) ordered an investigation into the case. Survivors of the action were traced and interviewed and the result was a recommendation for a posthumous VC. Writing in support of honouring Tisdall's actions, Charles Walker, a senior official at the Admiralty, commented:

> Many knew that an Officer of the RND had shown conspicuous bravery but hardly anyone seems to have known his name … If the story as pieced together had been represented at the time, doubtless rewards would have been given, possibly a VC to Sub Lieut Tisdall and CGMs to the four men [Perring, Curtiss, Malia and Parkinson] … It is proposed that, whether rewards are given or not, the services of Sub Lieut Tisdall and the four men should be recognised by gazetting their names and that a special letter should be written to the relatives of the Sub Lieutenant.

Sixteen days later the *London Gazette* announced the posthumous award of a VC to Tisdall and CGMs to Perring, Malia and Parkinson. Sadly, Curtiss's death in action on 4 June rendered him ineligible.

Fifty-five years after his courageous actions at Cape Helles, Tisdall's brother and sister presented his medals on loan to the London Division, RNVR. They were subsequently displayed at the Royal Naval Museum in Portsmouth but have since been sold privately. Today, Arthur Tisdall's selfless example is remembered at HMS *Raleigh*, at Torpoint in Cornwall, where a training block bears his name, and at Deal, where an impressive Celtic cross honours a life that promised greatness but was cut off in its prime.

E.C. BOYLE

Sea of Marmora, 27 April–18 May 1915

On 14 April 1915 a select group of naval officers gathered in the after cabin aboard the battleship *Queen Elizabeth* in Mudros harbour. Present among them were two submarine captains, together with Charles Brodie and Cdre Roger Keyes. There was only one subject on the agenda: the question of a submarine penetrating the mine-infested Narrows to reach the Sea of Marmora, a stretch of water regarded by the Turks as their own private lake. For some time Brodie's was the only voice, as he traced the likely route on a chart, outlining the navigational as well as the military hazards. Perfectly spaced rows of mines, five in all, indicated in red above and below Kephez underlined the Turkish determination to prevent any breakthrough, while Brodie was able to speak from experience about the dangers posed by the many searchlights that nightly swept the channel. The question of difficulties of trim owing to the different densities of fresh and salt water where the Marmora met the Mediterranean was little understood and hardly touched upon. As Brodie's briefing petered out in a flurry of questions and answers, Keyes, who had said barely a word, cut them short. 'Do you think an E-boat can make it?' he asked.

Of those present, only one answered in the affirmative: Brodie's twin brother T.S. Brodie, captain of *E15*. The other submariner was Courtney Boyle, the cool and efficient commander of *E14*. Both were recent arrivals in the Dardanelles and their subsequent fortunes could not have been more different.

Within four days of that portentous conference, Brodie had been killed and his boat wrecked in the first attempt to exceed Norman Holbrook's great coup, and inside a fortnight Boyle had become only the second submariner to enter the Marmora, following in the wake of Hew Stoker's *AE2*, which safely negotiated the Dardanelles bottleneck on 25 April to signal the beginning of one of the most successful submarine campaigns ever waged.

E14 made her passage past the Gallipoli beach-head as the rattle of rifle-fire drifted across the water in the early hours of 27 April. The crew's mood was similar to that in *B11* four months earlier. 'I think really that we were all resigned for the worst and hoped for the best,' wrote Edward Stanley, *E14*'s first lieutenant. Ahead, where the water narrowed, the white glare of searchlights turned night into day. To Stanley it all looked 'very weird and threatening', but Boyle, standing alone and exposed on the open conning tower, appeared unruffled. Determined to travel as far as possible on the surface, he held his course until a searchlight at Suan Dere picked him out. Only then, with shells churning the sea ahead, did he take *E14* under.

Diving to 90ft, *E14* passed under one minefield before rising to 22ft a mile south of Kilid Bahr. Contrary to the prevailing wisdom that favoured a slow, underwater passage, Boyle had decided to gamble on surprise and speed. Trimming *E14* so that the conning tower was awash, he surged through the dark, passing Chanak at 5.15 a.m., with all the forts blazing at him. The channel was alive with enemy patrol boats, but what might have overawed some merely served to whet Boyle's appetite. He reported:

> I saw one torpedo gunboat, 'Berki-Satvet' class, which I fired at range about 1600yd. I just had time to see a large column of water as high as her mast rise from her quarter where she was presumably hit, when I had to dip again as the men in a small steam boat were leaning over trying to catch hold of the top of my periscope.

Unusual though this encounter was, Boyle was fortunate that the men aboard the steamer were not armed. Rounding Nagara Point at 6.30 a.m., he passed beneath three pairs of patrol boats searching for him, and at 9 a.m., while taking a navigational fix, he spotted a battleship, which he took to be the *Muin-I-Zaffer*, about a quarter of a mile astern heading for Nagara. Unable to get a shot at her, and with the sea speckled with patrol boats, he pressed on, passing Gallipoli at 10.15 a.m. to reach the Marmora. However, such was the state of alert that Boyle was forced to remain submerged for another five and a half hours. The cat and mouse game had begun.

Boyle's first full day in the Marmora was a frustrating one. Enemy patrol boats and destroyers, maintaining a careful watch, appeared to be all around and every time *E14* broke surface, she attracted fire, which forced her under from 9 a.m. to 7.30 p.m. Needing to recharge his batteries, Boyle eventually sought out safer waters in the vicinity of Marmora Island, though even there a destroyer forced him to dive.

The next day brought a change of fortune. Having sighted four destroyers at 12.30 p.m., Boyle spotted more smoke at 1.15 p.m. This time there were two troopships, with three escorting destroyers. With the sea glassy calm, conditions were hardly ideal for an attack, but the targets were too tempting to pass up. Almost as soon as *E14*'s periscope popped up, she was spotted and the destroyers turned towards her, firing as they came. Boyle held his nerve. He wrote:

> I fired at one transport, range about 1500yd, but had to dip before I could see the effect of the shot. (One periscope had had the upper window pane broken by a shot the day before and was useless, and so I could not afford to risk my remaining one being bent). However, I heard a thud and the depth gauges flicked 10ft, and when I was able to put the periscope up about half an hour afterwards I saw two destroyers and one ship proceeding on their original course and the remaining ship and destroyer making for the shore ...

Dense columns of yellow smoke pouring from the transport, later identified as the 921-ton steamer *Ittihat*, confirmed *E14*'s torpedo had found its mark. But what Boyle did not know was that one of the Turkish destroyers, thought to have been the *Muavent-I Milliye*, had made an attempt to ram him. Unaware how close he had come to disaster, Boyle continued with his patrol and, a few hours later, enjoyed an altogether different encounter when he unexpectedly made contact with Stoker's *AE2*. In stark contrast to *E14*, the Australian boat had suffered a run of bad luck. After a brief discussion, arrangements were made to meet again the next day. It was a rendezvous *AE2* was unable to keep. Early on 30 April, *AE2* encountered the Turkish torpedo boat *Sultan Hissar*. In attempting to escape, the submarine lost control and was fatally holed by two shells. Stoker and his crew were able to swim away, the majority being taken prisoner.

Turkish pressure was mounting. Twice on 30 April *E14* came under attack and was forced to dive hurriedly. After a night spent sheltering at the bottom of Karabuga Bay, and frustrated by the lack of transports, Boyle decided instead to sink a patrol boat for the simple reason that 'they were always firing at me'. It did not take him long to exact his revenge: 'At 10.45 I fired at and sank a small gunboat which looked as if she was fitted as a mine layer ... She sank in less than a minute.

I remained in the vicinity, and a larger gunboat ... came up and I fired at her. Unfortunately the torpedo did not run straight ...'

Boyle's victim was the minelayer *Nour-el-Bahr*, and the explosion of her deadly cargo was sufficient to give *E14* a severe shaking. It would be another nine days before his next success, but in that interval Boyle's very presence was sufficient to spread alarm throughout the Marmora, with ships scurrying back to port rather than running the risk of encountering *E14*. Days of fruitless chasing and searching ended on 10 May in dramatic fashion near Kalolimno Island. While Boyle's crew were taking a swim, a destroyer was sighted. They quickly scrambled back on board and *E14* dived; the destroyer passed overhead. *E14* waited until 6 p.m. when a second destroyer hove into view, followed by two transports. Boyle wasted no time in lining up a target:

The torpedo fired at the leading transport did not run straight and missed astern. The second torpedo hit the second transport, and there was a terrific explosion. Debris and men were seen falling into the water. She was a three-masted and two-funnelled ship and about twice as large as any other ship I saw there. Unfortunately it was 7.35pm when I fired, and in ten minutes it was quite dark, so I did not see her actually sink. However, she was very much down by the stern when I last saw her, and must have sunk in a very short time.

According to one of *E14*'s crew, Leading Stoker John Haskins, troops aboard the transport were seen jumping overboard 'in their hundreds', prompting a loud cheer. The 5,017-ton former White Star liner *Germanic*, rechristened *Guj Djemal*, was, indeed, seriously damaged. However, contrary to British accounts, which credited Boyle with her destruction, Turkish records show that *E14*'s most celebrated victim actually survived the torpedo attack. *Guj Djemal*, with 1,600 troops aboard and not the 6,000 men trumpeted by an exultant British press, was apparently able to limp into Constantinople with the assistance of two Bosphorus ferries.

Irrespective of the transport's escape, the damage to Turkish morale was immense. Constantinople was gripped by submarine hysteria. Many ships remained in port rather than risk an encounter with *E14*. Those that did dare to venture out of their Marmora ports were prone to scuttle back at the first, and often erroneous, report of a submarine sighting. Even enemy naval vessels appeared to be running scared. Writing on 14 May, Boyle observed: 'I think that the Turkish torpedo boats must have been frightened of ramming us, as several times when I tried to remain on the surface at night they were so close when sighted that it must have been possible to get us if they had so desired.' In such circumstances it scarcely mattered that his last torpedo was found to be faulty. The threat that *E14* posed was enough, and even without armament, her value to the Allied cause was out of all proportion to her actual successes. For three more days, *E14* continued to prowl the Marmora with a dummy gun rigged by her crew until, finally, on 17 May, she was ordered home.

Boyle's return passage was every bit as eventful as his journey into the Marmora. Setting off at 4.40 a.m., he once again relied on speed. Twice before reaching the Narrows he had brushes with patrol boats. Charging full speed for Gallipoli, he came under attack from three vessels. The chase lasted nearly an hour before Boyle took *E14* down, with shells bursting too close for comfort. His pursuers, however, were not easily shaken off. 'The gunboat, TB and tug shepherded me to Gallipoli,' wrote *E14*'s captain, 'one each side and one astern, evidently expecting me to get caught in the nets there ...' They were to be sorely disappointed. Over the course of the next seven hours *E14* eluded every defensive obstacle placed in its path: nets, mines, patrol boats (Boyle even caught sight of the battleship *Torgud Reis* north of Nagara) and shore batteries. At 3.40 p.m. she surfaced abeam of a French battleship whose crew responded with 'a rousing cheer'. It was a fitting end to a trail-blazing twenty-two-day patrol in which *E14* had accounted for a troopship, a transport, a patrol boat and a minelayer.

As only the second British submariner to penetrate the Narrows and the first to make it safely back, Courtney Boyle was immediately fêted. Within twenty-four hours word reached him that he had been awarded the Victoria Cross, the telegram beating the *London Gazette* announcement by two days. Keyes, for whom *E14*'s epic patrol represented the vindication of his daring policy, wrote of the award: '... isn't it splendid! They gave it to him on the strength of a wire we sent on the night of the 14th saying that he deserved the greatest credit for his persistent enterprise in remaining in the Sea of Marmora, hunted day and night ... *E14* simply disarranged the whole Sea of Marmora.'

One of the most experienced of all British submariners, Edward Courtney Boyle was born on 23 March 1883 in Carlisle, Cumberland, the son of Lieutenant-Colonel Edward Boyle of the Army Pay Department and Edith (née Cowley). He was educated at Cheltenham College and *Britannia*, where, as a cadet captain, he was remembered by Charles Brodie as having the 'deep chest and long limbs of a runner'. A fine athlete, he excelled as a rugby wing three-quarter, possessing 'the knack of looking unruffled when others were muddied oafs'. In fact, Boyle did most things with an apparent, and to some, infuriating ease that was occasionally mistaken for arrogance. An early submarine convert, Boyle joined the depot ship *Thames* for instruction on 4 July 1904 as a sub-lieutenant. So quickly did he master this new mode of warfare that he was promoted lieutenant within five months of his arrival and given his first command, a Holland boat, at just 21. From the very beginning, Boyle stood out from the crowd. Brodie wrote:

> In the period 1905–8 submarines and motor bicycles were new and fascinating if grubby toys, and specialists were often dubbed pirates. Boyle knew his submarine as thoroughly and rode his motor cycle as fast as any, but was more courteous and tidy than most pirates ... He did not pose, but seemed slightly aloof, ganging his own gait.

After a spell in command of *C4*, Boyle returned to general service in the battleship *Ocean* before taking over *C29* in 1910. Much the same pattern followed, with Boyle skippering the *D2* and serving in St Vincent before embarking on six years of unbroken submarine service. Commanding *D3* in the Harwich-based 8th Flotilla at the outbreak of war, Lieutenant Boyle made a number of patrols into the North Sea, including one that Keyes described as a 'first class reconnaissance' off the north German coast and which resulted in a mention in despatches. His skill was further recognised by promotion to lieutenant-commander and his appointment in October to command the new *E14*, one of three E-boats sent to the Dardanelles in March.

Boyle became a national hero within the space of two extraordinary months. In all, between April and August 1915, *E14* made three successful cruises into the Marmora, each successive foray made more dangerous by improved Turkish defences. Returning from his third patrol, Boyle narrowly evaded two torpedoes fired from the shore, scraping beneath the minefields to safety. Having spent seventy days in the Marmora, Boyle and his crew, all of whom had been decorated for the first patrol, were withdrawn and rested, never to return. With the evacuation of Gallipoli, *E14* was ordered to the Adriatic, where conditions were not to Boyle's liking. The clear waters coupled with the enemy's well-sited observation posts led him to make a formal protest, complaining that he could spend no more than two days on patrol at a time because 'the strain on the captain was too great'.

His spell there was brief. In August 1916, Boyle, who had been made a Knight of the Legion of Honour by the French (*LG*, 7 April 1916) and given the Italian Order of St Maurice and St Lazarus (*LG*, 14 July 1916) to add to his VC, returned to England to take command of the *J5*, part of the 11th Flotilla at Blyth. Echoes of the Dardanelles, however, trailed after him. That year, he fought and lost a £31,000 claim in an Admiralty prize court for 'sinking' the *Guj Djemal*. Ironically, the case was thrown out, not as a result of any new information regarding the transport's fate, but because she had not been 'offensively armed'. Even more bizarrely, shortly after the war, the decision was reversed by an Admiralty still convinced of the ship's destruction.

After the war, Boyle, who had been promoted commander at the height of his fame, was loaned to the Australian Navy and appointed to HMAS *Platypus* in charge of a submarine flotilla. It was his last submarine posting. Promoted captain on 30 June 1920, he commanded the light cruisers *Birmingham* and *Carysfort* between 1922 and 1926, and spent the next two years as King's Harbour Master at Devonport. His last active appointment was commanding the veteran battleship *Iron Duke* from 1929 to 1931. He retired on 19 October 1932, a day after being promoted rear admiral. Returned to the Active List in 1939, Admiral Boyle spent the next three years in *Pembroke* and *President* as Flag Officer in Charge, London, before finally retiring in 1943.

Boyle lived in retirement at the Sunningdale Hotel, Sunningdale, and was a keen member of the local golf club. A childless widower, he died on 16 December 1967, after being knocked down by a lorry on a pedestrian crossing. His family presented his VC to HMS *Dolphin*, headquarters of the 1st Submarine Squadron, at a ceremony in Fort Blockhouse in 1988, eighty-two years after the then Lieutenant Boyle took over the fort from the army as one of the first submarine stations. Today, the Cross is one of the treasures in the care of the Royal Navy Submarine Museum, Gosport.

M.E. NASMITH

Sea of Marmora, 19 May–7 June 1915

At last had come our turn. Should we get through? Where should we be the next night? These were the questions we asked ourselves, but there 'twas. Orders are orders and need I say that not one man was afraid, but it was nerve-trying …

Such were the emotions of Edgar Lohden, leading telegraphist of HM Submarine *E11*, on the night of 18 May 1915. His captain had just returned from a short conference aboard the battleship *Lord Nelson*, anchored in Kephalo harbour, Imbros. The meeting with a tired but elated Courtney Boyle, Vice-Admiral de Robeck and his chief of staff Roger Keyes had been a short one, ending with Keyes's memorable exhortation to 'go and run amok in the Marmora!'

Martin Nasmith needed no second urging. Supremely fit, innovative and charismatic, he was said to possess the best 'periscope eye' in the navy. But luck, that crucial and most elusive of all commodities, had been sadly lacking in his war career to date. Thwarted in his attempt to reach the Baltic, he had suffered further mishaps en route to the Dardanelles which cost him the chance to be the first man to reach the Marmora. It speaks volumes for his reputation that even after so many setbacks his colleagues considered him to be a submariner without equal. The first Dardanelles patrol of *E11* proved beyond question the correctness of that assertion.

From the outset Nasmith's intention was not merely to repeat his *Britannia* term-mate's success, but to eclipse it. Greatly assisted by having flown over the Narrows shortly before embarking on his mission, Nasmith made quick and, by Boyle's standards, relatively quiet progress as far as Kilid Bahr during the early hours of 19 May. But the sight of two battleships steaming towards Nagara was too tempting and, despite being in the midst of the most heavily protected strip of water, he prepared to attack. Unfortunately for him, the current was strong and the wash caused by his protruding periscope 'attracted an unpleasant amount of attention from the numerous patrol craft'. Though the torpedo tubes were readied for firing, the Turks were, in Nasmith's words, 'too clever' and surged past while their patrol boats kept *E11* down.

Eventually, having shaken them off with a long dive, *E11* passed Nagara and the minefield off Gallipoli, and at 1.45 p.m., its battery almost exhausted, Nasmith took her to the bottom and waited for dark. *E11*'s first full day, spent exploring the western Marmora, passed off uneventfully with sightings of only small craft. Nasmith decided to investigate the eastern side, towards Constantinople itself. The following morning *E11* stopped a small sailing vessel, liberated a deck cargo of chickens and eighty eggs, and lashed the boat alongside its conning tower to act as camouflage. By 8 p.m., having sighted nothing, Nasmith slipped his cover and headed west for the night. The next day yielded more contacts but no successes, and it was not until 23 May that *E11* opened its account. The destruction of the 'gaily painted' gunboat *Pelenk-i-Dria*, riding at anchor off Constantinople, was, however, not without incident. As pandemonium broke out aboard *E11*, with shouts, cheers and clapping, the sinking vessel hit back. Tel. Lohden wrote:

> Our officers were all anxious to see the ship sinking and the periscope was unwisely kept up too long. Bang! A shot hit the water near us. Bang! 'By Jove! He's hit us,' said the Captain, as indeed he had. The Gunner must have been an excellent shot and had a good nerve …

According to Nasmith, it was the first shot which did the damage, but whichever one it was the result was the same: the foremost periscope was rendered useless. Embarrassing setback though this was, it did nothing to hamper Nasmith's adventurous instincts. Indeed, the attack off Seraglio Point served merely as a foretaste of things to come. First, though, there was an entertaining interlude. The following morning *E11* stopped a steamer and ordered its crew to abandon ship, which they did in 'reckless haste' and in such comic-opera fashion that all but one of the boats capsized. At that point, Nasmith reported, 'an American gentleman' appeared on the upper deck, introduced himself as a reporter on the *Chicago Sun* and declared that he was 'pleased to make our acquaintance'. Nasmith's first lieutenant, Lt Guy D'Oyly Hughes, boarded the steamer and, before sinking her with a demolition charge, gave the journalist an unlikely scoop in which he declared *E11* to be merely one of eleven submarines operating in the Marmora.

Hardly pausing to observe his men's handiwork, Nasmith immediately set off in pursuit of another vessel. *E11* chased the heavily laden steamer *Hunkar Iskelesi* into Rodosto harbour, putting a torpedo into her as she lay alongside the pier. Once again the submarine's periscope became a target as she bumped through the shallow waters. Fortunately, the only direct hit was scored by a rifle bullet which left a big dent in the lower tube. The drama, however, was not yet over. *E11* sighted a paddle-steamer, the *Kismet*, its deck festooned with coils of barbed wire. Hailed to stop, she turned sharply and boldly attempted to ram the submarine. Having avoided the potentially disastrous collision, Nasmith chased her on to a beach. But just as the submariners were preparing to mount their second boarding operation of the day, they found themselves under attack from a party of horsemen on the clifftop above the stricken vessel. With the conning tower exposed to 'hot rifle fire', *E11* was forced to beat a hasty retreat with yet another bullet, according to Lohden, narrowly missing the only working periscope, and a further one 'piercing the Skipper's cap'. Nasmith's parting shot, a torpedo fired from a safe distance, missed, exploding harmlessly on the shore.

Content with his tally, Nasmith now decided to carry out an attack that had been in his mind from the very beginning of his patrol. It was what Signalman George Plowman called 'the grand splash': an attack into the very heart of the Ottoman empire. Diving unobserved near Oxia Island at 6 a.m. on 25 May, *E11* dodged a guardship and nosed into Constantinople harbour, Nasmith taking care to follow the course taken by a steamer during his reconnaissance two days before. From an array of targets, he selected a large vessel, later identified as the *Stamboul*, which was moored alongside the arsenal, together with a smaller ship lying ahead of her. In his report, he described his audacious attack:

12.35pm. Fired Port Bow Tube. Torpedo failed to run. Fired Starboard Bow torpedo and observed track heading for larger vessel. Unable to observe the effect owing to being swept ashore by cross tide and the presence of what I took to be a Brennan torpedo ... Two explosions were heard, so it is probable that the stray torpedo found a mark as well as the one directed at the ship lying alongside the arsenal ...

Diving away, *E11* grounded heavily, bouncing up to 40ft; only by flooding her internal tanks and going full astern did Nasmith prevent her breaking surface. Even then she was in trouble. Gripped by the fierce harbour currents, *E11* was swung round before her captain regained control to bump into deeper water. More by luck than judgement, *E11* eventually scraped her way out. Only after twenty minutes did Nasmith dare bring her to the surface, and by then he was well clear. It had been a close run thing. As D'Oyly Hughes admitted: 'The good God brought *E11* out of Constantinople – because none of us knew where we were going.'

E11 left behind a city seized by panic. Troopships were emptied, and many ordinary people fled to the country for fear of an allied landing. The material damage, by comparison, was relatively modest: a troop barge sunk, a damaged steamer run ashore and a section of wharf blown away by the first torpedo which had gone haywire and been mistaken by Nasmith for a defensively fired Brennan.

In the days after, *E11*'s score steadily mounted. A large supply ship, the 474-ton *Bandirma*, was clinically dispatched on 28 May with the loss of 250 lives, with another vessel crippled three days later and an ammunition ship, the *Tecilli*, destroyed on 2 June. But Nasmith did not have things all his way. On 3 June *E11* was almost run down by a destroyer, evading her only by means of a 'spectacular dive at full speed'. Time was beginning to run out for Nasmith, though he tried to prolong his effectiveness by setting his dwindling stock of torpedoes to float at the end of their run so that any which missed their target might be recovered. The strain on men and machines, however, was beginning to tell. Nasmith and D'Oyly Hughes were laid up for the best part of a week with 'fever, headaches and an awful lassitude'. Even more disturbing was the wear and tear on the boat. Finally, in the face of mechanical troubles which included a cracked main starboard shaft, Nasmith decided it was time to go.

His journey out on 7 June was in keeping with all that had gone before. Finding an empty transport in his sights, Nasmith ignored it in the hope of finding something better nearer the Narrows. But having reached there and found the anchorage deserted, he unhesitatingly went about and sank the transport after all. The crew faced the usual struggles to maintain control of the boat as she passed through the narrow waters off Kilid Bahr, but the biggest scare came when something was heard scraping alongside the hull. Rising to 20ft, Nasmith found 'a large mine preceding the periscope at a distance of about 20ft', its moorings having snagged the port hydroplane. Saying nothing to his crew, Nasmith took *E11* down and went on his way, safely negotiating

the Turkish defences before launching into a series of strange manoeuvres which finally saw the mine break free. As destroyers clustered
round, their decks were lined with cheering seamen in a scene repeated
in Imbros. The compliment was well deserved. Nasmith's nineteen-
day patrol had surpassed even Boyle's great achievement. Eighteen
days after his return, the *London Gazette* announced the award of the
Victoria Cross to Martin Nasmith. As in the case of Boyle's submarine,
E11's other two officers, Lieutenants Guy D'Oyly Hughes and Robert
Brown, RNR, received Distinguished Service Crosses and the men
Distinguished Service Medals. Still greater success, however, lay ahead.

Martin Eric Nasmith, whose exploits in the Marmora were to make
him the most famous of all Britain's First World War submariners, was
born at 13 Castelnau Gardens, East Barnes, London, on 1 April 1883,
the eldest son of Martin Nasmith, a stockbroker, and Caroline (née
Beard). His two soldier brothers were both decorated for their war services, one receiving the Distinguished Service Order and Military Cross
and the other a DSO before his death.

Educated at Eastman's, Winchester, he entered *Britannia* in May
1898, and joined *Renown* as a midshipman. Promoted sub-lieutenant on
15 February 1903, he began his spectacular career in submarines on 4 July
1904 when he went to HMS *Thames* in Portsmouth for training. Made
lieutenant on 15 May 1905, he gained his first command, *A4*, within
two months. His promising career was almost ended that October when
near-disaster struck. The wash from a passing steamer spilled through the
boat's open ventilators, causing the boat to fill with water. She surfaced
just in time to save boat and crew. Court-martialled, Nasmith escaped
with a reprimand on account of his actions after the accident.

Apart from a two-year interlude spent in the armoured cruiser
Indomitable, Nasmith, nicknamed 'Nazims', spent the rest of the pre-
war period in submarines, commanding *C7*, *C18*, and *D4* (in which
he dived with the king aboard), before taking a key post at Fort
Blockhouse, training submarine officers. In this role he oversaw a
number of innovations and was chiefly responsible for introducing a
more scientific approach to undersea operations.

On 3 August 1914 Nasmith, who had been made lieutenant-
commander the previous year, moved to Harwich to command
the newly completed *E11*, which was commissioned the following
month. In October Nasmith joined two more E-boats in an attempt to
force the passage into the Baltic. *E1* and *E9* made it, but mechanical

mishaps delayed *E11* and Nasmith was forced to abort the operation after making strenuous attempts to evade the already alerted German defences. More misfortune followed. In December, while attacking an enemy battlecruiser returning to base after the bombardment of Hartlepool, he watched despairingly as his torpedo passed underneath. The failure prompted him to vow never to touch either alcohol or cigarettes until he had sunk a battleship.

His run of bad luck was conspicuously ended by his headline-grabbing feats in the Dardanelles. In all, he completed three remarkable patrols into the Marmora, the two that followed his VC cruise being every bit as successful, although a niggardly Admiralty gave no further recognition beyond accelerated promotion to commander. His second patrol (5 August–3 September 1915) was marked by the sinking of the elderly battleship *Barbarossa*, a vessel he had narrowly missed on his first foray, and a daring 'commando' raid by his second-in-command, Lt D'Oyly-Hughes, which resulted in a stretch of the Ismid railway track being blown up. But even these coups were overshadowed by his third cruise (6 November–23 December), at forty-seven days the longest ever mounted in the Marmora. Despite being faced by much stronger and more elaborate defences, Nasmith accounted for a destroyer, eleven steamers, five large sailing vessels and thirty smaller craft. He also staged a second raid on Constantinople, sinking a large steamer lying inside the harbour breakwater.

On 15 January 1916, a week after the last British troops were brought off Gallipoli, Nasmith received his Victoria Cross at Buckingham Palace. He deserved much more. At the very least his two subsequent patrols should have brought him a DSO and Bar, and an argument could even be made for him receiving a Bar to his VC. Instead, he had to make do with being made a Knight of the French Legion of Honour (*LG*, 7 April 1916) and promotion to captain, the youngest officer of that rank in the navy, while waiting to command the new submarine *J4* at Blyth. Nasmith took part in a number of North Sea patrols before taking command of the 3rd Flotilla's six D-boats in the Firth of Forth in February 1917. Further submarine commands took him to Lough Swilly, Bantry Bay and Southbank on Teesside. The Armistice brought no let-up. In May 1919 he took the 7th Flotilla into the Baltic during the war against the Bolsheviks, supplying the coastal motor boats with torpedoes for their successful raid on Kronstadt harbour. His services were recognised by his being made a CB (*LG*, 8 March 1920) and the same year he married Beatrix Justina Dunbar-Rivers, taking the name Dunbar-Nasmith.

After attending a senior officers' technical course, he was appointed Flag Captain to the C.-in-C. Mediterranean and commanding officer of the battleship *Iron Duke*, serving in her from 1921 to 1923. Following spells as Director of the Trade Division at the Admiralty and Captain of *Britannia*, his old training college, Dunbar-Nasmith was promoted rear admiral, one of the youngest officers to achieve flag rank. His active career continued with command of the Submarine Service (1929–31), a spell in Colombo as C.-in-C. East Indies (1932–34), and promotion to Second Sea Lord and Chief of Naval Personnel (1935–38). At the outbreak of the Second World War he was in command of Plymouth and Western Approaches, a key role he held until 1941.

Sir Martin Dunbar-Nasmith VC (he was knighted in 1934) officially retired in 1942, though he was still employed on the Active List until 1946, having succeeded his submariner friend Courtney Boyle as Flag Officer-in-Charge, London. His Second World War services were recognised by a number of foreign awards, including the Dutch Order of Orange Nassau, Grand Commander, the Polish Order of Polonia Restituta, 1st class, and the Norwegian Royal Order of St Olaf, Grand Cross.

In retirement, the navy's most distinguished submariner served as vice-chairman of the War Graves Commission and as deputy lieutenant and later vice-lieutenant of Morayshire, where he settled with his wife. Created a Knight Commander of the Order of St Michael and St George in 1955, Martin Nasmith, who listed his hobbies as sailing, skiing and forestry, died in Dr Gray's Hospital, Elgin, on 29 June 1965, and was buried in Holy Trinity churchyard.

His death marked the passing of arguably the most daring and resourceful of the navy's first generation submariners. Although critics found weakness in his unwillingness to delegate, fellow officers noted that he was 'extravagantly admired by his crews'. William Guy Carr knew him better than most. A submarine chronicler who served under Nasmith, he wrote: 'He had that rare combination, a delicate sense of the incongruous and an almost ferocious insistence on efficiency.'

F.D. PARSLOW

*Atlantic, 90 miles south-west
of Queenstown, 4 July 1915*

The *Anglo-Californian* was a modern
vessel, handy and reliable, with a fair turn
of speed. Built in 1912 for the London-
based Nitrate Producers Steamship Co.,
she had joined the war effort with a different cargo and a new commission,
transporting horses across the Atlantic
under Admiralty charter. She was unarmed
but unquestionably a military target of
some importance. Beneath her decks, on
the morning of 4 July 1915, were 927
horses in specially built stalls complete
with fodder stores, bound for Avonmouth
en route to the Western Front. Thus far her
passage from Montreal had been uneventful. All being well, she could
be docked and disgorging her equine cargo before the day was out. But
such hopes were to prove premature. At around 8.30 a.m., some 90 miles
south-west of Queenstown, Ireland, an alert look-out sighted the outline of a submarine breaking surface on the port bow. He estimated her
to be about a mile distant, though in all likelihood she was probably
about 3 miles away. At that range, positive identification was impossible.
But the *Anglo-Californian*'s 59-year-old Master, Frederick Parslow, was
taking no chances in waters known to be a favourite hunting ground
for U-boats. Ordering his engineer to 'crowd on all speed possible', he
altered course in an attempt to keep the submarine astern, thus reducing
the target area. As he did so, the dark, menacing shape, still a distant
speck, followed suit. It was the beginning of a chase that would result in
one of the most gallant engagements in the war at sea, and an encounter destined to have far-reaching repercussions for the country's highest
award 'for valour'.

The war was precisely eleven months old when Frederick Parslow made his unfortunate rendezvous. The first submarine campaign in history was still in its infancy. Early on, U-boats prowling British coastal waters had scorned merchantmen in favour of warships, but in February 1915 the Kaiser retaliated against the blockade inflicted on German maritime traffic by proclaiming 'all the water surrounding Great Britain and Ireland and all English seas ... to be a war area'. His words signalled the first direct assault on what Admiral Sir Percy Scott called 'our most vulnerable point' – the maritime trade routes vital to the country's survival. U-boat commanders were instructed to prosecute the campaign against Allied commerce 'with all possible vigour'. Merchant ships were to be sunk on sight, with only ships flying neutral flags, hospital ships and vessels belonging to the Belgian Relief Commission being spared the new ruthlessness.

German efforts were concentrated in three main areas: the English Channel, the north-east coast around Newcastle and the southern Irish Sea. With only a few submarines available, sinkings were, at first, uncommon. Five weeks into the campaign only 28,000 tons had been destroyed. But the figure soon rose sharply. Losses during May, which included the Cunard liner *Lusitania*, sunk off the west coast of Ireland, amounted to 106,293 tons. An alarmed British press branded the U-boat crews 'pirates' and hailed every ploy to defeat them. Captain John W. Bell, master of the small collier *Thordis*, was fêted as a hero for ramming a U-boat off Beachy Head. He was awarded a Distinguished Service Cross and £500 prize money and was given a commission in the Royal Naval Reserve before it was realised his 'victim' had survived to limp home. Other ships' masters made no secret of their determination to resist the new threat. Following a much-publicised encounter between the steamer *Vosges* and a U-boat, which ended with the merchantman being sunk only after a two-hour chase, the ship's captain reportedly declared: 'I had always made up my mind to make a fight of it in an emergency.' While it is not known whether Frederick Parslow was acquainted with the *Vosges'* captain's remarks, he undoubtedly shared his sentiments. According to an account of the action compiled by the ship's owners, Parslow instantly appreciated the 'seriousness' of his position. Even as the *Anglo-Californian* showed her stern to the U-boat, he 'ordered every man to his post'.

There were approximately 165 men aboard the *Anglo-Californian*, including 'horsemen', veterinary staff and thirty Russian reservists who were heading home to fight for their country. The ship's company was no less cosmopolitan. Counted among their number were Canadians, Irish, Italians and Swedes, some of whom were to prove of dubious quality when the crisis came. Parslow could at least rely on his officers, not least his eldest son, Frederick, who was serving as second mate.

After changing course, the *Anglo-Californian* soon reached her top speed of almost 13 knots, while her wireless operator repeatedly tapped out SOS messages. Within fifteen minutes of the first sighting, Parslow's call for assistance was answered by the *Princess Ena*, a former London & South West Railway vessel converted into one of the navy's earliest anti-submarine decoy ships. Together with two destroyers, *Mentor* and *Miranda*, which also picked up the signal, she made haste to the transport's aid. It was a race against time to reach her before the U-boat could close the gap sufficiently to make an attack. In the ship's log, Chief Officer Harold Read recorded the unfolding drama:

> 9.20am. Submarine fired one round, the shot falling 50 yards on Port Quarter. She slowly gained on *Californian*. Range about 7 cables [1,400yd]. From 9.20am onwards *Californian* was continually altering course and practically turning circles to try to keep Submarine astern. Continuous fire was kept up by Submarine, about thirty rounds being fired altogether. Range between Ten and Three Cables. Rough percentage of hits was about 80 per cent ...

As the range closed, the ship's crew got a clear view of their assailant. The submarine was 'very long, showed no number, carried two guns and displayed no colours'. She was, in fact, *U-39*, commanded by KL Walther Forstmann. Unbeknown to the men aboard the *Anglo-Californian*, she had fired her last torpedo at another vessel shortly before sighting the transport. In a colourful account published in the United States a few months later, one of the U-boat's crew, Carl Franz List, recounted the frustration caused by Parslow's persistent manoeuvring:

> We went for her without a single torpedo in our tubes, and with but a handful of shells for the deck gun. That meant surface work. We fired into her rudder, hoping to disable her, but she kept on steering in circles. *U-39* was doing almost trial speed. The gun was eating up our last shells. But the wily commander on the *Anglo-Californian*'s bridge kept working in spirals to escape. Our captain ordered the gun to aim at the bridge and sweep the deck underneath ...

The damage was appalling. Shells wrecked the upper bridge, pierced the funnel and severed winch steampipes, while shrapnel riddled lifeboats and ventilating cowls. The bombardment left a grisly trail of dead and wounded and provoked near-panic among a section of the crew. A report by the ship's owners stated that: 'Many of the bodies were horribly mutilated, which, added to the piteous groans of the wounded, created consternation, with the result that a number of the horsemen and stokers who had come on deck made a rush for the boats and were deterred at the point of the revolver.'

Parslow, 'instinctively a peculiarly silent man', according to his managers, remained resolute. His whole attention was focused on saving his ship. With his son manning the wheel beside him on the shattered remains of the bridge, he continued to outwit the U-boat commander. The action was moving inexorably towards its awful climax when, around 10.05 a.m., according to the ship's log, *Princess Ena* was sighted. Roughly half an hour later, she joined the fight, opening fire from 9,000yd on the surfaced submarine. According to a naval report of the encounter, the Q-ship's long range intervention coincided with the *U-39*, then within 800yd of the *Anglo-Californian*, hoisting a signal ordering the transport's crew to 'abandon ship as fast as possible'. At the same time Parslow received a message from the fast-approaching destroyer *Mentor*, urging him 'to hang on as long as possible', though by that stage it is doubtful that the *Anglo-Californian*'s master had any other intention.

The events following the U-boat commander's final demand are recounted in the ship's owners' graphic report:

Evidently as a ruse, Captain Parslow merely answered that the signal had been read and telegraphed to the Chief Engineer to stop the engines, he having decided to let anyone on board, who thought he was safer in the boats, have a chance of leaving the steamer. He did not, however, send up the pennant agreeing to abandon ship. After waiting ... about five minutes, during which period two boats were lowered and got away, the submarine again started to shell. As a consequence the subsequent boat fell into the water, owing to the davits being carried away by a shell, and the occupants were either killed or precipitated into the sea, while another capsized. The Captain at this time called for volunteers to go into the stokehold and offered £20 per man as an inducement, but without avail. He was greatly distressed at the refusal of the men to assist in the emergency, but the Chief Engineer, Second Engineer, and Donkeyman ... gratuitously volunteered to do their utmost in the stokehold. Before returning to the Bridge, the Captain went to his cabin and gave the Chief Steward the ship's papers, certain trinkets, and also photographs of his wife and children, which he affectionately kissed and asked the Steward, in the event of the worst happening, to convey to his family the assurance that his last thoughts were of them, and to give them his love. The Steward, who had a great affection for the Master, asserts that he begged of him to be allowed to remain, but the request was refused and he ordered him instantly to proceed to one of the boats. He left ... to return to the Bridge and gave the Chief Engineer orders to go full speed ahead. He then instructed the Chief Officer to send a wireless message to the patrol steamer [*Princess Ena*], which was nearer than the Destroyers, to start firing shots at random as soon as possible, thinking this might possibly frighten the submarine off, and also to give the patrol steamer the exact position of the submarine. Meantime, the commander of the latter, evidently enraged at Captain Parslow's refusal to abandon ship, continued savagely to direct shell after shell on the Bridge. Captain Parslow having no protection, lay down flat, while the Second Officer (his son), in a similar position, manipulated the wheel from the lower spokes. Ultimately the submarine got close up and thirteen of her crew took up positions on her deck and fired volley after volley with rifles, and also endeavoured to snipe individual members of the crew, but without much success. As the submarine kept dodging round, Captain Parslow mentioned to his son, while giving him steering orders, that his purpose was to manoeuvre for an opportunity to ram her, but owing to the submarine's agility in steering, he on each occasion found it impossible for the *Anglo-Californian* to get round quickly enough ...

Of the two boats lowered aft, while the ship was stopped around 10.50 a.m., one managed to pull clear while the other capsized as it was being got away. A third boat was lowered even as 'the ship was gathering headway', while a shell struck the davit holding the fourth boat, sending it crashing into the sea with seven men aboard. Parslow's sudden move had taken the *U-39* completely by surprise. 'It was a mystery how they were kept from being swamped, as the *Anglo-Californian* never slowed once,' wrote List. To the submariners it was clear that someone was steering the ship while 'lying flat on his stomach'. Time and shells were fast running out, but the frustrated Forstmann was reluctant to give up his quarry. List wrote:

We were ordered to count the few remaining shells and aim accurately. We riddled the bridge and funnels [*sic*] with a furious fire,

but the last round of ammunition was gone and there was no surrender of the *Anglo-Californian*, which was still zig-zagging. As a
last resort a Maxim was brought on deck and clamped to the top
of the conning tower. It began to fire bullets by the beltful. Less
than a couple of hundred yards away we picked off the … crew
whenever a head showed itself. Our fire was returned, rifle shots
dropping on the deck and spattering our conning tower …

By then, the *Anglo-Californian* was in a sorry state. Shells had smashed
the deck and bridge, but the most alarming damage was below deck, in
No. 4 hold, where water was rushing through two holes torn along the
waterline on the port side. The steamer's plight was desperate. To make
matters worse, she was gradually slowing and losing steering way.
But still Parslow – his hopes raised by a message from the destroyers
reporting that they had seen his smoke – remained defiant. For perhaps the first time, he even allowed himself to believe they were out of
danger. Turning to his son, lying on the bridge alongside him, he said
he 'believed they had succeeded in saving the ship and the lives of those
who had remained on board'. He was right, but sadly he would not live
to see the success he had engineered.

At around 11.20 a.m., almost three hours after the chase began, a
shell tore through the bridge, killing him outright. The ship's owners'
report stated:

It was necessary for him occasionally to raise himself in order to
verify the steamer's position, and also that of the submarine, and
on one of these occasions, when so occupied, he was struck by a
shell which carried half of his body overboard, part of the same
shell carrying away the peak of his son's cap and slightly injuring
his forehead …

Only two more shots were fired by *U-39*. With her captain dead, the
transport came to a stop again and her crew were ordered on deck.
Three minutes later, according to the *Princess Ena*'s report (but thirty
minutes according to Chief Officer Read), the U-boat, then lying
barely 50yd off the steamer's port side, hurriedly dived. List recorded:
'A grey patrol yacht turned up … followed by a swarm of destroyers.
Like lightning we scattered pellmell for the conning tower hatch, and
we were unshipping the Maxim and handing the rifles below, just as
a shell whizzed over our heads and struck the water within 15ft. We
dropped below the surface like a rock and we could hear the sound
of the propellers of our pursuers overhead …' Too late for Parslow

but just in time for the *Anglo-Californian*, the hunter had suddenly become the hunted.

Fortunately for the *U-39*, however, the destroyers were more concerned with saving the transport than chasing the submarine. Leaving *Miranda* and *Princess Ena* to recover the men in the lifeboats (*Princess Ena* alone accounted for fifty-two men, plus two bodies), *Mentor*, low on fuel, set about escorting the *Anglo-Californian* towards Queenstown. With one of her more serious holes plugged and deliberately listing to starboard in an attempt to limit the flooding, the steamer eventually limped into port at 10.30 p.m.

Casualty figures vary. Where Read listed nine men dead, seven wounded and nine missing, feared drowned, the navy's report gave the number of men unaccounted for as twenty-one. There was, however, no disagreement about the courage and skill displayed by *Anglo-Californian*'s father and son team. Commander R.G. Rowley-Conwy, *Mentor*'s captain, thought the action of the master, officers and men of *Anglo-Californian* 'deserving of great praise'. It was a view shared by Thomas Scott, secretary of the Mercantile Marine Service Association. Having read a report of the action in *The Times*, Scott wrote to Arthur Balfour, First Lord of the Admiralty, suggesting that the 'courageous efforts of the master of the steamer *Anglo-Californian*' were worthy of 'public recognition'. Further endorsement came from an unlikely source. Concluding his account of the encounter, published in the American press, Carl List declared: 'Our crew agreed that the *Anglo-Californian*'s captain ought to have the Iron Cross.'

By then, in fact, the first moves to honour the men of the *Anglo-Californian* had already been made. Two days after the action, Vice-Admiral Sir Charles Coke, having inspected the ship and read the initial accounts, reported the gallant behaviour of Captain Parslow, his son, Chief Officer Read and the ship's wireless operators, John Rea and William Williams. He described the master as 'a most gallant gentleman', but reserved most praise for his son:

> He steered the ship throughout the action, the Captain having ordered everyone off the Upper Bridge except his son. The Submarine concentrated his fire on the Upper Bridge and how Mr Parslow escaped death is a marvel. The Upper Bridge was riddled, the wheel he was at had a spoke knocked off, the binnacle was struck, the peak of his cap knocked off; yet he and his father stuck to their place of duty and when the latter was killed by his side Mr Parslow was there alone till the action finished. If ever a man deserved the Victoria Cross this man does.

Captain Richard Webb, Director of the Trade Division on the Admiralty War Staff, concurred. Writing on 23 July, he stated: 'A VC conferred on Mr Parslow as suggested by Admiral Coke would have an excellent effect on the Merchant Service generally.' In the event, however, Frederick Parslow jr, second mate of the *Anglo-Californian*, was commissioned as a sub-lieutenant in the RNR, awarded the Distinguished Service Cross and presented with a gold watch. Similar watches were sent to Captain Parslow's widow, Chief Officer Read, the two wireless operators and First Engineer James Crawford. Two other members of the crew, the Italian donkeyman Giovanni Badano and Second Engineer Henry Suddes, who had both volunteered to work in the stokehold, were awarded £5 each for their gallantry. The rest of the crew made do with pieces of shell fragments as souvenirs of their remarkable escape.

The recognition afforded Captain Parslow himself seemed particularly niggardly. A letter from the Admiralty accompanying his watch informed his widow: 'Had your husband survived ... [we] would have recommended him to HM the King for the award of a decoration.' Frances Parslow replied, thanking them for the gift, and added: 'It will remain an emblem to me and my family of how a brave man can die.' More than a year was to pass before further tangible recognition came. On 19 December 1916 it was announced that Frederick Parslow had been awarded the Lloyd's Medal 'for meritorious service' for his 'extraordinary exertions on the occasion of the *Anglo-Californian* encountering an enemy submarine'. And there, seemingly, the matter rested, the Admiralty's letter of the previous year apparently inferring that Parslow's actions were not considered worthy of the VC, an award that could have been granted posthumously.

That this was not the case is clear from Admiralty papers released long after the war. They revealed that attempts to honour Frederick Parslow had been delayed by concerns about the wartime position of merchant seamen. The Admiralty's dilemma was revealed in documents relating to the case of Archibald Bisset Smith, captain of the SS *Otaki*, who met his death during a gallant encounter with a German surface raider in March 1917. The papers show that the Admiralty, anxious to avoid compromising the Merchant Navy's civilian status, had embarked on a policy of subterfuge. Awards to the Mercantile Marine were camouflaged by supplying recipients with ante-dated ranks in the Royal Naval Reserve and deliberately obscure citations. Such deception, they argued, could not be applied to the VC, where any award was bound to excite enormous interest. The Admiralty's position, though not universally accepted, remained unaltered for the rest of the war. Behind the scenes, however, changes were being made.

During discussions by the Interdepartmental Committee to draw up a new VC warrant in 1918, the Admiralty successfully pressed for members of the Merchant Navy to be made eligible for the award. Not completed until 1919, the warrant was eventually signed at the beginning of March that year. Although the king ordered that publication of the change must await the formal end of hostilities, the Admiralty saw no reason to delay bringing forward the outstanding cases of Parslow and Smith. Both awards were gazetted the same day, on 24 May, more than a month before the Treaty of Versailles officially brought the war to a close. The citation accompanying Frederick Parslow's overdue honour concluded: 'He set a splendid example to officers and men of the Mercantile Marine.' King George V presented his widow with the Cross in the quadrangle of Buckingham Palace on 10 July. More than four years had passed since *Anglo-Californian*'s encounter with *U-39*.

Frederick Daniel Parslow, the first officer of the Mercantile Marine to be awarded the VC, was born at 16 Salisbury Terrace, Islington, on 14 April 1856, the son of Charles and Eliza (née Pizey). He was born barely ten weeks after the institution of the Victoria Cross.

Little is known of his early life. His father was serving in the Merchant Navy, his profession being given as 'oilman (Master)', and it would appear likely that Frederick followed in his father's footsteps straight from school, just as his own eldest son would do in his turn. He gained his master's certificate (no. 02007) in 1882 and spent the remainder of his working life at sea aboard a succession of ships, culminating in his appointment to the *Anglo-Californian* in May 1912. Over the course of the next three years, he completed no fewer than twenty voyages in her, eight of them after war was declared.

Frederick Parslow married Frances at St Mary's, Islington, on 18 November 1885. They had six children, three boys and three girls. The war took its toll of the Parslows. In the same year that witnessed Frederick's death, Frank, their second son, was killed in action on the Western Front. More tragedy followed after the war. In March 1938 the *Anglo-Australian*, a British steamer bound for Vancouver out of Cardiff, with every modern safety device installed, vanished without trace after passing the Azores. After days of searching, the vessel was listed as 'missing' along with crew and master, Frederick Parslow DSC.

The sea did not claim the other leading protagonist in the *Anglo-Californian*'s gallant struggle for survival. The body of Frederick Parslow VC was brought ashore and buried, along with other members of his crew, in Queenstown (now Cobh) Old Church Cemetery. His headstone bears the immortal lines: 'At the going down of the sun, And in the morning, we will remember them.' In his native London, the grimly impressive Tower Hill Mercantile Marine Memorial bears mute and sobering testimony to the cost of what a shipping company executive described as 'one of the gamest and most unequal fights ever put up by a shipmaster'.

E.C. COOKSON

Es Sinn, Mesopotamia, 28 September 1915

Mesopotamia, 'the land of the two rivers', resounded with echoes of the Old Testament, of Adam and Eve, the Garden of Eden, Noah and Father Abraham. It was also the land of fable, of glittering minarets and golden palaces that provided the glorious setting for the fantastic tales of the Arabian Nights. Yet the reality could scarcely have been more different for the men compelled to campaign there during the First World War. 'When Allah made Hell, he did not find it bad enough,' the Arabs were fond of saying, 'so he made Mesopotamia as well – and added flies.' To the British, it was a God-forsaken place, rife with disease and full of murderous tribesmen who owed allegiance to none but themselves. Moreover, it was a country defiled by some of the most squalid settlements known to man. Of them all, none was worse than Kut-al-Amara.

Filthy beyond description, Kut was a drab clutter of mud-houses set within a maze of alleys. The town's strategic importance, however, belied its physical appearance. Located in a loop of the Tigris, where it forms a junction with the Shatt-al-Hai, Kut was not merely a centre of grain traffic but a vital link in the chain of communications upon which the people in this forlorn corner of the Ottoman empire depended for their survival. By the late summer of 1915, however, Kut had acquired far greater prominence in British thinking. Having been selected by the Turkish army as a key defensive position, it represented the last great obstacle barring the way to Baghdad, the glittering prize in a campaign that had begun with the seizure of Basra, Sinbad's fabled port, ten months earlier. Since then, an Anglo-Indian force had secured its primary objective, the region's oilfields, and gone over to the offensive. Easy victories and spectacular advances followed until Baghdad, ancient city of the caliphs and seat of Turkish power, appeared within reach. British commanders, seduced by their success, stretched resources and supply lines to the limit.

On 29 August Major-General Charles Townshend, GOC 6th (Poona) Division, was instructed to 'disperse and destroy' the enemy forces preparing to make a stand before Kut. It promised no cheap victory. Intelligence revealed a well-constructed position straddling the Tigris 8 miles downstream from Kut at Es Sinn. Roughly 2½ miles of trenches, broken by marshes and laced with barbed wire, minefields and pits of sharpened stakes, stretched across the left bank with similar defences tracing a line along an ancient canal on the right bank. The defences, which the Turks considered impregnable, were completed by a river block consisting of two iron barges linked by wire hawsers to a maheilah (a shallow-draught dhow) in midstream. To defend these fortifications, the Turks had amassed 11,000 men, supported by artillery, with reinforcements on the way. Townshend's force consisted of three infantry brigades, supported by cavalry, artillery and one of the strangest naval forces ever to see action.

The Tigris Flotilla was a motley collection of gunboats, paddle-streamers, stern-wheelers, armed launches, tugs and barges. It added up to what one historian called 'an amazing gallimaufry of vessels' and yet was also the linchpin of British operations in Mesopotamia. During the flood season, when the great rivers burst their banks, turning desert and marsh into an inland lake, their impact on the fighting was out of all proportion to their number. In the course of operations which became known as Townshend's Regatta, the Tigris navy sank a gunboat and two steamers and seized the important town of Amara, together with 2,000 PoWs and an abundance of stores.

In the advance on Kut the flotilla was once again assigned a crucial supporting role. The vessels involved were the *Comet*, a paddle-yacht armed with a 12-pounder, a 6-pounder and two 3-pounder guns, the tugs *Shaitan* and *Sumana*, two floating gun batteries mounted on horse barges, and a pair of steam launches, *RN1* and *RN2*, each of which carried a single Maxim gun. For the first time since the start of the offensive the Tigris boats had a new man at the helm. Captain Wilfrid Nunn had departed to Ceylon for rest and recuperation. His deputy, Captain Colin Mackenzie, had barely taken over when he fell sick with malaria, leaving Lieutenant-Commander Edgar Cookson, second-in-command of the sloop *Clio*, in overall command just as final preparations were being made.

Cookson was a 31-year-old career naval officer of more than sixteen years' service, much of it spent on the China Station. His Mesopotamian experience was brief but eventful. Less than a month after his arrival he had been seriously wounded in a river skirmish that resulted in the award of a DSO, which was announced on 13 September. By then Cookson, recovered from his wound, was directing naval operations against Kut from the *Comet*, having relinquished his temporary command of the flotilla's horse barges.

Townshend had devised a subtle plan, involving a feint designed to tie the Turks down in the centre while turning the position with a strike between the line of trenches and the northernmost swamp. The objective was nothing if not ambitious; to deal a crushing blow that would not only destroy the forces barring the way to Kut but seal the fate of the Turkish army of Mesopotamia. The navy's role was to protect the army's flank, provide covering fire and, when the breakthrough had been achieved, lead the pursuit up-river.

After a ten-day wait, Townshend put his plan into action. On 26 September British and Indian troops advanced along both banks of the river. A two-hour unopposed march brought them to within 3 miles of the Turkish defences at Es Sinn, on the right bank. There they stopped and pitched tents. The Turks, believing this to be the main thrust, reinforced the right bank. At dawn on 27 September a preparatory attack, supported by the guns of the naval flotilla, was launched on the left bank, with a demonstration on the opposite bank. Then came Townshend's master-stroke. At midnight, under cover of darkness, the majority of his force on the right bank slipped across a hastily constructed pontoon bridge and launched an enveloping attack. Fighting, intense in places, continued through a broiling day in which strong winds fanned clouds of dust that enveloped the battlefield. At one point Cookson's flotilla of riverboats halted a Turkish attempt to forestall Townshend's plan with close-range fire. Then they turned their guns on the redoubts that the British and Indian units were striving to outflank. That they did not have everything their own way, however, is clear from an account written by one of the *Comet*'s ratings which appeared in the British press under the byline of a 'West Country RNR':

> The Turks were ready for us, for they had quite as many guns as we had and four of them were a little bigger. We had a very lively time for a few hours, but, as usual our gunboats kept creeping up closer and closer until it got too warm for them. Then they ran away and left their guns. But they had stuck out well ... as it was dinner time before we shifted them. Our ship had several hits but

very little damage – one of their shells went through our funnel, and that was the most damage they did to us. We silenced all their guns but one big one, but the gunners had us weighed off, and as soon as we attempted to get round ... we had to drop back under cover again ...

Half-swallowed by the dust-storm, the two armies slugged it out until sunset. A final bayonet charge eventually sent the Turks reeling, but the victorious troops were in no condition to follow up. Exhausted and parched with thirst, many were on the brink of collapse. But the gateway to Kut had been prised open. 'Now,' wrote the Official Historian, 'was the time for the flotilla to make the success decisive.'

At around 7 p.m., an RNAS seaplane plopped down alongside Cookson's flagship. According to *Comet*'s seaman correspondent, it brought news that the 'Turks were on the run' and orders from Townshend to clear the river block below the fast-dissolving front-line and give chase to Kut's routed defenders. The idea was simple enough: a waterborne cavalry charge against a disorganised enemy. As soon as it was dark, the *Comet*, captained by Lieutenant W.V.H. Harris, supported by the launches *RN1* and *RN2*, under the overall command of Cookson, crept upstream. All lights were extinguished, but it made no difference. Surprise was impossible and they were soon sighted by Turks who, contrary to Townshend's report, were resolved to fight and fight hard. As the boats neared the obstruction they came under a hot fire that signalled what *Comet*'s 'West Country RNR' called 'the liveliest time I have had since we have been fighting'.

He wrote: 'It was very dark. We took the lead, being the biggest boat. When we got round the headland the Turks opened fire with rifles, but we steamed right up to the obstruction. The Turks were then close enough to us to throw hand bombs, but luckily none reached the deck of our ship ...' Unfortunately, the same good fortune did not extend to the rifle and machine-gun fire that poured at them from both banks. The lightly armoured craft were peppered with bullets from less than 100yd range. *Comet* bore the brunt of the fusillade. One man described the bullets as 'pattering' on the vessel's steel plating 'like raindrops on a window-pane'. Cookson, however, held his course and charged the centre of the obstruction, hoping to punch a hole through the block. The dhow buckled under the impact, but the hawsers held. Amid an inferno of fire, *Comet* drew away with the intention of using her guns to destroy the block.

As the sounds of battle reverberated across desert and marsh, the exposed paddle-yacht was lashed by fire. Despite being a sitting target for every Turk in the vicinity, *Comet*'s crew stuck to their task. But it was useless. The obstruction remained defiantly in place. Cookson might have considered withdrawing, but if he did the notion was quickly rejected in favour of a daring gamble which, if successful, was liable to turn the Turkish retreat into a rout. His plan was to lay the *Comet* alongside the central maheilah and cut the steel moorings holding her in place.

Having issued his orders, Cookson set the paddle-yacht thrashing upstream into a hurricane of fire that not even her steel cladding could withstand. *Comet* shuddered under the welter of blows. One shell blew away the 6-pounder's gun shield, leaving Private Arthur May, a marine gunner, to fight on without a shred of cover. There were many other acts of bravery. Gilbert Wallis, a signaller, was wounded and unable to stand, but propped himself up and carried on, while Leading Seaman Ernest Sparks somehow managed to keep his gun in action despite the bolts that held it to the deck working loose. But for sheer cold-blooded courage none could match Edgar Cookson.

As the bullet-riddled *Comet* came up against the obstruction, he was heard by Lt Harris to shout for an axe. Ignoring a hail of close-range fire, Cookson made his way along the deck towards the bow. The crew of the fo'c'stle gun were among the few eyewitnesses to what followed and their account was later recorded by Cyril Cox, a paymaster lieutenant-commander in the Tigris flotilla:

> They saw the SNO, axe in hand, leaning over the *Comet*'s steel plating in an endeavour to reach the wire hawser. Then they saw him get over the plating and step on to the maheilah itself. Immediately afterwards they saw him fall between the ship and the maheilah, and they hastened to extricate him and bring him back to the ship ...

According to Cox, 'there were more bullet holes in him than they cared to count'. Cookson, though, was still conscious. *Comet*'s 'West Country RNR' reported: 'Our SNO was shot in seven places, and when we dragged him in his last words were: 'I am done. It is a failure. Return at full speed.' Ten minutes later, he was dead.

As *Comet* drew back, Lt Harris signalled the launches to retire, which they did successfully and without further casualties. The gallant enterprise had ended in failure and with the loss of the flotilla's senior officer. Incredibly, given the ferocity of Turkish resistance, Cookson would appear to have been the only fatality among the boats' crews, though a number were wounded. Details of the casualties are contradictory. Captain Nunn put the figure at twelve injured, including four men of the Royal West Kents who were on board, and two Goanese seamen. *Comet*'s anonymous seaman, however, listed only six wounded, 'none seriously', while the Official Historian insisted that 'hardly a man was touched'.

Whatever the truth, there could be no denying the suicidal courage shown by Edgar Cookson. Struck by his senior naval officer's self-sacrifice, Townshend sent a special despatch to GHQ detailing the known facts of the affair. His report closed: 'He found that he could not send a man over the ship's side to cut away the obstruction, because it meant certain death, so he took an axe and went himself.' Whether Cookson's death served any purpose, however, is a matter of conjecture. Next morning aerial reconnaissance reported the Turkish forces in full retreat and their positions, including the river block, deserted. Had Cookson's desperate attack contributed to their flight? Or was it merely the inevitable consequence of Townshend's enveloping manoeuvre? The *Comet*'s crew were in no doubt. One seaman wrote:

We must have frightened the Turks because on going up again at daybreak (after we had buried our officer), when we reached the obstruction again, we found the Turks had cleared out ... So we steamed up-river after them. When we reached Koot Amara [*sic*] ... we found the cavalry there. This is the first place to which the Army has got before the Navy ...

On 21 January 1916 the *London Gazette* published a list of awards to men of the Tigris flotilla for their part in the operations at Kut. They included DSMs to Pte May, LS Sparks and LSig. Wallis and were headed by the posthumous award of the Victoria Cross to Lt Cdr Edgar Christopher Cookson DSO for an 'act of most conspicuous gallantry'. Less than four months had passed since his death, yet in that time the whole complexion of the campaign had been transformed. The road to Baghdad had been closed and the remnants of Townshend's victorious army lay besieged in the town that cost Cookson's life. The scene was set for even greater tragedy.

Edgar Christopher Cookson was born at Cavendish Park, Tranmere, in Cheshire, on 13 December 1883, the son of Captain William Edgar de Crackenthorpe Cookson RN, Admiralty pilot on the Mersey, and his wife, Louise Helene. He was educated at Hazlehurst in Kent, and entered HMS *Britannia* in September 1897, aged 13. Within two years he was promoted midshipman (15 February 1899) and inside three years he received his baptism of fire as part of HMS *Dido*'s naval brigade engaged in suppressing the Boxer Rising. Promotion followed slowly. He was made lieutenant on 30 September 1906 and advanced to the rank of lieutenant-commander seven years later. At that time he was serving as second-in-command of the sloop *Clio* on the China Station, where his father had served before him, and it was in her that he arrived in Basra in 1915 to reinforce the Navy's small flotilla operating in Mesopotamia and the Persian Gulf.

The supporting role given to *Clio* was nothing new to her crew. Shortly before joining Capt. Nunn's force, they had helped ward off a Turkish attack on the Suez Canal and, during *Clio*'s passage to Basra, she had been diverted to Bushire to counter the activities of German agents fomenting revolution in the Gulf. She eventually joined the Mesopotamian force in mid-April after a month spent in Bushire. While *Clio* was assigned to the gunboat flotilla supporting an advance towards Amara, Cookson was given command of the newly commissioned stern-wheel riverboat *Shushan*. It did not take him long to make his mark.

On 9 May he was ordered to carry out a reconnaissance of the El Huir Creek, a reed-fringed tributary of the Euphrates about 3 miles south-west of Kurna. The patrol soon ran into trouble as the *Shushan* was ambushed by Arabs hidden in the reed beds. Three men among a thirty-strong party of the Oxfordshire & Buckinghamshire Light Infantry were wounded and Cookson was shot through the right side of the chest. With his wound roughly bandaged, however, he insisted on resuming command and, with the assistance of F.W. Lyte, *Shushan*'s civilian captain who was aboard as pilot, extricated the vessel from the creek under covering fire of the *Clio*.

His wound meant he missed the lightning advance on Amara, but it had healed sufficiently for him to return to duty in late summer. Given command of a pair of horse barges converted to carry gun batteries, he found himself rapidly elevated, owing to sickness among senior officers, to command the entire flotilla. His role as senior naval officer of the Tigris Flotilla lasted less than a month and ended with his death at Es Sinn.

In the space of five months his name had become a byword for bravery among the seamen of the Mesopotamian navy. Twice honoured, he did not live to receive either award. Capt. Nunn wrote of him: 'His dash and bravery had shone conspicuously even amid the high level of those qualities which obtained in the Naval forces that I had the honour to command.'

Cookson was unmarried and his father had died some years earlier, leaving his mother, as the only close relative, to receive his VC from the king on 29 November 1916.

Edgar Cookson was buried in Amara War Cemetery, but the grave was subsequently destroyed and his name is now among those listed on the cemetery wall. Thousands of miles away in Dorset, a plaque in Whitchurch Canonicorum, a church he 'knew and loved' from his childhood, recalls his heroic sacrifice. Its inscription closes:

This is the happy warrior: this is he
that every man in arms should wish to be.

H.O.B. FIRMAN
AND C.H. COWLEY

Magasis, nr Kut-al-Amara, Mesopotamia,
24 April 1916

The Tigris was aflame with the dying embers of the sinking sun as a
fretful Vice-Admiral Sir Rosslyn Wemyss and his staff gathered on
24 April 1916 to bid an emotional farewell to the small river steamer
and her volunteer crew. Their mission, little more than a forlorn hope,
represented the final, desperate attempt to stave off the capitulation of
General Townshend's starving army, besieged 24 miles upstream in Kut.
Wemyss found himself drifting back. It was a year, almost to the hour,
since another, far greater force, had embarked from Tenedos bound for
the shores of Gallipoli. And as he walked among the steamer's crew,
shaking hands and thanking them for what they were about to do, he
hoped against hope that the anniversary might hold some portent of
success. 'They were so nice and cheery and gallant,' he wrote. But try

as he might, he could not shake off a deep sense of foreboding. No one was under any illusions about their chances of reaching Kut with their precious supplies. Wemyss rated them no better than 'one in a hundred' – and he told them so. In his diary, he confided: 'They were perfectly well aware of what they were doing, for I never disguised from them the fact that only by a miracle could they succeed, and that I never could have permitted the project had it not been our last and only chance.'

In the seven months since Edgar Cookson's suicidal charge at Es Sinn, the situation in Mesopotamia had been transformed. Forestalled at Ctesiphon, 22 miles short of Baghdad, Townshend's force, plagued by sickness and a chronic shortage of supplies, fell back on Kut. By 7 December the town was cut off and in the months that followed all attempts to lift the siege were bloodily repulsed. The plight of Townshend's 10,000-strong garrison was worsening by the day. Only by cutting rations to starvation levels could he hope to prolong resistance. Primitive attempts at air supply proved futile. In desperation, the army turned to the navy.

Wemyss, making his first visit to Mesopotamia since taking up his post as C.-in-C., East Indies, was initially reluctant. 'The conditions,' he wrote, 'were all unfavourable. No available vessel could make more than 6 knots against the strong current, and she would have to run the gauntlet of several well-placed and well-served batteries ... and it was almost certain that a heavy chain had been laid across the river to foil just such an attempt.' Only the army's assurance that the mission's success 'would help to save Townshend and not merely prolong the agony' persuaded him to consent to so risky an undertaking.

The vessel selected to run the gauntlet was the SS *Julnar*, a twin-screw shallow-draught oil-fuel steamer of 750 tons. Before the war the *Julnar* had plied the Turkish-controlled Mesopotamian waterways under the flag of the Euphrates and Tigris Steam Navigation Company, operated by the British firm of Lynch Brothers. Since August 1915 she had been employed in transport work along the Tigris, under the command of Lieutenant-Commander Charles Cowley RNVR.

Cowley was no ordinary officer. The son of an Irish riverboat captain and a half-Armenian mother, he had spent almost his entire adult life in Mesopotamia, working, like his father and grandfather before him, for Lynch Bros. As the company's senior captain, with his home in Baghdad, Cowley was regarded by the Turks as one of their own, even though a colleague described him as 'thoroughly British in sentiment and in no sense an Arabicised foreigner'.

To the British his expertise and unrivalled navigational knowledge were a godsend and such was his daring reputation in support of military operations that he had been commissioned a lieutenant-commander in the RNVR. To the Turks, however, he was the 'pirate Cowley', a traitor condemned to death in his absence by a Baghdad military court. There were even rumours of a price being placed on his head and of a bungled assassination attempt. Either way, he was a marked man, with no doubts as to his likely fate if captured, which made his decision to volunteer for the *Julnar* all the more remarkable.

Although loath to let any 'civilian' take part, Wemyss was prepared to make exceptions in the case of Cowley and *Julnar*'s chief engineer William Reed, in the hope that their involvement might sway the 'overweighted balance in our favour'. Reed was made a temporary Engineer Sub-Lieutenant, while Cowley was appointed pilot and second-in-command with the promise that his widowed mother would be granted a pension in the event of his being killed. Overall command was given to Lieutenant Humphrey Firman, a regular naval officer and captain of the recently commissioned gunboat HMS *Greenfly*. At 29, he was fifteen years' junior to Cowley.

Cowley received orders to take *Julnar* to Amarah on 14 April. The following day a call for volunteers to crew her resulted in every man of the Tigris Flotilla stepping forward. Twelve unmarried men were selected: Leading Seaman William Rowbotham, Engine Room Artificer Alexander Murphy, Leading Stoker Herbert Cooke, Able Seaman Montague Williams, Stoker Charles Thirkill, Stoker Samuel Fox, Able Seaman Herbert Blanchard, Able Seaman John Featherbee, Able Seaman Harold Ledger, Stoker George Forshaw, Able Seaman Alfred Veale, and Able Seaman William Bond. And on 19 April Wemyss reported *Julnar* commissioned 'for special duty'. Like Reed's rank, the steamer's new status was to be a brief one, lasting only as long as the mission.

Six days were spent in Amarah fitting out. Reed wrote: 'All cabin woodwork was removed from the inside, and the mast and top-deck stanchions were cut away. The ship was plated with armour $\frac{3}{8}$-inch thick round the bridge and over the boiler and engine rooms, bags of atta [flour] being placed between the armour and the ship's sides to give additional protection against bullets and shell splinters.' The steamer was then carefully loaded with around 270 tons of food and medical provisions until, in AS Bond's description, she resembled a floating 'pyramid'. *Julnar* left Amarah on 21 April and, with the river in flood, made good progress en route to her last staging post, between Arab Village and Fallahiya (referred to by Wemyss as Abu Roman Mound). She arrived in the afternoon of 23 April, just as an Easter Service was drawing to a close.

Originally, it was intended to mount the operation that same night, but it was postponed for twenty-four hours, adding to the consternation of those who suspected the mission to be already compromised. That night Firman dined aboard HMS *Dragonfly*. Seated alongside him was Colonel Aubrey Herbert MP, a noted Turcophile attached to Wemyss's staff. Herbert, a gifted linguist and veteran of Gallipoli, had volunteered to join *Julnar*'s crew, but his request was turned down. He thought Firman 'an attractive, good-looking fellow', who seemed 'very glad to have got the job, and felt the responsibility'.

The following day Herbert, together with Wemyss and the rest of his staff, wished Firman and his men well. Cowley, an old friend of Herbert's, was in great spirits. 'He is a proper Englishman,' Herbert wrote in his diary. 'He laughed and chafed with Philip Neville [Wemyss's flag lieutenant] and me …' Cowley made a deep impression on Wemyss, too. 'Such a charming man,' he recorded, 'the very best type of a gallant, middle-class Englishman who couldn't make out that he was doing anything out of the way in volunteering for this business.' By 8 p.m. on 24 April all was ready aboard the heavily laden steamer and Herbert stood among a crowd of soldiers and seamen to see her off:

> No cheers were allowed. They pushed off, almost stationary, into the river, that was a glory of light with the graceful mehailahs in an avenue on both sides of it, with masts and rigging a filigree against the gorgeous sunset. The faint bagpipes and the desert wind were the only music at their going …

Steaming slowly into the gathering darkness, the *Julnar* soon passed out of sight. About five minutes later she negotiated a floating pontoon bridge. Not long after the night sky ahead was filled with the blaze of Turkish flares. *Julnar* maintained her course, her crew uncertain whether the pyrotechnical display was in response to them or a feint attack designed as a diversion. Whatever the reality, enemy reaction was weak in the early stages, with only a few bags of meal being set alight. Indeed, little damage was sustained during the first hour, although AS Williams, at the helm, had a narrow escape when 'a shot went right over the bridge' hitting but not wounding him.

Julnar steamed on 'without further incident', according to Reed, until she reached the enemy position at Sannaiyat. 'Here,' he wrote, 'very heavy rifle fire was opened on the *Julnar* from both banks … and before we had gone much further the ship was riddled with bullets. They kept penetrating the engine-room and falling down among the engines.' Leading Stoker Cooke and Seaman Blanchard were both slightly wounded and the crew were only spared heavier losses by what Murphy described as 'wretched' shooting. Reed wrote:

> After we had passed Sannaiyat, the enemy fire slackened off considerably, although there were occasional bursts of rifle fire and sniping from both banks. The *Julnar* made a good run until we arrived opposite the Turkish position along the Sinn Bank, where the ship came under heavy fire, this time from artillery as well as from rifles. A fragment of shell penetrated the boiler-room and put the oil burners out, but otherwise did no damage of any consequence. Hostile fire still followed us upstream and at about 11.40pm, five minutes after passing the Sinn Bank position, I could hear the Turks, during a lull in the firing, bringing down guns to the riverbank some distance ahead. Three or four minutes afterwards the enemy opened a heavy and effective fire on the *Julnar* from guns on the river-bank near Magasis Fort ...

Murphy, one of a number of men cut by flying splinters, had been subconsciously measuring the Turkish response ever since leaving Arab Village. It ranged in ferocity from 'murderous shell fire' to 'most systematic artillery fire', but at Es Sinn he adjudged the reception 'greater than ever'. Three shells 'passed clean through the ship', he wrote, before another struck the bridge, killing Lt Firman instantly. According to Reed the shell pierced *Julnar*'s armour 'with ease' and her captain, standing on the right of the bridge, had no chance. Cowley, who was standing near him at the time, was also hit in the back, though not seriously according to Murphy. Also wounded, if not then, shortly after, was Williams. *Julnar* was now drawing heavy fire and with no room for manoeuvre there was little opportunity for taking avoiding action. One shell smashed into the stern and fires flared along the top deck where piles of protective atta bags were set alight by the hail of splinters and bullets. On each occasion LS Rowbotham darted out from cover to douse the flames. 'How we survived such a fire I cannot tell, and how our casualties did not become larger I don't know,' wrote Murphy.

With Firman dead, Cowley took control, though still feeling the effects of his back injury. He must have known their chances were bleak against a thoroughly alerted enemy, but he would not countenance abandoning the mission. With the stoic Williams at the wheel, *Julnar* ploughed on through a storm of fire. For five more minutes she defied the odds, until the old mud fort at Magasis loomed up on the right bank.

Here the river broadened briefly, the strong current flowing north for almost 2 miles before twisting south-west for the final run-in to Kut.

Julnar was nearly opposite the fort, where the river curved sharply, when disaster overtook the brave crew. Unbeknown to Cowley, an underwater chain straddled the Tigris at this point. It is not clear whether it was placed there as an obstruction or was used to operate a ferry, but the effect was the same. *Julnar* struck the cable head-on, the current swinging her stern round towards the right bank, where it grounded below Magasis Fort, within sight of Kut.

Julnar had already slipped a similar wire in the early stages of her mission, but on that occasion the cable was clearly visible and enemy fire almost non-existent. At Magasis, *Julnar* was trapped within easy reach of gun batteries at the water's edge. As shells burst around him, Cowley made desperate attempts to pull clear, with Williams putting the helm first hard a-port and then hard a-starboard. But it was all to no avail. *Julnar* was stuck fast and nothing they tried could free her. Like a sitting duck in a shooting gallery, *Julnar* was peppered. Every few seconds shells crashed through the atta bag walls. The damage was bad enough, but it would have been infinitely worse but for the fact that many shells failed to detonate. One dud actually landed on the bridge, close to Cowley, and Williams promptly picked it up and threw it overboard, before making a last attempt to pull the boat clear.

His failure signalled the end of *Julnar*'s mission. With shells reducing her superstructure to matchwood, Cowley and Williams took shelter and remained under cover for almost three-quarters of an hour while the bombardment continued unabated. Bullets by the score tore through the ship's hull to carpet the engine-room. By the time the fire eventually slackened, *Julnar* resembled a sieve. Her upper decks were 'absolutely riddled', her crankshafts were wrecked and the bridge was scorched and scarred by fire. But her Colours were never struck. Instead, remembered AS Bond, 'we watched them burn down'. Their fate no longer in any doubt, Cowley ordered a white lamp hoisted as a sign of surrender, only to see it shot away. A red lamp was raised in its place, and, soon after, the firing ceased.

Reed, who had been down below throughout *Julnar*'s passage, then received a message to go up on the bridge. 'There,' he later stated, 'I found Lt Cdr Cowley with several Turkish officers. He explained to me that finding it impossible to get the ship under way again, he had decided to surrender in order to avoid useless loss of life.' All hands were mustered on deck and taken ashore, to be greeted with the comment: 'You are very brave but fools; we knew you were coming 48 hours ago!'

The prisoners were led on to a raft and ferried to the opposite bank, where they were placed in a camp, under armed guard, about 100yd from the river. Just before leaving *Julnar* for the last time, Lt Cdr Cowley was heard by Seaman Williams to remark, 'I am finished now; I shall be killed.' Initially, however, they were well treated. The injured, including Cowley, had their wounds daubed with iodine and around 3 a.m., Reed and Cowley were placed in a tent together. Reed recorded:

> Next morning we were all marched to another camp about 5 miles distant, where we were again placed in tents, Lt Cdr Cowley and I still being together. About an hour after our arrival Lt Cdr Cowley was sent for and after an absence of about 20 minutes, he was brought back and informed me that he had been interrogated by a Turkish Staff Officer. Shortly afterwards a Turkish officer came to the tent and said that they could not allow two officers to remain in the same tent. I was accordingly moved to a tent by myself a few yards away. Half an hour later I was informed that I had to proceed to Baghdad at once with the crew of the *Julnar*. I requested permission to go and say good-bye to Lt Cdr Cowley before I left, but I was told by a Turkish officer that that was not necessary, as they were waiting for a horse for Lt Cdr Cowley, who would probably catch us up on the way. That was the last time I saw Lt Cdr Cowley. He was walking up and down in front of his tent and except for two very slight wounds, one on his face and the other in his hand caused by shell splinters, he was in perfect health ...

As the *Julnar*'s crew set out on their long march into captivity, Admiral Wemyss began piecing together the story of the gallant failure. During the morning aerial reconnaissance reported the riverboat 'lying against the bank at the turn of the Magassiz [*sic*]', thus confirming his worst fears. That same morning he received a wire from Townshend, expressing his 'heartfelt sympathy ... for the heroic attempt'. The commander of the beleaguered garrison had spent the night on the roof of his headquarters 'anxiously' watching and hoping for *Julnar*'s arrival. 'At midnight,' he later wrote, 'we heard a terrific musketry. It lasted for an half an hour; then all was silent.' Six hours later, he saw *Julnar* lying alongside the riverbank. With her loss, Kut's last hope had gone. On the morning of 29 April, the garrison's guns having been spiked, launches scuttled and stores destroyed, Townshend ordered the white flag raised over the town. There was one final bitter irony. In answer to a request for urgently needed food, the Turks allowed a party of British officers to take a launch downriver to salvage some of the stores from the abandoned and bullet-riddled *Julnar*, which the Turks had already rechristened 'The Gift'.

Wemyss knew nothing of the crew's fate, though her position, moored alongside the riverbank, led him 'to hope that they have not paid the extreme penalty for their courageous and gallant action'. In his diary, he noted: 'I have every reason to hope that they are prisoners, and I feel sure that they will be well treated by the Turks, who are gallant and can recognise gallantry in their enemies …' It was in every regard an overly optimistic assessment. The first of those hopes was soon dashed. A Turkish report on 15 May, in response to a plea for information about the Kut prisoners, stated that the *Julnar*'s 'first and second captains were killed' and five sailors wounded 'when we were firing at the ship in order to stop her'.

By then, Wemyss had already recommended awards for *Julnar*'s gallant crew. In a telegram sent to the Admiralty on 26 April, he outlined the mission and concluded: 'Although unsuccessful I consider the case worthy of the Victoria Cross and accordingly recommend Lt Firman, Lt Cdr Cowley and Eng. Sub-Lt Reed for the Victoria Cross and remainder of the crew commensurate rewards.' The Admiralty remained, at first, unimpressed. Not only did they regard such 'wholesale' issue of Crosses – 'viz 3 for 3 officers engaged' – as likely to reduce the award's value, but they felt it drew a 'most undesirable' distinction between officers and men. The Naval Secretary suggested, instead, a ballot under Rule 13 of the VC Warrant as being more appropriate, although he maintained that it should await a full report 'as it would be ridiculous to award our highest distinction if the operation ultimately turned out to have been badly executed'. Wemyss, however, was not to be put off. Writing a more detailed account, stressing the many hazards, he argued that 'each Officer and man has fully earned the Victoria Cross'. Given that only fifteen men were engaged and that the survivors were all prisoners, he contended that Rule 13 did not apply. 'Under these circumstances,' he added, 'I find it impossible to make any nominal recommendation and would ask to leave any nominal selection in the hands of their Lordships, merely observing that if the Victoria Cross is not awarded to each individual those who are not recipients should be granted the next highest reward applicable.'

It took the Admiralty seven months to act on Wemyss's report. During that time *Julnar*'s last mission had been the subject of much discussion and considerable praise. Two accounts, in particular, one from the C.-in-C. in Mesopotamia and the other contained in a despatch by General Sir Percy Lake, who commanded the attempts to relieve Kut, mentioned both Firman and Cowley in 'very high terms'. Yet neither the Admiralty nor anyone else on the British side was any the wiser as to what had really happened. Even the manner of the two officers' deaths was uncertain. The only indirect information concerning either of them was an entirely erroneous report of Cowley's last moments based on hearsay and taken from an account written by an artillery officer who was captured at Kut and later released in a prisoner exchange. He stated:

> We heard that every member of the crew was killed by rifle fire and the navigator, Captain Cowley, had dropped at the wheel with a bullet through his groin just as he was steering the ship through the most critical place in the whole river ... While consciousness lasted he hung on, but the boat was swept into the bank and grounded. No one will ever know the agony Captain Cowley must have suffered trying to steer the boat with a bullet in the groin. When the Turkish officers boarded the boat they found him unconscious with his hands still gripping the steering-wheel and in spite of all the efforts of the Turkish doctors to save him he died without regaining consciousness.

Whether the Admiralty was in any way influenced by the report is not known. What is clear, however, is that despite the paucity of reliable evidence, earlier concerns were set aside along with doubts about awarding VCs only to *Julnar*'s officers. Discussion, though, was confined to the merits of Wemyss's case for Firman and Cowley. Charles Walker, the Admiralty's Assistant Secretary, thought Firman as leader should be honoured 'even if no more Crosses are given'. The Naval Secretary, Admiral Allan Everett, maintained, however, that two VCs were justified. Writing on 19 January 1917, he stated: 'Considering the nature of this forlorn hope, and the reasonable presumption that both these responsible officers were fully alive to the extreme danger of their task, I submit that they are both deserving of being awarded the posthumous honor [*sic*] of the VC.' He went on to suggest that Eng. Sub-Lt Reed be 'earmarked' for the award of the DSO or DSC and the remainder of the *Julnar*'s survivors the CGM or DSM, provided that a postwar investigation confirmed 'the presumption that they are each deserving of honours, and if so of what degree'. With that, events moved swiftly. On 2 February 1917 the *London Gazette* announced the award of posthumous VCs to Lt Humphrey Firman RN and Lt Cdr Charles Henry Cowley RNVR.

Five weeks later British and Indian troops marched into Baghdad, where rumours were circulating about the fate of one of the city's most respected pre-war residents. Although differing in detail, they told substantially the same story: that Charles Cowley had been captured alive – and was subsequently murdered by the Turks.

Humphrey Osbaldeston Brooke Firman was born on 24 November 1886 at 26 Queensferry Place, Kensington, the son of Humphrey Brooke Firman, whose family owned the Gateforth estates in Yorkshire. His short life, from the day he joined the Royal Navy as a cadet on 15 May 1901, followed the course of a career naval officer. As a midshipman and then sub-lieutenant, he served aboard the battleship *Glory* on the China Station, in the battleships *Albion* and *Illustrious* in the Channel Fleet and in the Royal Yacht *Victoria and Albert*. Promoted lieutenant on 31 August 1908, he saw service in the Persian Gulf and off the Horn of Africa before the war brought him to Mesopotamia to join the navy's motley fleet of river boats.

In early 1916 he was given his first Tigris command, the new gunboat HMS *Greenfly*, one of sixteen 'Butterfly'-class vessels assembled, launched and commissioned at Abadan for the navy. Armed with a 4-inch gun, a 12-pounder, a 6-pounder, a 2-pounder AA pom-pom and four Maxims, the shallow-draught vessel with its crew of two officers and twenty men was specifically designed to provide gunnery support to the army. In April *Greenfly* did just that, participating in the bombardment of Turkish positions at Sannaiyat prior to the last (and unsuccessful) attempt by the army to break through to Kut. Shortly after the failure of that attack, Firman left to commission the new steamer *Julnar* in readiness for her desperate mission to run the Turkish blockade.

Firman's body was said to have been found in the cabin of the *Julnar* and buried by the Turks at Magasis. The grave, if it was ever marked, was subsequently lost, and he is commemorated on the Basra Memorial. His Victoria Cross was presented to his father by the king at Buckingham Palace on 28 February 1917.

The fate of Charles Cowley would tax the naval authorities and war crimes investigators for more than four years after his mysterious death. It was an inquiry that would ultimately implicate the Turks' senior officer at Kut, and one in which questions about Cowley's unusual status and highly unorthodox role in the campaign would be fundamental to the British case.

Charles Henry Cowley was born in Baghdad on 21 February 1872, the eldest of ten children, to Henry Vereker Cowley, senior captain of the London-registered Euphrates and Tigris Steamship Navigation Company, which had been established by Lynch Brothers in 1840, and

Mary Elizabeth (née Holland). His mother was half Armenian, being the daughter of Captain Anthony Charles Holland, a former officer in the Indian Navy and later a Tigris river boat captain, and Sushan Minas, a refugee from Persia, who had fled with her brothers and sisters to Baghdad in the 1830s following the murder of their parents. Under English law at the time of his birth, Cowley was a British subject, although that would not have been the case had he been born after 1914.

He was educated in Liverpool, joining the training ship HMS *Worcester* as a cadet in January 1885. An able student, he gained a first class extra and ordinary certificate and was apprenticed, in July 1888, to McDiarmid & Co., with whom he gained his first sea-going experience in the sailing ship *Pendragon*. Four years later, on the death of his father, 20-year-old Cowley returned to Baghdad, his mother's adopted home. Now head of the family, he took over the financial responsibilities and followed his father and grandfather into Lynch Bros' employ on the waterways of Mesopotamia, where they had been granted exclusive rights to steam navigation.

Cowley threw himself into his new role with enthusiasm, soaking up the customs and language while retaining the appearance and lifestyle of a thorough-going Englishman. So great was his knowledge of the country and its people that Arthur Tod, a fellow employee with Lynch Bros, considered him to have 'more influence' over the Arabs 'than any other man in Mesopotamia, native or European'.

By 1914 Cowley was the steamship company's senior captain. When war broke out between Britain and Turkey in November, he was directed by Lynch Bros to take a steamer from Basra to Baghdad to evacuate all those British nationals who wished to leave. That same month the company's steamers and their crews were requisitioned by the British government for use during the campaign.

In command of the steamer *Mejidieh*, Cowley, despite having no military rank and still flying the red ensign, was to play a critical and combative part in British strategy as it moved from defence to offence. Using to the full his knowledge of the waterways, he was able to deliver troops and artillery to points along the Tigris and Euphrates where they could do most effective damage to the Turks, who came to hate and fear him in equal measure. In December 1914 the Turks, who had already condemned him to death *in absentia* at a military court hearing in Baghdad, sent a message to Cowley declaring him to be a 'pirate' and 'threatening to have his blood'. The charge of piracy was repeated by the captured Turkish commander of the Kurnah garrison, Subhi Bey, while he was being shipped by Cowley to a prison camp. All of this appealed to his sense of humour. Far from being perturbed, he appeared to revel in his notoriety and even took to flying the 'skull and cross-bones' flag when in Basra.

In British circles Cowley's reputation grew with every action. At the capture of Kurnah, the *Mejidieh*, sporting two 18-pounders, manned by RGA crews, on its forward deck house, braved enemy fire to shell the Turks out of their positions, materially influencing the outcome of the battle. Cowley's 'meritorious conduct' was recognised by a letter of 'high appreciation and thanks from the Admiralty'. During the rapid advance the following spring and summer, Cowley's river boat was a leading participant in 'Townshend's Regatta', frequently acting as a floating headquarters for the general and his staff. Later, after the tide turned at Ctesiphon, the *Mejidieh* was the means by which hundreds of wounded men escaped to Basra.

By the autumn of 1915 Cowley had become an infuriating thorn in the side of the Ottoman empire's Mesopotamian army. According to a report compiled after the war, the Turks were determined to rid themselves of a man considered not only to have great influence among the native population, but of being 'brave to the verge of rashness'. In a plot plucked straight from the pages of the 'Arabian Nights', they resorted to an attempt at murder. On a November night, when the *Mejidieh* was moored opposite Turkish positions along the Tigris, 'an assassin boarded the ship and, with a dagger, seriously wounded Captain Wingate, who was sleeping on the bed usually occupied by Cowley'. According to witnesses, 'there was no doubt that the Turks meant to kill Cowley'.

Recognising the dangerous position in which Cowley and the other Lynch company men had been placed by their actions, the British authorities insisted the boats be placed under naval control with white ensigns and their officers given ranks in the RNVR. But it was all too little too late as far as the Turks were concerned. Cowley knew as much, and that is what made his decision to volunteer for the *Julnar* doubly heroic. He, more than anyone, realised that he would not be allowed to slip through their grasp a second time. And so it proved.

Within days of the doomed enterprise, lurid stories began to spread that Cowley had been murdered in cold blood. In stark contrast to the official Turkish account which spoke of him being killed in action, it was variously alleged that he had been shot after attempting to escape, killed by a Turkish officer after an argument during which he drew a revolver, executed as a traitor on the instructions of Khahlil Pasha, commander of the Turkish forces besieging Kut, and, most astounding of all, that he had been murdered personally by Khahlil in a drunken rage.

Following the capture of Baghdad, investigations started by Cowley's colleagues among the naval flotilla and taken up by his friends and relatives began yielding the evidence that formed the basis for the war crimes inquiry that was to continue after the war ended. Among many interviews was one in which a Turkish PoW claimed that when Cowley was brought before Khahlil, he was asked: 'How dare you come back to these parts? Did you not realise that we, aware of your knowledge of this country, would regard you as a spy?' To these questions Cowley was said to have responded with a show of defiance, insisting he was British, that he was acting under orders and that 'it was no affair of Khahlil's'.

In trying to reconstruct his last movements, the most compelling evidence appeared to come from a captured officer, a Jewish interpreter who was attached to the Turkish 13th Army Corps when Cowley was brought ashore. Cowley 'seemed quite well and was talking Arabic with Turkish officers'. The following morning, together with other members of *Julnar*'s crew, he was taken across the river to the Turkish HQ at Fallahiya. There he was questioned by a staff officer about his nationality. During this interview Cowley was said to have given 'unfortunate' answers. A heated argument followed, during which Cowley allegedly warned his interrogator that the 'Ottoman Government would be held responsible for any bad treatment'. But his words had no effect. What followed, according to the Turkish interpreter, was never confirmed beyond doubt, although British investigators were clearly convinced of its veracity. In summarising his conclusion, they reported: 'On leaving the tent in which Cowley was lying, the Turkish officer ordered the Guard over the tent to shoot Cowley through the canvas. This was done.'

Cowley's body was said to have been buried at Fallahiya near the scene of the murder, although no grave was ever found. His Victoria Cross was presented to his mother by Rear Admiral Drury Wake, Senior Naval Officer, Persian Gulf, in Basra, on 25 August 1917, by which time she was well aware of the rumours about her son's death.

At the end of the war survivors of the *Julnar* emerged from an ordeal even more harrowing than the desperate mission to bring succour to Kut's defenders. Three men, Stokers Thirkhill and Fox and AS Veale, died in captivity, the victims of callous Turkish neglect. But their courage and that of their crewmates was not forgotten. Every member of the *Julnar*'s crew was decorated: Reed received a DSO, Murphy and Rowbotham a CGM apiece, and the rest DSMs. Yet if justice was done in respect of the gallantry of *Julnar*'s 'one-trip' company, it was certainly not done in the case of the war crime that followed. Investigations rumbled on until 1920 when they were quietly wound up. No one was ever prosecuted for the murder of Charles Cowley VC, the 'pirate of Basra'.

F.J.W. HARVEY,
E.B.S. BINGHAM,
L.W. JONES AND
J.T. CORNWELL
Jutland, 31 May 1916

The arguments still rage, churning the waters as furiously as the mighty guns that thundered off Jutland Bank more than eighty years ago. The epic battle fought on 31 May 1916 marked the climax of a decade of Anglo-German naval rivalry. The last of the many actions fought by long lines of closely spaced ships, it was also the only great sea battle to be fought with guns between post-dreadnought capital ships. But to the dismay of a British public beguiled by the illusion of naval supremacy, it produced no outright victory. In fact, British losses outnumbered by far those of the German High Seas Fleet: 6,000 dead to 2,500, and three capital ships, three cruisers and eight destroyers lost against one battlecruiser, one pre-dreadnought battleship, four light cruisers and five destroyers. Yet the bald statistics do not tell the whole story. If the British had lost this battle, then, as one historian has commented, the Germans could 'hardly be judged to have won anything but an escape from annihilation'. For while the Grand Fleet was largely intact and ready to continue the struggle on 1 June, the High Seas Fleet was unfit for further action.

The result in part of German naivety and British code-breaking skills, the Battle of Jutland reflected the desire of the world's two most powerful fleets to confront one another only on terms favourable to themselves. Vice-Admiral Reinhard Scheer's plan was to lure Vice-Admiral Sir David

Beatty's battlecruisers to their destruction. As an adjunct to the scheme, Zeppelins were to provide early warning of any unwanted encounter with heavier forces. Poor weather led to the plan being redrafted, but the goal remained the same. Vice-Admiral Franz von Hipper's battlecruisers were to make a feint to tempt Beatty to give chase, leading him into the killing range of the main fleet lying in wait. Unfortunately, the plan took no account of the Royal Navy's ability to read the German codes. Aware that a major operation was being mounted, though without knowing precisely where or in what strength, Admiral Sir John Jellicoe ordered the Grand Fleet out from its bases with the intention of turning the tables on Scheer.

Beatty's force comprised the 1st and 2nd Battlecruiser Squadrons, Fifth Battle Squadron, First, Second and Third Light Cruiser Squadrons and the First, Ninth, Tenth and Thirteenth Destroyer Flotillas. As vanguard, they cleared the Firth of Forth by 11 p.m. on 30 May and headed for a point 120 miles west of Jutland Bank. This would place them 69 miles ahead of the main fleet which, having rendezvoused 90 miles west of Norway's southern tip, was to steer for Heligoland Bight. If no enemy ships had been sighted by 2.15 p.m., Beatty was to turn away and join forces with Jellicoe.

In the event the rival forces clashed by chance almost precisely at the point when the British battlecruisers should have made their pre-arranged move north. Sent to investigate a Danish steamer, two light cruisers sighted two enemy vessels engaged on the same mission and signalled: 'Enemy in sight'. Another hour passed before Hipper was able to make out the British force, and it was a further five minutes before Beatty, who had the worse of the light, could see the Germans. Hipper immediately reversed course to fall back on Scheer, and took care to align his five battlecruisers so that the funnel and gun smoke of his leading ships would be blown away from the ships bringing up the rear. The opposite applied to the British ships, already hampered by poorer visibility. Buoyed by past success, however, Beatty surged towards the enemy, confident that his six battlecruisers could achieve the complete victory that had eluded him at the Dogger Bank sixteen months earlier.

By 3.45 p.m. Beatty had formed line of battle with *Lion* leading and *Princess Royal*, *Queen Mary*, *New Zealand* and *Indefatigable* following. To Cdr Georg von Hase, gunnery officer in *Derfflinger*, they resembled 'a herd of prehistoric monsters ... spectre-like, irresistible'. At 3.48 p.m. tongues of flame shot from *Lutzow* at the head of the German line, followed almost instantaneously by a rippling flash from the British ships. Although the British had more powerful guns, the

Germans had the advantage of superior range-finding equipment. According to Lieutenant W.S. Chalmers, on the bridge of *Lion*, the enemy fire was 'phenomenally accurate'. Within three minutes *Lion* and *Princess Royal* had both sustained two hits, with *Tiger* taking four blows. But as the British ships bored through a forest of shell splashes, the Germans were untouched. Not until 3.55 p.m., with the range cut to 12,900yd, did *Queen Mary* succeed in landing two hits on *Seydlitz*. *Lion* on the other hand was taking frequent hits. Chalmers saw one lifeboat disintegrate in 'a cloud of splinters', and peering into the 'white mist' he hoped the enemy were 'being similarly punished'. At about this time he was surprised to see a 'bloodstained sergeant of Marines' appear on the admiral's bridge:

> He was hatless, his clothes were burnt, and he seemed to be somewhat dazed: on seeing me he approached and asked if I were the captain. While directing him to the compass platform above my head, curiosity got the better of me, and I asked him what was the matter: in a tired voice he replied, 'Q turret has gone, sir. All the crew are killed, and we have flooded the magazines.' I looked over the bridge. No further confirmation was necessary: the armoured roof of Q turret had been folded back like an open sardine tin, thick yellow smoke was rolling up in clouds from the gaping hole, and the guns were cocked up in the air awkwardly. It was evident that Q turret would take no further part in the battle. Strange that all this should have happened within a few yards of where Beatty was standing, and that none of us on the bridge should have heard the detonation ...

Even more incredible was the narrow margin by which catastrophe had been averted thanks to the quick thinking of the turret's dying commander, Major Francis Harvey RMLI, a 43-year-old gunnery specialist and veteran of the Heligoland Bight and Dogger Bank battles. Subsequent investigation showed that the shell which came within an ace of destroying Beatty's flagship was almost certainly fired by *Lutzow* around 4 p.m. Q turret had fired just twelve rounds when a large calibre shell struck the joint between the thick front armour and roof plate, peeling it back like a tin can to wreak havoc inside. *Lion*'s gunnery officer wrote:

> Six inches higher and the shell would have struck a glancing blow on the roof plate and bounced away; six inches lower and it would have struck the thick front armour plate, and in all probability failed to penetrate; but striking at the weak point, as it did,

the shell entered the gun-house and detonated over the centre line of the left gun ...

Marine H. Willons was down below in the turret's magazine, selecting the cordite, when he felt the impact of a 'heavier explosion than usual' and 'dense smoke came down the trunk'. Work stopped briefly while the men quickly put on respirators.

> Two men were then brought up from the Shell Room [Willons later wrote]. Both had been working in the Gun house and were badly wounded. They were passed along the mess deck to the medical station. Standing by the Magazine Door I heard the Officer of Turret give the order (CLOSE MAGAZINE DOORS! Q TURRET OUT OF ACTION). The Corporal and I closed the port magazine door and clipped it up. By the time we had finished, the hand[l]ing room crew had gone up the iron ladder to the switchboard flat which is immediately above and, being rather a small place, was rather crowded ... About then, the Chief Gunner came along to see everything was in order. Finding the turret was out of action, he ordered several of us to put out fires on the mess deck. Just as he and I got clear the ignition of the cordite occurred and the blast pushed us along ...

According to Willons, some ten minutes had elapsed between the initial shell blast and the ignition of the cordite in the cages, hoppers and possibly the handling room. The carnage was terrible. Every man in the gun house was either killed or seriously wounded, as were all those toiling in the silent cabinet and working chamber directly below.

Major Harvey had been at his command post in the silent chamber, behind the gun breeches, when the shell struck. Fatally wounded by the blast and the burns, which covered most of his body, he nevertheless had the strength and presence of mind to ensure that the disaster that had befallen his turret did not lead to an even greater tragedy. Conscious that Q Turret was immobilised and that the fire raging in its shattered hulk might reach the magazine, he staggered as far as the voice pipe linked to the handling room below and ordered the magazine doors closed and flood valves opened. It was almost, but not quite, his last act. A professional to the end, he recognised the need to inform the bridge of his actions and the extent of the damage. As he lay dying, therefore, he instructed a sergeant to take the message aloft, and it was this man, his uniform shredded black, who delivered the news to a dumbfounded Chalmers.

Harvey's orders had prevented the 'flash' from the guns' cordite charges reaching the magazine, but just how close *Lion* came to disaster was revealed by the post-battle investigation. It showed that the turret fire had, as Willons reported, ignited cordite charges in the loading cages. Chalmers wrote:

> The resultant flash passed down the trunk into the magazine handling room and thence escaped through the 'escape trunk' on to the mess deck, where it finally dissipated itself. By the time the flash reached the handling room, the crew of the magazines had just closed the doors; some of them were found dead afterwards with their hands on the door clips. Their work was done, and the ship was saved ...

What might have been *Lion*'s fate but for Harvey's selfless act was amply demonstrated within minutes when first *Indefatigable* blew up in 'a colossal pall of grey smoke' and then *Queen Mary* exploded 'like a puffball'. Both battlecruisers were almost certainly victims of 'flash' fires igniting open magazines.

That Hipper made no attempt to exploit his advantage was due in part to the menacing approach of a swarm of British destroyers. Even before *Queen Mary* had been dealt her death blow, Beatty had sought to relieve the pressure on his ships by ordering the 13th Flotilla and any other destroyers favourably placed into the attack. By 4.15 p.m. these little ships were a mile ahead of *Lion*. At much the same time, and with the opposite intention, a flotilla of German destroyers was steaming full tilt for Beatty's line. Emerging from the disengaged side of Hipper's battlecruisers, they charged through 'a mad turmoil of white water spouts' to collide head-on with their opposite numbers in 'a fast, disorganised mêlée'.

Leading the British charge were three destroyers of the 13th Flotilla's 2nd Division, *Nestor*, *Nomad* and *Nicator*, under Cdr the Hon. Barry Bingham, the 34-year-old son of an Anglo-Irish nobleman. His ships were new and untested in battle. *Nestor*, his own command, was only a month old, and while the majority of the ship's company had served with him in his previous destroyer, few of the eighty-four officers and men had seen action. Indeed, the orders sending them to sea had taken most of them by surprise, not least Bingham, who had been enjoying a round of golf with his first lieutenant, Lieut Maurice Bethell, at the time. Less than twenty-four hours later, they were converging on the enemy fleet at a rate of thirty-five knots.

For thirty minutes the British destroyers forged on at full speed in the hope of reaching a point on the enemy's bows from which to launch their torpedoes. In the process they spotted an estimated fifteen enemy destroyers making for Beatty's depleted line. Bingham turned north to cut them off, and they responded by turning on to a parallel course. This battle within a battle began at a range of 10,000yd and rapidly closed as Bingham's destroyers forged on under a hot fire. Most of the enemy shells overshot *Nestor* and *Nicator* to burst around *Nomad*, bringing up the rear. One shell wrecked *Nomad*'s wireless gear and another burst in the engine-room, bringing her to a standstill. Supported by the crippled destroyer's guns, *Nestor* and *Nicator* closed the enemy and what Bingham described as 'a vigorous action' ensued. 'Before long,' wrote Bingham, 'two enemy TBDs were observed to sink, and a third to be heavily damaged, steaming at very slow speed'. At least one, according to Bingham, fell to *Nestor*'s guns and, after ten minutes of furious action, the enemy broke off the fight and retreated, pursued by the British force. Braving a deluge of shells from the light cruiser *Regensburg*, Bingham led his depleted division after those enemy destroyers making for the head of the German battlecruiser line. 'Just then,' wrote Bingham, 'the enemy's battlecruisers altered course four points to port; that is 45 degrees to the left. Most probably this manoeuvre was prompted by the warning splashes that marked the discharge of the British torpedoes, of which the *Nestor* had just fired her first two.' Bingham thought it likely that one of these torpedoes had struck the *Lutzow*, but analysis of the fighting suggests that the battlecruisers' turn allowed them to evade Bingham's bold attack.

With *Nicator* still following, Bingham then surged towards the line of enemy battlecruisers. In his official report, he stated: 'Here we were subjected to the heaviest shell fire from the secondary armament of most of their BCs, but we pressed on fully determined to drive home our torpedo attack at the closest possible range; when within 3,000–4,000yd, and on the beam of the leading BC, the *Nestor* fired her third torpedo. Then, having accomplished my two objectives, I turned back followed by *Nicator* ...'

His gallant effort was in vain. All the torpedoes missed and as *Nestor* turned to escape she was smothered by shells, one of which tore through the ship's no. 1 boiler. Six minutes later no. 2 boiler was hit and the ship was enveloped in a cloud of steam. Slowing to a crawl, *Nestor* eventually came to a standstill at 5.30 p.m. *Nicator*, which had to swerve to avoid hitting her, came alongside and offered assistance, but was waved away by Bingham.

While efforts were made to repair her engines, more destroyers passed by on their way to attack the enemy line. As they fell back, one slowed to offer *Nestor* a tow. Not wishing to endanger another ship,

Bingham again declined. By then resigned to his fate, he was neverthe-less determined to fight to the last, as an unwary enemy destroyer soon discovered to its cost. Surgeon Probationer Alec Joe noticed Lieutenant Bethell running toward the bridge to find out what was wrong with *Nestor* when another officer spotted the German destroyer approach-ing. Bethell immediately dashed back to his position at the after gun and, according to Joe, 'put his gun into local control with such purpose that the German turned and went off at full speed without coming into action at all with us and with several 4-inch prodgies [shells] into him …' The reprieve proved short-lived. 'No sooner had the two BC lines disappeared to the NW hotly engaged, than the German High Sea [*sic*] Fleet was observed approaching,' wrote Bingham. 'It became obvious that they would pass within three or four miles of our position.' Even Bingham was 'dumbfounded'. 'This,' he remarked, 'was more than I had ever bargained for.'

Scarcely ten minutes later the stationary *Nomad*, 2 miles away to the east, disappeared beneath a welter of shells. Bingham knew it could only be a matter of time before *Nestor* followed her sister-ship to a watery grave. 'From the time that we realised that our destruction was imminent, all preparations were made with a view to saving as many lives as possible.' Bingham disposed of his charts and confiden-tial books, while his first lieutenant made preparations for the crew's evacuation. As *Nomad* was being pounded, *Nestor*'s motor boat and whaler were being loaded with biscuits and water and lowered to the water's edge and Carley floats hoisted out. At the same time, to keep the men's minds occupied, cables were got ready on the fo'c'stle in 'the unlikely event of a tow being forthcoming'. The end was not long in coming. From roughly 5 miles distance, the High Seas Fleet opened fire with its secondary armament. Despite being straddled, *Nestor* fought back, firing her last torpedo in a gallant if futile gesture, before being buried beneath a 'whirlwind of shrieking shells'. Repeatedly hit aft, she began to settle by the stern and then took an alarming list to starboard. At this point, with his ship clearly doomed, Bingham gave the order: 'Every man for himself!'

As the motor-boat filled with wounded and two Carley floats worked their way clear, shells continued to bracket the ship. Only Bingham, his first lieutenant and an injured seaman remained. In a letter to Maurice Bethell's mother, Bingham described the final moments aboard *Nestor*:

After the men had all got into the boats I turned to him and said 'she's sinking. We'll get clear of her – where shall we go?' meaning which boat should we go for. Maurice said, 'We'll go to Heaven, sir!'

'All right,' I said and started down a rope's end, hoping he was following me, but he didn't follow. He was standing by a dying signalman. It was madness! Salvo after salvo was hitting the ship. At last he was seen to jump …

Bingham managed to get off in the whaler, but the gallant Bethell was lost. Whether he drowned or was struck in the water by a splinter was unclear, but Bingham was certain 'he died like a Hero'. Seconds after shoving clear, Bingham watched as *Nestor* 'stood up, bows in the air, then dived absolutely perpendicular, stern first'. In a letter written to his wife, Bingham said: 'We gave her three cheers as she went down and then sang 'Tipperary', then 'the King' [national anthem].' Not long after, the whaler, which had been holed, sank also, leaving Bingham in the water, kept afloat by his 'life-saving waistcoat':

> It was not very cold [he wrote to his wife] and I struck out for the motor-boat and was pulled aboard. We thought she was buoyant but, no, she began to show signs of sinking. Over-loaded, we realised. She might float for an hour and then it would be the 'ditch' for good and all. Somehow we all experienced that wonderful hope that something would turn up, someone come along and pick us up. And it materialised; a division of German destroyers closed round and came along and picked us up, 75 out of 83.

Bingham, cold and dripping wet from his immersion, was treated to an impromptu but fruitless interrogation aboard the *S16* before being placed under guard in the ship's wardroom while the battle raged around them. 'We felt like rats in a hole,' he wrote, 'as we were quite sure the British destroyers would come up and sink us, and it tested one's loyalty to the utmost to wish it so, at the expense of our own lives …'

Even as *Nestor*'s defiance was drawing to a close, the main units of the Grand Fleet were preparing to enter the fray. First visual contact was made with Beatty's force at 5.33 p.m. The two main fleets were converging oblivious of each other's location. The situation was no clearer on the opposite flank where Admiral Hood's 3rd Battlecruiser Squadron was also racing through thickening patches of mist to support Beatty. Hood's force was about 25 miles ahead of the main fleet, with the light cruisers *Canterbury* and *Chester* scouting 5 miles further forward and the destroyers *Shark, Christopher, Acasta* and *Ophelia* forming an anti-submarine screen. But unbeknown to Hood, a signalling error meant they were headed in the wrong direction, away from Beatty and dangerously close to Admiral Boedicker's Second Scouting Group.

At 5.27 p.m. the distant rumble of heavy guns was heard aboard *Chester*. Having reported to Hood, Captain Robert Lawson turned south-west to investigate, increasing speed in the process.

Like *Nestor*, *Chester* was a recent addition to the fleet. A Birkenhead Class light cruiser of 5,185 tons originally intended for the Greek navy, she was commissioned on 2 May and formally adopted by her namesake city. Acceptance trials completed, *Chester* joined the Grand Fleet at Scapa on 15 May. A fortnight's intensive exercises ended the day before the fleet steamed out of its northern anchorage. The training had gone well. Commander Charles Forbes, second-in-command, wrote on 28 May: 'the ship's company generally are a No 1 lot, the Executive POs especially are Very Good, not a dud amongst them ...' But Lawson had reservations. In particular, he was bothered about the 'deplorable lack of experienced ratings'. One-third of the ship's company and half of the guns' crews were what he termed 'raw and inexperienced hands'. Given the cruiser's design, with its open decks and exposed guns, Lawson had serious misgivings 'about the proportion of youngsters' among *Chester*'s draft: fifty-one boy seamen, with another seventy-one 'hostilities only' ratings, out of a complement of 430. A large percentage of *Chester*'s most 'immature seamen' were to be found manning the ship's open gun batteries. Included among them was a 16-year-old Londoner whose short life was soon to be raised to the status of a national icon.

Jack Cornwell was a sight-setter on one of *Chester*'s ten 'uncase-mated' 5.5-inch guns. Only 5ft 3in tall and weighing just 7st 12lb, Cornwell looked every inch the boy rating he was. Eager and enthusiastic, he had impressed his instructors at Devonport. His certificate of General Efficiency recorded high marks for gunnery and seamanship and concluded with a simple, two-word character reference: 'Very Good'. Promoted Boy First Class on 19 February 1916, his nine months' training was completed on 1 May when he was drafted to *Chester*. As the newly commissioned vessel continued its 'working up' exercises, the crew were assigned their various jobs. In his last letter home, dated 23 May, Cornwell informed his father 'they have just put me as sight-setter at a gun ...'

His role was an important one. The gun's accuracy depended on him. He was the vital link between the gunnery officer and the ten-man crew. Instructions were relayed to him via a telepad fixed across his head and over his ears. On receiving his orders, he had to make certain adjustments to the mechanism of the gun. In front of him was a brass disc, pinned through the centre, and in some respects resembling an old-fashioned telephone dial. As the disc, which was calibrated in yards, was manually turned it raised or lowered the gun's muzzle, thus altering the range. It was a job which called for a cool head as well as quick and precise hands. It was also one that required considerable courage. For in order to carry out his duties without interfering with the work of the gun crew, he was compelled to stand outside the protective shield, thus making his the most exposed post of all.

Boy Cornwell had taken up his post, to the left of one of f'c'stle guns, as *Chester* steamed into the mist in the late afternoon of 31 May. The dull flash of gunfire lit the murk and at 5.36 p.m. the dim outline of a three-funnelled cruiser, with what seemed like one or two destroyers in close proximity, was sighted roughly 4 miles away. *Chester* immediately challenged the 'stranger', who made no reply. Lawson was in a quandary. Although the presence of destroyers made it likely she was an enemy, her appearance was not unlike that of a British cruiser. Taking no chances, Lawson altered course to starboard to guard against the threat of torpedoes. But as *Chester* was still manoeuvring on to a parallel course, two more 'ghost-like' cruisers emerged astern of the leading vessel. All doubt was removed moments later when the nearest one opened fire, just as *Chester* was completing her high-speed turn. Even before Lawson's instructions reached him, Lieutenant Charles Simeon, *Chester*'s gunnery officer, ordered fire to be returned. But with the ship 'under helm' vital minutes were lost. Two salvoes had already screamed over *Chester* by the time her port battery burst into life in what proved her first and last broadside of the action. Before the guns could be reloaded, a third salvo from the enemy's 5.9-inch guns dealt *Chester* a devastating blow. Almost all the shells struck the area around the foremast, disabling the port no. 1 gun and the nos 1 and 2 guns on the starboard side. Casualties in the batteries were appalling, with a high proportion of the young crews killed or maimed by the hail of shrapnel sweeping across the open decks. From the holed and splintered f'c'stle past the riddled funnels as far as the stern, *Chester* was swallowed by smoke from a rash of cordite fires. In those moments of screaming confusion, it appeared certain she would be destroyed. Looking down from the foretop, Lt Simeon expected at any moment to see the battered bridge shot away.

In eight shattering minutes *Chester* had been rendered almost defenceless. Most of her guns were out of action, with forty-seven out one hundred men manning the exposed batteries killed or wounded. The dead included the ship's chaplain, sent down to the port battery 'to encourage the younger men'. Though Lawson saw 'no case of actual flinching or deserting a post', the effect of such carnage was obvious:

Confusion undoubtedly occurred among gun crews – utterly inexperienced in all that appertains to sea life – when they found themselves on an open deck, with mutilated men all round, officer of the battery either killed or wounded, and apparently no enemy to shoot at. Nothing to do, in fact. The natural and sensible instinct in such case is to take cover. The only apparent cover was the light bulkheads of superstructures, which appear to afford protection, but are in point of fact most efficient shell bursters. And disengaged gun crews endeavoured to take such shelter. The only real shelter is the off side of the gun shield. And had a larger proportion of seamen been among the crews, it is not improbable that valuable lives would have been saved ...

With communications wrecked and the range-finder blown overboard, Lt Simeon decided against bringing up extra crews. To do so, he insisted, would merely have meant 'additional carnage, with no compensating advantage', a view shared by Lawson, who, from the moment his ship had been smothered by the enemy's fire, was intent only on saving *Chester* from destruction. Retreating at high speed to the north-east, Lawson steered a zig-zag course, deliberately turning towards each fall of shot in order to upset the enemy's aim. 'This,' he wrote, 'was apparently successful as regards saving the ship from a large amount of further serious damage. In the last few minutes I believe she was seldom hit, but the changes of ship's course rendered it impossible for the after guns to make effective shooting, even if the gun crews had been in a fit state and sufficient number to do so ...'

By 5.54 p.m., when *Chester* turned into safety, she had been under sustained fire from three, then four, enemy cruisers for nineteen minutes, during which she had been hit eighteen times. As she passed Hood's flagship, four jagged holes were clearly visible along her side. That she had survived her baptism of fire was a miracle that owed much to her captain's brilliant handling. His skill in dodging salvo after salvo 'like a snipe' was matched by the steadfast courage displayed by his crew, most of them in their first action.

Among numerous acts of individual gallantry the behaviour of some stood out. Lieutenant Arthur Curtis left the after control to tour the open batteries after they were hit. Finding 'many men stupid from shock', he took over spotting the after gun, independently firing eighteen rounds at the chasing cruisers. Burnt about the face, Temporary Captain Edward Bamford RMLI, commanding the port and starboard no. 3 guns, scrambled clear of the after control when it was wrecked by a shell to help the crew manning the starboard gun. Later, he helped extinguish a fire abaft the after funnel.

But of all the selfless acts it was the performance of Boy Jack Cornwell, in his first and last action, which made the deepest impression on *Chester*'s captain. Writing to the youngster's mother, Lawson told of his 'splendid fortitude and courage':

> The wounds which resulted in his death ... were received in the first few minutes of the action. He remained steady at his most exposed post, waiting for orders. His gun would not bear on the enemy: all but two of the crew of ten were killed or wounded, and he was the only one who was in such an exposed position. But he felt he might be needed, as indeed he might have been; so he stayed there, standing and waiting, under heavy fire, with just his own brave heart and God's help to support him. I cannot express to you my admiration of the son you have lost from this world. No other comfort would I attempt to give to the mother of so brave a lad but to assure her of what he was and what he did and what an example he gave ...

Jack Cornwell was found still standing at his post on the fo'c'stle when the 3rd Battlecruiser Squadron drew off the enemy fire. Carried below, he endured the terrible agonies of his wounds without complaint through a long night of unremitting drama.

As *Chester* drew out of harm's way, it was the turn of her pursuers to suffer. With the fire power of Hood's battlecruisers dwarfing Boedicker's light cruisers, retribution came swiftly. Firstly, *Wiesbaden* was hammered to a smoking wreck and then *Pillau* was hard hit. In an attempt to relieve the pressure on the hard-pressed cruisers, Commodore Heinrich ordered every available torpedo-boat into the attack. Once again the opposing destroyer forces had chosen the same moment.

Having been left on Hood's port quarter by the battlecruisers' turn towards Boedicker, the four destroyers comprising the Fourth Flotilla under Commander 'Willie' Loftus Jones sighted the retreating enemy cruisers heading towards them, half-hidden by shell splashes. Realising his great opportunity, Cdr Loftus Jones, in *Shark*, led off 'to make the most of it', followed by *Acasta*, *Ophelia* and *Christopher*. In a repeat of Bingham's action, the four British destroyers met the charge of a large portion of three enemy flotillas. The action was fast and furious with quick-firing guns stabbing the swirling smoke and flurries of torpedoes lost in the confusion of battle. In the wild mêlée, the enemy destroyer *B98* had its mast shorn off by one shot.

But it was the British destroyers, outnumbered and outgunned, which came off worse. Within minutes *Shark*, her progress obscured by a torrent of water spouts, was smothered by shells. According to Stoker Thomas Swan the first hit wrecked the fore steering gear, and was quickly followed by another in the stokehold that killed two stokers and a petty officer. *Shark*'s fo'c'stle gun got off about eight rounds before a direct hit sent it crashing overboard along with its captain, Sub-Lieutenant Patrick Vance, and all but one of its crew. Moments later, the bridge was hit by a shell which carried away the telegraph mast and wounded the coxswain, Petty Officer William Griffin, and his captain, standing alongside him.

PO Griffin later recorded: 'Cdr Jones staggered back with an intake of breath. He had been wounded in the leg. It was then that I became conscious that I, too, had received a wound. There was blood dripping from my right hand.' Quickly recovering, Jones ordered the after-wheel manned, and the survivors of the bridge party scrambled down the ladder to reach the new steering position. Griffin recalled:

> On all sides there was chaos. Dead and dying lay everywhere around. The decks were a shambles. Great fragments of the ship's structure were strewn everywhere. At the foot of the ladder I met Tom Shepherd, a torpedo instructor and a particular friend of mine. 'What's up, 'swain?' he asked … 'Foremost wheel's gone,' I said as I hurried away; 'telegraph too.' Salvo after salvo was coming over. I had just reached the foremost funnel when a shell burst overhead and I was thrown to the deck …

Wounded in the head and eye, Griffin lapsed into unconsciousness. Jones, his thigh roughly bandaged, connected the after steering gear only to discover that a shell had ruptured the oil pipes feeding the boilers. Attempts to hand-pump the oil were useless and efforts to locate the damaged pipes proved impossible in the flooded confines of the forward stokehold. Petty Officer Charles Filleul made his way back to the after stokehold where his desperate attempts to pump oil yielded only saltwater. 'At this juncture,' he wrote, 'the engineer transmitted the order from the Captain for the hands in the stokehold to come on deck since we were stopped and at the mercy of the enemy …'

No sooner had Filleul reached the deck than the after gun was smashed and most of its crew wiped out. The men manning the after torpedo tubes lay dead at their posts with the exception of Able Seaman Charles Smith who had single-handedly fired off one torpedo at the *Regensburg* before lending a hand with the wounded.

Acasta, drawing away from the fight, offered to put a towline aboard, but Jones would have none of it. 'Look after yourself,' he shouted. In those moments, *Acasta* was hit and holed but managed to pull clear, leaving *Shark* to her lonely and inevitable end. A diversion by the cruiser *Canterbury* brought a brief stay of execution, during which rafts and Carley floats were readied. Like Bingham, Jones had every intention of going down fighting.

He did not have long to wait. Shortly after 6.30 p.m. two German destroyers, returning from their unsuccessful attack on Hood's battle-cruisers, closed to deliver the *coup de grâce*. *Shark* appeared dead in the water, but as they neared they discovered too late their mistake. A shell from *Shark*'s only gun still in action brought the *V48* to a standstill, ensuring she would eventually share her intended victim's fate. This success put fresh heart into the crippled destroyer's crew as they met the next assault from an estimated force of fifteen cruisers and destroyers who used *Shark* for target practice as they passed by.

Their only means of defence was the midship 4-inch gun which kept up a furious fire, despite man after man falling dead or wounded. Eventually, the gun team was reduced to Midshipman Thomas Smith, acting as gun trainer, Able Seaman Joseph Howell, the gunlayer, and Able Seaman Charles Hope, his no. 2. But they were joined by a steady flow of reinforcements, including a signaller who was twice blown overboard, PO Filleul, Able Seaman Smith, Stoker Swan and *Shark*'s wounded captain. With nothing left but to lead by example, Jones took command of the exposed gun, acting as sight-setter. 'All the Captain could do was to direct me and tell me where to fire,' wrote Howell. 'My gun having been reduced to two hands, firing became slow, and I found that the new percussion firing gear did not act at all nicely, but nevertheless [*sic*] we managed to give them a warm time …'

Their resistance could not last. Enemy destroyers were battering *Shark* from 600yd. Howell fell with a serious leg wound, struggled to his feet and carried on until, weakened by loss of blood, he collapsed again. Not long after, a shell severed Jones's left leg above the knee. Carried aft by Hope and Griffin, he was placed on a cork fender, from where he continued to give orders while Chief Stoker Hammel applied a tourniquet to his thigh. Glancing up, Jones saw that the White ensign was no longer flying. 'What's wrong with the flag?' he called. AS Hope was first to respond:

> I climbed on to the shelter constructed over the after wheel and unbent the ensign from the gaff. I passed it down to Midshipman Smith, who then hoisted it at the yard-arm. Commander Jones seemed then to be less worried when he saw the flag was hoisted again.

Shark's fight was almost over. Cdr Jones, his lifeblood ebbing away, ordered the survivors to don their cork lifebelts, calling out: 'Save yourselves!' Moments later, with the midships gun still returning fire, the first of two torpedoes slammed into *Shark* abreast the after funnel. According to PO Filleul, the impact shook 'half of our number over the side'. *Shark*, her colours still flying, quickly began to heel over.

As the survivors abandoned ship, Jones was helped into the water, where he was seen 'supporting himself on a raft' with two other men. 'I went to his assistance,' wrote Filleul, 'and tied a cork lifebelt around him, telling him that our ships were coming towards us.' Griffin, Hope, Howell and Swan managed to scramble aboard another Carley float. From his raft, Jones shouted, 'Let's have a song, lads!' The first lieutenant began to sing 'Nearer My God to Thee', and others joined in until they were exhausted. When some ships came into sight, Jones was heard to ask if they were English or German. When told they were English, he replied: 'That's good'. They were thought to be his last words. As darkness fell, the floats drifted apart. Filleul recalled:

> Nine survivors, or thereabouts, as far as I can recollect, were upon each of two Carley floats; some of whom were very badly wounded and, of course, could not control their craft to get to the Captain and effect his rescue. We all floated down together for some time; my own support in the water consisting of a cork belt and a round lifebuoy; but after the fall of darkness I could not tell what became of the two Carley floats and the wooden raft to which the Captain was clinging for upwards of three hours ...

Exhaustion and cold took their toll of the survivors, until fewer than ten remained. Then, with hope fading, a small group of men clinging to a Carley float saw a ship's lights. Hope ignited a flare and waved it frantically.

The SS *Vidar*, a Danish steamer out of Copenhagen, was making for a 'two-masted man o'war' that was on fire when her captain, Ole Christiansen, noticed a light on the water in the opposite direction. Turning about to investigate, he brought his ship alongside the float. Three men were clinging to it, calling out for help, and a fourth man lay apparently dead. And all around, the sea was covered with the bodies of dead seamen, kept afloat by their lifebelts.

As *Vidar* searched the water around the float, they found four more survivors, including PO Filleul. Alone in the water, he had seen the *Vidar*'s lights, but hardly hoped to be seen in the darkness. 'I waved my hand and must have been seen for I was picked up by the boat she had lowered,' he wrote. 'However, I do not remember my rescue as I lost consciousness after waving my hand to the steamer, and did not regain my senses until about 9 a.m. on the morning of the first of June.' By then, Chief Stoker (Pensioner) Francis Newcombe had died from exhaustion, leaving just six survivors from a crew of ninety-two. Joseph Howell, the wounded gunner, commented: 'It is a marvel there is anyone left to tell the tale.'

The same might have been said for the hundreds of seamen aboard Beatty's flagship. Only later did the full extent of *Lion*'s damage and narrow escape become clear. Marine Willons, who had spent much of the engagement fetching and carrying the wounded, recalled sloshing through four inches of water, striking matches to light the way as he stumbled across mess decks strewn with boots and clothing. Then came a more grisly duty:

> The Chief Gunner and I went down to the Shell Room ... to find out if it was possible to salve any of the ammunition. The Hand[l]ing Room, Switchboard, Flat and Shell Room were completely burned out. The crew were lying in all directions, some still hanging on the ladder in a last attempt to get out. On finding that it was impossible to salve any of the projectiles for use in the other turrets the shell room was flooded. The Captain of Marines sent for me then to go to the Gun house to find the Major and remove some of the casualties. I got into the Gun house through the manhole on top and, assisted by another marine, got out seven people from the right cabinet. The Chaplain was one of these. The Major was in the range-finder position close by the voice pipe. There was a great deal of smoke coming from behind the ready use shell bin and we gave the alarm that four common shell were being roasted and were likely to cause another explosion. With the assistance of several more marines the fire was put out and the remainder of the casualties were removed. They were then taken aft, identified if possible and sewn in hammocks ...

All but three of the hundred or so officers and men in the silent cabinet, gun house, working chamber, handling and shell rooms were dead. In some areas, searchers were surprised to find no evidence of any fire, though that was not the case in the gun house, where signs of a fierce blaze were reflected in the burnt and charred paintwork. It was here, 'in the poor light of a torch', that Francis Harvey's body was found. Captain F.R. Jones, RMLI, who helped carry him out, noticed that, although very badly burnt, 'he was not dismembered in any way,' thus giving the lie to one of the battle's more enduring myths.

As day dawned with the North Sea cleared of enemy ships, *Chester*, holed along her hull and funnels, her pocked decks stained with blood, was ordered back to the Humber. On board, in her cramped sickbay, were forty-four wounded men, many of them with injuries below the knee caused by shell splinters spraying across the open decks. Among the 'seriously wounded' was Boy First Class Cornwell. Still clinging to life when *Chester* docked at 5 p.m., he was among those transferred to Grimsby Hospital. Although in great pain and very weak, he could still talk in whispers. When the matron tending him asked how the battle had gone, he was said to have replied, 'Oh – we carried on all right!' Later, he asked for the matron and whispered: 'Give my mother my love. I know she is coming.' And so she was. Alerted by an Admiralty telegram, she hurried to Grimsby, arriving just too late. On his death certificate, a doctor gave as the cause of death 'intestinal perforation due to wounds received in action. Injuries received in the naval battle between the British and German navies in the North Sea.'

Eight days later, with details about the battle still obscure, news was received of the safe arrival in Germany of survivors from *Nestor* and *Nomad*. Disembarked at Wilhelmshaven on 1 June their number was greater than might have been expected. Indeed, Bingham listed only seven fatalities among *Nestor*'s stout-hearted company, with a further eight men wounded. He considered they owed their incredible escape to the fact that many of the enemy shells had struck the after-part of the ship, while almost all the crew were engaged forward. 'Had the fore-part of the ship met with the same treatment,' he wrote, 'very few of us would have been left alive.'

For weeks after the battle the sea continued to give up its dead, each tide bringing with it doleful reminders of the fearful price paid for a struggle without a victory. The bodies of hundreds of seamen were scattered by wind and current across a wide area of southern Scandinavia. A number were washed ashore on the small Swedish island of Fiskebackskil where, in the fourth week of June, local people found the mutilated body of an English officer, a cork lifebelt still strapped around his lifeless corpse. 'Willie' Loftus Jones had made his final landfall.

Francis John William Harvey, the only Royal Marine to earn a Victoria Cross during a 'big ship' action, was born on 29 April 1873 at Kirkdale Villa, Upper Sydenham, Kent, the son of Commander John William Francis Harvey RN and Elizabeth Edwards Lavington (née Penny). At the age of 11, his family having moved to Courtney Lodge, Southsea, he entered Portsmouth Grammar School, following in his brother's footsteps. Both were accomplished scholars, Francis showing a particular talent for languages and debating. He once proposed the motion that war was the only effective means of settling international disputes on the grounds that arbitration always proved unsatisfactory to all sides. He passed out 33rd of 693 candidates for Sandhurst and second out of twelve accepted for officer training in the Royal Marine Light Infantry.

He chose the Marines, thus maintaining his family's ties with the military, and the navy in particular, stretching back more than a century. His great-great-grandfather, Captain John Harvey, was mortally wounded while commanding HMS *Brunswick* at the Battle of the 'Glorious First of June' in 1794, his great-grandfather was Admiral Sir Edward Harvey GCB, and his grandfather, Captain John Harvey, had served in the 9th Foot (later the Royal Norfolk Regiment). Appointed second lieutenant in the Portsmouth Division RMLI on 1 September 1892, Francis Harvey attended the Royal Naval College and, on his return, in the following July, was promoted lieutenant. Before taking his first sea-going appointment aboard HMS *Wildfire* in October 1894, he found time to gain a qualification in military law. Within a year, however, he was back, immersing himself in the theory and practice of naval gunnery. It was a field that was to dominate his career and one in which he would become thoroughly expert. Following courses at HMS *Excellent*, he passed as an instructor (first class) in January 1896 and, after nearly two years aboard HMS *Phaeton* during which he earned the approbation of the Admiralty for a report on San Diego, he was appointed Assistant Instructor of Gunnery at Plymouth Division.

A brief spell in HMS *Edgar* was followed by an appointment to HMS *Diadem* of the Channel Fleet, during which time he was promoted captain. After a gunnery refresher course, he joined HMS *Royal Sovereign*, the first of a succession of big ship appointments that between 1903 and 1909 would include the *Duke of Edinburgh*, *St George* and *Inflexible*. In 1910 he became Instructor of Gunnery at Chatham, being promoted major the following year. His marked professionalism and ability to pass on his knowledge was soon recognised. An inspection report by the Commander-in-Chief, The Nore, in 1911 praised his 'thoroughness', while the following year's report was even more laudatory: 'Degree of efficiency in Gunnery Establishment at Chatham is very high both as regards general training and attention to detail. Great credit is due to all concerned particularly to Major F.J.W. Harvey, the I of G.' Such glowing reports undoubtedly helped to land him a plum job in the new battlecruiser HMS *Lion*, which he joined as senior marine officer on 12 February 1913, two weeks before Admiral Beatty hoisted his flag. It was to be his last appointment.

After twenty-two years, peace-time service, Francis Harvey finally went to war in August 1914. By the end of the month, he had received his baptism of fire at the Battle of Heligoland Bight when *Lion*'s guns helped account for the cruisers *Koln* and *Ariadne*. In January the following year he was in action again at he Battle of the Dogger Bank, where *Lion* contributed to the destruction of the battlecruiser *Blücher* and narrowly missed sinking the *Seydlitz*. Despite being badly hit herself, *Lion* succeeded in scoring a direct hit on Hipper's flagship. A 13.5-inch shell penetrated the rear turret, sparking a fire that spread from the loading room via two ammunition chambers to a neighbouring turret. In an extraordinary pre-echo of Harvey's dying act at Jutland a year later, a catastrophic explosion aboard the *Seydlitz* was only averted by the heroism of three crewmen who flooded the after magazines.

Francis Harvey's entire war service, spanning twenty-two months, was spent in *Lion*, and it was from her quarterdeck that his body, together with ninety-eight others, was committed to the deep in a moving ceremony attended by Beatty and his fellow officers in the forenoon of 1 June 1916. As chance would have it, it was the 122nd anniversary of his illustrious forebear's mortal wound. Harvey, who was married and had a son, was posthumously mentioned in Admiral Jellicoe's Jutland despatch. His Victoria Cross, gazetted on 15 September 1916, was presented to his widow, Ethel (née Edye), at Buckingham Palace on 29 November. In time, the Cross, together with his 1914–15 Star, British War and Victory Medals, passed to his son, Lieutenant-Colonel John Malcolm Harvey, the King's Regiment. Six years before his death in 1979, he presented them to the Royal Marines Museum at Eastney Barracks, where they are displayed to this day beneath a portrait of the man whose last action was to save his ship and the lives of hundreds of his crewmates. As Winston Churchill wrote: 'In the long, rough, glorious history of the Royal Marines there is no name and no deed which in its character and consequences ranks above this.'

The Honourable Edward Barry Stewart Bingham had the distinction of being the only member of the Royal Navy to be awarded the Victoria Cross while in captivity during the First World War. He was born at Bangor Castle, Bangor, in County Down, on 26 July 1881, the third son of John, 5th Baron Clanmorris, JP, DL, ADC to the Lord Lieutenant of Ireland, and his wife, Matilda Catherine (née Ward), Lady Clanmorris, daughter and heiress of a wealthy builder. He was educated at Arnold House, in Llanddulas, Wales, and on the Dartmouth-based navy training ship HMS *Britannia* before being commissioned as a midshipman in 1897. Promoted lieutenant on 30 June 1903, Bingham, who was a fine horseman, was a member of the Royal Navy polo team, which won the Inter-Regimental and Ships Annual Challenge Cup in Malta.

At the outbreak of war, he was serving as a lieutenant commander aboard the Admiralty yacht *Enchantress*, a miniature liner of some 2,000 tons complete with its own boardroom and wine cellar. The following morning he joined the Dreadnought battlecruiser *Invincible* as fourth most senior officer in command of A turret. His duties also involved taking charge of the ship's midshipmen and acting as boarding officer.

Despite undergoing an extensive refit when war was declared, *Invincible* was at sea by the middle of August 1914 and by the end of the month had taken part in the successful action at Heligoland Bight. Dispatched to the South Atlantic in November, *Invincible* and Bingham played a prominent role in the defeat of Vice-Admiral Graf von Spee's Pacific Squadron at the Battle of the Falklands on 8 December 1914. Having fired Admiral Sturdee's first sighting shot at the retreating *Leipzig*, Bingham's gun crew scored a number of hits during *Invincible*'s destruction of the *Sharnhorst*. In recognition of his services, Bingham was promoted to commander on 31 December and was promised a destroyer command. That promise was kept on 12 February 1915 when he took charge of the 850-ton *Hornet* and a division of destroyers which formed part of the First Flotilla based at Harwich and, from the following month, the Firth of Forth. For the next fourteen months *Hornet* was engaged in essential, though largely uneventful, patrol work, often in company with Beatty's battlecruisers or a squadron of elderly pre-Dreadnought battleships. His most notable service during this time was the hazardous rescue of 500 crewmen from the cruiser *Argyll* which had run aground on the Bell Rock off the Forfarshire coast. In what he described as a 'delicate and ticklish' manoeuvre, he put *Hornet*'s fo'c'stle alongside the stricken vessel's quarter-deck and held her there, against the wind and sea, while the crew leapt to safety. It was a remarkable piece of seamanship that earned him praise at the subsequent Court of Enquiry.

Earlier that year, during a 48-hour leave from *Hornet*, Bingham had married Vera Temple Patterson, only daughter of Mr Edward Temple Patterson, of Culford Gardens, South Kensington (the marriage was dissolved in 1937). They had two children, John Temple and Lavinia Mary.

In the spring of 1916 the First Flotilla began to replace its existing ships with new M-class destroyers. Bingham's new command, HMS *Nestor*, arrived in the Firth of Forth on 30 April and the following day the bulk of Bingham's 'Hornets' transferred en masse. It proved a short commission. Within a month, they would be dead, wounded or prisoners of war. *Nestor*'s survivors were held initially in Mainz, before being transported a few days later to Friedburg in Hessen. After a stay of nine and a half months, roughly a third of the prisoners, including Bingham, were transferred to Augustabad, Neubrandenburg.

It was while incarcerated at Friedburg that Bingham received news that he had been awarded the Victoria Cross for his 'dauntless courage' in pressing home his attack in the face of the 'concentrated fire' of the High Seas Fleet's secondary batteries. What he did not know was that the award, gazetted on 15 September 1916, had been the subject of considerable bureaucratic debate. In examining the recommendation, the Naval Secretary had urged that the question of Bingham's VC be postponed until the war was over. Writing on 28 August, he declared that Cdr Bingham, 'being a prisoner of war, is not by the accepted rules eligible for an honour until his release and subsequent enquiry into his conduct.' But Arthur Balfour, the First Lord of the Admiralty, disagreed. Two days later, he retorted: 'I see no sufficient reason why ... Bingham should not receive VC at once.' With that, the recommendation went forward and was duly approved by the king on 2 September. The following June, Bingham, by then a captive in Augustabad, learned that the Russian government had awarded him the Order of Stanislaus, 2nd class with swords, for his exploits at Jutland.

During his two and a half years' captivity, first in German hands and later in a Dutch internment camp, Bingham occupied himself by preparing his wartime memoir, which was published in 1919 with an introduction by Admiral Beatty, under the title *Falklands, Jutland and the Bight*.

In May 1918, at Bella Vista internment camp, Scheveningen, he compiled a series of copious reports of his final action containing a lengthy list of men from the *Nestor* cited for gallantry. Among them were recommendations for two CGMs, seven DSMs and a posthumous DSO to Maurice Bethell, his gallant first lieutenant. Of these, only three DSMs were granted, including one downgraded from a CGM.

In his absence Cdr Bingham had already become a celebrity in his home town. The first anniversary of Jutland was marked in Bangor with a holiday for pupils of Ward School, which took its name from his mother's family. In a ceremony performed on the lawn beside Bangor Castle, the band of the Royal Garrison Artillery played martial airs and Sir Robert Kennedy recalled the hero's childhood. Bingham's father had died the previous November, but his mother joined in the speeches, while pupils presented parcels of cigarettes to be sent to the commander and his crew. Writing to thank them from Germany, Bingham urged the boys to consider the navy, 'the finest profession in the World', as a future career and entreated them to 'remember the great example of Boy Cornwell VC'.

On his return to Britain, Bingham was presented with his Victoria Cross by the king in the ballroom of Buckingham Palace on 13 December 1918. Bangor gave him a hero's homecoming. Stepping from a train decorated with the flags of the Allies, he was greeted by loud cheers and, following a tour through the streets crowded with townspeople, he was carried shoulder-high to the gates of Bangor Castle. That night, a torchlight procession led to Dufferin Hall and a civic reception, during which Bingham proclaimed: 'Anything I was able to do for my country was all in a day's work.'

Later, in further recognition of his 'valorous conduct', the Admiralty presented the townspeople with a German naval gun taken from the submarine *UB19*, which was sited in Ward Park. The record of the Binghams had been an impressive one. Five of Lord Clanmorris's sons took up arms: Denis, the second eldest, rose to lieutenant-colonel and earned a DSO in the Tank Corps, and Gerald, the youngest, was killed while serving with the Royal Flying Corps. After the war Bingham resumed his naval career. Promoted captain on 31 December 1919, he was awarded the recently instituted Order of the British Empire and, the following year, was appointed to command the Admiralty yacht *Enchantress*, in which he had served before the war. After taking a senior officers' course, he returned to destroyers in 1923 as captain of the *Montrose* and commander of the Fourth Flotilla, part of the Mediterranean Fleet. This was followed by command of the Nore Destroyer Flotilla from 1925 to 1929 and then the battleship HMS *Resolution*.

In 1931 he was made Naval ADC to King George V and appointed senior officer of the Devonport Division of the Reserve Fleet. It was his last active appointment. The following July he was promoted rear admiral on his retirement and settled at Evershot in Dorset.

Barry Bingham, the only one of the quartet of Jutland VCs who lived to receive his honour, died in a London nursing home on 24 September 1939. His body was cremated in a private service at Golders Green Crematorium. Two years later, following the death of his mother, his birthplace was bought by Bangor Borough Council and eventually converted into the Town Hall. More than forty years later, on 13 October 1983, Bangor further cemented its proud ties with the Bingham family with the purchase for £18,000 of the only VC to be won by one of its citizens. Bought from a private collector by North Down Borough Council, the Bingham VC group was placed on public display in Bangor Castle in a heritage centre. They were replaced by replicas in 2001 after a thief made off with the medals, only to be caught by an off-duty policeman.

Loftus William Jones was born into a naval family on 13 November 1879, the second son of Admiral Loftus Francis Jones and Gertrude (née Gray), of Hylton House, Petersfield, Hampshire. With an admiral for a father, it was hardly surprising that 'Willie', as he was known in the family, should join the Senior Service, which he did via Eastman's Royal Navy Academy, Fareham, an establishment he detested, and HMS *Britannia*, which he entered in 1894. Two of his three brothers, Lewis and Frank, served in the Navy, Frank taking part in the Battle of Jutland, while the third, Charles, broke with tradition and entered the Indian Army.

Jones's career points to a certain restlessness. From 1896, when he joined the *Royal Sovereign* as a midshipman, until taking command of *Shark* in 1914, he had no fewer than twenty-eight appointments. Most lasted little more than a year. In one of his shortest spells aboard any ship, he was temporary watchkeeper aboard the cruiser *Argonaut* for just ten days during 1903, a year in which he served in five different ships!

Big ships were not, it would appear, much to his liking, and when, towards the end of 1903, he was appointed, at the relatively youthful age of 21, to command the gunboat *Sandpiper* on the China Station, it marked the beginning of an association with small ships that would last, with one short interruption, until his death at Jutland. His appointment in 1905 to the *Success* was the first in a line of destroyer commands – *Chelmer* (1908–10), *Gurkha* (1910–13) and *Linnet*, an appointment he took up in June 1914, after being promoted commander. Professionally and domestically, his future appeared settled and assured. Four years earlier he had married Margaret Annie Dampney, of Netherbury in Dorset, and before the end of 1914 they would celebrate the birth of a daughter, Linnette, named after his new destroyer. By then, however, his long experience of destroyer work was being put to the test in the white heat of combat.

The opening months of war proved busy ones for Jones. *Linnet* was among four destroyers from the Harwich Patrol's Third Flotilla involved in the sinking of the German minelayer *Konigen Luise* on 5 August 1914, the navy's first victory. And the following day she had the unhappy duty of helping rescue survivors of the hapless *Amphion* after she struck one of the recently laid mines. It was in the course of this work that *Linnet* suffered her first war casualty, a gunner who was hit by a hatch cover from the exploding cruiser. August closed with *Linnet* sharing in the victory achieved in the Battle of the Heligoland Bight.

It was Jones's last major action before being appointed to command *Shark* on 11 October. Two months later, as leader of the 2nd Division of the Fourth Flotilla based at Cromarty under Admiral Beatty's command, he was heavily engaged in the enemy raid on the Yorkshire coast. In the pre-dawn darkness of 16 December, *Shark* was one of a number of destroyers which clashed with the advance guard of a portion of the German High Seas Fleet which, though it included a light cruiser, they boldly proceeded to attack, resulting in the enemy turning tail. Despite the foul weather and superior German force, Cdr Jones pressed on to make contact again, shadowing and reporting the enemy's position. It was an example of courageous leadership that earned a commendation from Beatty and which served to presage his final, gallant action eighteen months later.

In the immediate aftermath of Jutland, the captain of *Shark* emerged as one of the first 'heroes' of the battle. Weeks before the public had ever heard of Boy Cornwell, the name of Cdr Jones was headline news. For days, national newspapers vied with one another for the most graphic description of *Shark*'s brave fight against hopeless odds. 'Captain Fought

On Though His Leg Was Shot Away' ran one typical headline. In another version, published within a week of the battle, comparison was made with the *Titanic* as survivors recounted the moment they sang the hymn 'Nearer My God To Thee'. To the popular press, it was the stirring stuff of legend. The navy's response, however, was more restrained. Having interviewed the survivors, Rear Admiral Stuart Nicholson, commanding the East Coast of England, wrote a bland report in which he briefly outlined *Shark*'s struggle and the extent of Cdr Jones's injuries. He made no recommendations for awards, other than to suggest that the 'kind action' of the *Vidar*'s captain should be 'suitably recognized'. In due course Captain Christiansen was presented with a gold watch, his chief officer a silver cup and four seamen awards of money for their part in the rescue of the men from *Shark*.

By then Cdr Jones's name had appeared in the Jutland honours list on 15 September among those officers and men mentioned in dispatches. He had been recommended, though by whom is not clear, for a post-humous honour: 'For fighting his ship until she sank after having been serious wounded.' To this, however, was appended a terse note: 'Cdr Jones is not entitled to any posthumous honour except the VC. As this paragraph will appear in the gazette it seems that nothing more can be done in his case, unless he is considered for a VC and this seems inappropriate.' And here, undoubtedly, the matter would have rested, but for the intervention of the redoubtable Mrs Jones.

Motivated, no doubt, by a desire to have her husband's well-publicised heroism officially recognised, she set about visiting and interviewing as many of *Shark*'s survivors as she could find. From their stories she then wrote a narrative, a copy of which she sent to Captain E.O. Gladstone, an officer in her husband's old flotilla. The 'consistency' of the men's accounts left her in 'no doubt as to its accuracy'. Merely noting that he had received private information from 'a reliable source' that 'great bravery and gallantry were displayed by the late Commander Loftus W. Jones and one or two of the crew of HMS *Shark*', Gladstone wrote to Commodore James Hawksley, Grand Fleet Flotillas, on 13 October, urging that the survivors be 'officially interrogated with a view to any such meritorious and exemplary deeds ... being brought to the notice of the Commander-in-Chief'.

Over the next six weeks all six men were traced and signed statements taken. Armed with these, Gladstone wrote again to Hawksley on 3 December, asking him to forward the evidence to the C.-in-C. in the hope that recognition for Jones's 'noble example ... might be shown even now'. With the reports he enclosed a copy of Mrs Jones's narrative. The response was almost immediate. Hawksley ended his letter to the newly appointed C.-in-C., Admiral Beatty: 'I feel sure that the posthumous award of a decoration to the late Lt Cdr Jones [*sic*] would be very highly appreciated by the survivors as a recognition of their behaviour in action.' Beatty agreed wholeheartedly. 'This is a fine story and I strongly recommend the behaviour of the ship's company of *Shark* be recognized by rewards to the survivors,' he declared. 'The example of Lt Cdr Loftus Jones was of such a character as to warrant his recommendation for the posthumous award of the Victoria Cross.' Later, he would add: 'No finer act has been produced in the annals of His Majesty's Navy.'

'Willie' Loftus Jones's VC was gazetted on 6 March 1917, and on the last day of the month his widow went to Buckingham Palace to receive the honour she had done more than anyone to secure. Four years later Margaret Jones took her daughter to Fiskebackskil to see the fine memorial erected by local people in honour of her father.

Linnette Sheffield returned to Sweden in 1991 for a ceremony marking the 75th anniversary of the battle. Her father's grave had been moved to Kviberg Cemetery in Gothenburg during the 1960s, but the people of Fiskebackskil had not forgotten. Earlier that year, she had presented her father's VC on loan to the Royal Naval Museum in Portsmouth, saying: 'I'm so very proud of this medal, but I did worry about being burgled.' Subsequently withdrawn from the museum and sold privately, it is now part of the Lord Ashcroft VC Collection.

In death, Jack Cornwell achieved a kind of fame he could not have dreamt of during his short life. His action, coupled with his extreme youth, touched off a wave of popular sentiment and public mourning that was unparalleled during more than four years of war. Myth and reality became so intertwined as to be almost inseparable and the 'boy hero of Jutland' came to stand as a symbol for a generation of doomed youth.

John Travers Cornwell was born on 8 January 1900 at Clyde Place, Leyton, Essex, the son of Eli Cornwell and his wife Lily (née King). His father had spent fourteen years in the Royal Army Medical Corps, serving in Egypt, Sudan and South Africa, and had worked variously as a milkman, a male nurse in a mental hospital and a tram driver. He had married twice, first to Alice Carpenter, by whom he had a son and daughter, and then to Lily King, who bore him three sons and another daughter.

Jack, as he was always known in the family, was the second eldest of his father's second family and grew up in Leyton and then Manor Park. From May 1905 to July 1910 he was educated at Farmer Road School (which by a remarkable coincidence was later renamed George Mitchell School after one of its pupils who won a VC during the Second World War) and then, following his family's move to 10 Alverstone Road, Manor Park, he attended Walton Road School, which would take his name in 1929. Quiet and reserved, he was an average student who seldom gave any trouble. One teacher said of him: 'We always felt we could depend on him.'

Leaving school at 14 he worked as a delivery boy on a Brooke-Bond tea van, but his ambition from an early age was to join the navy. His parents were against the idea so he concentrated instead on his other passion: scouting. A member of the 11th East Hall Scout Troop, attached to St Mary's Mission, he revelled in the quasi-military regalia and training, undertaking with enthusiasm each new test. His scoutmaster would remember him as a 'daredevil' for whom 'nothing was too hard'. By the time the troop was disbanded because its leaders had enlisted, Jack had gained his Second Class Badge and was well-prepared for the fulfilment of his dream.

Shortly after the outbreak of war Jack, armed with character references from his headmaster and employer, tried to join the navy, but was rejected as being too young. Eventually, on 27 July 1915, he was accepted and sent to Keynsham Naval Barracks, Devonport, where his training began four days later. By then, his father, aged 63, had also wangled his way back into uniform, serving initially in the 2/6th Essex Regiment and then the 57th Company, Royal Defence Corps, the First World War equivalent of the Home Guard. As Boy Seaman 2nd Class (No. J/42563), Jack embarked on a service career of less than ten months' duration, of which only the final twenty-nine days would be spent in his first and last ship, the light cruiser *Chester*.

Following his death from wounds received at Jutland, his body was brought home to London, at the request of his mother, and interred without fuss in Manor Park Cemetery. With his family unable to afford a headstone, the grave was marked simply by a small wooden peg bearing the number 323. A largely anonymous life had reached an anonymous end. But not for long. From the countless acts of individual gallantry displayed by hundreds of men in the ships under his command, Admiral Beatty chose to highlight only one in his despatch published on 7 July 1916. This was the 'splendid instance of devotion to duty' performed by Boy (1st Class) John Travers Cornwell. Based on the report written by *Chester*'s captain, Robert Lawson, Beatty's account of his action was a model of brevity, summed up in three short sentences, and concluded with the comment: 'I recommend his case for special recognition in justice to his memory, and as an acknowledgement of the high example set by him.'

Seized upon by the newspapers, the story of the 16-year-old hero, the only non-officer singled out by Beatty, instantly became headline news. Unfortunately for the navy, the story that appeared the next day was not simply one of virtuous bravery, but of official neglect and the scant regard paid to the country's fallen heroes. Beneath a front-page photograph showing Jack Cornwell's grave, covered with flowers but marked only by a numbered peg, the *Daily Sketch* declared: 'England will be shocked today to learn … that the boy-hero of the naval victory has been buried in a common grave. The flowers were sent by his schoolmates – they in their humble way paid the honour that the Admiralty failed to give the young hero.' Furthermore, and no doubt to the navy's embarrassment, the same newspaper promised to see 'that his memory and his family are not forgotten'.

Captain Lawson was furious. As relatives and friends posed for what seemed like carefully staged photographs alongside the 'still nameless' grave, the man whose report of Boy Cornwell's 'fine pluck' was responsible for his name being brought to public notice complained bitterly: 'What was (and is, essentially) a clean, fine, simple story of devotion to duty has been besmirched by the paws of the Press.' More to the point, he maintained, it was not the navy who were to blame for the state of Cornwell's grave, but his unwitting mother:

If Mrs Cornwell had not elected to have his body moved from the hospital to her own house, there would have been a funeral with full naval honours. As it was, she wished to take the body away for a private funeral, and the cost of the journey is paid by the Admiralty, but not, I believe, the cost of the funeral also. Perhaps poor Mrs Cornwell hardly understood all that, but felt she would like to have her neighbours at the funeral; then discovered that she couldn't afford to pay for a separate grave. Meanwhile, the pressmen discover this, and instead of helping quietly, publish half the story far and wide. Well, well. Many of his shipmates were more fortunate in resting in the

North Sea where not even a ghoulish pressman can disturb your mortal remains.

Fuelled by a display of self-righteous indignation in the Press and cynical political manipulation, the saga of the 'boy hero' took on a momentum all of its own. Questions were asked in the House. Lord Beresford wanted to know if it was proposed to recognise his courage with a posthumous VC. No recommendation had been made, came the reply. There were calls for special tributes, memorials to be built and a suggestion that Cornwell's body be exhumed and reinterred with full naval honours at Devonport. His mother was averse to the idea. 'It was a consolation to know that he was buried near her, and that she could at any time visit his grave,' she said. But Jack Cornwell had become public property, a national hero to be mourned by one and all. In the end, a compromise was reached. The youngster would be laid to rest again with all the pomp and pageantry associated with a State funeral, but in Manor Park, close to where he grew up.

The funeral which took place on 29 July was unmatched by any event of its kind during the war. Shops were closed and dense crowds lined the route as the coffin, draped in a Union Jack and resting on a gun carriage, was drawn to the cemetery by a team of boys from the Crystal Palace Naval Depot. In the following carriages were Dr F.J. Macnamara, Financial Secretary to the Admiralty, the Bishop of Barking, the Mayor of East Ham, Sir John Bethell, MP for Romford, and members of East Ham Borough Council. Six boy seamen from *Chester*, who had all taken part in the fighting at Jutland, carried wreaths from the ship's company. Among countless other floral tributes was one from the Lord Mayor of London, with the words: 'With Deep Respect.' In a moving eulogy at the graveside, Dr Macnamara sought to find inspiration out of noble sacrifice: 'It has been written that what good men do is often interred with them. Not so here! This grave shall be the birthplace of heroes ... Boy Cornwell will be enshrined in British hearts as long as faithful, unflinching devotion to duty shall be esteemed a virtue amongst us.'

The ceremony marked not so much the end of a life as the beginning of an exercise in hero worship. Six weeks after his second funeral, the *London Gazette* of 15 September merely confirmed Cornwell's status among the ranks of the nation's bravest with the announcement of his Victoria Cross. What the respected naval historian John Winton has called 'a convulsive spasm of collective commemoration' duly followed. His face appeared everywhere, in paintings by such distinguished artists as Sir Frank Salisbury, who used Jack's elder brother Ernest as a model, and F. Matania, on stamps which sold in their millions and in a stained-glass window thousands of miles away in Kingston, Ontario. Framed portraits of the young hero were hung in classrooms the length and breadth of the country. While his old school in Walton Road made plans to put up a brass memorial to be unveiled by Lady Jellicoe, it was announced that 30 September 1916 would be known as Jack Cornwell Day, when elementary schools all over Britain would pay homage to his valour. His name was exploited for fund-raising campaigns, raising money for a Star and Garter Home at Richmond, naval scholarships and six cottages for retired sailors. The latter were built at Hornchurch, under the auspices of a memorial committee formed as early as July 1916, and opened on the 13th anniversary of Jutland by Earl Jellicoe.

Among the more notable posthumous honours were those initiated by the Scout Movement. Awarded the Bronze Cross, the highest award for gallantry, Jack Cornwell had his name perpetuated with the instigation of a new badge, to be awarded to scouts of high character who have shown devotion to duty, courage and endurance, while the Chief-Scout Sir Robert Baden-Powell added a personal touch by painting a water-colour depicting his gallant action.

Yet even as Jack Cornwell was being venerated, his family was being quietly forgotten. While his heroic image helped generate thousands of pounds for all manner of causes, they slipped towards poverty, with hardship heaped upon further sacrifice. The wave of admiration that swept across the country had barely begun when the Cornwells were shaken by another tragedy. On 25 October 1916 Jack's father Eli succumbed to bronchial catarrh while on active service with the Royal Defence Corps, and was buried in the same grave as his son. Two years later Arthur Cornwell, Jack's elder stepbrother, was killed in action in France. By the end of the war Jack's widowed mother, with two children under 18 to support, was in dire financial straits and struggling against ill health. With only Jack's meagre pension of 6s 6d and 10s a week from the Navy League to sustain her, she was no longer able to pay the rent on her home in East Ham, and was forced to take some rooms in Stepney. Not even a public outcry could persuade the Memorial Fund set up in her son's name to help, and on 31 October 1919 Lily Cornwell was found dead in her bed, an exhausted woman at 48.

After her death the Navy League stepped in with a grant of about £60 a year to support the upbringing of the two younger children. Even so, theirs was little more than a subsistence life and in 1923 Lily Cornwell, the youngest at 18, having been unable to find work, decided to emigrate to Canada with her half-sister Alice and her family. Later, they were joined by George Cornwell, who had taken a job as a steward on the *Aquitania*, and Jack's elder brother Ernest, who had doubled for him in Salisbury's heroic painting.

They left behind a host of memorials and monuments dedicated to their brother which have not merely stood the test of time but actually grown in number. His medals, presented on 'long loan' by his elder brother's widow, are displayed in the Imperial War Museum, together with a 5.5-inch gun said to have been the actual one by which he stood, while a portrait is exhibited in the National Maritime Museum. Jack Cornwell's name also lives on in the solidly working-class area of London where he grew up. Amid the bleak high-rise blocks of flats in E12, the Jack Cornwell Community Centre stands adjacent to Jack Cornwell Street, within sight of the Victoria Cross pub. Most impressive of all the enduring memorials, however, remains one of the earliest: the sculpted cross and anchor which rises above his grave in a crowded corner of Manor Park Cemetery now called Cornwell Crescent. Paid for by contributions from 'scholars and ex-scholars of schools in East Ham', the memorial, which also carries the names of Jack's father and stepbrother killed in France, was unveiled by Dr Macnamara on 28 December 1920. The inscription carved on its face reads:

It is not wealth and ancestry
but honourable conduct and a noble
disposition that makes men great.

A fitting epitaph to a boy who found in death a kind of immortality.

G. CAMPBELL
South-west of Ireland, 17 February 1917

R.N. STUART AND W. WILLIAMS
South-west of Ireland, 7 June 1917

C.G. BONNER AND E.H. PITCHER
Bay of Biscay, 130 miles south-west of Ushant, 8 August 1917

By January 1917 the anti-submarine campaign, once considered little more than an irritating diversion by the Admiralty, had assumed the gravest importance. In six months the monthly losses of British and foreign merchant vessels had more than trebled to 368,521 tons. By contrast, U-boat losses during the whole of 1916 amounted to just twenty-five, of which five were due to accidents and a further four to action by our Russian ally. The unpalatable truth was that the Royal Navy was not merely failing to check the submarine campaign, it was actually in danger of losing it and, with it, the war itself. Depth-charges, mined nets, deep minefields, hunter-destroyers and specially equipped P boats, fixed and floating obstructions, armed decoy ships and special patrols of submarines had all been employed, but none of the counter-measures had proved effective in reducing the danger. 'Perhaps no conclusive answer will be found,' an Admiralty memorandum despondently noted. 'We must for the present be content with palliation.'

Not everyone, however, shared their pessimism. During a spell of leave in that first month of 1917 a 30-year-old naval commander took it upon himself to carry out his own review of anti-submarine tactics. Gordon Campbell, bluff, pugnacious and independently minded, was unusually well placed to assess the situation. As one of the earliest recruits to the navy's growing fleet of Q-ships, tramp steamers, colliers and sailing ships heavily armed with hidden guns, torpedoes and depth-charges and designed to lure submarines to their destruction, he had already acquired a matchless reputation for daring and skill. His ship's company, drawn largely from the Merchant Navy and RNR, had been trained to behave in the manner of the crew of a typical tramp: to misread the enemy's intentions and invite attack, before lying to and abandoning ship with a practised display of panic, leaving on board only the captain and a few concealed gunners ready to man the masked battery as soon as the target presented itself within range. In this way, over the course of the past year, the elderly 3,200-ton *Loderer*, rechristened *Farnborough*, had accounted for *U-68*, one of only two enemy submarines destroyed by Q-ships during 1916, and damaged another a month later. Still unsatisfied by his return and increasingly doubtful of the ruse fooling any but the most inexperienced U-boat commander, Campbell now decided upon a course of action that appeared to take the concept of Q-ships as 'live human bait' still closer to the realms of suicide mission. He wrote:

> I came to the conclusion that the only way for us to ensure decoying the enemy to the surface was deliberately to get torpedoed and trust to still being in a position to fight with our guns afterwards. On the two previous occasions when torpedoes had been fired at us, we had merely taken our chance, but now I decided we must ensure getting hit. It can easily be seen that if a torpedo missed just ahead ... it would have hit the ship provided we had been going a bit faster; so the idea now was that the ship would be manoeuvred so as to make the torpedo hit.

Campbell did not have long to wait to test his theory. Following a refit, he set course for his old hunting-ground off the south-west coast of Ireland. The declaration of unrestricted submarine warfare on 1 February had brought a new intensity to the struggle. Reports poured in of ships being sunk, sometimes as many as a hundred a day. To Campbell it seemed only a matter of time before they, too, would be targeted. 'The whole crew were waiting for it with enthusiasm,' he wrote. 'There is a good deal of difference between being in a ship where you know that if a torpedo is seen approaching, you are going to avoid it, and in being in one where you know you are going to make it hit; and yet I never saw a crew more anxious for a fray. They realised that if the Germans' intensified submarine warfare was a success, then England would be beaten.' Their opportunity duly came on 17 February, eight days into a gruelling patrol out of Queenstown. The rough weather of the past few days had relented. On a fine morning the homeward-bound *Farnborough*, officially restyled *Q5*, was steaming at 7 knots on an easterly course across a placid sea, approximately 35 miles west-south-west of the Great Skellig. Suddenly, at 9.45 a.m., a torpedo was seen approaching on the starboard side. Clearly fired from extreme range, it could easily have been avoided, but that was the last thing on Campbell's mind:

> Nothing ... was done till it was close to the ship and coming straight for the engine-room. At the last moment, when it would be too late for the enemy to see our movement, I put the helm over to avoid unnecessary loss of life and brought the torpedo just abaft the engine-room, which undoubtedly saved the lives of those below, but caught us on the bulkhead and flooded, in consequence, two-thirds of the ship.

The torpedo struck no. 3 hold, slightly injuring an engineer sub-lieutenant and bowling over a number of the crew, including Campbell. Well-rehearsed pandemonium ensued except in one small quarter of the ship. Scrambling to his feet, Campbell saw a group of men on the foredeck 'smoking and lolling over the ship's side when they ought to have been "panicking".' Cursing them with a volley of Anglo-Saxon invective, he demanded to know what they were doing. 'Waiting for the order, sir. "Torpedo hit",' came the reply!

Even as they joined the pantomime, the submarine's periscope was sighted about 200yd away, watching events. As yet no signal had been sent, for fear, as Campbell later reported, of 'some ship arriving before we had done our work'. Amid considerable chaos, two lifeboats and a dinghy crammed with suitably distressed seamen were sent away, and a fourth boat partially lowered. Within a short while the ship had been 'abandoned' by everyone except those required for action. All this time the engine-room was filling with water and the ship settling by the stern. Campbell's gaze, though, was fixed on the periscope. From his hidden look-out on the starboard side of the bridge, he watched the U-boat come closer:

He ... came past the ship on the starboard side, about 5 yards off the lifeboats and 10 yards off the ship, so close that I could see the whole hull of the submarine distinctly,' he reported. 'The temptation to open fire was almost unbearable. He passed close across the bow and broke surface about 300 yards on the port bow at 10.05am and I then made the signal 'Torpedoed'. He came down on the surface past the port side; I waited till he was on the only bearing on which all my guns could bear, and opened fire at point-blank range.

In that moment the wheel-house collapsed, the ship's sides fell away and the Maxim spluttered into life from the hen coop. Barely 100yd separated *Farnborough* from her victim and scarcely had the White Ensign been run up than the first shot – from the 6-pounder – struck the conning tower, decapitating the U-boat's captain. Campbell reported:

The submarine apparently never recovered from his surprise as he remained on the surface whilst we shattered his hull. His conning tower was continually hit, some of the shells apparently going clean through it. Altogether 45 shells were fired in addition to the Maxim. He finally sunk with his conning-tower open and shattered, and with the crew pouring out. When the submarine had disappeared I ordered 'Cease fire'; there were about 8 men in the water and one of my lifeboats went to their assistance, and were in time to save one officer and one man. The water was thick with oil and blood, and air bubbles were very conspicuous ...

The grisly slick marked the watery grave of *U-83*, her commander Kapitainleutnant Bruno Hoppe and more than thirty crewmen. Donning a naval cap and jacket, Campbell received the two survivors on the bridge. One had sustained serious injuries from which he would later succumb and both were in a state of shock, though, in a strange aside, Campbell later wrote that neither had any complaints! Campbell's main concern was saving his own vessel. Recalling his 'panic party', he made a quick inspection. The prognosis was not good. In his report he stated:

The engine and boiler-rooms, nos 3, 4 and after holds were rapidly filling, and I considered she was sinking by the stern. I therefore signalled for assistance and placed all hands on the boats except a few men I kept on board, and I also gave orders to destroy all confidential and valuable books and charts, etc.

Before doing so, Campbell sent Admiral Sir Lewis Bayly a coded farewell that was destined to become enshrined in naval history: 'Q5 slowly sinking respectfully wishes you good-bye.' It was not, however, the end of the story, nor the end of Q5. Within an hour of his signal, the destroyer *Narwhal* arrived, followed shortly after by *Buttercup*. With the ship's stern awash, Campbell transferred all his crew to *Narwhal*, and discussed the possibility of *Buttercup* taking Q5 in tow. 'As the ship appeared to have assumed a definite position, and the water only gained slowly, I returned with twelve officers and men and told him to take us in tow, which he did in a most seamanlike manner. The tow parted, probably owing to my helm being jammed hard over and immovable, but I was raising steam in the donkey boiler, so told *Buttercup* to wait till I had steam and could steer ... We finally got in tow about 5pm.' By then, the swell was breaking over the after deck. At times the after gun house was completely submerged. Even so, the ship towed 'fairly well', although all the time she was taking on water.

At dusk the destroyer *Laburnum*, which had taken over from *Narwhal*, closed and suggested that Campbell and his skeleton crew should transfer. But he had not given up yet. 'I decided to remain as long as we could steer and assist tow,' wrote Campbell. He remained until 2 a.m., when a sudden inrush of water extinguished the donkey boiler and made the ship heel over. Campbell just had time to heave her amidships, before the last 'drop of steam' vanished. After groping through the flooded bunkers with his engineer-lieutenant, he ordered the remainder into the motor boat that had been kept alongside. Campbell prepared to take one last look around his sinking command. The explosion of a depth-charge in the submerged stern, however, soon sent him scurrying back. Waiting for him was his First Lieutenant Ronald Stuart, who had ignored his order to get into the boat. 'He thought it part of his job to see I was "all right",' observed Campbell.

Mistaking the exploding depth-charge for a torpedo, *Buttercup* slipped her tow and retreated back to port, reporting Campbell and his men 'probably lost'. In fact, they drifted about in their defective motor boat until picked up by *Laburnum*, which continued to stand by until daylight revealed the derelict *Farnborough* still afloat. Taking five men Campbell went aboard again and re-established a tow. 'There being nothing to be done aboard and the condition of the ship being critical', they then made their way back to *Laburnum*. Towards evening, as they neared Berehaven, Campbell returned with a few men. By then, *Farnborough*'s stern was under 8ft of water and the ship had taken on a list of nearly 20 degrees. As they approached the harbour entrance, the harbourmaster came on board and told them where to beach her.

The faithful *Laburnum* then slipped her tow and the trawler *Luneta* and the tug *Flying Sportsman* eased alongside and pushed the gallant *Farnborough* on to the beach at Mill Cove at 9.30 p.m. Admiral Bayly's signal was a model of brevity: 'Very good piece of work. Well done.'

In rewarding Campbell and his ship's company for their 'skill, nerve and gallantry', the Admiralty displayed unusual largesse. As well as £1,000 shared among the crew, there were forty individual awards. The gallant dozen who formed Campbell's skeleton crew were all decorated, including Lt Stuart and Engineer-Lieutenant Len Loveless, who both received DSOs. Three more officers won DSCs, while twenty-four men were given mentions. The list, however, was deservedly led by Gordon Campbell. Already the holder of a DSO for his action against *U-68* a year earlier, he was awarded the Victoria Cross. The circumstances were left deliberately vague, the citation simply stating: 'In recognition of his conspicuous gallantry, consummate coolness and skill in command of one of HM ships in action.' The excessive secrecy proved counter-productive. Far from escaping attention, Campbell, who had been cited in a Court Circular as having received the award even before it was officially announced, found his name plastered all over the Press as 'the mystery VC'. Enemy suspicions were immediately aroused. 'They connected it with another episode altogether,' wrote Campbell, 'and I understand put a price on my head. From that moment I repeatedly received information from various sources that they intended to "get me".'

After a brief and not altogether happy period spent inspecting potential decoy vessels, under the auspices of the Admiralty's Anti-Submarine Department, Campbell was given a new command. Such was his reputation, he was allowed not only to select his own ship but to take with him all those members of his old crew prepared to take the risk. Among those who did so were his trusty Number One, Ronald Stuart, and chief engineer Len Loveless, two vastly experienced merchant seamen whose sound advice had proved invaluable to Campbell both as captain of the *Q5* and during his short-lived roving commission as an Admiralty inspector.

The ship he eventually chose, with the help of his loyal lieutenants, was the tramp steamer SS *Vittoria*, soon to be rechristened *Snail* and, finally, *Pargust*, the name under which she would achieve undying fame. An ordinary-looking trader of 2,817 tons, barely capable of 8 knots, with two well decks and a poop, she was a slightly more modern vessel than the *Loderer* and altogether more solid. Commissioned on 28 March, she underwent a dramatic conversion that took the best part of two months. In that time the once harmless tramp was transformed so that by completion she had sprouted a 4-inch gun, four 12-pounders, two Maxim guns, two 14-inch torpedo tubes and depth-charge rails on the stern. The 4-inch gun was mounted aft on the poop, hidden by a dummy boat and a fake cargo hatch, designed to collapse at a moment's notice. Two 12-pounders were sited on either side in 'houses' built on to the existing cabins, and Campbell made the most of the latest innovations by placing two specially modified 'tilting' 12-pounders amidships, one on the fo'c'stle shrouded by canvas and the other hidden by deck lumber. An appeal for a further gun to be openly displayed in the manner of a growing number of merchant vessels was turned down. Undeterred, Campbell had a dummy 12-pounder constructed out of wood and fitted aft in a position where it would be plainly visible. Towards the end of May *Pargust*, complete with extra bulkheads, five watertight departments and her holds filled with timber and casks, sailed for Queenstown. Before the month was out Campbell and his crew were back in their favoured patrol zone, hoping to attract another submarine.

The chances were all too promising. Submarine activity in the waters south-west of Ireland was intense. One of Campbell's first tasks was to pick up survivors from a torpedoed merchantman. Transferring them to some destroyers, he continued with his patrol, steaming west by night and east by day. 'We had no orders about returning to harbour this time,' wrote Campbell, 'and we all felt confident we should have another engagement before we did so.' To one member of *Pargust*'s crew, it was pre-ordained. On 6 June Chief Petty Officer George Truscott, a mariner of superstitious bent, assured Campbell they would find a submarine the next day. His prediction was based on the fact that a bird had that day flown into Campbell's cabin, something that had happened prior to all of their past U-boat encounters.

The next day found *Pargust* in familiar waters, close to the scene of *Farnborough*'s last encounter. Conditions, though, were in sharp contrast. Rain was falling heavily from a mist-shrouded sky and the sea, whipped by a fresh southerly breeze, was uncomfortably choppy. *Pargust*, her make-believe gun manned, was plodding slowly eastwards at 8 a.m. when a torpedo was seen, streaking out of the gloom on the starboard beam. Apparently fired at 'very close range', there was no need on this occasion to do anything to ensure a successful torpedo strike. Campbell reported: 'It jumped out of the water when 100 yards from the ship and struck the engine-room near the water-line – making a large rent and filling the boiler-room, engine-room and no 5. Hold. The starboard lifeboat was blown in the air, pieces of it landing on the aerial.' A stoker petty officer died instantly, but the duty engineer officer had an incredible escape when he was blown through the engine-room hatch.

He was found staggering in a concussed state towards his boat station to join the panic party.

What Campbell did not know until later was just how close the blast had come to wrecking his plans. The force of the explosion had freed the weights holding the starboard gun ports in place, and it was only a combination of quick-thinking and sheer physical strength on the part of one of the 12-pounder gun team that prevented *Pargust*'s cover from being blown. Seaman William Williams, a tall, powerfully built Welshman awarded the DSM for his part in the destruction of the *U-83*, took the entire weight of the port on himself, thus preventing it falling down and prematurely exposing the gun. As the usual, rehearsed mayhem ensued and the panic party, complete with stuffed parrot, tumbled into the two remaining lifeboats and dinghy, the 26-year-old seaman single-handedly shouldered the strain, waiting for the submarine to show itself.

In fact, it was not until a quarter of an hour after the torpedo struck that the periscope was seen, about 400yd away on the port beam. Campbell, hidden in his usual spot on the bridge, watched as the submarine turned and steered straight towards *Pargust*. In his report he noted the U-boat's cautious approach as the leading lifeboat drew clear:

> At 8.25am, when about 50 yards off the ship and close to the stern of the lifeboat, he submerged. Periscope was again sighted directly astern a few minutes later and he steamed to the starboard quarter, then turned round and went across to the port beam, turned again towards the ship and lifeboat, and at 8.33am, when about 50 yards or less off the ship, he partially broke surface, the conning tower and ends being visible. He was heading parallel and opposite to the ship; the lifeboat in the meantime was pulling away and round the stern. The submarine followed, passing close under the stern, and by the time the lifeboat was on the starboard beam the submarine was close astern abaft my beam; one man was on top of the conning-tower and kept shouting down directions through the conning-tower. I watched this man carefully, as, as long as he was on top I knew I could withhold my fire …

At this point Acting Lieutenant Francis Hereford DSC, leader of the panic party, realising Campbell could open fire whenever he chose, ordered his men to row for *Pargust*. According to Campbell, this action so annoyed the commander of the submarine that he 'came right up and started to semaphore to the boats'. Another U-boat crewman emerged on to the conning tower and trained a rifle or machine-gun at the nearest lifeboat. Two men were now outside; the submarine was a sitting duck, barely 50yd abeam of *Pargust*, within range of all her guns. 'There was nothing more to wait for,' observed Campbell. At 8.36 a.m., more than half an hour after being torpedoed, he ordered his gun crews to break cover and open fire. As a no doubt relieved Seaman Williams thankfully relinquished his crucial hold on the starboard gun port, *Pargust* reverberated to the sound of gunfire. Campbell reported:

> The first shot from the 4-inch gun hit the base of the conning-tower and also removed the two periscopes. The close range enabled many hits to be obtained, nearly all in the conning-tower. The submarine almost immediately on opening fire assumed a list to port, and several men came out of the hatch abaft the conning-tower. She steamed slowly across my bow with a heavy list to port, stern nearly under water, oil squirting from her side, and the crew coming out of the conning-tower and after hatch. When close on the port bow they held up their hands and waved.

Campbell immediately called to his gunners to cease firing. But no sooner did they comply than the U-boat began to draw away at 'a fair speed', leaving those crewmen who had scrambled on to the after casing floundering in the water. The submarine was still listing to port and her stern had disappeared beneath the water, but, crippled though she was, it seemed as though her captain was making a last desperate attempt to escape into the mist. Campbell was taking no chances. He ordered his gunners to resume firing, although for half a minute his fo'c'stle 12-pounder was the only gun that could bear on the retreating target. He need not have worried. Hardly had the U-boat drawn clear of *Pargust*'s bows, allowing her other guns to join in, than an explosion ripped through the submarine's fore end. Rolling over on to her side, she sank some 300yd away. The last Campbell saw of his victim was her sharp bow, end up, about 3ft out of the water, with one man clinging on as it plunged beneath the waves.

It had taken the well-drilled gun teams aboard *Pargust* just four minutes to send *UC-29*, her commander, Kapitanleutnant Ernst Rosenow and twenty-two of his crew to the bottom. During that time Campbell had expended thirty-eight rounds, most of which found the target, and one torpedo, which missed astern.

Several men were left in the water, which was thick with oil, and Campbell sent his panic party to their assistance. Struggling against the wind, they reached them in time to save one officer and one man, prompting Hereford to report: 'We've again got a sample of each.' The captured officer was brought before Campbell and promptly threw up in the chart-room.

Pargust 'lay inert' for almost four hours, until the sloop HMS *Crocus* arrived to take her in tow. They were joined by the USS *Cushing*, America having entered the war two months earlier, and HMS *Zinnia*, which took on board the prisoners. After an uneventful tow *Pargust* reached Queenstown at 3 p.m. on 8 June having already received the congratulations of Admiral Bayly.

As in the case of the destruction of the *U-83*, the crew were awarded £1,000 for sinking the *UC-29*. The submarine, a minelayer, had been in service for less than a year. The report of the action, however, appears to have left the Admiralty in something of a quandary. Once again, Campbell's crew had displayed 'admirable discipline and courage' in an encounter worthy of the highest recognition. But being unable to decide who should be singled out, it was left to the king to approve the first 'elected' VCs to a ship's crew, one to go to an officer and the other to a man, the recipients to be selected by the officers and men respectively, in accordance with Clause 13 of the Victoria Cross Warrant.

Campbell read out the award to his assembled crew and gave them twenty-four hours' notice for the ballot, which was supervised by an 'outside' officer. Names were written on chits and handed in for counting. 'Personally,' wrote Campbell, 'I took no part in the voting, beyond noting down the name of an officer and man which were only to be used in the event of an even draw. Neither was necessary. The balloting officer only gave out the names of the selected ones so that no one should know how near he might have been ...' *Pargust*'s officers had initially expressed their wish that Campbell should be the officer recipient, which would have made him the first and only naval officer to receive a Bar to the Victoria Cross. Campbell, who considered that this was never the Admiralty's intention, later wrote: 'I, of course, could not agree to this as I already felt that the Victoria Cross I wore was on behalf of my crew and through no special act of my own.'

As a result of the historic vote Victoria Crosses were awarded to Lt Ronald Stuart DSO, *Pargust*'s second-in-command, and Seaman William Williams DSM, who Campbell felt had saved the show. But for Williams's intervention, he wrote, 'the action might never have taken place'. Fourteen members of *Pargust*'s crew were decorated and a further eleven mentioned in despatches. The awards included a DSO for A/Lt Hereford and a DSM to Petty Officer Ernest Pitcher, a senior member of the ship's gun crews. Campbell received a Bar to his DSO and was promoted captain over the heads of five hundred officers.

Meanwhile, every member of *Pargust*'s crew had their participation in the VC ballot entered in their service certificates.

Pargust having been docked, cleared and paid off, Campbell lost little time in finding another ship to fit out. Once more he turned to Cardiff and its fleet of colliers. His selection was the *Dunraven*, and he decided to keep the name. Slightly bigger than *Pargust*, with a double well-deck and a much larger poop, Campbell thought her ideal for her intended role. Fitting out began swiftly at Devonport. In the converted *Dunraven*, the art of subterfuge was to reach new heights of sophistication. Among a host of new gadgets were a specially armoured bridge look-out with slits cut and a perforated pipe designed to let off steam in order to give the impression of having suffered a hit in the engine rooms. As well as the dummy 12-pounder salvaged from *Pargust*, Campbell was also, at last, given permission to carry a real defensive gun, a 2½-pounder sited right aft on a raised platform, which was to be manned by a three-man crew, including Seaman Williams VC, DSM, in deliberately wretched fashion. For the most part, however, *Dunraven*'s main armament resembled in size, quantity and positions that found in *Pargust*: a tilting 12-pounder on the fo'c'stle, one each side housed in cabins, another tilting 12-pounder on the after end of the boat deck and a 4-inch gun on the poop.

Of all the disguises, none was more elaborate than that designed to mask the 4-inch gun and its crew. To begin with, the deck had been slightly lowered to reduce its height. Then, following the *Pargust* model, it was mostly hidden in a hatch, with a washing line of clothes and drying canvas sheets screening the remainder of the gun. The transformation from harmless-looking deck cargo to potentially lethal submarine-killer was achieved by a complex system of wires operated in the manner of a stage set so that at any given moment the hinged hatch sides would fall outwards at the same instant as the poop rails dropped inwards and a counter-weight raised the washing line clear. To reach the gun hatch, the crew, consisting of PO Ernest Pitcher, the gun captain and gunlayer, Able Seamen Dennis Murphy and Richard Shepherd, Seamen William Bennison, John Martindale and James Thompson, and Wireless Telegraphist Tom Fletcher, had to climb up through a trapdoor. It was an operation that demanded steely nerves and split-second timing. Fortunately, these were qualities in abundance. Of the seven, four wore the ribbon of the DSM – Martindale, Pitcher and Thompson for their part in the destruction of the *UC-29*, and Fletcher for his role in the sinking of *U-83* – and two had been mentioned in despatches. Control and direction of the gun was in similarly safe hands in the shape of Lieutenant Charles Bonner RNR. A Q-ship veteran, his adventurous spirit – earlier in the war he had rowed across the Scheldt estuary to avoid internment with the majority of the Royal Naval Division following the ill-starred Antwerp operation – and varied seagoing experience appealed to Campbell, who hand-picked him for decoy work. The days following the *Pargust* action were particularly eventful for the 32-year-old Lt Bonner. In the space of six weeks he got married, was awarded the DSC and, following the departure of Ronald Stuart to command of his own Q-sloop, was promoted from second to first officer. He combined his new responsibilities with command of the 4-inch gun, his 'action station' being a steel drum, complete with specially mounted periscope and slits cut in the side, which was made to look like hawser reel and which could only be entered via a trapdoor from below. Both Bonner's post and the gun itself were sited above a mini arsenal consisting of the 4-inch magazine and shell-room together with the 2½-pounder magazine and, on either side of the poop's interior, two large depth-charges, each containing 300lb of explosive.

Conversion completed, *Dunraven* was duly commissioned on 28 July. A week later, after a few days spent 'working up' in Plymouth Sound, Campbell sailed not for Queenstown, as originally intended, but for the Bay of Biscay, where reports of intense submarine activity held out the promise of more gainful employment. As an added temptation and to complete her deception, *Dunraven*, sailing in the guise of a Blue Funnel steamer, carried on her upper deck four collapsible railway trucks in the style of a cargo vessel bound for the Middle East. Three days passed without any sightings. On the night of 7 August Campbell decided to retrace his course, the railway trucks having been laid flat in keeping with a homeward-bound steamer. The manoeuvre paid off. At 10.58 a.m. the following morning, while *Dunraven* was zig-zagging northwards at 8 knots, approximately 130 miles west of Ushant, the dim form of a submarine, later identified as *UC-71*, was sighted on the horizon about two points forward of her starboard beam. Pretending not to have noticed, Campbell stuck to his course as the submarine steered towards him. Then, almost twenty minutes after the first sighting, the submarine submerged, raising hopes aboard *Dunraven* of an impending torpedo attack. But it was not to be. At 11.45 a.m. the submarine surfaced on the starboard quarter, approximately 5,000yd away, and opened fire. Campbell responded immediately with his well-prepared decoy plan, hoisting the Red Ensign and returning wildly inaccurate fire from his 2½-pounder while the remainder of the crew took 'shell cover':

> I ordered much smoke to be made but at the same time reduced speed to 7 knots (with an occasional zig-zag) to give him a chance

of closing (had I been a merchant ship I could probably have escaped). I was steaming ahead to sea and the submarine's firing was very poor, shots were right for direction but bad for elevation, nearly all falling over. At 12.10 he ceased firing and came on at full speed; owing to the sea he was apparently unable to fire whilst chasing me. At 12.25 he turned broadside on and reopened fire; in the meantime my gun was intentionally firing short. During this period I made 'en clair' signals for the submarine's benefit such as 'Submarine chasing and shelling me', 'Submarine overtaking me, help, come quickly'. 'Submarine (position). Am abandoning ship'. At 12.40 shells were now falling close. I made a 'cloud of steam' to assume boiler trouble and ordered 'Abandon ship', at the same time stopping, blowing off steam, and turning my broadside so that he could see me abandon ship ...

Having exhausted almost every trick in the book for luring the U-boat within killing range, Campbell now resorted to the tried and tested 'panic stations'. The crew of the 2½-pounder, including the hero of the *UC-29* fight, fled in cowardly fashion and one of the boats was lowered 'end up'. For a moment, it seemed as though Campbell's ploy was working. The submarine was drawing ever closer, although wary enough to maintain a steady fire. Soon, though, she would be filling the sights of *Dunraven*'s hidden armoury.

But then came disaster. Three shells in quick succession struck the poop. The first exploded a depth-charge, severely injuring two seamen and blowing Bonner clean out of his post inside the fake hawser reel. Such was the severity of the blast that Campbell thought at first that the magazine had blown up. Bonner, having regained his senses, crawled into the hatch to join the 4-inch gun crew. It was, quite literally, a case of 'out of the frying pan and into the fire'. A fiery smog of flames and thick, choking black smoke engulfed the poop, offering only fleeting glimpses of the approaching submarine. Knowing full well what munitions lay beneath the poop deck, Campbell faced an agonising dilemma. 'It was obvious,' he reported, 'that an explosion must soon take place, so I had the option of opening fire on an indistinct object with a minimum chance of success or waiting till he got on the weather side – I waited.' What was obvious to Campbell was doubly so to Bonner and the 4-inch gun crew huddled in the hatch 'with a fire raging below and the deck getting red-hot'. All communication with the bridge having been wrecked, they made up their minds to await the inevitable rather than run the risk of 'spoiling the show' by moving. It was an act of self-sacrifice of the highest order that Campbell felt could only have stemmed from 'intense discipline and loyalty'. In a letter to the naval historian E. Keble Chatterton, he added: 'One man (believed to have been Seaman Martindale) tore up his shirt to give pieces to the gun's crew to stop the fumes getting into their throats, others lifted the boxes of cordite off the deck to keep it from exploding and all the time they knew they must be blown up ...' That awful moment was not long in coming. At 12.58 p.m., as the submarine was passing *Dunraven*'s stern and approaching a position within 400yd of Campbell's three 12-pounder guns, the ship 'shivered' under the force of a 'terrific explosion' that shattered the poop and sent gun and crew cartwheeling through the air. To those who saw it, it seemed impossible that anyone could have survived such a blast. But, by a remarkable stroke of good fortune, all of them did. One man landed in the water, where he was promptly rescued by the 'panic party', and the others had their fall cushioned by the collapsed wood and canvas railway trucks. Pitcher, who was wounded in a number of places, ended up near the engine-room. Bonner, bleeding from a severe head injury and with burns to his hands, somehow managed to find his way to the bridge where he reported to Campbell with the words: 'I am sorry, sir, for leaving my gun without orders. I think I must have been blown up.' Clearly nonplussed by being blown up for the second time in less than twenty minutes, he then asked who they were in action with. When Campbell told him, he replied, 'Is that all? I thought it was at least a battlecruiser.'

The explosion, thought to have been caused by the detonation of the remaining three depth-charges, set off the ship's 'open fire' buzzers, prompting the gun on the after bridge, the only one able to bear, to loose off two shots before the submarine slipped beneath the surface. The gun crew believed they had scored a hit on the conning tower but as she disappeared, well and truly alerted to the collier's true identity, Campbell could see that no serious damage had been done. The trap having been sprung, Campbell could have been forgiven for cutting his losses and scurrying for home. But that, he later remarked, 'savoured of running away', and so he decided to make one last desperate attempt to decoy his attacker to destruction. In his official report of the action, he stated:

> Realising that a torpedo would probably follow, I ordered the doctor to remove all the wounded and lock them up in the cabins, etc, so as not to spoil the next part, hoses were also turned on the poop which was one mass of flames, the deck being red hot and the magazine still, apparently, intact. I also signalled to a

man-of-war, who had answered my signal for assistance when the explosion took place, to keep away, as I realised the action was not yet ended.

He was right. At 1.20 p.m. a torpedo was seen approaching from the starboard side. Fired at an estimated range of 1,000yd, it struck the burning *Dunraven* abaft the engine-room, hurling hatches and railway trucks about the decks. As seawater rushed in, Campbell played his last trick. Ordering 'Q abandon ship', a second panic party fled, making their rapid exit aboard a raft and the boat which had been left dangling 'end up' following the failure of the first ruse. Their departure left on board two 12-pounder crews, to man the fo'c'stle and one or other of the cabin guns, two torpedomen, four men on the bridge, the chief engineer and a stoker and the nine wounded men together with the ship's surgeon. All they could do was to remain hidden and wait and hope that the by now wary submarine commander might be tempted to approach close enough for them to exact revenge.

Twenty minutes after the torpedo hit, the submarine's periscope was spotted on the starboard bow, and for nearly an hour she carried out the most careful examination of the apparently deserted and burning Q-ship and the boatloads of survivors. As she circled *Dunraven* at various ranges, Campbell could have tried a torpedo attack. But he had little faith in the weapon and preferred to rely on his guns. Throughout this agonising wait, the plight of the ship grew steadily worse. The fire in the poop was blazing out of control, the intense heat setting off a series of explosions as boxes of cordite and 4-inch shells were detonated. At the same time the ship was slowly but surely foundering under the relentless weight of seawater pouring in through the gash in her side.

The eventual surfacing of the submarine at 2.30 p.m. brought no end to *Dunraven*'s ordeal. Either by luck or design, she broke surface dead astern, in a position that none of the ship's guns could reach, and began a steady bombardment that went on for twenty minutes and which Campbell, with grim understatement, described as 'a most unpleasant experience'. Two shells wrecked the bridge, Campbell's life being saved only by the thickness of the recently fitted armour-plating. Almost all the shells fired, from a range of a few hundred yards, scored direct hits, wreaking further damage to the sinking vessel. But still Campbell and his skeleton crew kept their nerve and for a fleeting moment it appeared as though their courage might be rewarded. Around 2.50 p.m. the submarine edged to a position where one of the ship's guns could just about bear, only to suddenly submerge before a shot was fired.

The chance having gone, and with the submarine keeping a periscope watch about 150yd off the port side, Campbell finally decided to engage his weapons of last resort. He reported:

At 2.55pm I fired a torpedo when 'on', set at 22ft (maximum depth), the bubbles passing just ahead of the periscope. He did not notice it, as he steamed very sharp round the bow – according to the boats his periscope only missed it by about 6 inches – and he came very slowly down the starboard side. At 3.02pm, allowing a speed of 3 knots, another torpedo was fired, the bubbles passing a couple of feet abaft the periscope – maximum depth was on, but I suppose it must have passed over the top. The submarine saw it and at once submerged. I therefore signalled for urgent assistance as he would probably have either torpedoed or shelled me till we sank …

Thus ended what Keble Chatterton justly described as Campbell's 'greatest' Q-ship fight, though the forlorn struggle to save the battered *Dunraven* would last another thirty-six hours. Eventually, in the early hours of 10 August, even Campbell was forced to admit defeat. With the after deck awash, he ordered the ship to be abandoned. Towlines were let go and the destroyer *Christopher*, expertly captained by Frederick Thornton Peters DSO, DSC, himself destined to win a Victoria Cross twenty-five years later, came alongside and took off the last twenty members of *Dunraven*'s crew. Among them was the indomitable and seemingly indestructible Charles Bonner, his head swathed in bandages. When the bulk of the ship's gallant company had been transferred some seven hours earlier, he had appealed to his captain to let him stay. 'He was unfit for duty,' wrote Campbell, 'but we gave him a chair on the bridge and his cheery disposition bucked us all up.' By the time Campbell joined Peters on the bridge of *Christopher*, the *Dunraven*, her poop gutted, her hull ruptured and decks riddled, had gone, her colours flying to the very last.

Yet again a ship commanded by Campbell had been involved in a Herculean struggle, a fact reflected in another flood of honours. The total awards announced on 2 November 1917 surpassed even that for the *Pargust*: no fewer than forty-one members of the crew were cited for decorations with a further fourteen mentioned in dispatches. Among those recognised were Campbell, who received a second Bar to his DSO, and Seaman Williams VC, who added a Bar to his DSM. Once again, the list was headed by two Victoria Crosses. The first was an award for exceptional bravery to *Dunraven*'s first lieutenant, Charles

Bonner, who had an early inkling he might be in line for the highest award. In a letter to his parents written four days after the action, the injured commander of the ship's poop deck gun wrote:

> Am out of the Doctor's hands now except for a few dressings. Had dozens of small wounds and burns but not one of any account and am quite well again now. In fact have not been bad ... I half believe I shall get the V.C. but please don't say anything about it until it comes this time as it is not certain of course till the Admlty [*sic*] decides. I was quite the star turn in the fight, and by every law and regulation was killed on 3 different occasions by shells and explosions. Am feeling quite unkillable now, though I don't want another dose quite so bad as that again for a day or two ...

In keeping with the two previous awards to Stuart and Williams, the second VC was an elected award to Petty Officer Ernest Pitcher DSM, gun captain and gunlayer of the four-inch gun, who was selected to receive it on behalf of the gun crew, each of whom received a well-earned CGM.

The decision to award a VC to so small a group as a single gun's crew was unprecedented. Yet while it may have stretched the terms of the VC Warrant, few could argue that such an honour was not justified. In a letter to Campbell, the American Admiral W.S. Sims wrote: 'I know nothing finer in naval history than the conduct of the after-gun crew.' Campbell himself thought their bravery 'hard to equal'. Not only had they stuck to their posts, in the certain knowledge that they would be blown up, rather than betray the ship's identity, but they had endured the subsequent struggle as Campbell attempted to lure the submarine to her doom. He wrote:

> They were ordered to remain quiet in various places during the second action, they had to lie there unattended and bleeding, with explosions continually going on aboard and splinters from the shell fire penetrating their quarters. Lieutenant Bonner ... did what he could for two who were with him in the wardroom. When I visited them after the action, they thought little of their wounds, but only expressed their disgust that the enemy had not been sunk ...

The British were not alone in fêting their heroes of the Biscay encounter. To the German navy the destruction of one of the Royal Navy's deadly 'trap-ships' was cause for jubilation. The captain of *UC-71*, Oberleutnant-zur-See Reinhold Salzwedel, was decorated with Imperial

Germany's highest honour, the Pour le Mérite. One of the Flanders Flotilla's foremost submariners, he was eventually credited with the destruction of more than 150,000 tons of Allied shipping. Less than four months after his most celebrated victory, his luck ran out when his new command, *UB-81*, struck a mine off the Isle of Wight. There were only six survivors and Salzwedel was not among them. Campbell may well have been spared a similar fate by Admiral Bayly's decision to retire him from Q-ship duties. His last epic fight had been a close-run affair in which disaster was avoided by a tiny margin. A classic encounter of its kind, the four-hour struggle between *Dunraven* and the *UC-71* marked a watershed in the Q-ship campaign. Bravery, even when allied to the rarest skill and cunning, was no longer enough. As the Q-ship historian Carson Ritchie stated, 'the struggle had been magnificent, but it was hardly war'.

Gordon Campbell counted himself 'thoroughly fortunate' to be invited to go in for some 'special service', and it is not difficult to understand why. Just one of many ambitious young lieutenants seeking some desperate glory at the beginning of the war, he was, by its conclusion, one of the youngest and most famous captains in the Royal Navy, with a VC and three DSOs garnered from a fighting career unequalled in the history of the Senior Service.

The first and most successful of all the 'mystery ship' recipients of the Victoria Cross, Campbell was born at Upper Norwood, Croydon, on 6 January 1886, the ninth son and thirteenth of the sixteen children of Colonel Frederick Campbell CB, VD, JP, a Royal Artillery veteran of the Maori wars, and his wife, Emilie Guillaume (née MacLaine). He was educated at Dulwich College and passed into HMS *Britannia* as a naval cadet in 1900, although it was a close call. Expected to pass in the first seven, he actually passed 59th out of a total of sixty-five. His first ship was the *Prince George*, which he joined as a midshipman in 1902.

Over the course of the next few years he served in a variety of ships in the Channel Fleet, the Pacific, the Mediterranean and on the China Station. During that time he was off duty for six months with a serious leg injury dating back to his rugby-playing days at *Britannia*. Despite fears that he might be left with a 'stiff' leg for the rest of his life, he made a good recovery and resumed his career, being made sub-lieutenant and then appointed first lieutenant of the destroyer *Arun*. Promoted lieutenant in October 1907, he was appointed to the recommissioned *King Alfred*, flagship on the China Station, where his old injury recurred, eventually leading to a further operation.

Campbell showed his resilience and determination to regain his fitness. He also gave early evidence of his self-assurance and willingness to buck authority by rejecting the advice of his commanding officer and marrying Mary Jeanne Davids on 14 January 1911. After two years in *Impregnable*, the boys' training ship at Devonport, he was given his first command, the elderly destroyer *Ranger*, part of the same port's own flotilla. Six months later he turned over to the *Bittern*, in which he was serving when war was declared. After a spell of rather unexciting escort duties, his command was suddenly curtailed by a chase after a suspicious-looking vessel which turned out to have been a new seaplane carrier undergoing trials. The encounter ended with *Bittern* in dry dock, needing a complete refit, and the crew being paid off.

Restless for action and fearful of the war ending without him firing a shot in anger, Campbell applied for a destroyer at Harwich or a gunboat in the Persian Gulf, but was instead offered a 'special service' appointment under Admiral Sir Lewis Bayly, at Queenstown. On Trafalgar Day 1915 he commissioned the ex-collier *Loderer*, and in her converted guise as the Q-ship *Farnborough* enjoyed the first of his successes, the destruction of *U-68*, on 22 March 1916. The action, fought off the west coast of Ireland, was reported to Bayly in a flurry of signals, laced with Campbell's own brand of humour:

From *Farnborough*. 6.40. Hull of submarine seen …
7.05. Ship being fired at by submarine.
7.45. Have sunk enemy submarine.
8.10. Shall I return to report or look for another?

Campbell's morale-boosting victory was recognised by the award of his first DSO and promotion to commander over the heads of many others on the Navy List. A long lean spell followed, during which he was involved in only one other submarine encounter, before he embarked on his record-breaking run of success that would bring him a VC, two Bars to his DSO, the French Legion of Honour and the Croix de Guerre with Palm (both gazetted in 1918), as well as a glut of awards to his crew. If luck had played a part in his joining the Q-ships, it was his skill and courage, together with that of his crew, that was responsible for him accounting for more than a quarter of the eleven U-boats sunk by decoy vessels. According to Bayly, Campbell 'had a genius for fore-telling whereabouts a submarine was likely to be found and what its further movements were likely to be'.

During two years commanding Q-ships, Campbell, described by Bayly as 'a born leader' for whom 'life and honours seemed to count nothing', dedicated himself to the work of hunting and sinking sub-marines. The relationship between admiral and his 'ace' commander was one of mutual trust and respect. 'The only time we came near to a disagreement,' wrote Bayly, 'was when I told him that as a Captain RN at an exceptionally early age, with the honours His Majesty had given him, he must give up the dangerous game of mystery shipping and must take up the ordinary duties of a naval officer in war.'

Campbell served as Bayly's flag captain in the light cruiser *Active*, taking charge of all anti-submarine operations in the Irish Sea. Early the following year, he was appointed Bayly's representative in Holyhead, where he saw out the rest of the war with the dual status as Senior Naval Officer and commander of a flotilla of destroyers.

Peace-time saw Campbell return to his pre-war training role, first as commander of the cadet training cruiser *Cumberland* and then the boys' training establishment *Impregnable*, in which he had served before the war. Subsequently appointed captain-in-charge of Simonstown dock-yard, his last sea-going role was as captain of the battlecruiser *Tiger* from 1925 to 1927. The following year, he was peremptorily retired as a 42-year-old admiral with a letter he described as 'less gracious than one would send to a cook who had served you for two years'.

His response was to take a trip to the Sahara Desert, where 'I sat by myself for two days and said goodbye to the Navy'. Then he began writing his war memoirs. Published in 1928, *My Mystery Ships* became a worldwide bestseller, resulting in lecture tours throughout Britain and North America. More books followed, mostly on nautical matters, including his highly entertaining and richly anecdotal autobiography, *Number Thirteen*, published in 1932.

By then Campbell, who had been made an ADC to the king for a short period, had embarked on a new career as a Member of Parliament for Burnley. Having been rejected by the Conservatives as being 'too Socialistic' in 1928, he was persuaded to stand as a National candidate against the Socialist stalwart Arthur Henderson, then Secretary of the Parliamentary Labour Party and a former foreign secretary, in the 1931 general election. A fluent and popular speaker, Campbell gained a sen-sational victory, with a majority of more than 8,000. A loyal supporter of Stanley Baldwin and the League of Nations, Campbell spoke mainly on defence matters, supporting national service and opposing the use of submarines. His hard work as a constituency MP, however, was not enough to save him from defeat in the 1935 election when he stood as a Liberal-National candidate.

Campbell, who had suffered a serious heart attack the previous year, took on more book commissions and public-speaking engagements, until the Second World War brought an unexpected recall from his old friend Winston Churchill, esconced again at the Admiralty. At Churchill's behest Campbell, who had been elevated to vice-admiral on the retired list seven years earlier, was given the task of requisitioning and fitting out a new fleet of Q-ships. Amid a climate of jealousy and high-level wrangling about a 'navy within a navy', Campbell's decoy ships proved a dismal failure. Having enjoyed little success and suffered a number of losses, he resigned his command in April 1940, following an argument over the deployment of his ships. The scheme was abandoned. His critics insisted that 'he lived too much in the past', though that conflicted with the comments of officers 'astonished at his knowledge of up-to-date equipment and strategy'. The hero of 1916–17 spent the rest of his active Second World War service, until his health broke down in 1943, as Resident Naval Officer at Padstow, in the lowly rank of commander.

Retired for a second time Campbell returned to writing. In association with I.O. Evans, he wrote a textbook on flags, which was published in 1950. His health, however, was beginning to fail. In appearance a bluff, ruddy-faced sailor, he was in reality a sick man, his constitution weakened by the strain of his Q-ship experiences. The man who had defied all that the elements and enemy submarines could throw at him lost his last battle in the West Middlesex Hospital, Isleworth, on 3 October 1953.

Vice-Admiral Campbell, the greatest of all Q-ship commanders, was buried in All Saints' churchyard, Crondall, in Hampshire, his medals later passing to Dulwich College, where a display serves as a lasting memorial to its most distinguished old boy.

Ronald Neil Stuart, the first Royal Navy officer to receive a Victoria Cross by ballot, came of an old seafaring family. He was born at 31 Kelvin Grove, Toxteth, Liverpool, on 26 August 1886, only son and youngest in a family of six children to Neil Stuart, a master mariner of Scottish ancestry from Prince Edward Island, Canada, and Mary Harrison (née Banks), a master mariner's daughter who gave up her dressmaking business and became a captain's wife, sailing with her husband between England and Australia.

Stuart's parents were married in Montreal and their first child was born in Quebec, before they sailed for the Mississippi where Neil Stuart became a river boat skipper. There are some suggestions he may also have served a spell in the US Navy, before the family settled in Liverpool. After a spell as a dock superintendent, he ventured into the grocery trade, selling 'Stuart's prize teas' from a store in Prescott Street. The change of direction proved an unhappy one. When Neil Stuart died, following an accident while preparing to return to sea, his family was said to have been 'quite poor and absurdly proud'.

At the time, Ronald was attending a public school, Shaw Street (later Liverpool) College. But his father's death changed everything. He was forced to leave school and take a job in an office. 'He hated it,' wrote his son, Ian Stuart. 'He hated Liverpool.' Rescue, however, came in the shape of an aunt who secured for him an apprenticeship with Messrs Steele & Co in 1902. His first ship was the sailing barque *Kirkhill* and he was aboard her in 1905 when she struck a rock and foundered off the Falklands. He lost everything, but managed to reach shore safely. Later, he had another narrow escape when his ship was wrecked off the coast of Florida during a cyclone. Having completed his time, he joined the Allan Line, voyaging all over the world in a variety of ships. When the company was taken over by the Canadian Pacific Steamships Company, he continued in the service of the new proprietors.

By then, however, the war had intervened. Stuart spent almost two years in the 'clapped-out' destroyer *Opossum*. It was a grindingly dull appointment. When she wasn't in the repair yards, *Opossum* was employed mainly on patrol work in Plymouth Sound, reporting 'stray logs and boarding Dutchmen'. His attempts to seek more active commands (according to his son he even asked for a transfer to the Army) were rejected. One senior officer responded to his request by telling him to 'Go to hell! And shut the door behind you.' Stuart's misery ended in the late spring of 1916 when he was selected to join Campbell's crew as a replacement Number One for a decorated officer who had shown signs of cracking under the strain of decoy work. Campbell counted himself 'lucky' to have found Stuart. Though a 'different type of man' to his original first lieutenant, he thought him 'equally efficient'. 'He had the advantage of having everything in running order, instead of starting at the beginning,' added Campbell, 'and so was "on the top line" by the time we sailed.'

Stuart quickly showed himself to be an imperturbable character. Short and stocky with light blue eyes which could turn 'very bleak and penetrating', he was described by Campbell as 'blond, ruddy, powerful'. As is the way of so many seamen, he was also blunt and bluff, a man shaped by his rigorous sea-going experiences, as hard on himself as he was on others around him. Campbell came to rely on him for his expertise in handling and fitting out merchant vessels to ensure their decoy role was not compromised. Relations between the two, however, were not entirely cordial. Although Stuart rarely spoke of his war experiences, he left his family with 'the clear impression that he did not get on well with Campbell'. Their contrasting backgrounds, one Royal Navy and the other Merchant Navy, each with their own class codes, may have played a part, but the most likely cause of strain was their difference in temperament. While Campbell was to prove himself a master self-publicist, Stuart was a model of reticence who always played down the risks, contending that Q-ship crews 'were lucky and far better off than the poor fellows in the lines'.

No amount of modesty, though, could disguise his understated heroism under the most testing of circumstances. His contribution to the successes of the *Q5* and the *Pargust* were justly recognised by the awards of the VC and DSO and his elevation, in the summer of 1917, to his first command, the Q-sloop *Tamarisk*. In her, Stuart not only enhanced his reputation, but added to his list of honours as a result of a remarkable feat of seamanship in October 1917, when *Tamarisk* went to the aid of a torpedoed American destroyer, 20 miles off the Irish coast. Despite a near gale and in total darkness, Stuart succeeded in working *Tamarisk* close enough to get a line aboard the rudderless and badly damaged USS *Cassin*. Although the tow parted twice during the night, the *Cassin*, her stern virtually blown off, was eventually brought in to Queenstown behind a trawler. In recognition of his 'extreme bravery', Stuart was awarded the only US Navy Cross given to a VC holder during the war, although, unaccountably, it was not announced until 14 October 1927, almost ten years after the episode.

After the war, Lt Cdr Ronald Stuart resumed his career with Canadian Pacific. During the 1920s, he rose steadily through the ranks. Prior to taking his first command, the freighter *Brandon* in 1927, he was staff captain aboard the *Empress of Australia*. He later served as master of the *Minnedosa* and was appointed to command *Duchess of York* when she was commissioned in 1929. He remained in her until July 1934, when he was made Commodore of the CPS fleet and given the prestigious appointment of master of the company's flagship, the 42,500-ton *Empress of Britain*. At 47, Stuart was one of the youngest men ever to attain such a high rank. Two years later he was promoted to the post of superintendent at Montreal and, in December 1937, returned to Britain to take up the appointment of general superintendent. His distinguished career in the merchant service was capped in July 1938, when he was made Canadian Pacific general manager in London, an appointment which spanned the difficult years of the Second World War and which ended with his retirement in 1951.

His success in the merchant service was mirrored by his rise through the ranks of the RNR. Promoted commander on 30 June 1928, he was awarded the Reserve Officers' Decoration in November 1929, and further promoted Captain on 1 July 1935. Ronald Stuart was also Honorary President of the RNR Officers' Club, the Sea Urchins, was appointed Naval ADC to King George VI in 1941 and, as a mark of distinction, was authorised by special Ensign Warrant on 14 May 1927 to fly the Blue Ensign on any ship under his command.

Ronald Stuart's life, however, was not without its share of tragedy. In 1931 his wife, Evelyn, whom he married in Toxteth in 1919, died, leaving him with three sons and two daughters to bring up. His four surviving sisters, none of whom married, took over the running of his house and children, while he single-mindedly pursued his career, never taking a holiday and never again indulging in any kind of social life. Two of his sons eventually followed in the family tradition, serving at sea in the Royal Navy and Royal Canadian Navy (one earned a DSC for his part in the sinking of a U-boat and the other was mentioned in despatches), while Stuart himself lived out his retirement with his sisters at Beryl Lodge, Charing, in Kent. It was there, on 8 February 1954, that the most highly decorated RNR officer of the First World War died, aged 67.

A complex man, who detested pomp and snobbery, he was greatly affected by the death of his wife. He became increasingly dour and his defensive fear of any strong emotion (which he dismissed as 'mush') grew ever stronger. His son, Ian, recalled: 'His recreations were reading, walking, the weather and the natural world, and the "movies" every Saturday afternoon, where he enjoyed comedies and action films, and where he used to jeer embarrassingly loudly at falsely heroic, sentimental or emotional passages (mush!)'

No doubt he would have reacted in much the same way at the decision to name a road after him in Lee-on-Solent. Together with the display of his VC in the National Maritime Museum, Stuart Close, however, serves to ensure his memory is kept alive.

William Williams, the most highly decorated seaman of the war, came from a well-known Anglesey seafaring family. He was born at 6 Well Street, Almwch Port, on 5 October 1890, the son of Richard Williams, a longshore fisherman, and his wife Ann (née Thomas). Educated at Almwch Port School, he grew up in conditions of near-poverty as his father struggled to make a living off the north coast. As soon as he was old enough, Williams, like so many of his friends, found work at sea, in the Beaumaris schooners *Meyric* and *Camborne*. Powerfully built and over 6ft tall, he was a hard-working and thoroughly reliable seaman. Between August 1910 and December 1913, he made three round trips to Rio Grande in Brazil, receiving 'very good' reports for his ability and conduct on each trip.

Having taken his discharge at Ellesmere Port, he enlisted in the Royal Naval Reserve as a seaman/gunner on 29 September 1914, and was mobilised for service three days later. Details of his early war career are scant, but it seems he was among the earliest recruits to Q-ship work, joining Gordon Campbell aboard the converted tramp steamer *Loderer* in the autumn of 1915. During a little less than two years under Campbell's command, Williams was to serve aboard three more 'mystery ships' – *Farnborough*, *Pargust* and *Dunraven* – and would win a bravery award in each of them. In fact, his VC, DSM and Bar were all earned in a remarkable six-month period during which he helped account for two enemy submarines and survived being torpedoed on three occasions, at the cost of one ship sunk, another beached, and the third forced into dry docks for extensive repairs.

The sinking of *Dunraven* in August 1917 marked the end of Campbell's distinguished career in Q-ships, but Williams carried on in this hazardous service. As Campbell's crew went their separate ways, Williams found himself transferred to *Eilian*, a three-masted auxiliary schooner boasting two hidden 12-pounders, which was commissioned on 24 September 1917. One of the last three Q-ships operating under Admiral Bayly's command, *Eilian* survived the war. Williams's service career, however, ended five days short of the Armistice, when he was discharged from the RNR as 'medically unfit for further service'. Few had served longer, or shown more consistent valour, than Williams. But not even the stoutest heart could go on forever. After almost three years of unbroken Q-ship service, it appears the strain had finally taken its toll. The talk at the time was that he returned home suffering from exhaustion.

By then he was a leading seaman, with the French Medaille Militaire (gazetted on 25 January 1918 and awarded for the same action which resulted in his VC) added to his three British bravery awards, making him the country's most highly decorated serviceman of the war. As such, he was fêted wherever he went. Crowds turned out at Llangefni on 31 October 1918 to see him presented with £150 of War Bonds and the people of his home town saluted his heroism by giving him a gold watch and an illuminated address.

After the war Williams returned to his humble roots, moving to Holyhead, where he worked as a seaman on the Holyhead–Greenore cross-channel ferries, before taking a shore job in the LNER docks. Later he worked at a coal merchants until ill health forced him to retire. He married twice, first in 1925 to Elizabeth Jane Wright, by whom he had a daughter, and secondly in 1946 to Annie Hanlon, a widow.

Throughout his life he kept close ties with the British Legion. A founder member of the Holyhead branch, he was also for many years its standard bearer, regularly attending civic functions and Armistice Day parades. His 'long and devoted service' was marked in 1963 by the award of a special certificate. The year previously he had attended, with his wife and stepdaughter, the garden party at Buckingham Palace for members of the VC and GC Association.

Though proud of his many decorations and distinctions, William Williams, or 'Will VC' as he was known to many on Anglesey, maintained a dignified silence about his wartime exploits. Tudor Roberts, a member of the Holyhead branch of the British Legion, recalled:

He was a very quiet, very unassuming and very gentle man. You would never have known about his VC unless somebody had told you. As a young boy in Holyhead during the Second World War,

I remember him well. He had the ribbon of his VC stitched into his ordinary suit. We all thought the world of him.

William Williams's last years were marred by illness. After some time in hospital, he died from a combination of cancer and heart disease at his home at 31 Station Road, Holyhead, on 23 October 1965. He was buried in Amlwch Cemetery and his medals were later put on display in the National Museum of Wales. More than thirty-five years after his death, memorials in the Royal British Legion Club at Holyhead, Amlwch Sailing Club, Amlwch School and a housing estate named after him in his home town reflect the heartfelt pride in a tough Welsh seaman whose actions marked him out as one of the bravest men in an exceptionally brave ship's company.

Aside from his captain, Lt Bonner was the only recipient of a non-elected VC among Gordon Campbell's highly distinguished crew. Charles George Bonner was born at Shuttington, Warwickshire, on 29 December 1884, the youngest son of Samuel Bonner and his wife Jane (née Hellaby), formerly of Bramcote Hall. While Charles was still an infant, his father, a farmer and JP, uprooted the family and settled at Aldridge, near Walsall, in Staffordshire. Educated at Bishop Vesey's Grammar School, Sutton Coldfield, and Coleshill Grammar School, Bonner joined the training ship *Conway*, moored in the Mersey, in 1899 as the first step towards a career in the Merchant Navy.

He left in 1901 and joined the firm of George Milne & Co., and served his apprenticeship aboard the sailing ship *Invermark* out of Aberdeen. His rise was swift. After spells as second mate and then chief mate, he passed all the necessary examinations for the master mariner's certificate by the age of 21. Joining the Johnston Line, Bonner exchanged sail for steam. He served on the company's Black Sea trade routes, and was aboard the *Incemore* when she was involved in a collision with the *Kaiser Wilhelm* off the Isle of Wight shortly before the outbreak of war. The German liner was soon to be armed and converted for her

1. Artist's impression of Cdr Ritchie steering *Goliath*'s steam pinnace through a storm of fire at Dar-es-Salaam.

2. Lt Holbrook (back row, third from left), with the crew of *B11* after their successful mission. LS 'Fred' Mortimer is seated in the front row, second from left.

3. The *River Clyde* hard ashore after the capture of V Beach. The spit of rocks is clearly visible on the collier's starboard side.

4. Artist's impression of Midshipman Malleson winning his VC.

5. Artist's impression of Nasmith's raid into Constantinople harbour.

6. The crew of HM Submarine *E11*, 'scourge of the Marmora'. Martin Nasmith is seated centre on the conning tower with his number one, Lt Guy D'Oyly Hughes, on his left and his third officer, Lt Robert Brown, on his right.

7. Artist's impression of Cookson's gallant single-handed attempt to cut a way through the Turkish obstruction at Es Sinn, near Kut.

8. A Mesopotamian VC investiture. Seamen of the Tigris Flotilla parade in Basra for the presentation of Charles Cowley's posthumous honour to his mother.

9. HMS *Nestor* goes down under a welter of shells from the High Seas Fleet. Before abandoning ship, her captain, Barry Bingham, said to his number one, 'Where shall we go?' He replied: 'We'll go to Heaven, sir!'

10. Lt Cdr Loftus Jones' widow and daughter visiting his grave in Sweden after the First World War.

From a Water-coloured Drawing by the Chief-Scout of Cornwell's Heroism

11. 'Faithful unto death'. Chief-Scout Sir Robert Baden-Powell's impression of Boy First Class Jack Cornwell's action at Jutland.

12. Cdr Gordon Campbell (centre front) and the officers of the Q-ship *Pargust* in their clandestine 'rig'. Lt Bonner is in the front row, second from right, and Lt Stuart is in the back row, second from left.

13. Gus Bonner and Alice 'Cissy' Partridge on their wedding day, 20 June 1917, some seven weeks before his VC action.

14. Swathed in bandages, Gus Bonner in the immediate aftermath of *Dunraven*'s epic duel with *UC-71*. 'I was quite the star turn,' he told his parents, 'and by every law and regulation was killed on 3 different occasions.'

15. This painting of *Otaki*'s gallant struggle against the armed commerce raider *Moewe* was commissioned by the New Zealand Shipping Company via P&O.

16. Artist Charles Pears'
version of the encounter
between HMS *Prize* and
the *U-93* on 30 April
1917.

17. Lt William Sanders,
right, with his first
lieutenant, William
Beaton, aboard *Prize*.

18. The crew of *Gowanlea* (FR105/N4) before her famous fight. Fred Lamb is seated in the centre, wearing a white shirt.

19. Joe Watt's unique medal group: the Victoria Cross, 1937 Coronation Medal, Serbian Gold Medal, Italian Al Valore Militaire Silver and French Croix de Guerre (Spink).

20. Skipper Tom Crisp, the future fisherman hero, with his wife and children in a studio portrait photograph taken in the early years of the twentieth century.

21. *E14* under way off Salonika. Lost in a gallant but ill-starred attack on the Turkish battle-cruiser *Goeben*, she had the unique distinction of being involved in two Victoria Cross exploits almost three years apart.

22. HMS *Vindictive* bound for Zeebrugge on 22 April 1918, the gangways by which the marine and seamen landing parties were to storm the mole clearly visible.

23. Sgt Norman Finch, hero of the foretop, on the left, returns after the war to place a wreath of violets in the shape of *Vindictive* at the foot of the Zeebrugge Memorial unveiled by King Albert.

24. Lt Cdr Arthur Harrison   25. Lt John Howell-Price

26. A.B. McKenzie, still on crutches, given a hero's welcome in Southwark after his investiture.

H.M.S. "VINDICTIVE" SUNK AT OSTEND. MAY. 9TH 1918. COPYRIGHT COZENS PORTSMOUTH.

27. An artist's impression of *Vindictive* scuttled across the entrance to Ostend harbour.

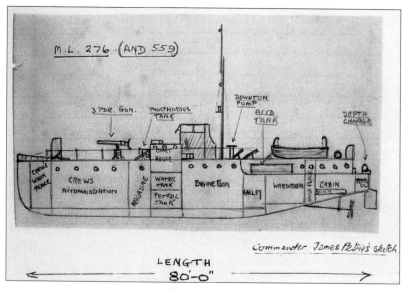

M.L. 276 . (AND 559)

3 PDR. GUN.   PHOSPHOROUS TANK   DOWNTON PUMP.   ACID TANK   DEPTH CHARGE

CREWS WASH PLACE   CREWS ACCOMMODATION   MAGAZINE   CHART HOUSE   WATER TANK   PETROL TANK   ENGINE ROOM   GALLEY   WARDROOM   WASH PLACE   CABIN   PETROL

Commander James Petrie's sketch

LENGTH
80'-0"

28. A cutaway sketch of Rowley Bourke's *ML276* drawn by James Petrie, who served aboard the launch during the second attempt to block Ostend harbour in May 1918.

29. Lt James Petrie outside Buckingham Palace after receiving his Distinguished Service Cross on 11 September 1918 for the action in which Bourke was awarded the Victoria Cross.

30. RowleyBourke with his bride, Rosalind Barnet, *c.* 1919.

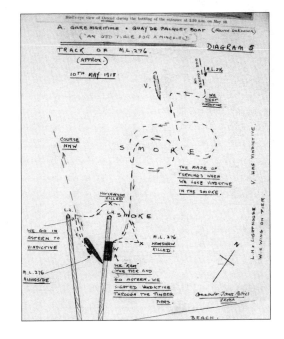

31. How a VC was earned. The circuitous route of *ML276* into Ostend as charted by Lt Petrie.

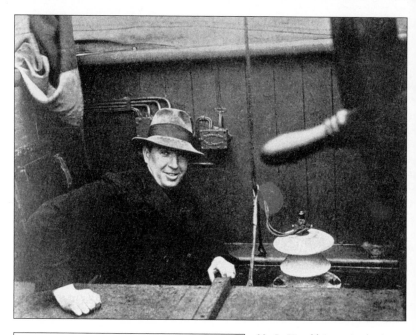

32. Lt Harold Auten in classic Q-ship pose.

33. A cartoon of Harold Auten reflecting his careers as a highly decorated naval officer and a successful film distributor.

short-lived career as a surface raider. Bonner's path to Queenstown and the Q-ships of Bayly's command, however, proved a circuitous one, as was explained by Campbell in his memoir, *My Mystery Ships*:

At the beginning of the war he was in a tramp steamer at Antwerp, and being anxious for a scrap, he took the shortest path and joined the Belgian Army. He was removed from that as a suspected person, came over to England, and volunteered for the RNR. Volunteers not being required at that time, he joined the RNVR at the Crystal Palace; being a fine-looking fellow, he found himself a Petty Officer, and back again in Antwerp with the Naval Division. He didn't see the fun of being interned with the remainder, so, making his way down to the Scheldt, he secured a boat and rowed himself down, and in due course got back to the Crystal Palace. His conduct not meeting with approval, he was sent to a cruiser in the 10th Cruiser Squadron as an ordinary seaman; but after a few weeks of this it was discovered that RNR officers were required after all, and he got his commission as Sub-Lieutenant RNR, and joined the Trawler Section at Larne.

Campbell, who had run into Bonner by chance, was impressed by his varied service and thought him 'cut out for the job' of decoy work. He took him on as his second officer and it was in that role aboard *Pargust* that he earned the Distinguished Service Cross for his part in the destruction of *UC-29* on 7 June 1917 (gazetted 20 July 1917). Barely a month later he had been wounded, had seen his ship sunk beneath him and had performed prodigies of heroism which resulted in the nation's highest military honour.

Bonner's VC was notable for being presented to him by the king even before the official announcement of the award had been published in the *London Gazette*. The break with tradition resulted from Campbell's fears for his friend's safety. Having recovered from his injuries, Bonner had been given command of his own Q-ship, the auxiliary schooner *Eilian*, whose crew included William Williams VC, DSM. But Campbell, concerned about a repetition of the disaster that overtook W.E. Sanders, urged the Admiralty to ask for an early investiture, before Bonner's 'dangerous-looking' ship went out on patrol. Unexpectedly summoned to the Admiralty from his digs in Saltash, Bonner soon found himself on a train bound for Wolferton on the royal Sandringham estate, with nothing more than a small bag and his sword. Met off the train by 'two huge men in Green Liveries', he was taken, on the evening of 7 October, to York Cottage, and led into the study, where the king waited to present him with his hard-won honour. Having been entertained to dinner, Bonner joined the royal party for the following morning's church service, and, following a courtesy call to Queen Alexandra, headed back to London. By 2 November, when the award was announced, he was already back on duty.

Thankfully, Campbell's fears were to prove unfounded. Charles Bonner survived the war and resumed his career in the Merchant Navy. For a couple of months he served as a first officer with the Furness Withy Line, before joining the Leith Salvage and Towage Company, based at Edinburgh. During a career spanning twenty-one years he became an acknowledged expert in ship salvage. Among his more memorable achievements were the refloating of the Danish steamer *Elizabeth* from a reef at Johnstone's Point, Campbeltown, in Argyll, in 1925, and the salving of the *Caledonia* in the Firth of Forth during the Second World War. Such was his reputation in this field that in 1948 he was flown to Norway to act as adviser on the salvage of the German battleship *Tirpitz*, which, having been damaged by midget submarines (for which two VCs were awarded), had been sunk by the Royal Air Force.

Bonner had married Alice Mabel Partridge, a solicitor's daughter from Walsall, at St Matthew's Church, Walsall, on 17 June 1917. They had one son, whom they named in memory of Bonner's former captain and the ship in which he survived almost certain death to win his VC. Gordon Dunraven Bonner followed his father into the navy, serving as a surgeon-lieutenant in the RNVR.

Charles George Bonner died at his home at 12 Netherly Road, Edinburgh, on 7 February 1951. He was 66. After a funeral at Warriston Crematorium, Edinburgh, his ashes were buried at Aldridge, his childhood home, where a headstone was later raised in his memory and that of his wife, who died twenty-two years later. The inscription reads: 'Love alone is eternal.' Perhaps the finest epitaph to one of the most distinguished Q-ship men, and certainly one of the luckiest, was provided by his former captain, Gordon Campbell, who dedicated his 1938 book *Abandon Ship* 'to my old friend and shipmate, Captain Charles George Bonner VC, DSC, the bravest man I ever met'.

Like Bonner, Ernest Pitcher did his best to ensure the heroic legacy of *Dunraven* lived on. Indeed, he went one step further than his former officer, naming his house as well as his daughter after the ship in which he enjoyed his finest hour.

One of only a handful of regular RN sailors among Campbell's crew, Ernest Herbert Pitcher was born on 31 December 1888 at Mullion, in Cornwall, the son of George and Sarah Pitcher (née Beverstock). While he was still an infant, his family moved to Swanage in Dorset, where his father continued his service as a coastguard. Educated at the local board school, Charles joined the navy at Portsmouth, aged 15, on 22 July 1903. At the outbreak of war, he was serving in *King George V*, the flagship of the Second Battle Squadron based at Scapa, and in 1915 he became one of the earliest recruits to join the Q-ships. Most of the crews were RNR men, bolstered by regular navy seamen with experience in gunnery. As a petty officer, Pitcher quickly emerged as one of Campbell's steadiest hands, a gun captain whose coolness under fire was successively recognised by a mention in despatches, a Distinguished Service Medal and the Victoria Cross, all earned within a matchless six-month period.

PO Pitcher received his Cross from King George V at an investiture in Buckingham Palace on 5 December 1917. Like Williams, his astonishing bravery was marked also by the award of the French Medaille Militaire (gazetted on 28 August 1918), which he added to the Croix de Guerre he already held.

With an old-fashioned black beard of a type that was fast disappearing from the naval service, Pitcher had what his captain described as 'a very striking appearance'. A photograph taken of him in 1918, sandwiched between Queen Mary and Queen Alexandra, with the king on one side and the elderly courtier Sir Dighton Probyn VC peeping through a plant on the other side, shows him in all his awkward splendour, a fish out of water, his jersey awash with medal ribbons. Strangely, little fuss appears to have been made of him in the port where he grew up.

That same year, he married Lily (née Evers) at Wareham and they had one daughter, Ruth Mary Dunraven.

After the war Pitcher carried on in the navy. Rated up to chief petty officer on 1 August 1920, he eventually retired on a pension on

30 December 1927, one day short of his 39th birthday. He had completed twenty-five years in a distinguished career capped by the award of the Naval Long Service and Good Conduct Medal. Returning to Swanage, he found work at a boys' preparatory school as a groundsman, PT instructor and part-time teacher of woodwork. Later, he appears to have operated an off-licence, being listed in trade directories as a 'beerseller', but ultimately he was reduced to eking a meagre living as a commissionaire, maintaining discipline in a local amusement arcade.

During the Second World War, with the country threatened by invasion, he rejoined the navy on 5 August 1940 and spent the remainder of the war in naval establishments at Poole, Portland and finally HMS *Attack* at Yeovilton. In early 1946 his health gave way. Seriously ill with tuberculosis, he was admitted to the Royal Naval Auxiliary Hospital, Sherborne, where he died on 10 February 1946.

Pitcher had spent his last years in a house called Dunraven, at 4 Richmond Road, Swanage, and the body of the 57-year-old seaman, who had served his country through two world wars, was brought back for burial in Northbrook Cemetery. The Commonwealth War Graves' headstone marking his grave is engraved with his last appointment, HMS *Attack*, and bears the memorable inscription:

At the going down of the sun and in the morning
we will remember them.

Ernest Pitcher's heroism is variously commemorated, by a modest plaque in St Mary's parish church, Swanage, and by two portraits commissioned shortly after his most celebrated action. They are held by the Imperial War Museum, where his outstanding medal group is displayed as part of the Lord Ashcroft Collection, having been purchased by the billionaire businessman and politician for £28,000 in 1997.

A.B. SMITH

350 miles east of the Azores,
10 March 1917

On 23 February 1917 Fregattenkapitan Nikolaus Burggraf und Graf zu Dohna-Schlodien addressed the crew of the armed commerce raider *Moewe* on the after deck. They had been at sea for sixty-three days and had taken their toll of Allied shipping to 92,000 tons, surpassing the outstanding success of their first cruise which had seen them fêted as national heroes and their captain awarded the Iron Cross, first class, and the Pour le Mérite, Germany's highest honour. Dohna-Schlodien feared the net was closing in. Only a week earlier he had narrowly evaded an armed British merchant cruiser. But before returning home, he told the *Moewe*'s assembled company that he wanted to reach the 100,000-ton mark of ships destroyed. His speech provoked loud cheers, the sound carrying across the grey waters of the Atlantic.

By the morning of 10 March *Moewe* had added two more victims to her score and taken her tally to 99,291 tons. But Dohna-Schlodien was growing anxious. The easy pickings of the South American trade routes were behind him. Blue skies had given way to a grey smother and wild seas where British warships regularly patrolled. As *Moewe* ploughed on, with 442 prisoners of war crammed into her holds, he ordered all guns and torpedo tubes to be manned. For hours she stuck to her course, lashed by squalls and Force 8 winds, until around 2.30 p.m., when a look-out spotted a grey shape through the murk.

Anxious to prevent his position being broadcast to any British warships in the area, Dohna-Schlodien altered course towards the ship, which immediately turned north. Dohna-Schlodien later wrote:

A merry chase now commences in a rough sea. The Englishman is going very steadily whilst we are rolling and labouring heavily. She is considerably larger than our vessel and is going so fast that we cannot overtake her, and once she even disappeared in a squall. When the weather clears she is 1,000m further ahead – a proof that she has smelt a rat ...

The 'Englishman' was, in fact, the 9,575-ton New Zealand Shipping Company steamer SS *Otaki* whose master, Archibald Bisset Smith, a 38-year-old Scot with more than twenty years' seagoing experience behind him, had indeed 'smelt a rat'. With a crew of seventy-one, the nine-year-old refrigerated cargo liner was bound for New York out of London, in ballast, when her look-outs sighted the *Moewe* some 350 miles east of Sao Miguel in the Azores.

According to a seaman aboard *Otaki*, *Moewe* was at first mistaken for another 'dirty old tramp' steamer. But Smith's suspicions were aroused the moment she turned towards his ship. Although not a fighting man, he had a clear sense of his duty – and that was to save his ship. His best hope lay in trying to outrun his pursuer until darkness. But it was a tall order. Nightfall was more than three hours away and Smith must have known that if he were overhauled any contest was liable to be an unequal one. His only armament was a single 4.7-inch gun mounted on the stern poop deck, whereas the *Moewe*, a 4,788-ton freighter originally designed to carry bananas from Africa, boasted seven guns and two torpedo tubes. And while unaware of the precise disparity, Smith had already decided on the tactics that he felt offered the best chance of survival. Ordering the helm turned, *Otaki* drove into a head sea, thus giving his own gun team the opportunity to engage the chasing raider while making life as difficult as possible for the enemy gunlayers.

At first unwilling to risk more damage to his already strained boilers, Dohna-Schlodien ordered only a slight increase in speed. The ship was pitching badly and taking heavy seas, but with the gap showing no sign of closing he was compelled to increase speed to 14 knots. By around 4 p.m. according to German accounts, or half an hour later according to the British version, the *Moewe* had closed to within 2,000m, five points to port astern of the *Otaki*. Dohna-Schlodien could wait no longer. He signalled *Otaki* to stop, firing a warning shot across her bows for good measure. That had usually been enough to cow her prey into submission. But Captain Smith was made of sterner stuff. His response was to order his gun team to open fire. Seconds later, and 'without showing a flag', according to a German account, a water-spout 500m short of the *Moewe* signalled *Otaki*'s intentions. Dohna-Schlodien promptly ordered: 'All guns ready for action. Open fire!'

As Smith had hoped, however, the head sea made aiming difficult for the enemy, reducing to some extent the impact of *Moewe*'s superior armament. The raider's gunnery officer, Hermann A.K. Jung, wrote in his diary:

> Our gunlayer's task was considerably bedevilled by the strong pitching of the ship. With the height above water only 6m, the muzzles of the two 15cm guns did such a dive in the direction of the rolling sea that it was really only chance to be thanked that we did not have any barrel bursts. For the same reason, the speed of fire of our quick-firer couldn't be made full use of. On the other hand, the steamer was nearly twice as big as we were and, as a result, lay more steady in the water; and his gun, standing on the after deck, could be served more steadily and fired without hindrance ...

According to Jung, the encounter lasted twenty minutes, although a seaman aboard *Otaki* claimed it was nearer an hour, in the course of which the *Moewe* registered twenty-two hits on the steamer. In return, Able Seaman Thomas Seamer counted eight direct hits out of nine shots fired at the raider. Though possibly exaggerated, there was no doubting the remarkable accuracy of *Otaki*'s single gun, nor the 'great damage' done to *Moewe*. Jung's blow-by-blow account bears testament to the ferocity of the action:

> Hit on the *Moewe*. Waterline. Forward penetration of the hull on the weather side. The shell explodes in the ship and kills two men. The splinters penetrate the hull on the lee side under water and tear two irregularly shaped holes in the hull; there is a fierce inrush of water; the *Moewe* begins to settle by the head and develops a 15 degrees list to port ...
> Hit ... in the signal bridge; no one hurt.
> Shot at the *Moewe*. 10m short. The splinters fly over the captain's bridge without harming anyone.
> Hit on the *Moewe*. Two metres above the waterline in the engine room bunkers. A violent explosion in the bunker; the flash penetrates even the neighbouring boiler room and severely burns six stokers (four of them later died) and simultaneously strikes up through a ventilator on to the bridge, without doing any harm there. In the engine room bunker the coal sacks and baskets that are lying on top of the coals catch fire together with some

material in the Indians' quarters above the bunker. Several Indians are killed [or] badly wounded. Individual fragments penetrate the lee side above the waterline …

What made the performance of *Otaki*'s gunners particularly remarkable was that for much of the time they were themselves under heavy fire. Jung saw one shell burst just below the gun platform and three more fell close by on the stern before a 10.5cm shell struck the gun pedestal. Momentarily, as smoke enveloped the gun, it seemed as though the crew had vanished, but suddenly four more men appeared and the gun continued firing. 'In the face of this obstinate defence,' noted Jung, 'it is now going to depend on which of the two ships first manages to disable the other's capacity to carry on the fight.'

Otaki, her midships hidden by a pall of coal-dust, was already hit on the waterline beneath her funnel. Then, in quick succession, five more shells penetrated her hull aft. Slowly but surely, she began to take water, but still she resisted, even though her sinking deck angle made it impossible for the gunners to aim. In an attempt to deliver the *coup de grâce*, *Moewe* fired three torpedoes, but all missed. Not that it affected the outcome. *Otaki*'s plight was by now hopeless. Shells were steadily pounding her. One struck the gun platform, the blast throwing two men off the poop deck. But once again an astonished Jung saw two more men take their places 'after setting the English Merchant flag on the flagstaff'. *Otaki*'s desperate defiance was almost over. With his ship sinking, Capt. Smith gave his last orders 'to get all boats out and ready for leaving [the] ship as it was no good staying too long'. Jung recorded *Otaki*'s end:

At first black and then thick white smoke pours out from the after part of the English ship and completely veils the gun. The enemy fire ceases. The crew of the steamer take to the boats and lower them into the water. Fire is stopped at 4.30pm. Thirty-five 15cm and twenty-three 10.5cm shells had been fired. The steamer is now lying very severely down by the stern. The poop is submerged to the upper deck – the bows of the ship standing high out of the water …

Not everyone had abandoned ship. Four dead – apprentices Basil Kilner and William Martin who served the gun, Deck Boy R. Keneston and the Third Engineer, A.H. Little – were left behind as the boats pulled away, along with three men, seen standing near the ship's rail. They were Capt. Smith, Chief Officer Rowland McNish and the ship's carpenter. As darkness fell and fire engulfed the wallowing *Otaki*, they each made their own decisions. According to the company's historian, 'it was expected that they would all leap into the water together. In fact, only two jumped. Captain Bisset Smith turned away and is presumed to have gone down to his cabin. He was not seen again and no doubt preferred to die with his ship, which went down shortly afterwards, her flag still flying.' The two men who jumped were picked up, but another member of the crew, H.J. Willis, *Otaki*'s chief steward, who had missed the boats, was drowned. Among those saved was the master's 17-year-old stepson Alfred Smith. He had begged to be allowed to stay with him, but, wrote AB Seamer, 'was not allowed to do so'. Seamer added:

> After we were in the boats for about two hours, the raider picked us up, but we did not like the idea of going on board as she was so badly damaged, and on fire and [had] a heavy list to port; they were trying to plug the holes up caused by the *Otaki* gun fire. The *Moewe* captain was very anxious and waiting for Captain Smith to come on board. I really believe they would have torn him limb from limb if they had got hold of him, but they did not have the chance.

Undoubtedly feelings were running high aboard the raider, but such a reaction seems unlikely given Dohna-Schlodien's chivalrous record. Indeed, Jung wrote: 'Although his resistance as a merchant ship as against a war vessel cannot be reconciled with existing law of sea warfare, nevertheless, it must be admitted that he defended himself bravely …'

Bravely and skilfully. With a little more luck, Smith might even have beaten off his heavily armed opponent. By the end of the fight *Moewe* resembled a floating wreck. As the steamer's survivors came aboard, the raider's crew, who had also been forced to repel an attempted breakout by the prisoners, were heavily engaged fighting fires. Holed amidships and in the stern, she was low in the water and there were fears she would not survive. Ammunition and explosives were jettisoned and the fires burned throughout the night, during which she resembled, according to Jung, 'a smouldering volcano'. Not for three days was *Moewe* back in trim and able to continue her run north.

Her fretful voyage home ended at Kiel on 22 March. In a triumphant four-month cruise *Moewe* had accounted for twenty-two steamers (including two captured) and three sailing ships, making a grand total of 119,600 tons. Dohna-Schlodien had achieved his goal, but at some cost. In the fight with *Otaki*, five of his men were killed and as many as forty wounded. *Otaki*'s losses were fewer: five dead and nine injured. In return, they had given Germany's leading commerce raider its greatest-ever scare. And while British and German versions vary slightly, both agree on the courage shown by Capt. Smith, whom the faithful Seamer described as 'a true British hero'.

Both the Admiralty and Mercantile Marine agreed, though neither seemed to know how best to translate praise into recognition. As with Frederick Parslow, they were torn between rewarding gallantry and preserving the Merchant Navy's civilian status. Their solution was to opt for a posthumous mention in despatches awarded on 16 November 1917 'for good services whilst on Transport Duties'. Oblivious of the difficulties surrounding her husband's case, Edith Smith felt this reward was hardly commensurate with so brave a fight. Armed with Seamer's testimony, together with reports of the action taken from the Press, she urged the New Zealand government to press 'for proper recognition of my husband's heroic action'. The result was a recommendation for the Victoria Cross put forward by the Mercantile Marine Awards Committee on 31 May 1918:

> For conspicuous bravery and devotion to the Country in the presence of the enemy, when he fought a very gallant action against overwhelming odds and all but succeeded in destroying the enemy, finally going down in his ship with the British colours still flying.

The difficulty was that the colours in this case were the Red Ensign, and not the White Ensign. Among those opposed to the award were officials at the Department of Naval Intelligence who argued that it was important to maintain the Merchant Navy's civilian status not only for the sake of prisoners held by the Germans but to allow merchantmen as 'peaceful' vessels the 'free use of neutral ports'. And they concluded: 'These questions of principle far outweigh any advantage to be gained by awarding a VC ... however well the decoration may have been merited.' The Admiralty agreed, though one official came up with a novel alternative. 'A Knighthood,' wrote William Evans, 'which would give his widow such a title would be a very effective recognition if it was considered suitable ...'

Unimpressed by the wrangling, Rear Admiral N.C. Palmer, president of the Mercantile Marine Awards Committee, called for a change in the rules governing the award of the VC so that Merchant Navy officers and men could be made retrospectively eligible. In the end this was agreed, though the new warrant would have to wait until after the war, and even then the Admiralty insisted on maintaining the subterfuge by giving Smith and Parslow ante-dated commissions in the Royal Naval Reserve. It was, therefore, as Lieutenant Archibald Bisset Smith

RNR that *Otaki*'s master eventually appeared in the *London Gazette* on 24 May 1919. The list of awards included six members of his gallant company: Chief Officer Rowland McNish, who received the DSO, Acting Leading Seaman Alfred Worth RFR and Able Seaman Ellis Jackson RNVR, the two naval gunners who were each given a DSM, the ship's carpenter and the two apprentices, Basil Kilner and William Martin, who were mentioned in despatches. Uniquely, the VC citation ended with the verdict delivered by an enemy officer, Graf zu Dohna-Schlodien, who stated that Archibald Smith's defiant action was 'as gallant as naval history can relate'.

Archibald Bisset Smith was born at Cosie Brae, Cults, Aberdeen, on 19 December 1878, the second youngest in a family of three sons and two daughters to William and Annie Smith (née Nicoll). His father was an accountant and later a wholesale tea and dry goods merchant who, it was said, could trace his ancestry back to Bold Peter Smith, a Jacobite killed at Culloden and whose sword hilt became a treasured family heirloom.

As a teenager, Archie Smith spent two years at Robert Gordon's College, Aberdeen, from 1893 to 1895, before embarking on a career in the Merchant Navy. In 1903, while serving with the New Zealand Shipping Company, he gained his master's ticket (certificate No. 034635) and went on to serve aboard the *Waikato*, *Rakaia*, *Waimate* and *Turakina* before the war.

Archie Smith married Edith Clulee (née Powell) in about 1914 in a ceremony which, family sources suggest, may have taken place aboard a ship en route to England. It was her second marriage and her son Alfred (born in 1900), by her first husband, took his stepfather's surname. Archie and Edith are thought to have been introduced by her brother, a master mariner, then serving in the Union Steamship Co., in about 1906. At the time Edith was living in Port Chalmers with her parents, who had emigrated to New Zealand from Wales thirty years earlier.

During the war Smith served as captain aboard the *Rakaia*, *Hurunui* and *Otaki*. The latter, built by Denny's of Dumbarton in 1907–08, was something of a trail-blazer. She was the first merchant steamer to be fitted with triple expansion and turbine machinery. Her main peace-time cargo was New Zealand meat; she was built to carry 100,000 carcasses of frozen mutton. Archie Smith's first voyage in command of the vessel was in June 1915, and, after a spell in command of *Hurunui*, he returned to *Otaki* for what would be her last assignment in February 1917. On board with him was his stepson Alfred, serving as a Merchant

Navy cadet. He survived the battle and spent the rest of the war in German hands.

After the war Alfred Smith returned home and on 7 June 1919 accompanied his widowed mother to Buckingham Palace where she received her husband's posthumous VC from King George V. On her death in 1951, Alfred Smith, who was said to have been deeply affected by his stepfather's death and his own incarceration, sold the Victoria Cross, together with the British War Medal, Victory Medal and Mercantile Marine Medal, at Glendinings. They were bought by the New Zealand Shipping Company for £125. The medals were temporarily lodged in Robert Gordon's College before being displayed in the officers' dining saloon of a new *Otaki*, the fourth to carry that name, which was built two years later. When that ship was sold at the end of 1975, the Cross was brought ashore and, in August 1976 a replica was placed at the former NZ Shipping Company sports ground, the Maori Club at Worcester Park, while the original was held in the strongroom of the P&O Line, which had absorbed Smith's former employers.

Archibald Bisset Smith, who was described by one of his crew as 'a kind and generous man ... so brave and a great credit to the Mercantile Marine', is remembered on the Tower Hill Memorial dedicated to all those Merchant Navy officers and men who lost their lives in the war. His name also appears on the Aberdeen War Memorial and his parents' headstone in Rhynie Cemetery, where the inscription reads: 'Commander SS *Otaki* who, on being attacked by the German Raider *Moewe* on the high seas, refused to surrender and went down with his ship, after a most gallant resistance.'

Capt. Smith's most enduring memorial, however, is the Otaki Shield. Presented by his family to the governors of Robert Gordon's College in 1936, it is awarded annually to the scholar judged pre-eminent in athletics, character and leadership. Since 1937 the honour has included a travel scholarship to New Zealand given by Smith's old shipping company and later by its successor company, P&O, in recognition of a 'civilian' seaman who fought as bravely as any man o'war.

W.E. SANDERS
180 miles south-west of Ireland, 30 April 1917

The evening air was refreshing as Captain A.B. Burroughs emerged from the submarine's conning tower. The master of the SS *Ikbal* tugged his jacket around his body, while his companion, slim, fair-haired and neatly attired in German naval officer's uniform, fussed after him. The incongruity seemed not to affect either of them as they exchanged pleasantries. In truth, Burroughs had been given little time to reflect on the misfortunes of war. Barely thirty-three hours earlier he had been bound for Le Havre with a cargo of munitions and hay, and now he was accepting a cigarette from the man who had destroyed his ship. Yet rather than resenting his captor, he found himself admiring his courtesy and humanity.

Kapitanleutnant Adolf Karl Georg Edgar Freiherr von Spiegel und zu Pecklesheim was no ordinary U-boat captain. One of Germany's most distinguished aces, his exploits in *U-32*, propagandised in a notorious wartime book, had earned him command of one of the latest submarines. *U-93* was a formidable fighting machine. Some 235ft long and displacing 1,000 tons submerged, she could make 16 knots surfaced and carried six torpedo tubes and a pair of 10.5cm deck guns either side of the conning tower.

She had left Emden on her maiden patrol on Friday, 13 April 1917, and after a slow start fortune had smiled on her. By the evening of 30 April, with her torpedoes exhausted and her complement swollen by five prisoners, *U-93*'s tally stood at eleven ships sunk, six of them in the last two days. As von Spiegel shared a cigarette with Capt. Burroughs he had cause to feel satisfied with his patrol. All being well, he would be home in time to see his horses run in the Berlin races!

Suddenly, around 8.30 p.m., their conversation was cut short. A three-masted schooner had been sighted. Even in the fading light she was too tempting a target to let pass. Leaving Burroughs a hapless spectator, von Spiegel gave orders to attack. In moments, the deck guns were manned and speed increased. The sea was calm, the weather fine and visibility was plenty good enough. At 8.45 p.m. *U-93* fired the opening shots in what was to prove one of the most famous sea duels of the war.

The first shell splashed well ahead and the second threw up a fountain well astern of the schooner. Having delivered their warning shots, the gun crews awaited the response. Not long after, a boat was seen being lowered. As it pulled clear, von Spiegel ordered his guns to fire on the apparently abandoned sailing vessel. Within minutes, a fire broke out, wreathing the schooner in smoke. To all on *U-93*, her fate appeared sealed – but all was not what it seemed.

Far from being a deserted hulk, the schooner was in fact HMS *Prize*, a disguised man o'war equipped with two hidden 12-pounders, under the command of Lieutenant William Edward Sanders, a 34-year-old raw-boned professional seaman. Like so many of the men who manned the Royal Navy's decoy ships, Sanders was a member of the Royal Naval Reserve and had served at sea since he was a boy.

A first-generation New Zealander, born in Auckland on 7 February 1883, he was the eldest son of Edward Helman Cook Sanders, a boot-maker, and Emma Jane (née Wilson), who had both emigrated from England. He first went to sea aboard the small steamer *Kapanui* in 1897. Such was his proficiency that within twelve years he had gained his Extra Master's Ticket, and was serving as First Mate on the barque *Joseph Craig*, of J.J. Craig Ltd, when war broke out. Three days later, on 7 August 1914, the ship was wrecked inside the Hokianga Bar and Sanders showed great bravery and presence of mind in single-handedly steering a boat to shore through dangerous surf to bring assistance to the crew. Afterwards, he joined the Union Steamship Company, serving first as executive officer on the *Moeraki* and then, from December 1914, as extra Third Officer aboard HMNZT *Willochra*, engaged in the transportation of troops overseas. Such undemanding work, however, gave little satisfaction. In June 1915, during one such trip, Sanders passed a letter to an officer of the NZ Army Staff Corps. Addressed to the Admiralty, the note made clear his desire to join the Royal Naval Reserve. His wish granted, he was offered the rank of temporary sub-lieutenant on his arrival in the United Kingdom. Following a spell in another troopship, the *Tofua*, Sanders, impatient for more active employment, quit his job and worked his passage to Britain aboard the *Hebburn Jan*. Discharged at Glasgow on 7 April 1916, he was ready to open a new and extremely hazardous chapter in his adventurous career.

In response to increasing attacks by enemy submarines on sailing ships, the Admiralty had begun requisitioning a number of these vessels as 'trap' ships, with volunteer crews recruited mainly from the Auxiliary Patrol and Trawler Reserve. Commissioned sub-lieutenant on 19 April 1916, Sanders, by virtue of his experience in sailing ships, was appointed mate and gunnery officer of the *Helgoland*, a two-masted Dutch brigantine, refitted with four 12-pounders and a Maxim. During two patrols in September and October she fought two inconclusive actions south-west of the Lizard. In one of these encounters Sanders had given further evidence of his character, coolly freeing a jammed gun screen. His determination impressed senior officers and on 5 February 1917 he was promoted acting lieutenant and given command of *Prize*, then being fitted out at Falmouth. After undergoing special gunnery training, Sanders and his second-in-command, Lieutenant William Beaton, joined their new ship a week before commissioning.

Formerly the German-registered *Else*, the *Prize* had already earned a place in naval history as the first enemy vessel to be seized in the war. Sold to the Marine Navigation Company and rechristened *First Prize*, she was requisitioned by the navy in November 1916 and fitted for decoy work. Under her slightly amended name, the 112ft topsail schooner set sail from Milford Haven on 26 April to patrol the west coast of Ireland. For four days she ploughed a lonely course without glimpsing a single U-boat and by 30 April was about 180 miles south-west of Ireland, approaching the limit of her patrol area. Sanders, frustrated at finding nothing, had already decided to turn north around midnight. But then, just as he and Beaton sat bemoaning their bad luck over mugs of cocoa in the wardroom, the alarm gongs sounded, sending the crew scurrying to their stations.

Before making for his position at the foot of the foremast where he would control the forward gun, Beaton made certain the White Ensign was ready and placed the halyards in his skipper's hands 'so he could stand in the little iron deckhouse out of sight and watch his chance to open action'. But first they would have to bide their time. From his hidden post Sanders watched as *U-93* altered course towards him. Then, as soon as the submarine opened fire, the ship's well-rehearsed drill swung into action. Sanders later wrote:

> The 'Panic party', consisting of six persons in charge of a Skipper [William Henry Brewer], RNR, then launched the small boat to

the starboard side and left the ship with instructions to linger en route and not on any account to make straight for the submarine … so as to force the submarine to manoeuvre towards the boat and thus expose herself in a favourable position for me to attack.

The remainder of the crew were hidden away at their respective guns, viz. in after house and forward bulwarks. I … took up a position at the control station … amidships. From time to time I crawled backwards and forwards to instil into the men the importance of remaining quiet and out of sight.

The ship's head slowly fell away to the eastward and the enemy slowly followed us round, all the while approaching closer. He continued to fire at the ship in a deliberate manner until satisfied that she had been abandoned. Up to this time a total of sixteen rounds had been fired, two of which struck the water-line, exploded inside, and caused considerable damage. The motor was put out of action, the wireless room wrecked, the mainmast shot through in two places, and all the living rooms shattered. The lubricating oil tank was holed and the contents filtered on to the deck. The ship also began to make water at a fairly rapid rate …

Prize's plight was becoming desperate. The twenty-minute bombardment had left her engine room a mass of flames, yet even as the fire raged out of control the 'remarkably cool' crew held their nerve, waiting for Sanders's order to unmask their guns. Sanders himself braved the shelling to crawl across to Beaton, who was struck by his captain's 'unexampled courage and iron nerve'.

Throughout, von Spiegel had kept his glasses trained on the ship's decks, checking for any movement. But, convinced that no one could have endured such heavy fire without showing themselves, he ordered his boat towards the blazing ship. According to Beaton: 'the submarine commander could see that our ship was in a sinking condition, so he ceased fire, and slowly steamed up close to get particulars of the ship's name and tonnage, etc.' Nearer and nearer she came until the tension aboard the *Prize* was almost unbearable. Sanders wrote:

The enemy continued to approach from dead astern until she was within 150yd. My anxiety was great, as the after gun would not bear right astern owing to the position of the wheel. Fortunately at this moment she altered course several points to clear our stern, and when about three points abaft the beam and distant 80yd I considered that the critical moment had arrived. It was then 21.05, and the order was given to 'down screens and open fire' at point-blank range. I may add that, from the moment of going to 'stations' until fire was opened on the submarine, sights had been kept carefully adjusted by the estimated range of the approaching enemy. Almost as soon as our screens were downed the enemy fired with both her guns. One shell struck the water-line, passed through the side, and was deflected upwards through the deck. The other, as far as I could tell, hit the superstructure. As a result, three hands were wounded.

One man had just released the after gun screens and was manning a Lewis gun when shell fragments shattered his right forearm and smashed the gun. Sanders added:

A pause of barely two seconds elapsed and then both forward and after 12-pounder guns and the Lewis gun fired simultane-ously. A shell from the after gun hit the enemy's forward gun, blew it to pieces, and annihilated the gun's crew. The forward gun missed. The Lewis gun swept about 25 men off the decks of the submarine. [This figure was an exaggeration as subsequent events would prove.] The submarine then proceeded at full speed ahead with helm hard a-starboard. As she started to move a second shot from the after gun blew the conning tower clean off.

Beaton, who was in communication with Sanders by voice-pipe, reck-oned the first ten shots, all from the after gun, found the mark, while the forward 12-pounder also scored a number of hits. Amid the chaos aboard the submarine, he saw von Spiegel, in front of the conning tower, apparently signalling to swing the boat hard a-port. At first, Beaton thought he was making to ram the *Prize*, but then he saw him apparently countermand the order. Unaware that the U-boat's supply of torpedoes was exhausted, he feared she might be turning to get off a stern shot. Whatever the reality, Beaton maintained that von Spiegel never gave another order aboard *U-93*. 'A second later,' he wrote, 'a man's body – hit by a large portion of one of our shells – came in vio-lent contact with the commander and knocked him into the sea.'

Too late, von Spiegel had realised his mistake. Directing operations from the fore gun until it had been blown overboard, he had followed the survivors among its crew to the after gun. There they continued the fight, until a shell struck the barrel, decapitating the gunlayer and stunning and temporarily blinding the boat's captain. The next thing he felt was a cold sensation around his legs. 'We were up to our knees in water,' he wrote. 'A moment later we were swimming in the Atlantic.

The *U-93* had sunk beneath us. I could see her black shadow vanish in the depths of the ocean. A dreadful pang of anguish shot through me at the thought of my fine new boat and my crew going down to their last port on the cold silent bottom of the sea.'

The German commander was not alone in believing the *U-93* had been sunk. Capt. Burroughs, who was on the submarine's deck throughout the brutal engagement and received shrapnel wounds to his legs, saw two crewmen inflate lifebelts and leap overboard. He would have followed them, but for his inability to swim. Instead, he sought shelter behind the wrecked and blood-spattered conning tower.

Sanders, too, was convinced of his victory. He felt certain that the third shot from the after gun had disabled the submarine, ascribing her movement, as she continued to forge ahead, to the motors being jammed on. Attempts at pursuit were quickly forestalled by *Prize*'s own problems: one engine was smashed, and the second gave out after barely 100yd. Sanders wrote:

> The submarine finally came to standstill at about 500 to 600 yards away, slewed broadside on, heading in an opposite direction to mine. The after gun continued to find the target. Time after time a hit was registered, and out of a total of 14 rounds fired from this gun 12 appeared to find a billet. The forward gun was not so successful, and only scored an occasional hit which did not materially affect the result of the action. Altogether 36 rounds were fired before the submarine disappeared from sight. She settled down stern first, ablaze internally, the fire being distinctly visible through the wreckage. As she sank the jagged end of the conning-tower came into view for a moment and was lost to sight. Previous to sinking a white vapour was emitted from the hull, and her Commander (who was subsequently rescued) ventured an opinion that this was due to the salt water getting into the batteries.

Crippled though she was by the furious onslaught that lasted barely four minutes, *U-93* had not been sunk. With her hull pierced in at least a dozen places, her periscopes shot away and trailing oil from her ruptured fuel tanks, she managed to zig-zag away into the gathering gloom. Then began one of the most remarkable escapes of the war. Command having devolved on novice executive officer Wilhelm Ziegner, *U-93* made the perilous passage home entirely on the surface, evading mines and patrols, to reach Sylt nine days later. It was an outstanding feat of seamanship which had fatal repercussions for Sanders and the *Prize*, which faced a struggle of her own as night fell on 30 April.

Having rescued von Spiegel, his navigating officer and a petty officer, Sanders embarked on the no less desperate battle to repair the serious damage done to his ship:

> The water was pouring through the shot holes and had covered the flooring above the ballast to the extent of about a foot. The hold pumps and the portable Downton pump were manned and a bucket party told off. Another party was detailed to stop the leaks by means of mattresses, hammocks and hatches. The efforts to stop the leak were not successful, and water continued to gain on the vessel. The only course open was to list the ship, and to do this the small boat which was swung out on the davits was filled with water, both cables passed on deck and ranged in the starboard scupper-way, coal shifted from port to starboard side and port fresh water tanks emptied. The vessel was also put on port tack. These measures were instrumental in relieving the pressure, and the shot holes were left almost clear of the water. They were temporarily stopped; but the crew were forced to continue bailing and pumping night and day, until arrival at Kinsale on 2 May. Fortunately the weather remained calm, otherwise we could never have kept afloat ...

Emergency repairs having been effected at Kinsale, the *Prize*, minus two wounded crewmen who had been transferred by motor launch to hospital in Queenstown, left under tow for Milford Haven at 5 a.m. on 4 May, arriving safely the following day. Legend has it that in bidding Sanders farewell von Spiegel invited him to visit his Schleswig-Holstein estate after the war.

Although initially crestfallen at his sudden reversal of fortune and the apparent destruction of his boat and crew, von Spiegel 'marvelled at the bravery of these Britishers who in their hiding place could take [such] a shelling ... and then run their gun platform out and start to fight'. Sanders, in particular, made a deep impression. Describing him as 'a tall, slender chap [with] fine brown eyes and blond hair which sprawled over his head', von Spiegel was struck by his captor's bearing and consideration at a time when his ship appeared to be sinking beneath him.

The respect was mutual. Sanders, in his report, made a point of praising the prisoners for doing 'all in their power to assist us in saving the *Prize*, starting the motor, and attending to the wounded'. He stated: 'Immediately after he boarded the Commanding Officer gave me his word of honour that he would make no attempt to escape, and that he and his men would do all in their power to assist us on board. It must be admitted that he fully carried out his promise.'

Promoted lieutenant-commander, the New Zealander was offered command of another ship. But he chose to stay with the *Prize*, which was undergoing repairs. Unbeknown to Sanders, however, the hazards facing him had multiplied since the escape of *U-93*. By the time the *Prize* left Milford Haven on 27 May for a three-week Atlantic patrol, a report identifying the three-masted schooner as a 'trap-ship' had gone out to all submarine commanders operating in Irish waters. Indeed, the warning may well have been responsible for the behaviour of a submarine encountered by Sanders on the morning of 12 June. Employing the same tactics as he had used against the *U-93*, he sent off his 'panic party' and allowed the submarine – 'a very large type, armed with two guns' – to pound his vessel from a range of more than a mile. For half an hour the bombardment continued, until a shell burst on the starboard side, sending fragments through the deck near where Sanders lay:

> Putting up my arm to shield my face [I] received a piece of shell in my right arm just above the wrist. The force of the explosion knocked me over and carried me the other side of the deck, where I was picked up by Skipper Mead. I was just sufficiently conscious to give the order 'Action'.

The screens dropped and both starboard guns opened fire at a range of roughly 1,800yd. Only six rounds had been fired and one hit claimed, before the submarine slipped beneath the surface. In his report Sanders declared that the enemy commander had shown no sign of being lured to within killing range of the *Prize*. It was an unhappy augury.

Ten days later the *London Gazette* announced a long list of gallantry awards in respect of the desperate battle with *U-93*, although in keeping with previous Q-ship actions no details were given. The honours included a DSO for Beaton, DSCs for Skippers Brewer and Mead, DSMs for every member of the ship's company, and the list was headed by the Victoria Cross to *Prize*'s gallant captain. To this honour would be added a DSO, gazetted on 14 September in respect of his second unsuccessful action. But by then William Sanders was dead.

Having recovered from his wound, he took *Prize* out again in August to patrol north-west of Ireland. Freshly painted and flying the Swedish flag, the schooner carried a new threat – a D-class submarine with which she partnered in the hope of dealing with any U-boat that refused to be tempted within range of her hidden guns. *D6*, commanded by Lieut Cdr William Reynard Richardson, followed *Prize* in loose formation but was out of contact when, on 13 August, Sanders detected a submarine on the surface, 150 miles north-west of Rathlin Island.

Undeterred, *Prize*'s captain resorted to his old subterfuge and, in a brief engagement, came within an ace of success. At a range of 250m, *Prize* and the *UB-48* exchanged shots, the Q-ship sustaining one hit while inflicting damage to the submarine's wireless mast above the conning tower. It was a narrow miss that was to prove disastrous for *Prize* and her crew.

Chased by two more shots from Sanders's gun crews, *UB-48* slid beneath the surface while her commander, Oberleutnant zur See Wolfgang Steinbauer, plotted his next move. The hunted had become the hunter. Steinbauer's first attempt to stalk *Prize* came to naught, but he refused to give up. 'I decided to try and sink this ship because it was dangerous for all our boats,' he later recalled. He decided to bide his time until it was dark. *Prize*, meanwhile, met up with *D6* around 9 p.m. For the first time, Richardson learned of *Prize*'s fight. Sanders thought he had scored a number of hits on his opponent and was happy to continue the patrol. Darkness was closing in when the two parted company. It was the last time any of *Prize*'s crew would be seen alive.

Having lost sight of his prey, Steinbauer spent two hours in a vain pursuit. He had just about given up hope of finding her when he spotted a small light. It was apparent for less than a second, but long enough to betray *Prize*'s presence. Shortly after 3 a.m. on 14 August, with squalls of rain blowing over a phosphorescent sea, *UB-48* fired a bow shot from what he thought was a range of 400m but was in fact nearer 1,000m. It was the first time Steinbauer had ever attempted a night attack on the surface, and though it seemed impossible to miss, he did. Fortunately for him, the Q-ship's lookouts apparently saw nothing of the misdirected torpedo. Then, it occurred to him that the schooner was not sailing but using an engine:

I began a new attack [he later stated]. We were parallel ... and fired a bit nearer. I thought about 300 metres ... I counted when the torpedo left the boat. My observation – about 300 metres, 20 seconds and nothing happened, 30 seconds – nothing. 40 – nothing. At 45 seconds, the torpedo blew up. That was a distance of 700 metres – and I thought 300!

By a dreadful mischance, the torpedo had apparently struck the ship's magazine. The resultant explosion was terrible. As a fireball lit the night sky, it reminded Steinbauer of a 'firework' display. When *UB-48* reached the scene, there was nothing left of *Prize* but pieces of wreckage and the lifeless body of a seaman kept afloat by his lifebuoy. Thus ended the remarkable career of Willie Sanders VC, DSO, a man described by his former adversary, Frieherr von Spiegel, as 'a soldier, a sailor and a gentleman'.

On 19 June 1918, in a ceremony at Auckland Town Hall, the Governor General, the Earl of Liverpool, presented the Victoria Cross and DSO to William Sanders's father. Eighty years on the annual award of the Sanders Cup, New Zealand's premier sailing trophy, provides a fitting and lasting memorial to the only Kiwi naval VC winner of the First World War.

J. WATT

Straits of Otranto, 15 May 1917

Joe Watt's homecoming was a quiet affair. He made sure of that. Keeping the time of his return a secret, he caught the late train back to Fraserburgh, ensuring he arrived under cover of darkness. From the station, he slipped away unobserved and, once home, quickly discarded his naval uniform in favour of a fisherman's jersey and kersey breeks. But it would take more than a change of clothing to escape the public gaze. Like it or not, and Joe Watt didn't like it one bit, he had become a local hero to be fêted at every opportunity.

It wasn't long before his cover was blown and the first in a stream of journalists beat a path to his door. But he, like all those that followed, received short shrift. Having dodged an official welcoming party, complete with brass band and guard of honour, Watt was more than capable of handling a reporter bent on securing a headline-grabbing story. Watt was content to talk about his recent spell in a Maltese hospital and his memorable journey home, via Rome, Turin and Paris, but he refused point-blank to discuss the action which had made him famous throughout his homeland. 'I have firmly made up my mind to say nothing about that,' he declared. 'There has been too much said already and it should get a rest ... I'm ashamed to read the exaggerations that have been printed ...'

No amount of charm could persuade him to alter his mind either then or in the years after. Six months earlier, in far different circumstances, he had displayed similar obstinacy – with altogether different consequences.

Joe Watt was among hundreds of fishermen who, having volunteered to serve King and Country, found themselves manning a fleet of steam drifters in one of the war's more eccentric sideshows. Based in the heel of Italy, they formed the so-called Otranto Barrage, a mammoth maritime undertaking designed to prevent enemy submarines, operating out of Cattaro, 140 miles to the north, entering the Mediterranean via the straits separating Italy from Albania. As well as 120 drifters maintaining a net barrier day and night, the Anglo-French-Italian blockade comprised motor-launches, destroyers, cruisers, kite balloons and aircraft. Yet its strategic value was dubious. One historian has likened it to a 'large-scale sieve' through which U-boats passed with relative impunity. Though successes were few, they were sufficient to provoke the Austro-Hungarian navy into retaliatory hit-and-run raids.

During one such sortie, three days before Christmas 1916, four destroyers and a light cruiser attacked the barrage. Taken by surprise, the drifters, armed only with 6-pounder guns, were saved only by the intervention of six French destroyers. One Fraserburgh boat, in particular, enjoyed a lucky escape. The 87ft wooden vessel, delivered to its Inverallochy owners in the week war broke out, had one shell pass right through its cabin, narrowly missing the skipper and carrying away the funnel. Another shot sank a small boat that had just been lowered and a third penetrated the hull above the waterline. Miraculously, none of the crew was hurt and the boat was able to reach Fano Island, before limping into port two days later. Her name was *Gowanlea* (FR105) and her skipper was Joseph Watt.

By the spring, her damage repaired, *Gowanlea* was back on the drifter line. Her nine crewmen were a close-knit team. Mainly Fraserburgh men, they were bound by ties that transcended naval rank. As well as the 29-year-old quietly spoken Watt, they included Fred Lamb, a man of herculean strength renowned as a champion barrel-maker, who took charge of *Gowanlea*'s solitary gun, and William Noble, the engineman, who had proved his worth during the last fracas by nursing the wounded vessel back to port. The boat's complement was completed by a terrier dog, a replacement mascot for the monkey given to them by Italian seamen.

Nothing had changed as far as the barrage was concerned. Every day, from 3 p.m. till daybreak the following morning, eight groups of drifters, each comprising seven vessels, straddled the straits from Italy to Fano Island, a distance of 44 miles. At first light, in a daily ritual, one group would steam back to Taranto, leaving a 10-mile channel for Italian merchant shipping to pass through, with the gap being filled by a fresh group in the afternoon. Each week the line was altered slightly, but most of the time it was positioned just south of latitude 40 degrees. It was, for the most part, a thoroughly monotonous routine.

After weeks of little excitement, however, April saw a marked rise in the number of submarine sightings. None was actually destroyed, but a number were forced to turn back. It was enough to spur the Austrians into action. Having twice reconnoitred the barrage, the decision was taken to mount the strongest attack yet. The three cruisers *Helgoland*, *Novara* and *Saida* would teach the driftermen a lesson they would not forget, while a force of destroyers raided shipping around the port of Valona. The date set for the operation was 14–15 May.

That the Austrians were up to no good was plain. The Italian admiral was aware of the impending threat to the barrage, but its timing and the size of the enemy force assigned to the operation remained unknown. As a result, limited counter-measures were put in place, but none of these involved telling the driftermen of the threat. The first indication any of them had of the blow about to fall was the sound of gunfire carrying across the eastern straits around 3 a.m. Even then, they were not unduly alarmed. Temporary Lieutenant Robert Baunton RNR, the drifters' senior officer, mistook it for another submarine encounter and promptly steered towards the noise.

In fact, the rumble of guns heralded the start of the attack. An Italian convoy had blundered into the path of two Austrian destroyers and in no time an escort had been sunk, a munitions ship blown to smithereens, and two more vessels damaged. As Baunton closed the scene of the action, guided by a flurry of flares, he heard more firing, accompanied shortly after by signals of distress. They came from the south-west, in the direction of the drifter line.

The attack on the barrage began between 3.15 a.m. and 3.30 a.m. At the time, forty-seven drifters were stretched across the straits in seven groups. Identified by their code letters, the groups from west to east were N, B, C, T, E, O and S. Some of the driftermen had actually seen the cruisers pass through the line a half-hour or so earlier. But they assumed they were friendly vessels, so none of them had reported the sighting. It was only when the cruisers began their systematic destruction shortly before first light that they realised their costly mistake.

Having inspected the barrage without interference, the cruisers set about their task methodically: one working in from the west, a second from the east and the third dealing with the centre. In each case, the pattern was much the same, with the enemy approaching to within a hundred yards of their victims, then stopping and ordering the crews to abandon ship before they sank the vessels with gunfire. Given the huge disparity in weaponry – nine 3.9-inch guns and four of smaller calibre vs. the drifters' 6-pounders – little resistance was expected. And, not surprisingly, some crews were quick to accede to the enemy's demands.

But not all were of the same inclination. A remarkable number chose to accept the ridiculously long odds with displays of belligerence that bore comparison with Sir Richard Grenville's immortal fight. Prominent among these defiant driftermen was Joe Watt.

Part of N Division, *Gowanlea* (officially numbered N4), in company with *Admirable, Caledonia, Jean, Selby* and *Transit*, had slipped her nets as soon as firing was heard around 3.15 a.m. and steered for Cape Santa Maria di Leucha on the Italian side of the straits. After fifteen minutes, however, they ran into a four-funnelled light cruiser heading in the opposite direction. It was the 3,500-ton *Helgoland*, commanded by Linienschiffkapitan Erich Heyssler. Having achieved initial surprise by striking from the south, Heyssler had begun a destructive sweep along the westernmost portion of the drifter line. A trail of burning boats and floating wreckage marked his progress. By the time he encountered Watt's *Gowanlea*, he had already disposed of a number of drifters from ranges of as little as 200m. In keeping with her captain's orders to give the crews a chance to escape, *Helgoland* dipped her battle ensign and gave a loud blast on her siren to signal Watt's men to abandon ship. It was a chivalrous gesture that was rudely rebuffed.

Ordering full steam ahead, Watt called on his crew to give 'three cheers for a fight to the finish' and promptly steered straight for the cruiser. At the same time, *Gowanlea*'s gun team, comprising Deckhands Lamb and Godbold, opened fire. The Austrian response was immediate and emphatic. *Gowanlea* almost vanished beneath a welter of sea spouts. One shell struck the boat's top rail, deflecting upward without exploding, but two more heavy blows inflicted heavy damage. The port railings were torn away, the bulwarks smashed and the gun rendered useless by a shell that plunged through the deck, detonating a box of ammunition. Fred Lamb was blown away from the gun, the blast shattering his right leg and peppering his face and eyes with shell splinters. He had managed just one shot with such indeterminate results that no one aboard *Helgoland* even realised they had been under attack. But like the *Gowanlea*, Lamb was not quite finished. Incredibly, despite his injuries, he hauled himself back to the disabled gun, where he joined other members of the crew in a vain attempt to repair the damage.

The short-lived duel was effectively over, although two more shots struck *Gowanlea* before *Helgoland* continued on her way. Fortunately, there were no more casualties, though Watt, whose cap had been punctured by shrapnel, had a narrow escape. One of the shells hit the wheelhouse, splintering the framework, before passing through without exploding. Miraculously, *Gowanlea*, her decks and cabin riddled, was able to limp away under her own steam. Many of her fellow drifters were less fortunate.

Admirable, Transit and *Selby* were all sunk and *Jean* severely damaged amid scenes of unbelievable bravery. Led by their gallant skipper, D.S. Ralph, *Selby*'s crew stuck to their boat until she sank beneath them. Unequal struggle though it was, it was not wholly one sided. Some, like Watt, fought back. The resistance shown by one drifter left a lasting impression on Heyssler. This was almost certainly the *Admirable*, commanded by Skipper William Farquhar. Only after her boiler exploded and her wheelhouse was demolished was she abandoned by all save one man. With *Helgoland* barely 50m away, Deckhand Adam Gordon scrambled back on board the burning drifter, apparently with the intention of carrying on the fight single-handedly, only to be cut down by a shell as he ran toward the gun.

N Division's ordeal spanned roughly thirty minutes. The entire raid lasted little more than an hour. In that time, fourteen of the forty-seven drifters were sunk and more damaged. Hardest hit were those vessels stationed at either end of the straits. S Division, farthest away on the eastern extremity, lost four out of six boats with most of the crews taken prisoner. The neighbouring O Division lost two and had two more disabled. As the cruisers withdrew, a running battle ensued between the raiders and units of the British and Italian fleets based at Brindisi. In an inconclusive exchange, the *Novara* was struck on the bridge and in the engine room and had to be towed back to port. She left behind a scene of carnage as the shell-scarred survivors among the drifter line searched the debris-strewn waters for survivors.

In spite of her own terrible damage, *Gowanlea* reportedly joined the rescue effort. Among those vessels she assisted, according to official accounts, was the *Floandi*. The O Division crew had fought back bravely against the *Novara* but had paid heavily for its courage, losing four men killed and three more injured, including its thrice-wounded skipper. Watt was credited with taking *Gowanlea* alongside the battered drifter to recover her dead and wounded before making for port, though this version of events was later disputed by another drifter skipper, Andrew Lyall, who claimed that it was his boat, *British Crown*, that had gone to *Floandi*'s aid before towing her into Brindisi.

What is irrefutable is that the raid, while wreaking great physical and psychological damage, had met with a degree of resistance that none on the Austrian side had anticipated. Lauding the drifter crews' courage, one leading Italian newspaper said their actions 'gave proof of marvellous physical endurance and self-abnegation'. A flood of recommendations duly followed. Amid a welter of brave deeds, two were considered worthy of the highest honour. On 29 May, Rear-Admiral Mark Kerr, commanding the British Adriatic Squadron, telegraphed the Admiralty, 'strongly' recommending awards of the Victoria Cross to Skipper Watt, 'for greatest gallantry and example', and to Deckhand Lamb, for fighting his gun throughout the action under a hot fire 'after having [his] leg shattered by explosion of box of ammunition'. The rest of *Gowanlea*'s crew was among forty-five men put in for CGMs. In all, the list ran to 119 recommendations for awards, a degree of largesse almost without precedent in the annals of the Royal Navy. It was soon apparent, however, that the admiration felt in Italy for the drifter crews' fight was not universally shared in London. Senior figures at the Admiralty were highly critical of those who had so readily surrendered 'instead of upholding the traditions of the Navy by holding out and fighting to the last, irrespective of the odds'.

A report compiled by the navy's M Branch declared: 'The recommendations of the Rear Admiral go a good deal beyond any scale which the Admiralty have hitherto approved ... The CGM, in particular, was never intended to be awarded on the wholesale scale put forward. Only 54 have been given in the whole course of the war.' Rear Admiral Allan Frederick Everett, Naval Secretary to the First Sea Lord, went further. 'No doubt certain Drifters fought to the best of their ability and with pathetic ability against overwhelming odds, whilst others apparently made no fight,' he wrote. He urged that the recommendations be scaled down to six decorations and six mentions for the officers and fourteen decorations and fourteen mentions for the men. 'This makes 40 awards in all (or 6% of the numbers engaged), which is liberal for a rout,' he added. Everett was similarly dismissive of the recommendations for the highest award, noting: 'I do not consider that either of the proposed VCs comes up to the standard required.' He suggested that Watt should be awarded the DSC and promoted a step in rank with a CGM given to Lamb. He further proposed that both men be recommended for the Italian Silver Medal for military valour 'of which some have been placed at our disposal'.

While there was broad agreement about his proposal to limit the number of awards, opinion was sharply divided over the issue of the two VC recommendations. To Everett's intemperate report, someone, presumably another high-ranking member of the navy's honours and awards committee, appended the note: 'As regards the awards to Skipper Watt and Deckhand Lamb, I think both these deserve the VC, when the conditions are considered – a cruiser attacking a drifter – I am of the opinion their courage and example were most meritorious and deserving of the highest recognition.' In the end a compromise was reached. On 6 July the Admiralty advised Kerr, in a confidential letter, of their intention to recommend Watt for the VC and Lamb for a CGM. The greatly curtailed list of awards was duly published in the *London Gazette* on 29 August 1917. As well as the awards to Watt and Lamb, they included a DSM to Engineman William Noble and a Bar to the DSM for Deckhand Edward Godbold, both of the gallant *Gowanlea*.

Joseph Watt was born at 64 Denside, Gardenstown, a small fishing community hugging the shores of the Moray Firth, on 25 June 1887, the third child of a family of two boys and three girls to Joseph and Helen Watt (née Mair). The family's ties with the sea, and with fishing in particular, were already well established. Joseph Watt sr, one of a large family from nearby Crovie, was a fisherman, as were most of the village's menfolk, and his wife Helen was one of six sisters who came to Gardenstown to work during the herring season.

It was a hard and precarious existence touched with tragedy. Joe was just 10 when his father was drowned, while line fishing for haddock some 23 miles off Troup Head, in January 1898. Not long after, his mother married George 'Sottie' Noble and moved to Broadsea, now part of Fraserburgh. His education, which began at Bracoden, now continued at the local village school, but his future occupation was never in question.

Fishing was a way of life, and death, among the God-fearing communities clinging to the Moray coast. As a youngster straight from school, Joe served his 'apprenticeship' aboard the *White Daisy*. He soon proved himself a capable seaman, diligent, hard-working, temperamentally sound, a man who knew his own mind and was prepared to act on his judgement. In about 1907 he left home and moved to Fraserburgh, where a couple of years later he invested in the part-ownership of the Dundee-built steam drifter *Annie*. For the next five years he plied his trade, earning a reputation among his fellow driftermen for being 'a daring seaman, who never shrank from facing the wild North Sea in its most stormy moods'.

The war signalled an unexpected change from the usual routine. Volunteering for the Patrol Service, he was appointed skipper in the Royal Naval Reserve on 11 January 1915. Before leaving, later that same year, for the Adriatic with *Gowanlea*, he married Jessie Ann Noble, the ceremony taking place in Broadsea.

In January 1916 the wearisome pattern of patrol work was broken by the need to help the desperate men of the Serbian army. Forced to retreat through the mountains of Albania in the depths of winter, they straggled to the Adriatic coast, from where they were evacuated, at great risk, by a fleet of transports, including British drifters sent across from Italy to help guard against enemy submarines. For his services during the evacuation, Watt was awarded the Serbian Gold Medal 'for zealous service' which was gazetted on 1 March 1917. By then *Gowanlea* had been well and truly blooded, having survived by the narrowest of margins the Austrian raid mounted nine weeks earlier.

Watt's outstanding bravery during the attack on the drifter barrage in May 1917 resulted in two further awards, the Croix de Guerre from the French, presented a few months later but not formally gazetted until 4 May 1920, and the Al Valore Militaire Silver from the Italians, to add to the VC which he received from King George V at Buckingham Palace on 6 April 1918. Such honours, however, meant little to him, beyond causing considerable embarrassment. Newspaper reports published after his return to Fraserburgh, following six weeks spent in a Maltese hospital recovering from a bout of sickness, described him as 'an almost painfully modest man'. His shyness owed something to natural reserve, but rather more to his firm belief that reports of his exploit had been greatly embellished by the Press. All attempts to persuade him to set the record straight were doomed to failure. 'He refuses even to tell me anything about it,' his wife told one journalist. Not even the prospect of civic celebrations could make him break his vow of silence. If people wanted to make a fuss about it, that was their business. For his part, Joe Watt wanted only a return to normality. 'I wish it was all over,' he said ambiguously, 'and let us get back to the herring fishing again.' Long after peace came his determination to avoid the subject that had brought him his undesirable brush with fame remained unshaken. When the maritime author David Masters wrote to the Provost of Fraserburgh in the mid-1930s in the hope of obtaining an interview with Watt, the reply had a familiar ring. 'I know Joe Watt intimately and have the feeling that you would not succeed in getting information from him concerning his war exploits,' observed the Provost. 'He is very reticent and disinclined to give any information.' And so he remained for the rest of his life.

After the war Joe Watt did indeed go back to fishing for herring. His drifter *Annie* (FR420) having been sunk while clearing mines a few weeks after the Armistice, he bought another vessel, the 86ft steam drifter *Benachie* (FR15), named after the highest peak in Aberdeenshire. It was on her, between the wars, that a smiling Joe Watt famously forgot to remove his cap during a visit by the Duke of Kent. Later, he took a share in the *Linet* and for a while was skipper of the *Girl Alice*, before eventually becoming a shareholder in the *Flora Fraser*.

A small, quiet man, he was a popular skipper blessed with a happy disposition. According to one account, those who worked with him considered him 'a grand shipmate "an' afa easy to get on wi".' During the Second World War he commanded a drifter serving the Home Fleet, with a crew that included his son, invalided home in 1940 after being wounded while serving in the Gordon Highlanders. Useful though the work was, it lacked excitement. In 1942 the hero of Otranto was quoted in one newspaper as saying: 'Ah'm not allowed to go to sea and fecht, they think ah'm tae auld.'

'VC Joe', or 'Gamrie Joe', as he was known by fishermen all along the East Coast, died of cancer of the gullet at his home, 7 Finlayson Street, Fraserburgh, on 13 February 1955 and was buried in Kirktown Cemetery, in the same plot as his wife and her parents. As he lay dying, he was visited by his local MP, W. Duthie, who later said of their meeting: 'If ever anyone was conscious of the peace of God that passeth all understanding, I was, as I entered his sick room. He had wonderful faith and courage.'

The VC that he reportedly kept in a small drawer on his fishing boat now features in the Lord Ashcroft Collection at the Imperial War Museum. Auctioned at Spink of London in April 2012, it was sold for £170,000, together with his Serbian Gold Medal, Italian Al Valore Militaire Silver Medal, French Croix de Guerre, 1937 Coronation Medal and the gold pocket watch that was presented to him in December 1917 by George Walker, proud owner of the *Gowanlea*, in commemoration of one of the bravest and most unlikely naval engagements of the war at sea.

T. CRISP
North Sea, off the Jim Howe Bank,
14 August 1917

During the cheerless autumn of 1917, with the campaign in Flanders drawing to a close in the swamps around Passchendaele, Lloyd George paid tribute to the sacrifices made by the country's armed forces. In a vote of thanks delivered on 29 October, he drew on all his oratorical skills. He spoke of the 'sustained courage' shown by the British army undergoing its severest test and he praised the Royal Navy's hazardous services 'from the icy waters of the Arctic Ocean to the stormy floods of Magellan'. Turning to the prodigious though unglamorous endeavours of the Mercantile Marine, he singled out the example of an unnamed fisherman who commanded a 'trawler' in an unequal struggle with a U-boat:

> Though armed only with a 3-pounder gun and out-ranged by her opponents, she refused to haul down her flag, even when the skipper had both legs shot off, and most of the crew were killed or injured. 'Throw the confidential books overboard, and throw me after them', said the skipper, and, refusing to leave his ship when the few survivors took to the boat, he went down with his trawler …

It was stirring stuff and the Press were quick to take up the story. The following morning's newspapers were full of the tale of the gallant skipper, his last words rendered a glorious epitaph in banner headlines. Four days later the identity of the fisherman became public knowledge as the *London Gazette* of 2 November announced the posthumous award of the Victoria Cross to Thomas Crisp, 41-year-old skipper of the armed Lowestoft fishing smack *Nelson*. In a country grown weary of war, the martyrdom of Tom Crisp struck a chord, and his defiance in the face of hopeless odds became symbolic of a wider resolve to fight to the bitter end. However, there was more to the story than met the eye. Like all politicians, the prime minister had been economical with the truth. To begin with, the impression of a small boat strewn with dead and dying was wildly inaccurate. Crisp was, in fact, the only casualty. Nor was the smack quite the innocent vessel she may have appeared to newspaper readers. The clue lay in the reference to her 3-pounder gun – scarcely the norm for a fishing 'trawler', let alone a humble sailing smack.

In reality, *Nelson* was a 'Special Service' vessel, a submarine hunter masquerading as a harmless fishing boat. Furthermore, she was not alone. During her final action she was acting in company with a second armed smack, and Crisp, far from being the innocent at arms of the popular Press, was actually one of the most experienced skippers operating out of Lowestoft, a man whose skill and determination to close with the enemy was well noted and had already been recognised by the award of the DSC.

Like many of the fishermen volunteers, Crisp had a score to settle with the U-boats. His own sailing smack, *George Borrow*, was among those lost to the submarine 'strafe' which had decimated the East Coast fishing fleet in 1915. His enthusiasm and skill resulted in him being given command of the 61-ton *Nelson*, which as the *G & E* (LT649) was the first smack to be armed and to claim a hit on a U-boat. During Crisp's time in command, the smack, rechristened *I'll Try*, was fitted with a 13-pounder gun and credited with the 'possible' destruction of a U-boat 17 miles south-east of Southwold while she was operating with the armed smack *Boy Alfred* (LT200). Post-war investigation later revealed that the submarine, though heavily damaged, had survived. Nevertheless Crisp had shown himself to be a determined commander, as adept at handling his boat's specially installed motor engine as he was at luring increasingly suspicious U-boat commanders to their doom.

Wednesday, 15 August 1917 found the same two decoy vessels operating together in the Jim Howe Bank fishing grounds. In an attempt to maintain their cover, both smacks had adopted new names: *I'll Try* became *Nelson* and *Boy Alfred* was rechristened *Ethel & Millie*. Crisp's partner was Charles 'Johnsey' Manning, a fisherman from Oulton Broad, who had recently taken command. On board *Nelson* with Crisp were eight men: Leading Seaman Percival Ross DSM and Able Seaman

Edward Hale, both regular seamen, who were responsible for manning the gun; a Royal Marine, Private George Cox RMLI, who had with him his service rifle; four RNR fishermen volunteers, Frederick Corrie, Alfred Pease, William Boon and Edward Fenn; and Crisp's 18-year-old son Thomas, who was serving as second hand.

Following the excitement of that February encounter their patrols had been frustratingly uneventful, and 15 August promised more of the same. In keeping with their subterfuge, they spent the morning herring fishing. After a break for dinner, they resumed work, so that shortly after 2 p.m., with the beam trawl still shot and *Nelson* on the port tack, the crew were variously engaged in routine chores. The skipper was below, with Ross and Hale, packing the morning's catch. Fenn, the 18-year-old cook, was on deck, cleaning fish for breakfast, as were Cox and Pease, who in between passing down baskets of fish, were keeping watch.

Around 2.30 p.m. Crisp came up for a breath of fresh air. Almost immediately he noticed a strange speck on the horizon, apparently moving north-west of the Jim Howe Buoy, 3 or 4 miles away. The *Ethel & Millie* was only 100yd distant, but her crew seemed oblivious of the threat. Calling for his binoculars, Crisp quickly dispelled any doubts. Turning to Marine Cox, he called: 'Clear ship for action – Submarine.' Cox passed the word down to the men below decks. The men were still scrambling for their positions when the submarine opened fire. To LS Ross it appeared, momentarily, as though the enemy vessel had exploded in a 'white puff of smoke'. Seconds later, a water plume 100yd off *Nelson*'s port bow heralded the start of the action. As Hale took his place alongside Ross, Boon started the motor, only to be told by his skipper 'not to gear up'. Crisp knew his only hope lay in maintaining his harmless pretence long enough to draw the submarine within range of his gun. His only concession was to order the fishing gear cut away to assist manoeuvrability. But hardly had the warp been slipped than a shell, the third or fourth fired by the U-boat, struck the *Nelson*, passing through the wooden bow just below the waterline, narrowly missing Fenn and the boxes of ammunition stowed below the gun.

As seawater rushed through the hole, Crisp shoved the smack round and called out to the gun team. 'It's no use waiting any longer, we'll have to let them have it.' Ross, whose aiming was made difficult by the lack of telescopic sights, recounted:

> As it was such a long range I opened fire at 6,000yd. My first shot went to the left and I put on 5 knots right deflection. I fired again and the shot was still left and I could see that it was short. I put the sight up another thousand yards making it 7,000.

That shot was still left and I put on 5 knots making it 10 knots. This I thought … was as near the range as I could get. I kept on firing when the sights came on and when I could get a shot in, but I could not get anyone to spot to tell me if the shots were hitting or going over. I carried on firing until the gun would not bear owing to my ship settling down in the water …

The U-boat's gun crew had no such difficulties. One shot ripped through the mains'l before the seventh struck *Nelson* a savage blow. Crisp, standing at the tiller, was cut in half as the shell passed through his left side, partially disembowelling him and severing both legs at the thighs, before passing through the deck and out the other side without exploding. His son and Ross immediately went to his aid, but there was nothing either could do. Still conscious despite his horrific wounds, he said to Ross: 'It's all right, boy, do your best.' With his son at the tiller, he continued to give orders, calling, at one point, for the 'secret books' and 'pigeon cyphers' to be thrown overboard. By then, *Nelson* was making water fast. Most of the crew were on deck, though Boon remained in the engine-room as long as he could. Crisp knew that the end could not be long delayed. Summoning his last reserves of energy, he dictated a message to be sent off by pigeon. It read: '*Nelson* being attacked by submarine. Skipper killed. Jim Howe Bank. Send assistance at once.' In all, four birds were sent, the first three circling the smack until the fourth was released. Crisp's son later reported:

After that we were making water fast and had used nearly all our ammunition, only having five rounds left, and we had to leave the ship because she was sinking. I asked the Skipper if we should take him in the boat with us but he said, 'No, throw me overboard'. This I would not do and so we had to leave him on board the smack as he was in too bad a condition to be moved. We got into the small boat, the smack sinking by the head about a quarter of an hour afterwards …

In an unpublished memoir, he added to his terse description:

All this was happening when shells were bursting around us … I then gave orders for the small boat to be got out … The crew soon did this and got into the boat leaving me and my poor father on the smack alone. I knelt down beside him and kissed him goodbye. He did not speak or make any sign that he knew what was happening, so I think my father had passed away. The crew

> ... were calling for me as the ship was on the point of sinking, so I jumped over the stern into the small boat and not long after the *Nelson*, taking my father with her, went to the bottom ...

The submarine continued to fire at the smack until the sea closed above her. Then, as the survivors rowed with the tide, she turned her attention to the *Ethel & Millie*. *Nelson*'s crew were near enough to hear 'Johnsey' Manning calling them to come aboard. But they decided it was safer where they were, a view quickly confirmed by a direct hit on the smack. What followed has been the subject of much controversy. Crisp's son later told the Naval Court of Inquiry:

> The submarine left off firing at the 'Ethel & Millie' and picked her crew up. We saw the submarine's crew line the 'Ethel & Millie's' crew up on the submarine foredeck. They tied the smack's boat up astern ... and steamed to the smack. The wind being from the south-south-east was blowing the 'Ethel & Millie' away from us into the north-north-west. We stopped rowing in case the submarine fired on us and the wind kept blowing the 'Ethel & Millie' ... Just before the 'Ethel & Millie' got out of sight a haze fell over her and we rowed into the south-east as hard as we could, the opposite direction in which the smack and the submarine were going ...

Nothing more was ever seen of Manning and his crew of six. Fearful of the consequences of being captured, *Nelson*'s crew pulled clear until, by a stroke of good fortune, a sea mist came down to hide them. Even then, Crisp took no chances. 'I thought the sub would think we would row towards the land,' he wrote, 'but instead we rowed out to sea. This we did till midnight and [then] we changed our course and headed for the land, which we knew was nearly 40 miles away.' Around daybreak they sighted a buoy, but the freshening wind was against them, blowing them further out to sea. That same afternoon they saw the Lowestoft fishery protection vessel *Dryad* and a group of minesweepers sail by. Crisp recalled:

> All the time we had a large piece of oilskin and pair of trousers tied on two oars to attract attention, but they did not see us. As night came the weather became finer and we kept pulling into the westward all night as hard as we could. At daybreak we saw some smacks straight ahead of us, but there was too much wind from the westward and we could not get to them and they went away from us in a south-westerly direction ...

Later, one of the men spotted a buoy in the distance which turned out to be Jim Howe Bank Buoy. 'We pulled up to it and made fast ... just as the tide turned about 10.30 a.m.,' noted Crisp. 'The wind was blowing hard.' They remained huddled in the boat, falling and rising with the buoy, until shortly after 1 p.m., when *Dryad* once more hove into view. Determined not to be missed again, Crisp scrambled to the top of the buoy, furiously waving his handkerchief. 'They were just going to turn away from us when they saw me waving,' he later recalled.

It was 1.45 p.m. on Friday, 17 August, almost forty-eight hours since their ordeal began and a day after one of the *Nelson*'s pigeons had brought back the first report of the fight. The following day, at a hastily convened Court of Inquiry, naval officers listened to the accounts of the eight survivors. In their report they concluded that '*Nelson* was handled in a seamanlike and brave manner' and that 'her skipper, Mr T. Crisp, RNR, died in action, giving orders to the last minute'. Three weeks later, on 7 September, the Commodore-in-Charge at Lowestoft wrote to the Admiralty recommending that Crisp's 'exceptionally gallant conduct' be considered for recognition by 'the award of a posthumous decoration, the VC, or otherwise'. He added: 'I think it would be of great interest to the Auxiliary Patrol and the country generally to hear of this Officer's gallant conduct and death.' Lloyd George plainly thought so too. His statement in the Commons pre-empted by four days the announcement of the Victoria Cross to Thomas Crisp. The same *London Gazette* carried news of the awards of a DSM to his son and a Bar to Percy Ross's DSM.

Nowhere in any of the accounts was mention made of the involvement of the *Ethel and Millie*. Her crew's fate remains uncertain to this day. The men were last seen as prisoners on the submarine's casing. Originally reported 'missing', they were officially given up for dead on 10 March 1918. In the circumspect words of the Admiralty, they were 'presumed to have lost their lives on 16 August 1917 [*sic*]'. A number of theories have been put forward as to their likely fate. They include the possibility that they may have been cast off in their small boat after questioning and subsequently lost. The most persistent speculation of all has it that they were either murdered or left to drown. One theory that can certainly be disregarded is that the crew of *Ethel and Millie* remained aboard and were lost when the submarine was sunk before reaching port, for German records show that the U-boat, identified as the Flanders Flotilla boat *UC-63*, not only made it safely back to her Bruges base but also returned with useful intelligence gleaned from the interrogation of *Ethel and Millie*'s crew. In his report of the action, Oberleutnant zur See Karsten von Heydebreck stated that he initially opened fire from a range of 5,400m. His version of the encounter continued:

Shots are close to targets. On one boat [the *Nelson*] a hit was noticed. Both vessels returned fire at once with a 5cm gun sited amidships. I increase distance to 6,000–7,000m. Both boats, of which one is fitted with an engine, try very skilfully to get closer … At 5.30 p.m. the motor boat starts sinking after pigeons have been released and the crew has abandoned ship. After a short pause the gunnery duel with the remaining vessel continues until the crew abandons ship at 7.20 p.m. having been hit … When I was certain that the vessel had been abandoned I closed in and sent over a demolition party … We captured a complete 5cm gun with a few shells, an underwater listening device, several lists … and orders of the Lowestoft Naval Base. The booty was transferred with great difficulty on the small rowing dinghy to the U-boat … The crew consisted of two Royal Navy gunners and four other men who, contrary to a found order, were undoubtedly wearing civilian dress. During the whole engagement the vessel flew the English Merchant Navy flag …

Though von Heydebreck made no mention of taking *Ethel and Millie*'s crew onboard *UC-63*, his report makes clear that they were remarkably forthcoming about their clandestine role. In addition to disclosing operational tactics, they apparently revealed the number of armed smacks based at Lowestoft, the nature of their disguise and the amount of ammunition carried. They also admitted that 'the gunners have strict orders to put on uniforms before leaving port', something *Ethel and Millie*'s gun team had signally failed to do. Yet for all his displeasure at what he regarded as a clear contravention of the rules of naval warfare, there was nothing in what he wrote to suggest that he had sought retribution or inflicted summary punishment on the hapless crew. To the contrary, he applauded their brave effort, observing that their gunnery was rendered ineffective only by the 'great distance'. In a fitting epitaph to the struggle, he concluded: 'The two crews … fought tenaciously and only abandoned ship after sinking following artillery [*sic*] hits or running out of ammunition …'

The sea was in Thomas Crisp's blood. His father was a master shipwright and boatbuilder, who at one time owned eight ships, and his grandfather was a master cooper, plying his trade on the beach. He was born in Alma Street, Lowestoft, on 28 April 1876, one of a large family of five sons and two daughters to William Crisp and Mary Ann (née Patteson). There was never any doubt that the sea and fishing would loom large in his life. He was educated at the Baptist School, and then St John's National School, where the close proximity of the harbour with all its bustling activity proved irresistible. His 'marked preference for quayside adventure to school routine' led him into trouble, and he was eventually removed by his father to the British School in London Road, 'where there were no tapering masts or gleaming iceblocks to lure him away'.

Attempts to interest him in pursuing his father's trade as a shipwright were all in vain. Boatbuilding held little fascination compared with sailing. His first sea voyage after leaving school was in a Lowestoft drifter around the west coast of Britain. After four or five years of herring and mackerel fishing, he decided to go in for trawling and soon became third hand on a Lowestoft sailing smack.

In search of wider horizons he joined the Merchant Navy, shipping aboard a liner plying between London and New York. Later, he was in the steamer *Mobile* when she narrowly escaped being sunk following a collision with another vessel. He remained a deep sea sailor for about two years, attaining the rank of quartermaster.

During one of his spells ashore he met Harriet Elizabeth Alp, a fisherman's daughter from Aldeby, near Beccles. They were married in 1895, settled in Burgh St Peter, a small village 6 miles inland from Lowestoft, and produced a family of two sons and a daughter. By then a senior seaman, much travelled and experienced but lacking the necessary qualifications for further advancement, Tom Crisp decided to return to trawling and quickly secured first a mate's and then a skipper's certificate.

In 1902 he joined the fishing firm owned by the Chambers family of Lowestoft. The latest addition to their fleet of smacks was a 61-ton wooden ketch named the *George Borrow* (LT956) and for the next thirteen years the greater part of his life would be spent in her, initially as mate and then, once he gained his ticket, as master.

It was a hard life, not made any easier by the 6-mile hike home across the marshes after every fishing trip. Eventually, in 1907, the family moved to Lowestoft, firstly to Tunning Street, then Essex Street and, finally, shortly before the war, to a house in Stanford Street. Like so many fishing families at the time, the Crisps were a close-knit unit, who lived frugally, made their own entertainment and occasionally supplemented their income by taking in holiday visitors. Described as 'a homely man', Tom Crisp had neither the money nor time to spend on hobbies; it was estimated that nine-tenths of his adult life was spent at sea.

An able skipper, well-liked and respected by his peers, Crisp had a reputation for never cheating or exploiting his crew. His eldest son

Tom, who joined the *George Borrow* as a 14-year-old apprentice in 1913, later recalled: 'Father was one of the best. He could always get a crew … He was a very fair man.' Much of his success was based on his knowledge of the waters off the East Anglian coast, and his almost intuitive understanding of the sea's changing moods. In common with most other skippers, he knew the fishing grounds, with their myriad sandbars, like the back of his hand, even though his only navigational instruments were a quadrant and a greased 'lead-line'. According to his son, 'All they did, to get from one place to another, was throw the lead-line overboard and when it hit the bottom, whatever was on the bottom adhered to the grease, and when they pulled it up they knew exactly where they were in the North Sea.' Such was his skill, said Tom jr, that his father could find his way back to port through the thickest sea mist. Superstition also played a part. As was the custom among Lowestoft fishermen, Crisp wore an earring, not for ornament but for the simple reason that it was believed to 'improve his eyesight'.

Tom Crisp was at sea, fishing in the *George Borrow*, on the day war was declared. His son later wrote:

We did not know there was a war on until we came in four days after and found the harbour full of smacks that were being kept in. This did not last many days, when off to sea again we went, not caring about the war, and did not think there was one on until one day we were reminded there was by [the sight of] three very large HM Ships passing very close to us. Their names were *Aboukir*, *Cressy* and *Hogue*. These three beautiful ships, as they were then, were sunk the next day by a German submarine with the loss of hundreds of lives. For several weeks after this calamity, we were reminded of it by the constant sighting of bodies floating about the sea.

Crisp continued fishing at least until the following February, when his son quit to join the navy, advancing his age from 16 to 18 in the process. By then, the fishermen's 'phoney war' was over. Increasingly their work was being disrupted by enemy submarines which would approach groups of trawlers and order the crews into their small boats while they sank their vessels with explosive charges or gunfire. The fishing fleet was being decimated. In July 1915 twenty smacks were captured and sunk off Lowestoft. The following month, the *George Borrow*, trawling some 15 miles east-north-east of Cromer, fell in with a submarine and was sunk by time-bomb. Whether Crisp was aboard her at the time is not clear, but it was around this time that he gave up fishing and undertook work for the Admiralty ashore. His time away from the sea, however, proved brief. At the request of some fishing skippers, the navy had begun arming some smacks with 3-pounder guns, with marked success. As the number of 'decoy' boats grew, so did the need to find volunteers to sail in them. Crisp was recommended as a likely candidate for a command to the port's naval intelligence officer, George Atkinson, who was charged with recruiting men for 'special service'. 'I found him temporarily ashore at the net factory baling nets for export,' wrote Atkinson.

Having been enlisted into the Royal Naval Reserve, Crisp went as an ordinary seaman in one boat, then as a mate in another, before being made skipper, the most junior commissioned rank, in command of one of the armed smacks. By September 1916 he was able to pull enough strings to get his son, who had been serving in drifters at Dover, back to Lowestoft, where he joined one of the decoy boats as a deck-hand. Eventually, they joined forces in early 1917, when Tom Crisp was given command of the *I'll Try*, a veteran of 'special service', with his newly promoted son acting as mate. Their first action together was a memorable one. It took place on 1 February 1917, the first day of Germany's campaign of unrestricted submarine warfare. *I'll Try* was operating some 17 miles south-east of Southwold in company with another armed smack, the *Boy Alfred*, commanded by Skipper W.S. Wharton DSC, when they sighted two submarines. Tom Crisp jr later recalled the encounter:

> The Captain of the Subs must have been very 'green' because he came right up to the *Boy Alfred* and told them to abandon ship as they were going to sink them. Of course, the *Boy Alfred* opened up with her 12-pounder and that was the end of that sub. But the other submarine, who [*sic*] was some distance off, and saw everything, took evasive action. The time was just after midday [and] this submarine apparently made up her mind to destroy us, so a hide and seek started with us and our submarine. First he would come up one side of us, then the other, with just the tip of his periscope showing. I suppose he was trying to get into a position to torpedo us, but as we had a motor in, we could easily turn and twist and each time we saw the periscope we went straight for it ...

The dangerous game of cat-and-mouse lasted more than two hours, before Crisp attempted to lure the submarine to the surface by steering for home. For half an hour there was no sign of the U-boat. But then, just as Crisp turned about to renew the search, he saw his quarry suddenly surface, roughly 150yd away on the starboard beam, heading straight for *I'll Try*. Tom Crisp jr recorded:

> As soon as he saw us he let go a torpedo which missed our stern by inches. It was the motor pushing us along that saved us. We trained our gun on to her ... By now she was only about 20yd away and we let her have a 13-pounder right between the conning tower and deck. It blew the whole part of the sub to pieces. The sub went down head first with her stern sticking up in the air and the sea now covered with oil ...

According to the official report, the submarine's plunge was so quick that there was 'no time for a second shot'. Based on the graphic evidence of the smacksmen who were convinced that both U-boats had been sunk, two claims were made. Although subsequent research has shown that no enemy submarines were lost that day, it had been a daring contest for which Wharton and Crisp well deserved the Bar to the DSC and a DSC (gazetted on 23 March), which they later received, together with grants of £200 apiece. So impressed were the naval authorities with Crisp's coolness and boat-handling skills that they offered him 'a responsible position' on board a larger Q-ship. But as his wife was then terminally ill, he chose to remain skipper of his smack, soon rechristened *Nelson*. Harriet Crisp eventually died on 12 June 1917 and Tom survived her by little more than two months.

His Victoria Cross was presented to Tom Crisp jr by the king at a Buckingham Palace investiture on 19 December 1917, during which he also received his DSM, awarded for the same action. The following July Tom, by then a skipper in charge of a drifter operating out of the Shetlands, proudly wore both his own and his father's decorations at his wedding.

Lowestoft itself showed similar pride in its most distinguished fisherman hero. In May 1919 a portrait of Tom Crisp VC, DSC, was unveiled by the town's mayor in the Lowestoft Free Library, and another framed photograph was placed in St John's School, before being removed to form part of a display in the local maritime museum. More memorials followed. In 1920 one of eight bells in St Margaret's Church, Lowestoft, was dedicated to his memory and became known as the VC Bell, and forty-two years later the town council named a road on the new Gunton estate after him.

One of the more unusual monuments to him was a seat made from the *Nelson*'s taffrail which was dredged up years after the war, with the original name 'G & E' still clearly visible. Placed in the Free Library, it was destroyed when the building was bombed during the Second World War.

His medals are in the safekeeping of Lowestoft town council, having been presented for public display by Tom Crisp jr on the 50th anniversary of the award of his father's VC, in a ceremony attended by another former member of *Nelson*'s crew, Ted Fenn. They were given as symbols of peace and remembrance for the sacrifices made by Lowestoft's fishermen. 'I should like to think,' Tom jr told the distinguished gathering, 'that all who look at these will be reminded how fruitless war is and of the misery it brings to everyone. And I hope they will try to prevent war.'

J.H. CARLESS
Heligoland Bight, 17 November 1917

In the early afternoon of 21 February 1920 a crowd gathered outside Walsall's Free Library. They came to witness the unveiling of a bronze bust of an ordinary seaman who had died in extraordinary circumstances. The ceremony was performed by Rear Admiral Sir Walter Cowan. Once described by Sir Roger Keyes as 'the gallantest little sportsman I ever met', Cowan had seen many courageous acts during his distinguished career, but none was more heroic than the exploit which gained for John Henry Carless the posthumous award of the Victoria Cross. It was, he told the crowd of onlookers, 'the bravest deed I ever saw'.

The action to which he referred had taken place in the mine-infested waters of the Heligoland Bight on 17 November 1917, in what was the last 'big ship' engagement of the war. Following the titanic, if inconclusive, Battle of Jutland a stalemate had settled over the North Sea. It was a sign not merely of caution on both sides, but of the subordination of the Royal Navy's 'big ships' to the more critical submarine campaign. While the Grand Fleet lost destroyers and light cruisers to anti-submarine work, the High Seas Fleet was increasingly employed in covering minesweeping operations designed to ease the passage of U-boats.

To Admiral Beatty such sorties represented a rare chance to lure a portion of the enemy fleet into a trap. His strategy was simple but effective: to establish more extensive minefields, thereby forcing the minesweepers and their battleship escorts to venture deeper into the North Sea. By the autumn of 1917 this strategy appeared to be paying off. Mine-clearing operations were reported on an almost daily basis, ranging as far as 150 miles from their home bases. The time was ripe for action.

At 4.30 a.m. on 17 November a British force, comprising 1st Cruiser Squadron, 1st and 6th Light Cruiser Squadrons and 1st Battlecruiser Squadron, bolstered by the battlecruiser *New Zealand*, under Vice-Admiral Sir W.C. Pakenham, left Rosyth in the hope of dealing a surprise blow. They were to rendezvous on the edge of the vast mine barrier, although it was accepted that any chase might carry them into the minefields. Beatty's plan, however, had one major flaw. Poor staffwork had resulted in commanders leaving port with charts showing the Bight's minefields at various stages of their development. Whereas Rear Admiral C.L. Napier, commanding 1st Cruiser Squadron, had charts showing a large danger area regarded as an 'absolute barrier', Rear Admiral E.S. Alexander (6th Light Cruiser Squadron) and Commodore Cowan (1st Light Cruiser Squadron) were blissfully ignorant of the wider threat. It was a recipe for chaos, but for a while fortune favoured Pakenham.

That morning, as luck would have it, the enemy were engaged in a *Stichfahrt*, a so-called 'thrust voyage', designed to sweep in the precise area that Pakenham's force had chosen for their rendezvous. The minesweepers had as their escorts eight destroyers and a covering force provided by the 2nd Scouting Group, comprising four light cruisers and the battleships *Kaiser* and *Kaiserin*, under Rear Admiral von Reuter.

Courageous, flying Adm. Napier's flag, was the first to sight the enemy force around 7.30 a.m. The Germans were taken completely by surprise. The first they knew was when a roaring storm of 15-inch shells splashed around the destroyers and minesweepers. But as so often, the uncertainty was not limited to one side. As the enemy retreated, masked by an effective smokescreen, Napier had no idea of what he was running up against. In those frustrating early moments, he reported only 'occasional and baffling glimpses' of the enemy. Suddenly, at 7.45 a.m., a look-out aboard *Caledon*, Cdre Cowan's flagship, sighted a ship's smoke. Five minutes later two German light cruisers hove into view. Opening fire at 'extreme range', Cowan 'proceeded in chase at full speed …'

For many in *Caledon* those opening shots in what became known as the Battle of Heligoland Bight represented a baptism of fire. The ship's company was a new one, with many young, inexperienced seamen bolstered by a few older hands. Cowan had raised his pennant on the ship in June, following his promotion. Among other arrivals that month was a young ordinary seaman, who had confounded medical opinion to enlist. Doctors feared that John Carless had a weak heart, but his determination to fight had eventually been rewarded. Following a spell in destroyers, he joined *Caledon*, becoming rammer on no. 2 gun, a 6-inch weapon, under Petty Officer George R. Greenfield. Like many of his shipmates, Carless had been caught unawares by the thrust into the Bight less than a week after his 21st birthday. His last letter home before sailing closed abruptly: 'Can't write any more – had a sudden call.'

The fighting that morning was, by turns, frenetic and frustrating. For the most part the action was contested amid a smother of smoke. Extracts from Cowan's report give an indication of the confusion:

> At 07.54 ... it became evident that the enemy force consisted of four Light Cruisers accompanied by Destroyers. At the same time they altered course ... and the 1st Cruiser Squadron turned to starboard with 1st Light Cruiser Squadron formed on their starboard bow, all still firing; then the enemy altered course ... under cover of a smokescreen, made by funnel smoke and smoke balls on the water. The enemy reappeared from the smokescreen at about 08.02, two Light Cruisers being sighted between the smokescreens ... range estimated at 13,000yd. We first came under fire at 08.04 and concentrated in pairs on the second of the four enemy Light Cruisers. This fire appeared to be effective and caused many alterations of course on their part, in spite of which they appeared to be drawing away and necessitated our firing deliberately at extreme range ...

To Roger Keyes, Cowan added:

> It was a good hard straightfor'd chase and shoot, bothered to death by smokescreens, far too busy & interested to think of torpedoes and mines of which there were plenty & at the latter end rather anxious about ammunition, my bow gun shot away all its outfit (200) & 20 as well, we'd 50 rounds a gun left ...

Caledon did not escape lightly. She was hit twice during the pursuit: first by a 6-inch shell that wrecked the upper chart house and exploded on the lower bridge, raining shards of shrapnel on to the exposed gun crews below. In that moment two signalmen were killed and the ship's captain, Commander Henry Harrison-Wallace, slightly wounded. But the heaviest loss was among the men around no. 2 gun. Two were killed outright and all but three were injured, some grievously. Incredibly the hand-worked gun was still operable, and despite the terrible carnage, PO Greenfield set about keeping it in action, helped by an uninjured 17-year-old sight-setter, Boy First Class George Mann, and John Carless, the gun's rammer.

Carless presented a pitiful sight. His stomach had been laid bare and he was bleeding profusely from a fatal wound to the abdomen.

How he managed even to stand with such horrifying injuries was a mystery. But he did, his sole thought to keep the gun working. What torture he must have experienced can only be imagined. For several minutes this tall, blood-soaked figure kept himself going on guts and determination alone. No accounts tell how long he persisted, but it was long enough to affect all who saw him. Officers manning the lower bridge watched in awe as he lifted one shell and then helped clear away the other casualties spread around the gun. 'He collapsed once but again got up, tried again and cheered on the new crew,' wrote Cowan. 'He then fell again and died.'

Throughout no. 2 gun's ordeal, the action raged. Elsewhere in *Caledon* exhausted gun crews toiled to the point of collapse. At one gun, Cowan said, the 'loaders were physically dead beat and had to be relieved'. For a while it seemed as though their sacrifice would be rewarded. Despite 'distractingly effective' smokescreens, one enemy light cruiser was seen to be 'well on fire aft'. Cowan turned his attention towards another vessel, lagging at the rear, which was 'frequently and well hit'. But just as victory seemed within his grasp, it was snatched away by the appearance of the battleships *Kaiser* and *Kaiserin*. Their sudden intervention effectively ended the pursuit. Cowan wrote: 'It was no good going on ... to let them score off us.'

By then the British light cruiser squadrons were the only units in action, Adm. Napier having abandoned the chase on the edge of what was marked on his chart as a 'danger area'. Under covering fire from *Repulse*, Cowan reluctantly retired. He later wrote: 'It is a matter of the very greatest regret to me that the rear Light Cruiser escaped, as it was only a question of sea room and we must have stopped her. Her firing towards the end was very intermittent and she was hit again and again, but the appearance of the two "Bayerns" just saved her.'

During the final stages *Caledon* had been hit again by a 12-inch shell from one of the two enemy battleships. It tore a hole just above the waterline, wrecking the warrant officers' mess and flooding adjacent flats. Characteristically Cowan dismissed it as 'nothing to matter much'.

Thus ended what the irrepressible Cowan called '2¼ hours ... shooting & steaming & hoping'. The following day, while still at sea, the British buried their dead. There were nineteen in all: the five from the *Caledon* included John Henry Carless.

The Heligoland Bight action was a close-run affair and, as far as the British were concerned, a missed opportunity. Having surprised an inferior enemy force far from its base, they had failed to bring it to decisive action. The failure was due, in large measure, to the confusion over the charts, though a degree of timidity had also been displayed by some commanders. It was not a criticism, however, that could be levelled at Cowan. His relentless pursuit of the light cruisers earned high praise from Beatty, while the fortitude of the crews was a redeeming feature of an otherwise disappointing engagement. In a long list of recommendations made four days after the action, Cowan described the behaviour of the officers and men of the *Caledon* as 'very steady and well drilled'. Most notable of all had been the performance of the men serving no. 2 gun. PO Greenfield, who had kept his gun in action, was awarded a CGM for his determined leadership, which ensured that only one salvo was missed during the entire fight. Boy Mann's bravery was also noted. But Cowan reserved most of his praise for John Carless. 'My feeling is', he wrote, 'that his memory is worthy of the Victoria Cross as he not only showed a very bright and memorable example but he also, whilst mortally wounded, continued to do effective work against the King's enemies.'

The Lords of the Admiralty agreed. On 17 May 1918, six months to the day after his gallant death, the *London Gazette* announced the posthumous award of the Victoria Cross to (ONJ 43703, Po) Ordinary Seaman J.H. Carless 'for most conspicuous bravery and devotion to duty'.

John Henry Carless was born on 11 November 1896 at Renwick Terrace, Frederick Street, Walsall, the second son of John Thomas Carless, a journeyman brass caster, and Elizabeth (née Smith). He grew up in the town's working-class Caldmore district and was educated at St Mary's, The Mount, Roman Catholic School, where he was noted for his sporting prowess. An enthusiastic and gifted footballer, as well as being a strong swimmer and keen dancer, Carless captained St Mary's team and in 1910 represented Walsall in the final of the English Schools Soccer Shield, earning a gold medal.

On leaving school he spent two or three years working at the Alma Tube Works, turning out for a number of junior football clubs in his spare time. At the outbreak of war Carless, although only 17, joined the rush to enlist. Surprisingly, and to his bitter disappointment, he was initially turned down, not on account of his age but because of his 'poor' health. Three or four times army medical boards rejected his application because of 'heart trouble', though Carless would always maintain that it was 'purely imaginary on the part of the doctors'.

He changed his job, joining Messrs Price of South Street, Walsall, as a currier, and, undeterred by his previous failures, continued with his attempts to follow his friends into the Services. Finally, at the fourth or fifth attempt, he was successful and on 1 September 1915 he joined the Royal Navy as an ordinary seaman, although how he managed to get through the medical examination was never made clear.

Carless served aboard HMS *Vindictive* and a number of destroyers, taking part in several minor actions off the Belgian coast, before being transferred to the *Caledon* in June 1917. His eventful service had already been marked by a high degree of selfless gallantry. When a hospital ship sank, he was among a party of volunteers who assisted in the hazardous rescue of hundreds of passengers. On another occasion he braved a serious boiler-room fire to save an injured stoker trapped by the flames. Yet he came through them all unscathed, his only injury being an accidental wound to his right hand sustained during gunnery drill. His good fortune, however, finally deserted him six days after his 21st birthday when the *Caledon* encountered units of the German High Seas Fleet in the Heligoland Bight.

His courage and spirited show of defiance made a deep impression on his shipmates. Many wrote to his parents, praising his actions. Among the letters was one from Stoker Waterfield, who also came from Walsall, who declared: 'He was a noble lad, worthy of a hundred VCs for he feared nothing as he stood at his post of duty with ram-rod in hand. He laughed the whole time, and died smiling. He was a son to be proud of ... ' *Caledon*'s captain agreed. Cdr Henry Harrison-Wallace described the young seaman as 'a good fellow'. He continued: 'He was straight, he took a great interest in games, and when it was time to have a skylark he was in the very first row. In the "sing-songs" on board he was always ready to amuse his shipmates, and the last song he sang just before his death was called "Long Live the King".' Writing to his parents before the VC was announced, Cdr Harrison-Wallace told them:

> He was a most gallant lad and very promising. We feel his loss on the ship very much, and all send their sincere sympathy to you and his family in your loss. You will be very proud and have the satisfaction of knowing that he did his duty so bravely and gallantly, fighting his King and Country's enemy – the finest death a man can have. I buried him at sea and he had a very impressive funeral, attended by all his shipmates and the Commodore.

Nine days after the VC was gazetted, St Mary's RC Church in Walsall was crowded for a memorial service attended by a host of civic dignitaries. The following month Mr and Mrs Carless travelled to London to receive their son's Cross from King George V at a ceremony in the quadrangle of Buckingham Palace on 22 June.

Following the award there was a call for 'some fitting and permanent memorial' in his home town. A public subscription was launched which culminated in the unveiling of the bronze bust by Adm. Cowan in February 1920. Created by R.J. Emerson and set on a base of Portland stone, the memorial bears the word 'Valour' and the VC citation. Replicas of the bust were given to his parents and Cdr Harrison-Wallace, who, in turn, presented the town with the battle-scarred White Ensign borne by the *Caledon* throughout the action. For decades after, the Carless bust was the scene of a poignant act of remembrance performed every Armistice Sunday by his sister, Dora, on behalf of the family.

John Carless's gallantry was further recognised in Walsall by the renaming of two streets, Oxford Street in Caldmore becoming Carless Street, and Regent Street in Pleck becoming Caledon Street. Later, a locomotive was to be named the John H. Carless VC in his honour and a painting was commissioned by the Walsall Services Memorial Club. It was hung there until the club's closure in 1961. It was eventually presented to the town, after being found in an antique shop.

The Victoria Cross earned at the cost of his life passed, in turn, from his parents to his brother William, and then to his nephew John Henry Carless, who was named after him. On his death from heart trouble in 1986, the medal was bequeathed to Walsall Council on behalf of the town, where it remains a proud symbol of sublime devotion to duty from another age. Such selfless loyalty was echoed by the Mayor of Walsall at the crowded memorial service held sixty-eight years earlier. In recalling John Carless's short and 'inspiring' life, he repeated a story told by one of his shipmates:

> Carless and another were once discussing how they would wish to die. Carless, pointing to his gun, replied: 'I wish to die standing by my gun.' The other said, chaffingly: 'People say a live cow is better than a dead hero,' and Carless replied: 'Let the others be the live cows; I will be the dead hero.'

G.S. WHITE

The Dardanelles, 28 January 1918

The captain of the British destroyer *Lizard* could scarcely conceal his irritation. For months Lieutenant Norman Ohlenschlager had patrolled the entrance to the Dardanelles in the hope that the *Goeben* and her consort, the light cruiser *Breslau*, might venture out. But such was the lack of activity that the prospect seemed only marginally less likely than the High Seas Fleet sallying forth in strength from their home bases. It was a measure of how deep-rooted that conviction had become that when a cruiser answering to *Breslau*'s description was sighted off the Dardanelles on Sunday, 20 January 1918, Ohlenschlager reacted in annoyance rather than excitement, so certain was he that it was a mistake.

But it was true – and as he scanned the waters beyond Cape Kephalo he received the rudest of awakenings. 'Where one usually saw an empty horizon,' he observed, 'there was, without any doubt at all, *Breslau*, steering almost straight towards us.' The unexpected had happened at last. Within seconds the pre-arranged warning signal 'Goblo' was flashed to the fleet, heralding the start of a calamitous sequence of events that would culminate in the last Victoria Cross action of the Dardanelles campaign.

Since the evacuation of the peninsula, British ambitions in the region had given way to containment. Minefields were laid and the number of ships reduced. Where once there was a screen of destroyers (four by day and six by night) guarding the entrance to the Dardanelles, there were now just two, supported by a single battleship, the out-dated pre-dreadnought *Agamemnon*, at Mudros. The only other vessels were two monitors in Kusu Bay and a collection of drifters. To add insult to injury, *E12*, the only submarine in the area, was out of action with engine trouble.

Vice-Admiral Hubert von Robeur-Paschwitz could scarcely have chosen a better moment to attack. His objective was to destroy British shipping near the entrance to the Dardanelles before raiding Mudros. Passing through the mist-shrouded Dardanelles at night, *Goeben* and *Breslau*, rechristened *Yavuz* and *Midilli* by the Turks, emerged with surprise complete. Before the British could react, *Goeben* had opened fire on the look-out station at Kephalo. Within minutes the monitors *Raglan* and *M28* were reduced to blazing wrecks. The way seemed clear to Mudros. But then disaster struck. Just as the two ships were preparing to open fire, the *Breslau* struck a mine. Despite the danger to herself, *Goeben* went to her aid, only to set off another mine. Minutes later any rescue was rendered useless as *Breslau* detonated four more mines and rapidly began to sink. Under attack from aircraft, *Goeben* retreated towards the entrance to the Straits, where she was shaken by yet another mine. Though listing, she was still able to make headway and would have made good her escape but for a miscalculation by her captain. Nearing Nagara Point he mistook a buoy and the cruiser ran aground.

For the next six days *Goeben* remained stranded despite frenzied efforts to free her. To the British, it was a heaven-sent opportunity to avenge past humiliations. Twice before, *Goeben* had evaded them with appalling consequences and they were determined not to let her slip away again. Vice-Admiral Sir S.A. Gough-Calthorpe, C.-in-C. Mediterranean Fleet, was instructed to take personal charge with orders that 'every effort should be made to destroy the *Goeben*'. Day after day aircraft braved heavy fire to drop 15 tons of bombs around the ship. But it was all to no avail. Although two direct hits were recorded, the attacks caused only superficial damage and merely hindered salvage work. An attempt to destroy her by long-distance bombardment proved no more successful. The only remaining option was to mount a submarine attack.

Despite her defects, *E12*'s commander had volunteered to have a go as soon as *Goeben* was reported aground. But he was turned down on the grounds 'of the additional risk he would have to take with only one engine available for recharging purposes'. Instead, it was decided to await the arrival of reinforcements: *E2* from the dockyards at Malta where she had been refitting and *E14* from Corfu. By 24 January the three submarines were assembled at Mudros where the final selection proved straightforward. *E12* was already ruled out while *E2* had the handicap of a bow tube being out of action and her crew was the least experienced of the new arrivals. That left *E14*, Courtney Boyle's old boat and a veteran of the Dardanelles.

Her commander was Lieutenant-Commander Geoffrey Saxton White, a 31-year-old submariner of long experience and a friend of Boyle, whom he had succeeded in the autumn of 1916. Described as a 'thick-set, quiet, competent and very modest man', White was well-liked by his crew. Calthorpe was impressed by his spirit. 'A more devoted officer could not have been found for such a dangerous task,' he wrote.

Neither man was under any illusions about the hazards to be overcome. As the Official History states, 'the obstructions off Chanak were far more formidable than they had been in the early days of the Dardanelles campaign'. Shore batteries covered every yard of the narrow waterway and since the glorious days of Holbrook, Boyle and Nasmith, additional minefields had been laid, including one between Cape Helles and Kum Kale as recently as 20 January. To these were added patrol craft armed with depth-charges and highly sensitive hydrophones designed to detect submerged submarines at a considerable distance.

It had been more than two years since a submarine had ventured through the Straits, but White was optimistic about his chances. At a conference in Mudros, he affirmed his conviction that *E14* could reach Nagara and deal a fatal blow to the *Goeben*. Determined to plan his attack down to the last detail, he flew as an observer on one of the bombing raids against the cruiser. His aircraft was forced to take evasive action, but White believed he had seen enough to convince him that, provided he could get through the Straits, a beam shot fired from close by the European shore could finish off the pride of the Turkish navy. In discussions with Commander K.M. Bruce, who was in overall command of the operation, White agreed that the defenders' heightened state of readiness meant that the passage would have to be made at night, thus adding to the difficulties of navigating. Precise timing would be difficult, but he hoped to be in a position to make an attack in the early morning while the defences were distracted by yet another air strike. In doing so, he risked being hit by a stray bomb, but on balance he considered the advantages outweighed the disadvantages.

E14 was a hive of activity as preparations for the attack intensified. As well as stocking up with fuel, provisions and water, new 'knives' and 'jumper wires' were fitted to help her clear the nets and obstacles that lay ahead. By Friday, 25 January, all was ready. According to Able Seaman Reuben Mitchell, an Australian submariner and veteran of the

AE2 who was fore-end torpedo man aboard *E14*, the crew was 'up to scratch with everything' and itching to 'do the dirty on "Monsieur Goeben"'. But then the weather intervened. A gale blew in, and a thick cloud brought a temporary halt to flying operations. *E14* was ordered to go alongside the seaplane tender *Ark Royal*. While doing so, she grounded on a mud bank and was stuck fast till the end of Saturday. There was a further delay as the fuel discharged to help free her was replenished, and it was only in the late afternoon of 27 January that the mission, described by Calthorpe as 'exceedingly hazardous', was finally able to get under way.

Heartened by the promise of fine weather the following day, White left Imbros at 6.30 p.m., accompanied by a single destroyer as far as the entrance to the Dardanelles. Five hours later, as the RNAS were preparing for their next bombing sortie, *E14*'s crew went to their diving stations, and at 11.45 p.m. she submerged to pass beneath the freshly laid mine-field guarding the opening of the Straits. Her presence had not gone unnoticed. From Mavro Island, close to the Asian shore, British lookouts, ignorant of the mission, reported sighting a U-boat and duly raised the alarm. Though swiftly cancelled, the message may well have been inter-cepted by the Turks, thus placing them on their guard. Either way, it was the last confirmed British sighting of *E14* for at least twelve hours.

Dawn broke to the roar of aircraft over Nagara. On time and according to plan, they swooped to attack only to make the shattering discovery that the sea was empty. *Goeben* had vanished. Nor was there any sign of *E14*, until around 11 a.m., when a seaplane flying over the lower Straits saw puffs of smoke from the shore batteries and white plumes marking the fall of shells. The observer could not make out who or what they were aiming at, but eventually, near Kum Kale, he noticed an explosion, followed by shockwaves spreading in a widening circle across the sea. Although he did not know it then, he had just witnessed the end of *E14*'s gallant odyssey.

Back at Mudros, in the absence of any news, the awful truth sank in that the operation had misfired. But it was another five months before the first hard facts emerged. They were contained in a letter written by *E14*'s coxswain, Petty Officer Robert Perkins, from a Turkish labour camp at Eski Hissar, Guebzeh, in Asia Minor. Outlining their mission's failure, he wrote of the outstanding heroism displayed by Geoffrey White:

> It was a credit to us all to think that we had such a brave cap-tain, and, sir, if only I could mention a few things about him; but owing to his coolness he saved the boat half a dozen times. It is a pity that no officer was saved to tell the tale ...

Only after the war when the survivors returned home could that tale be fully told.

After leaving Imbros, White made good progress into the Dardanelles. To avoid the newly laid minefields around Kephez, he took the boat down to 100ft. The night sky was jet black, and he was forced to rely on dead reckoning to reach Sari Siglar Bay. It was an agonising passage, hour after hour marked by the eerie scraping of mine cables along the boat's hull. Now and again, he took *E14* up to periscope depth in an attempt to check his position, but the darkness blotted out all landmarks. Instead, he was forced to take the boat deeper, to 150ft, until the scraping ceased.

At 3 a.m., *E14* passed the first net safely, but others were snagged, one of them forcing White to go astern before diving to 160ft to clear the obstruction. Around 5.30 a.m., he brought her to periscope depth. It was still dark, but the vague shape of cliffs to port and low land to starboard convinced him he was through the minefields and closing the Narrows. So far, according to Petty Officer Perkins, the various knocks and scrapes had caused 'no damage', and *E14* was able to continue unhindered until about 6 a.m., when she struck a net that deflected her onto a sandbank. Unable to manoeuvre free, and with daylight fast approaching, White decided to risk surfacing to investigate. Hurrying onto the conning tower, he searched in vain for the cause of the problem. Nothing being obvious, he called for one man to stand by the voice pipe to relay orders to his number one, Lieutenant Jack Blissett, while he climbed down onto the boat's casing and walked out along the bows to take a closer look. It was a desperately brave act. *E14* was within easy range of any number of Turkish shore batteries, and there were a number of craft visible in the darkness. That none noticed the stranded submarine was in part due to the fact that the shore lights were pointed skyward in search of aircraft. Even so, White was taking no chances. Before taking his lonely walk, he made it clear that the safety of the submarine and her crew should not be compromised, telling Blissett to 'dive at once if he sang out and leave him to look after himself'. In spite of the danger, he succeeded in removing the obstacle from the bows, calling back instructions to go 'full astern' until, at last, *E14* slid clear.

His hazardous foray also yielded an unexpected bonus: not only could he recognise Chanak opposite them, but he could also see the two buoys marking the entrance to the 'Gate', the channel through the minefields protecting the Narrows. Back inside the submarine, he took *E14* into deep water, descending to depths of 170ft and 190ft, until all the nets were cleared. So far as White was aware, nothing now stood between him and his quarry. 'Luck was with us,' observed Perkins. But not for much longer.

According to *E14*'s coxswain, the search for *Goeben* then began. He reckoned the submarine travelled a mile or two beyond Nagara in a vain hunt for the battlecruiser. The attack had been scheduled for 8 a.m., but half an hour before that *E14* was at periscope depth with White surveying the shore. In a letter written shortly after his release from captivity, AS Mitchell recalled:

> The skipper searched round and said: "God, she's gone". [Then] he measured off on the chart the distance to the Sea of Marmora, evidently weighing his chances of catching our prey on her way to Constantinople. But the battery was getting low and he had to abandon that idea ... "I'm not going back without firing a 'fish' after coming all this way. I'll have a look at Nagara" was the words the captain used. "There are a couple of ships," he said, "alongside the quay. Get the starboard tube ready".

In charge of the two bow tubes, Mitchell did as instructed, waiting until White gave the order to 'fire'. The timing of the attack on what was later discovered to be a Turkish auxiliary vessel that had been engaged in taking ammunition off the beached *Goeben* was variously given as 8.45 a.m. and 9.13 a.m. From a depth of approximately 21ft, the torpedo leapt from *E14*. Almost immediately – or in eleven seconds, in Perkins's precise reckoning – there was what Mitchell described as a 'terrific explosion', which left his ears ringing as a 'blue flash' passed through the boat:

> All the glass lamps and gauges shattered. Light woodwork, lockers, etc, split [he wrote]. And, worst of all, water was pouring in over my head like a river. I hadn't time to replace the firing gear on the tube. I dashed my hands to the clips on the hatch overhead and screwed them up, stopping the rush of water. For instead of being holed, as I thought we were, it was the hatch forced by the explosion. I reported it "right forward" and the skipper ordered: "Take her down to 125ft".

The cause of the explosion was unclear. Some accounts suggest a faulty torpedo was to blame. Others say the torpedo may have struck a mine. Mitchell, on the other hand, claimed to have discovered in captivity that it was a depth charge. Whatever the truth, the consequences were potentially disastrous. The force of the blast lifted *E14* 10 to 15ft, and as her conning tower broke surface, the Turkish shore defences were presented with a target they could hardly miss. Though visible for only a short time, Mitchell reckoned they 'must have put two or three rounds through the conning tower'. As *E14* dived to escape the bombardment, her crew could plainly hear shells hitting the water above them. For a while, it appeared as if they were actually striking the boat, so loud and close did they seem. Those shells that did hit, thankfully, did no damage to the hull, and White was able to regain sufficient control to submerge while Turkish gunboats rushed to the scene. From close to the bottom, *E14*'s crew listened anxiously as 'small, or perhaps big, power-driven boats' passed over them. 'Each time,' wrote Mitchell, 'we half expected another depth charge ...'

In the event, none was dropped, and *E14* was able to draw clear. For some hours, they made good progress down the Straits, though control was difficult as her trim and direction became increasingly erratic. Struggling to keep her at 150ft, White was forced to come up to periscope depth on a number of occasions to check her course. Despite all the difficulties and disappointment, it seemed as though they had miraculously evaded all the obstacles in their way. As the noise of their pursuers faded, *E14*'s crew began to relax. 'We told ourselves we must be well clear of the Narrows and [would] soon [be] coming up in safety outside!!' wrote Mitchell. White even found time to indulge in a game of cards.

'All was going well,' observed Mitchell, until 1.13 p.m., when White, apparently thinking that they were beyond the Narrows, ordered the boat up to periscope depth again to fix their position. The usual drill followed, but nothing happened. Reluctantly, he gave the order to 'blow ballast'. But the moment he called for pressure to be 'shut off', *E14* lurched violently out of control. 'The boat took a mighty heave to starboard, almost turning right over,' wrote Mitchell. 'Men and everything that would move fell into the bilge ...' White straightaway re-flooded external tanks 3 and 4 so that the boat righted before plunging again. Perkins managed to check the dive at 165ft, but only with more ballast being blown. With just three bottles of high-pressure air remaining, White took the decision to surface and hope for the best.

E14 shot to the surface in a matter of seconds in clear view of the Turkish forts ranged along both shores of the Dardanelles. Spotted immediately, it was quickly hit by a shell that 'came ... right into the boat'. Unable to dive, White ordered the hatches opened only to find the conning tower flooded. After a struggle, the fore-hatch was eventually opened, and White urged those men gathered forward to 'Go on up, my lads'. By then, the boat was well down at the bows and being straddled by shells. Mitchell clambered up with White and, as the heaviest fire was coming from the Sedd el Bahr side, took shelter on the port saddle tanks.

Attempts to steer the boat from the conning tower were rendered impossible. According to Perkins, who followed White and the boat's navigator up on deck, the steering gear spindle had been shot in half, though Mitchell reckoned the wheel was simply disconnected. Either way, orders were given to steer from below with directions being shouted by White, who was all the while standing exposed on the bows.

For what seemed like half an hour to Perkins, though was probably much less, *E14* 'ran the gauntlet', bracketed by shell geysers as the Turks poured an estimated 250 shells a minute at the slow-moving target. The result was inevitable and could not long be delayed. White realised this and ordered a turn to starboard to take *E14* toward the shore in an attempt to save as many men as possible. Moments later, a shell hit the muffler box, releasing steam into the engine room and badly injuring teenage telegraphist William Prichard, who collapsed unconscious. Mitchell, who was passing down White's directions, then heard his captain shout, 'Midships!' and that was the last he ever heard from him:

> Just as I was repeating his order to the chaps on the after hatch ladder a shell landed two feet away from me and tore the plating as if it were paper … The boat had been hit many times before … but this shell must have gone through and exploded in the beam torpedo tubes, killing about ten of the crew inside. Well, a piece of shrapnel from this shell just bruised my knuckle on the third finger [and broke a piece of a ring he was wearing] … The shrapnel must have been well spent. Probably, it had gone right up in the air and was just coming down again when it hit me with no more force than a boy could throw a stone. For I actually saw it and, in fact, picked it up and handed it to the Third Officer [Drew], saying "Here you are, a bit of shrapnel for a curio". He laughed and took it. The next moment I found myself alone on the tanks. All the men, Skipper and Third Officer had suddenly disappeared …

The shell had exploded on the starboard saddle tank, killing all who were there. Seconds later, having just heard White say, 'We are in the hands of God', Perkins watched his 'mangled' body roll into the water. The fatally hit *E14* was still turning rapidly as she began to go down. Mitchell was among those swept away by the rising water:

My first thought was to get clear of the propellers and, as I was facing the boat, I laid on my back and kicked out. Just as I got in line with the stern ... the after end lifted itself in the air and down it went ... Standing on her head for a second and her propellers whizzing round and pointing skywards, she plunged under as if she had been suspended from some huge airship and dropped head first!

As *E14* dived for the last time, Mitchell spotted the injured telegraphist in the water. Prichard was wounded in the jaw and appeared to be unconscious, so Mitchell swam toward him:

I caught his hand and discovered his thumb was just about blown off, so I collared him round the waist and told him to keep up spirits, but he kept saying "I can't. I can't. I'm done!" It was fearfully cold in the water and I was afraid of getting cramps. I looked to the shore, but there was no sign of a boat coming and the infernal Turks were firing as much as they were when the boat was afloat ... One could hear the 'zip, zip' of rifle bullets. In fact, poor Prichard put his hand up once, presumably to attract the attention of the people at Kum Kale as we were close to the shore, and I'm darned if he didn't get a bullet through his wrist.

Eventually, the firing ceased, and Mitchell, growing weary from his efforts to keep Prichard from drowning, called across to another survivor to help him. Signaller Charles Timbrell swam over, and together they managed to keep the injured youngster afloat until a motor boat came out to pick them up. Only nine men from *E14*'s gallant company of thirty-nine were rescued alive, a total that would have been one fewer but for the unselfish efforts of Mitchell and Timbrell. The recovery of the pitifully small number of survivors marked the end of an ill-starred enterprise, the pointlessness of which became clear only later when enemy sources revealed that the *Goeben* had been successfully refloated a full day before *E14* had set out from Imbros. Even as White was making final preparations for his gallant sortie, the battlecruiser was riding at anchor just off Constantinople. Rarely have so many brave lives been so needlessly sacrificed.

Once the survivors returned from captivity, recommendations for gallantry awards based on their reports were made. A few months later, the *London Gazette* of 24 May 1919 announced the award of the Victoria Cross to Lt Cdr Geoffrey Saxton White 'for most conspicuous gallantry and devotion to duty'. Included in the same list were

Distinguished Service Medals for AB Mitchell, RAN, and Signaller Timbrell. There then followed an inexplicable delay of eight more months before the same honour was conferred on Petty Officer Perkins, with Telegraphist Prichard receiving a Bar to the DSM.

Geoffrey Saxton White was born at Leecroft, Durham Road, Beckenham near Bromley in Kent on 2 July 1886, the second of three sons to William Henry White, a civil servant, and his wife, Alice (née Saxton). He was educated at Parkfield, Haywards Heath and Bradfield College before joining the Royal Navy as an officer cadet in 1901. Passing out from HMS *Britannia*, he was made midshipman on 15 November 1902, and over the course of the following six years, his career took him from the Channel to China with a succession of big ship appointments that included spells aboard the cruisers *Amphitrite* and *Glory* and the battleship *Venerable*. During this time, he was promoted sub-lieutenant (15 February 1906) and then lieutenant (1 October 1908).

His first contact with 'the Trade' came on 1 April 1909, when he joined HMS *Forth*, a sea-going depot ship for B- and C-Class boats, to begin training as a submariner. It was another two years, however, before he gained his first command, the elderly *A4*, before progressing a few months later to the *C27*, part of a flotilla stationed in The Nore command. A year earlier, in 1910, he married Sybil (née Thomas), with whom he would have three children – two sons, Peter (b 1911) and Anthony (b 1913), and a daughter, Sheila (b 1917).

White's initial spell in submarines came to an end in April 1914, when he joined the newly commissioned battleship HMS *Monarch*, in which he served during the early months of the war. He returned to submarines in September 1915, taking command of *D6* (11th Flotilla), the same boat destined to accompany HMS *Prize* on her tragic last voyage. Spells at Harwich, Blyth and Leith followed before, in August 1916, he was appointed to command *E14*. By then one of the most famous of all the Royal Navy's submarines, she was working out of Malta as part of the 12th Flotilla.

Promoted lieutenant-commander on 1 October 1916, White and *E14* were ordered to Brindisi two months later to carry out patrols in the Mediterranean. The following year, *E14* was one of four submarines ordered to Corfu, where a new base was established as part of Allied efforts to strengthen the Otranto Barrage. Conditions were primitive and the work unexciting. From a tented camp near an old Venetian gun battery, White and his crew ranged south of the drifter line that proved so vulnerable to attack in May. Though targets were sparse, White made an impression on his commanders, who reported on his boat-handling skills and excellent judgement. Kenneth Bruce, himself a Marmora veteran who would be in charge of directing the operation against the *Goeben*, was in no doubt about White's qualities. In a confidential report written on 9 October, he described *E14*'s captain as 'an exceptionally good and capable officer [who] makes very good attacks'. Overall, he considered *E14* under White to be the 'best-kept and run' boat in the flotilla and recommended him for 'better command'. Another senior officer, Charles Brodie, whose twin brother had been killed trying to take the *E15* through the Narrows, agreed and, having commented on his success in practice, noted presciently: 'Likely to do well in [an] emergency.'

Geoffrey Saxton White's death was the second tragedy to befall his family in the space of four months. His younger brother, Ronald, died in October while serving in France with 16 Squadron, Royal Flying Corps. Both are commemorated on the Horley War Memorial in Surrey, close to Charlwood Park, where their parents were living at the time. Geoffrey's body was never recovered, but in a strange twist, the boat he commanded with such skill and courage was discovered in June 2012, almost ninety-three years to the day after his widow travelled to Buckingham Palace to receive his posthumously awarded Victoria Cross from King George V. The boat, unique in the annals of the nation's highest award for valour in having been involved in two separate VC exploits, was discovered by Turkish divers in 20m of water about 250m off the coast at Kum Kale. Remarkably well preserved, despite evidence of its fatal shell damage, the coral-encrusted wreck was largely buried at an angle of 45 degrees on a sloping sandy bottom with the top part of the periscope protruding from the seabed. It stands as a ghostly reminder of one of the bravest and most futile submarine operations of the First World War.

A.F.B. Carpenter, A.E. McKenzie, A.L. Harrison, G.N. Bradford, E. Bamford N.A. Finch, R.D. Sandford, and P.T. Dean

Zeebrugge, 22–23 April 1918

In the fading light of Monday, 22 April 1918, a weird armada resembling, in the words of one officer, a 'bobbery pack', steamed steadily across the narrow waters of the English Channel. There were sleek, modern destroyers and ancient, slow-moving cruisers, a couple of obsolete submarines, a single picket boat, a swarm of motor launches and torpedo-boats and, most incongruous of all, two fat, stub-nosed Mersey ferry-boats. These last two vessels, bearing the singularly unwarlike names *Daffodil* and *Iris II*, occupied the centre column of three. In the wake of their tow was HMS *Vindictive*, a venerable, three-funnelled light cruiser plucked from dockyard obscurity to be given a leading role in a drama of epic proportions. To one observer, the sight of this strange triumvirate reminded him of 'a veteran hound on the trail with her two puppies on her flanks'.

At 8 p.m., with clouds beginning to billow on the darkening horizon, the force commander, Vice-Admiral Roger Keyes, in the manner of Nelson before Trafalgar, sent *Vindictive*'s captain, Alfred Carpenter, the signal: 'St George for England.' Mistaking it for a personal message,

Carpenter irreverently retorted: 'May we give the dragon's tail a damned good twist!' By ordinary standards, Carpenter later confessed, his reply was 'somewhat impertinent, but impertinence was in the air that afternoon.'

The 'impertinence' was the joint raid on the Belgian ports of Zeebrugge and Ostend, two of the most heavily fortified enemy bases in the lower waters of the North Sea. They provided the vital canal link between the sea and the docks, repair shops and reinforced concrete submarine shelters at Bruges which provided protection and sustenance to the troublesome Flanders Flotilla. Such was their strategic importance that the Germans sited twenty-six coastal batteries, with 229 guns ranging from 15-inch to 3.5-inch calibre, between Nieuport and Knokke. For years, successive plans had been put forward to take the sting out of the Flanders Flotilla. Most were rejected as too impractical or too hazardous. By the autumn of 1917 audacious thinking had given way to caution. Minefields were extended, a net barrage established and long-distance bombardment tried, but the passage of enemy submarines continued unaffected.

When Keyes became Director of Plans at the Admiralty on 28 September things began to change. An advocate for offensive action, he favoured breaking into the ports and sealing the entrances with block-ships. 'It can be done,' he told Admiral Beatty on 5 December. 'Salvage people say the possibility of removing blockships quickly – the excuse given always – is much exaggerated – and in the mean time 25 per cent of our losses continue to be caused by Flanders submarines.' But Admiral Sir Reginald Bacon, C.-in-C. Dover, was unconvinced. He came up with an elaborate scheme for a force to be landed on Zeebrugge's mole via a giant ramp, while the lock-gates were destroyed by gunfire from short range. He never had a chance to put his plan to the test, because on 1 January 1918 he was replaced by Keyes, who was made acting vice-admiral, and promptly set about turning his ideas into reality.

While rejecting the more absurd elements of his predecessor's plan, Keyes was astute enough to annex those parts he considered advantageous. Unlike Bacon, he elected to employ monitors in a subordinate rather than a leading role. The main players in Keyes's plan, and upon which all else hinged, were the blockships, which were to be filled with cement and scuttled to block the channels through the harbour entrances. To stand any chance of success at Zeebrugge, however, the formidable mole batteries would have to be overcome.

Reputedly the largest in the world, the mole had been transformed by the Germans into a fortress. Intended to protect the harbour from the North Sea's worst excesses, the curving barrier was festooned with defences. A battery of 3.5-inch and 4.1-inch guns pointed seaward from an extension, while at the end of the mole proper was sited a 5.9-inch battery protecting the harbour entrance. Beyond these lay a fortified zone, comprising barbed wire entanglements, machine-guns and trenches, straddling the 81yd-wide concrete and gravel mole. Even to reach these positions, any force attacking from the seaward side would have to scale a 16ft-high concrete wall, 10ft thick, which was further protected by a 4ft parapet wall. At high tide the top of the parapet stood 29ft above sea level. To land storming parties, therefore, would require a substantial vessel, capable of withstanding considerable punishment. Keyes originally considered a fast merchantman with a high freeboard, but after a visit to Chatham Docks he settled on *Vindictive*, then awaiting a decision about her future.

In the space of a few weeks the 20-year-old Arrogant class cruiser was transformed. Special guns were fitted for tackling the shore batteries and lock-gates and a diverse array of novel armament was added, including flame-throwers, Stokes mortars, pom-poms and Lewis guns. The foretop was converted to house two pom-poms and six Lewis guns to provide covering fire for the assault force. As well as extra armour and splinter mats, special fenders were fitted along the port side to protect the hull and fo'c'stle when she ran alongside. To speed the movement of storming parties, three wide ramps were built from the upper deck to the starboard side, while the ship sprouted fourteen narrow wooden brows which were to provide access on to the mole parapet.

Keyes selected Commander Alfred Carpenter, his chief of staff, to command *Vindictive*. A career officer, Carpenter was 36 and had spent much of the war as a staff officer, but he possessed a 'clear brain' and was, as Keyes declared, 'a 1st class navigator and seaman', skills that were vital to the success of one of the most daring operations ever mounted. Carpenter also had the advantage of possessing an intimate understanding of the plan, having worked on the draft proposal while serving at the Admiralty. Since then he had joined Keyes at Dover, where he toiled day and night on the final operational plan. On 19 February Keyes wrote to Beatty:

> I formed such a high opinion of him in the *Venus* that I got him built into the *Tiger*, but Sir J.J. [Jellicoe] took him for the *Iron Duke*'s staff where he got promoted, and splendid certificates, but he was not popular – from a service point of view for reasons which have raised him in my estimation … Anyhow I mean him to handle the *Vindictive* … when his main duty will be to lay her alongside and keep her there. I know no one better fitted to do so …

Keyes had intended to direct the assault personally from *Vindictive*, with Carpenter as his Flag Captain in command of the ship. Realising this was impractical, he was then left with a problem, since Carpenter was junior to the assault force commander who would also be in *Vindictive*. His solution was typically unorthodox: he promoted Carpenter acting-captain for the operation and made him responsible for conning *Vindictive* alongside the mole, while deferring to Captain Henry Halahan DSO, the landing force commander, in all matters relating to the assault.

The bulk of the storming parties was made up of men from the 4th Royal Marine Battalion, which was given en masse to Keyes, although every man was given the chance to withdraw. Originally raised to serve in Ireland, 4th RM had been used as a holding battalion, supplying reinforcements for RMLI units on the Western Front. For the raid the battalion was organised into three rifle companies (A, Chatham; B, Portsmouth; and C, Plymouth), each 165 strong. The battalion also included trench mortar and machine-gun sections, comprising two Vickers and four Lewis guns, all manned by Royal Marine Artillery and RMLI personnel under Captain Dallas-Brooks, one of two RMA officers in the unit. In overall command was Lieutenant-Colonel Bertram Elliot DSO. Joining the 730 marines was a volunteer force of eight officers and 200 bluejackets recruited from the Grand Fleet at Scapa, South Coast commands and units serving in France and Flanders. Commanded by Lieutenant-Commander Arthur Harrison, an England rugby international and gunnery officer in HMS *Lion*, they were divided into three seamen storming companies, each fifty-strong, with an additional fifty seamen and twenty-two marines forming a demolition party whose job was to destroy enemy installations and dock facilities.

While the seamen had volunteered for 'hazardous duties', their counterparts in 4th RM were told they were preparing for a large-scale raid on an enemy ammunition dump in France. Either way, it was widely accepted that their 'secret' mission would involve high loss of life. Officers took to calling themselves members of the Suicide Club. Even Carpenter admitted that 'none of us expected to come back'.

Preparations complete, the force which swelled to eighty-six officers and 1,698 men divided among 142 vessels (seventy-three bound for Zeebrugge and sixty-seven for Ostend) could only wait for suitable weather. Twice, on 11 and 14 April, they set out, only to be thwarted. Finally, on the afternoon of 22 April, Keyes gave the go-ahead, and from four different points the raiders converged on their allotted targets.

The daylight crossing passed without incident. By 9 p.m., with a light, drizzly rain falling, the force was within 30 miles of the mole. The night was quiet, the wind still blowing propitiously towards land.

Shortly after 10 p.m. the armada halted, surplus crews left the block-ships and the coastal motor boats slipped their tows. With Zeebrugge an hour away, the landing parties were ordered to put on equipment and at 11.15 p.m. the order, 'Action Stations' was passed along. 'Not a light was to be seen from the ships and silence reigned,' wrote Leading Seaman William Childs, one of the landing force in *Vindictive*. 'Onboard "chums" were saying goodbye in case they did not survive the action. The only noise to be heard was the throbbing of the motor-launches' engines. The artificial smokescreen had been started and one could scarcely see two yards ahead ...' At 11.30 p.m., as the monitors opened their bombardment, torpedo-carrying CMBs sped forward to engage enemy shipping in the harbour. *Vindictive* ploughed on, her progress masked by a smog of mist and smoke. 'Fortune', an officer wrote, 'was favouring us beyond our dreams.' Only at the last moment did the enemy react with a volley of star shells which turned pitch darkness into something akin 'the brightest moonlight and the middle period of early morning twilight'. Minutes later, the wind direction suddenly changed, and so, too, did *Vindictive*'s good luck.

Emerging from the pall of smoke at 11.56 p.m., *Vindictive* was exposed to a deadly close-range fire. The lighthouse extension of the mole was visible in the semi-darkness 300yd away on the port bow, but the smoke designed to cover her final run-in had been blown away. *Vindictive* was hit repeatedly. 'There were swift, shaking detonations close by, and one blinding flash of blue light right in our eyes,' wrote Lieutenant Hilton-Young. Later, looking back, he would recall the 'eruptions of sparks where the shells struck, the crash of splintering steel, the cries, and ... the smell of blood and burning'. Casualties were heavy, particularly among the landing parties. 'It seemed like hell let loose,' wrote LS Childs. 'The shrapnel and pieces of funnel caused havoc among the men, and the air was full of the cries of the wounded and dying. The Huns were hitting us every round they fired. At this time my sandbag dugout was demolished by two shells that hit us, taking away both sides, but not touching the front. These two shells wounded seven of us (myself only slightly) ...' Among those wounded beside him was his shipmate and no. 1 on the Lewis gun, Able Seaman Albert McKenzie. In those final terrible moments many of the senior officers were knocked out. Lt Col Elliot and his second-in-command, Maj. A. Cordner, were killed when a shell burst on the forebridge. Capt. Halahan, commander of the Bluejackets, died on the false deck, his deputy fell, shot through both legs and Lt Cdr Harrison, the next most senior officer, was hit by a shell fragment which smashed his jaw and left him unconscious.

As *Vindictive*, her upper decks torn to shreds and her funnels spraying fountains of flames, closed the mole, it seemed impossible she could escape destruction. Yet, despite the appalling punishment, none of her vitals were damaged. It was a miracle that Carpenter exploited. From his post in the *flammenwerfer* hut at the port end of the forebridge, only feet away from the point where Elliot and Cordner died, he prepared for the most critical landfall of his career. Nothing, not the 'terrific' noise, so deafening he could 'hardly hear himself think', nor the fearful carnage, was allowed to deflect him. With an excellent view from the starboard bow to nearly right astern, he conned *Vindictive* through an inferno of fire. Increasing speed and altering course to allow for a cross tide, he closed the shrouded mole:

> The ship was being steered from the conning tower, in which Lt Cdr Rosoman was stationed with full directions for taking over the handling of the ship immediately I should be rendered *hors de combat* ... In about 4 minutes after increasing to full speed the mole was within a few feet of the ship's side. Course was altered parallel to the mole and the telegraphs placed to full speed astern. When her weigh was nearly lost, the engines were stopped and the helm placed hard a-starboard. At 1 minute past midnight the ship bumped the mole, taking the blow on two fenders ... on the bulge of the port side of the forecastle. The bump was not felt and the fenders were not displaced. I immediately gave the order to let go the starboard anchor ...

Vindictive was one minute behind schedule, but, sadly for the storming parties, she was nearly a quarter of a mile west of her intended berth. In the circumstances, it was still an exceptional piece of ship handling. Lieutenant A.L. Eastlake RE, one of the *flammenwerfer* crew alongside the ship's commander, no doubt spoke for many when he wrote: 'Every survivor on the *Vindictive* owes his life to the remarkable skill with which Captain Carpenter navigated his ship through an extensive mine-field, and, in darkness, brought her alongside the mole at the appointed time.'

Carpenter's difficulties, however, had only just begun. Such was the din he failed to hear that the anchor had 'hung up'. Fearing that all the men on the cable deck had been wiped out, he sent Rosoman to take personal charge of letting go an anchor. What Carpenter called 'very rapid and drastic' orders to the engine-room were required to counteract the heavy backwash. The port anchor was dropped within a yard of the mole. With the helm to starboard her bow came in at once, but the brows would not reach the parapet. With the helm to port, she surged away. 'This was a very trying period,' wrote Carpenter. It lasted for three or four minutes, before *Daffodil*, already badly hit and her captain half-blinded, arrived to nudge *Vindictive* against the mole. Immediately, the only two landing brows to have survived the storm of fire were lowered. But the roll of the ship made crossing the swaying gangways a precarious business.

As *Vindictive* began disgorging its Bluejackets, *Iris II* shot ahead and bumped heavily alongside the mole 100yd away. On board the Mersey ferry, being tossed about 'like a cork', were the marines of Chatham Company, two Vickers sections, two mortar crews and D Company of the seamen landing force. Commanding the Bluejackets was Lieutenant-Commander George Bradford, whose 31st birthday it was that St George's Day.

An officer of great charm, popular with all ranks, Bradford combined strength of purpose with an immensely powerful physique. As a navy boxer, he was renowned as 'a splendid fighter'. Such courage seemed to run in his family. Of three brothers serving in the army, two had been killed, and their bravery recognised by the award of a VC, two MCs and a DSO. It was said of George Bradford that he never knew when he was beaten. It was a dangerous if heroic trait – and it was about to be fully realised.

When *Iris II* crashed against the mole at 12.15 a.m. her starboard anchor was immediately dropped. 'We went astern on it to bring us close in,' wrote 19-year-old Petty Officer G. Warrington, commander of a flamethrower party. 'There was an 8-knot current running along the wall, and the great hook fixed to the derrick was not strong enough to hold us in position.' Like the *Vindictive* before her, *Iris II* lurched back and forth, smashing a number of the scaling ladders needed to reach the mole. By now, the enemy was sweeping the wall with heavy machine-gun fire, causing a number of casualties from stray ricochets. But her captain refused to quit. Aware of the need to land quickly, his crew made desperate efforts to throw anchors over the parapet. Time after time they fell away. To PO Warrington, the situation looked hopeless. 'Finally,' wrote Lieutenant Oscar Henderson, the second-in-command, 'No. 1 anchor jammed on a telephone standard and was secured.' What followed was outlined in Henderson's post-raid report:

> We then endeavoured to catch with the fore derrick anchor (No. 2). To do this, Lt Cdr G.N. Bradford RN ... climbed up derrick and very gallantly placed anchor. While doing this he was shot and fell between ship's side and mole. This anchor bent and slipped

off immediately the strain came on it. At the same time Lt C.E.V. Hawkings RN (second-in-command of the *Iris*'s Bluejackets) got one of the ladders placed and swarmed up it on to the mole. When last seen he was defending himself with his revolver, and I fear was killed. At this moment No. 1 anchor tore away from the telephone standard and ship surged away from the mole ...

Later, in a meeting with Bradford's brother Tommie, Henderson added some detail to this bare account. He told how Bradford had leapt on to the mole, where he lay for about three minutes and 'shouted for those on deck to throw the grappling iron which they did and made it fast'. Relating their conversation to his mother, Tommie Bradford added: 'He thinks he must have been hit by a machine-gun bullet as he fell into the water. They threw him a line which he grasped but he thinks George died at that moment because his grip on the rope relaxed and he sank, dying after he knew he had done his work and without pain.' Gallant though it was, the story conflicts with other accounts. Having interviewed men of D Company, Lieutenant-Commander Bryan Adams, the senior surviving Bluejacket, reported that after being shot and falling into the water Bradford 'drew his revolver and fired three shots at the top of the mole and was then crushed between ship and mole'. Before he died, heroic efforts to rescue him were made, first by Petty Officer M.D. Hallihan, who died in the attempt, and then by Able Seamen Thomas Tuslar (who was subsequently awarded a DSM) and C.F. Clark.

Neither version, however, did justice to what the Official Historian called 'an act of desperate courage'. It took guts, agility and immense physical strength for Bradford to climb the derrick as it crashed repeatedly against the concrete wall. Then, having reached the top, he still had to lower himself on to the anchor swaying from the derrick high above the ferry. Timing his move perfectly, he completed the second stage. 'Here for a few moments he swung like an acrobat,' wrote the Official Historian, 'and then leapt on to the parapet and placed the anchor.' Only then, exposed in his moment of triumph, did he fall, 'riddled with machine-gun bullets', into the 'dark surging waters'. To many in *Iris*, it was a miracle he survived as long as he did. 'He hadn't a hope in hell's chance,' declared PO Warrington. But, as Carpenter observed: 'It was against his nature to give in as long as there was the remotest chance of winning through. His death brought us a great loss of a great gentleman.'

Even as *Iris* was struggling to land her storming parties, the mole was shaken by a tremendous explosion. 'Up went a huge tower of flame and debris and bodies into the black sky,' recorded Carpenter. 'I never saw such a column of flame. It seemed a mile high.' To LS Childs, on the mole, it appeared as though the flames 'would never stop going upwards.' The savage blast, which temporarily silenced the enemy batteries, signalled the fulfilment of the raid's most audacious mission: the destruction of the 300yd-long steel-girdered viaduct linking the shore-end causeway to the mole proper.

Keyes had planned this attack to prevent reinforcements from reaching the embattled mole. His original idea was to float rafts loaded with explosives against the piers. Then he thought of using CMBs armed with specially fitted depth-charges. Finally, at the suggestion of Lieutenant-Commander Francis Sandford DSO, a torpedo specialist, he agreed to employ two expendable C-class submarines. Manned with skeleton crews, these elderly craft were converted into floating bombs, with 5 tons of Amatol packed into their bows, to be detonated after ramming the viaduct. Even by the raid's own exceptional standards, it stood out as a mission teetering on the suicidal. The chances of escaping unscathed, even if they reached their objective, appeared infinitesimally small. Consequently, only unmarried volunteers were accepted, chosen – with one exception – from the crews of *C1* and *C3*, selected for the operation. The odd man out was Lieutenant Richard Douglas Sandford, recommended by his elder brother as a replacement for *C3*'s married captain.

Dick Sandford was an experienced submariner, though one whose career was as yet undistinguished. Dependable rather than outstanding, he considered himself 'a perfectly ordinary officer'. Where some found him rather dull, others thought him, in the words of one colleague, 'the perfect companion: interested, simple-hearted, faithful and wonderfully understanding'. With his thinning hair, Dick Sandford looked older than his 27 years, and he cheerfully played along with the gentle ribbing, his mock-old manners earning him the affectionate nickname 'Uncle Baldy'. His second-in-command and navigator for the operation was Temporary Lieutenant John Howell-Price RNR, a 31-year-old Australian with a colourful past, who was advised to delay his wedding plans. Like Sandford, a parson's son, he had run away to sea, served an apprenticeship aboard clippers and advanced to master mariner. Before volunteering for submarines, he had earned a DSC for his part in the sinking of the German raider *Greif*. The rest of the crew comprised Petty Officer Walter Harner, coxswain, Leading Seaman William Cleaver DSM, Stoker Henry Bindall and Engine Room Artificer Allan Roxburgh. Three more of *C3*'s crew took their places in a picket boat intended to rescue the submariners as they made their escape in motorised skiffs lashed to the conning towers. In practice, the submariners knew that if the means of rescue failed, as it had in the abortive attempt eleven days earlier, there was every chance that they would be killed in the explosion.

As it was, Unit K, as the viaduct force was officially styled, encountered problems of a different kind. According to Keyes's plan, the submarines were to be towed most of the way by destroyers, *C3* by *Trident* and *C1* by *Mansfield*. But *Mansfield* reached Dover late, leaving *C1* to proceed under her own power. *Mansfield* eventually caught her up, but *C1*'s misfortunes continued when the tow parted, forcing her captain to resort again to her own motors. Francis Sandford, in the picket boat, also had troubles. Twice his picket boat narrowly escaped capsizing only to foul its tow, resulting in a delay that lengthened when the tow eventually broke. As a consequence of all these mishaps, when *C3* slipped her tow at 11.35 p.m. she found herself perfectly alone in a gently heaving sea.

A light rain was falling as Dick Sandford cast around in vain for *C1* and his brother's boat. Knowing nothing of their fate or their whereabouts, he decided to press on, with or without a rescue launch. After a seven-minute wait, Sandford, standing alone on the bridge, ordered the antiquated petrol engines started and, with Howell-Price at the wheel, set course for Zeebrugge at 8½ knots. He intended to approach on the surface, submerging only as a last resort if attacked by enemy surface vessels. Furthermore, he had decided to dispense with the specially fitted gyro compass that might have allowed the crew to abandon the submarine once set on its final course. Instead, with the crew's support, he prepared to steer their floating bomb into the very jaws of the viaduct.

Shortly before midnight *C3* passed through a cloud of smoke, clearing it some three minutes later, just in time for Sandford to see the night sky turned a brilliant white by showers of star shells as flashes of gunfire tracked *Vindictive*'s final surge towards the mole. They were now within 1½ miles of their objective. Following his orders to the letter, Sandford altered course and steered straight for the viaduct. Till then his stealthy progress had been marked by an uneasy quiet. According to Stoker Bindall, *C3* had 'glided' into the shoal waters. Moments later, the peace was shattered as a star shell burst above them. Almost immediately shells splashed close by. Taking them to be 4-inch shells from one of the shore batteries, Sandford held his course and ordered LS Cleaver to turn on the smoke canisters in an attempt to mask their approach. But this proved counter-productive. According to Howell-Price, it 'only … obscured our view.' Sandford ordered it switched off. By then, the firing had inexplicably ceased. As *C3* ran on, unhindered and apparently unobserved, a flare burned on the far side of the mole, silhouetting the viaduct. Sandford estimated it to be about half a mile away, about two points on the port bow. 'Two searchlights were then switched on and picked up C3,' he noted. Briefly, the submarine was, as the historian Barrie Pitt observed, 'illuminated like the centrepiece in some naval tableau'. But still, the shore batteries held their fire. Stranger still, the searchlights were suddenly switched off. 'It was,' observed Henry Bindall, 'a silent and nervy business'. Sandford had no time to wonder about the defenders' erratic behaviour. The viaduct was looming ever larger, barely 100yd ahead. He shouted down to Howell-Price for a final course adjustment 'to ensure striking exactly at right angles'. Then, he ordered everyone up to join him on the bridge so that no one should be trapped below. Cutting through the water at 9 knots, and with the crew hanging on to the bridge rails, C3 smashed into the viaduct in a grinding screech of twisting steel. 'The boat', noted Sandford with characteristic precision, 'struck exactly between two rows of piles, and penetrated to the conning tower, riding up on to the horizontal girders of the viaduct … the hull being raised from the water bodily about 2 feet.' There was little opportunity for self-congratulation. 'I do not think anybody said a word except, "We're here all right",' observed Bindall.

LS Cleaver heard 'guttural shouts' and 'the trample of many feet' above them. Looking up, Howell-Price saw 'numbers of the enemy … on what apparently were gun platforms built on to the piles'. He also noticed a searchlight which C3 had almost rammed. As yet, beyond a good deal of shouting, there was no reaction from the Germans who evidently thought the submariners were as good as prisoners. The lull gave the crew time to release the skiff, while Sandford went below to light the three time fuses. As the skiff bumped heavily on to the submarine's bulges and splashed into the water, the crew scrambled in and waited for Sandford to join them. Cleaver later described their escape:

> We all … waited with bated breath. The shouting on the mole above increased. There was the clatter of rifles. At last we saw the figure of our commander. He was hurrying along the deck towards us bending low. 'Come on, sir,' we yelled in chorus. There was a fusilade of rifle bullets from the mole that whizzed menacingly past our heads. 'Everything OK,' said Lt Sandford as breathlessly he jumped aboard the skiff. He told us afterwards that his delay was due to difficulty in lighting the fuses. He had also seen that all the lights were out.
>
> It was now that we were faced with a fresh problem. Roxburgh announced that the propeller of the skiff … was permanently out of action. It was an awful situation. In less than three minutes

the first of the fuses to be lit if it functioned would reach the charge in the bows ... and destroy the viaduct and every living thing in the vicinity. 'The oars!' shouted someone. Bendall [*sic*] and Harner grabbed them from the bottom of the skiff and began to pull madly away from the mole. Less than two minutes to go now probably. And still the rifles cracked and bullets whistled all around. 'They couldn't hit a pussy cat,' said Lt Sandford derisively. And at that moment he sank back, wounded in the leg. What frantic strokes Bendall and Harner were making. One hundred yards! One hundred and fifty yards! Bendall rolled over with a groan. He was wounded in the thigh. I took his place with the oars. By this time the boat had been hit several times and was leaking badly. Roxburgh and Lt Howell-Price were having a busy time with the hand pumps. Had it not been for them the boat would undoubtedly have sunk. And then it was as though Heaven came to meet Earth in one momentary upheaval ... C3 and the viaduct were no more. Great chunks of masonry fell in the water all around us. The boat rocked and swayed as though possessed. Flames shot up to a tremendous height. In their glare was visible a great break in the mole ...

The blast threw debris 800yd, extinguished the two searchlights and reduced the enemy fire to a few spasmodic rounds. It was just as well. The motor boat, which had travelled between 200 and 400yd against the current, was in a parlous state, as were the crew. Hit in the leg and hand, Sandford lay slumped in the boat, along with the wounded Bindall and Harner. It was a marvel that none was killed. In the twelve minutes between the fuses being lit and the devastating explosion, the skiff was riddled by machine-guns, rifles and pom-poms. Ten minutes later the skiff, barely afloat, was found by the picket boat, just abreast the end of the viaduct. Her arrival, greeted by a shout of joy, was, in Bindall's words, 'in the nick of time'. With the sea lit by star shells and a desultory fire directed at them, the grateful submariners were hurriedly hauled on board. To Francis Sandford, it was clear they had been through 'a bad time', but he was nevertheless struck by their splendid behaviour, particularly that shown by his younger brother who, 'although in considerable pain and unable to move his leg or arms, insisted on the other wounded being attended to'. Their mission over, they headed away from the tangled wreckage that was all that remained of the viaduct.

On board *Vindictive*, the explosion prompted wild cheering. During the course of C3's isolated action, the fighting on the mole and around the expedition's assault ship had intensified. 'Every few seconds,' wrote Carpenter, 'the ship was being hit, chiefly in the upper works.' Shells burst on the funnels and bridges, scattering showers of deadly splinters on to the upper deck. For a time *Vindictive*'s only means of resistance came from the guns in the fore-top, a circular steel nest above the bridge and the only weapons platform above the height of the mole.

This tiny fortress, with its 2-pounder pom-poms and Lewis guns manned by eight marine artillerymen, was commanded by Lieutenant Rigby, whose second-in-command was a thick-set, 27-year-old sergeant by the name of Norman Finch. During the dash to the mole they were joined by Commander Edward Osborne, who was responsible for directing *Vindictive*'s fire. In the absence of normal communications, the fore-top guns represented the trigger for the rest of the ship's armament to open independent fire. Osborne wrote:

> We had decided not to fire till we were sure they had spotted us. Well, a shell burst close to [the] fore-top when we were about 200 yards off, I should say, and pinked Rigby and [my]self very slightly in the face; so we turned to the guns' crews of the fore-top and told them to open on the enemy's battery ...

As *Vindictive* bashed alongside, the fore-top pom-poms swept back and forth across the mole, engaging two destroyers moored on the opposite side and anyone foolish enough to show themselves on the bare breakwater. 'All along the mole and close under the 15ft parapet, there are dug-outs or funk-holes,' Carpenter later told an official correspondent. 'At first the Huns popped into these, but by-and-by it occurred to them that they would certainly be found and spitted if they stayed there, so the bright idea occurred to them of nipping across the mole and dropping down the side into their own destroyers lying there. An excellent scheme but for our fellows in the fighting-top, who picked them off with their Lewis guns as they ran.' For a time, the fire from the pom-poms and Lewis guns so cowed the defenders as to allow the first wave of Bluejacket landing parties to disembark virtually unopposed. As they poured ashore, Osborne departed, having given Rigby orders 'not to fire, unless he was certain that the target would not endanger our own men'.

By then the enemy were relentlessly pounding *Vindictive*, reducing her exposed upper decks and superstructure to a shambles. For a while the fore-top escaped the whirlwind of fire, allowing its gunners to give much-needed encouragement to the men fighting on the mole. But by then Rigby's men were a target for the enemy destroyers facing *Vindictive*. As shells peppered the upper works, the 'mad barking' of the marines' guns could still be heard, bursting out at regular intervals. For ten incredible minutes their luck held, before a shell struck the after end of the fore-top and burst inside. The crash and shower of sparks was followed by silence. Lieutenant Hilton-Young, in the starboard battery, was convinced they had been wiped out. However, he later reported:

> ... in a minute or two a single gun in the top broke out again, and barked and barked. Then there was another crash, and the silence of the top became unbroken. Words cannot tell with what a glow of pride and exultation one heard that last gun speak. It seemed impossible that there should be any one left alive in the top after the first shell struck it, and when the gun spoke again it seemed as if the very dead could not be driven from their duty.

The source of inspiration was a single, smoke-blackened marine sergeant. Despite wounds to his right hand and right leg, Norman Finch was far from dead. When the shell struck, killing Lt Rigby and five of his comrades and wounding the remainder, Finch had been hurled backwards and buried beneath a heap of bodies. 'We all went down in a bunch, and I had a job to get out from underneath,' he said. Struggling to his feet, he found one of the pom-poms still workable and carried on firing at any target that appeared in his sights until a second shell wrecked the gun. Of this, though, he had little recollection. 'I don't really know what I did,' he later insisted. 'One of my pals was badly hit, and I tried to get him down on deck. I know that. But it's a fact I don't really know what I did.'

Sgt Finch's brave defiance may have been short-lived, but it made a lasting impression on those who survived the night's fighting. Carpenter thought the fore-top's contribution 'invaluable', adding 'one cannot but attribute the complete success of our diversion very largely to these gallant men'. And none was more gallant than Norman Finch, who was eventually helped out of the shattered fore-top by Cdr Osborne and LS Childs.

Childs had led a charmed existence. One of Beatty's Grand Fleet volunteers, he had been invited to take part in the 'secret stunt' by Lieutenant Arthur Chamberlain, his officer in HMS *Neptune*. Told he would be lucky to return alive, he was asked if he knew of 'six suitable seamen' to accompany them. Chamberlain already had sixteen names, of whom only five had volunteered. After a few more interviews, they found their sixth man: Albert McKenzie, a strapping lad of 19, who was lightweight boxing champion of the 4th Battlecruiser Squadron.

Throughout their training Childs and McKenzie were inseparable. They practised bayoneting and bombing together – everything, in fact, that appertained to close-quarter infantry fighting. At the end of it all they found themselves in the same Lewis gun team, McKenzie as no. 1 and Childs as no. 3 ammunition carrier, the other places being filled by two men from HMS *St Vincent*, Able Seaman Frank White and Ordinary Seaman E. Ryan. Together with teams of bomb throwers, wire cutters and rifle grenadiers, they formed no. 1 Section, B Company, seamen landing party under Lt Chamberlain.

Once ashore, the company's role was to support A Company's assault on the 4.1-inch gun battery which threatened the blockships' approach. But heavy casualties sustained during *Vindictive*'s charge to the mole disrupted the attack. Even before *Vindictive* touched the mole, B Company's effective fighting strength had been seriously reduced, with Chamberlain among the dead and his second-in-command badly wounded almost as soon as he stepped on to the parapet. Childs and McKenzie were lucky to be alive.

As *Vindictive* ran alongside the mole, two shells shattered the sandbag shelter in which they lay, wounding all but one of the seven men forming A and B Companys' Lewis gun parties. Childs and McKenzie were peppered with shrapnel and a third, more seriously wounded, member of their team had to have a makeshift tourniquet applied. Moments later, as the mole loomed up, Childs was 'knocked silly' by a bullet which struck his helmet, tore through the rim and deflected into one of his puttees. Brought to his senses by someone shouting 'Over the top', he struggled, dazed, to his feet and made off after McKenzie. Their progress was slow, hampered by the weight of equipment. As well as his Lewis gun, McKenzie was burdened with eight trays of ammunition (each with forty-seven rounds), a revolver with 100 rounds, spare parts for his gun and a gas mask, making a total of 100lb. Childs had even more to carry, with sixteen trays of ammunition, a rifle, two bandoliers of fifty rounds apiece, a couple of hand grenades, an electric torch, wire cutters and gas mask. *Vindictive* was rolling heavily with the swell and they waited for the 'roll' before hopping on to the mole. 'Having landed,' wrote Childs, 'McKenzie and I advanced towards the end of the mole, our object being to fire upon some 5.5 [*sic*] guns. After about 50 yards we dropped down and opened fire ...'

Ahead of them were scattered parties of Bluejackets, portions of A Company, who had been led ashore by Lt Cdr Adams. Having helped secure *Vindictive*'s fragile berth, Adams had pushed on with a handful of men towards a concrete look-out station. A grenade was dropped in, but the shelter was found to be deserted, with an iron ladder leading down to the mole. From here, Adams could see the two enemy destroyers, neither as yet showing any sign of activity, tethered on the harbourside. A large, squat shed lay 50yd away and at the mole head, some 200yd ahead, he could make out a battery of three guns which stayed silent all the while he was on the parapet. Sandwiched between the guns and the end of the shed were barbed wire entanglements and what appeared to be a trench, about 100yd away, with a pile of white-stone, behind which a machine-gun was directing its fire at his party.

Under cover of a volley of rifle grenades, Adams took seven men and dashed along the parapet. Bullets splintered the wall as they rushed forward, bombing and shooting. But they were too few. With several men hit and no sign of support, Adams, his party reduced to four or five, retreated to the cover of the look-out station, where some wounded were sheltering. Desperately in need of reinforcements, Adams went back to fetch his Lewis gun team, only to find Able Seaman William Lodwick, the sole survivor, without ammunition. Sending him on ahead, he carried on until he found McKenzie and Childs.

With his reinforcements in tow, Adams sallied out again from the look-out station, McKenzie spraying the enemy machine-gun post and the mole beyond. But it was all to no avail. Despite McKenzie's brave efforts to provide cover from the open, Adams was beaten back. As far as he could make out, his party now numbered six men. Of B Company, who were to have supported him, there were only McKenzie, wounded again with his Lewis gun smashed, Childs and three others. Where, Adams wondered, were the marines? It was at this juncture, with his force pinned down behind the look-out station by a machine-gun in front and pom-poms to the side, that Lt Cdr Harrison arrived. His face bore the scars of the wound that had shattered his jaw and his sudden appearance came as a shock to Adams.

In the confusion that followed *Vindictive*'s arrival at the mole, Adams had been informed of Harrison's 'death' and assumed he had been a victim of the same shell which laid out so many of the Bluejackets' senior officers. Now, as bullets pelted the walls of the look-out station, he hurriedly brought Harrison up to speed with the situation and the urgent need for more men.

Harrison wasted no time. Telling Adams to carry on with his plan to bring up the marines, he took command of the sadly depleted Bluejackets. Later, in his report of the fighting, Adams told of his unavailing attempts to obtain help which persisted until he heard *Vindictive*'s siren signal the recall of the storming parties. Anxious to make certain his men were not left behind, he headed back to the look-out station where he found one of his section leaders, Leading Seaman

George Bush, but no sign of Harrison. Bush, one of a small number of Australian ratings who volunteered for the raid, had been prominent in every rush along the bullet-swept parapet and it was from him that he learned what had happened to Harrison:

Bush told me Lt Cdr Harrison had led another rush to the westward along the parapet beyond the look-out station, and he and several men had been killed by machine-gun fire. He was sure Lt Cdr Harrison was dead, being at his side when he was hit, and told me Able Seaman Eaves [actually AB Harold Eves], a rifle bomber, was trying to bring in his body when he was hit too. LS Bush was the sole survivor of the party. I then withdrew my men, got those from the mole by the iron ladder, and got all the wounded there were on the parapet between the brows and the look-out station on board. When my men were withdrawing I went out along the parapet beyond the look-out station to try to find Lt Cdr Harrison, and again came under machine-gun fire, so seeing nothing I came back and assisted to embark the men left on [the] parapet.

Adams's account was accurate in all but one detail. For while Bush may have been the only unwounded man to return from Harrison's last charge, he was not the only survivor. Eves, though badly hit, lived to receive a well-merited DSM, as did Bush. Also among the wounded survivors making their painful way back to *Vindictive* were McKenzie and Childs. In a letter to one of his brothers, McKenzie gave his own colourful rendering of the night's fighting, in which he compressed many of the incidents into a single vivid narrative:

Well, we got within about fifteen minutes' run of the mole, when some marines got excited and fired their rifles. Up went four big star shells, and they spotted us … They hit us with the first two shells and killed seven marines. They were still hitting us when we got alongside … I tucked the old Lewis gun under my arm and nipped over the gangway aft … I turned to my left and advanced about 50yd and then lay down. There was a spiral staircase which led down into the mole, and Commander Brock [Wg Cdr Frank Brock, who landed after the flamethrower post he commanded aboard *Vindictive* was rendered inoperable] fired his revolver down and dropped a Mills'. You ought to have seen them nip out and try to get across to the destroyer tied up against the mole, but this little chicken met them half way with the box of tricks, and I ticked about a dozen off before I clicked. My Lewis gun was shot spinning out of my hands, and all I had left was the stock and pistol grip which I kindly took a bloke's photo with who looked too business-like for me with a rifle and a bayonet. It half stunned him, and gave me time to get out my pistol and finish him off. I then found a rifle and bayonet, and joined up our crowd who had just come off the destroyer [*sic*]. All I remember was pushing, kicking and kneeing every German who got in the way. When I was finished I couldn't climb the ladder, so a mate of mine lifted me up and carried me up the ladder, and then I crawled on my hands and knees inboard.

Childs supplied more details of the struggle on the mole. After the misfortune of seeing their Lewis gun wrecked just as 'it was doing glorious work', they threw their spare ammunition drums into the sea and 'reverted to secondary armament', a revolver in McKenzie's case and a rifle for Childs:

This was better than nothing, so we opened fire on some Germans who were escaping from shelters underneath us, and were trying to reach the destroyers on the opposite side of the mole. Had these Germans remained where they were they would in all probability be alive now, but panic reigned amongst them, and they were shot down or bayoneted. We now advanced further, and came across a concrete sentry box. In here were some Germans who made a rush for it. In making a point with my bayonet at one of them, my blade finished up like a corkscrew ...

Graphic though they were, neither account shed light on the circumstances surrounding Harrison's headlong rush along the parapet. It has been suggested that it was an attempt to regain the initiative and give the stalled attack fresh impetus. If so, it was an act of extreme desperation. Of the reports that survive, none reveals how many men took part. But it is doubtful whether the dozen or so men Harrison inherited from Adams had been greatly reinforced nor the defences substantially weakened. Harrison must have known, therefore, that to try to advance with so pitifully small a force along that bare parapet, totally exposed to enemy machine-guns, was to court almost certain death. Yet if any man was temperamentally suited to lead such a forlorn hope it was surely Arthur Harrison, a man thoroughly imbued with the offensive spirit and dedicated to the principle of leadership by example. Unnecessarily heroic though it probably was, his charge 'down that narrow gangway of death' was, as Carpenter aptly observed, 'a worthy finale to the large number of charges which, as a forward of the first rank, he had led down so many a rugby football ground'.

Down below on the mole, the scattered remnants of the 4th Royal Marines, their number sadly depleted, began to dribble back towards *Vindictive*. During the final moments ashore, an attack launched against the fortified zone had made belated if limited progress towards the enemy battery before being brought to a premature halt by the recall siren. As the marines withdrew, small parties covering one another, the attack's failure appeared to one man to be symptomatic of a night full of frustration. Edward Bamford, commander of B (Portsmouth) Company, was convinced that none of the battalion's objectives had been achieved.

At 30, Bamford, a ginger-haired six-footer, straight-backed, with a wispy moustache adding to his military bearing, was reserved to the point of shyness. He had spent much of the war at sea as a gunnery officer, first in *Britannia* and then the modern light cruiser *Chester* (where we encountered him in the action that resulted in Jack Cornwell's posthumous award of the VC). His own performance at Jutland had been recognised by two bravery awards and promotion to captain and it was in this rank, on 20 February 1918, that he joined the 4th Royal Marines. Given command of the Portsmouth contingent, comprising four platoons numbered 5 to 8, he made a positive impression. His first words to B Company were, 'Well, fellows, if you will be right with me I'll be right with you.' And as one man later remarked, 'We got on very well indeed. Very strict. But [he had] what was very uncommon then in the forces – the Human Touch.'

The marines' main objectives were the destruction of the guns at the seaward end of the mole to ensure the safe passage of the blockships and to cause as much damage as possible to enemy port installations. Each company was given specific tasks in what was to be a four-phase assault. C (Plymouth) Company was to land first, two platoons establishing and consolidating a foothold on the shoreward end of the mole, while the other two headed left to capture the guns. Bamford's four platoons were to follow ashore, forming under cover of C Company's block before attacking along the mole, securing ammunition dumps, sheds and shelters, to a point about two-thirds of the way towards the shore. Bamford was told that the end of this sector, through which A (Chatham) Company was to advance to mop up the rest of the mole, was to be held at all costs. In the event, however, almost nothing went according to plan. The platoons earmarked for securing a firm base were decimated without even setting foot on the mole, and the men of A Company, aboard *Iris II*, were defeated in their attempt to land, and both these setbacks, combined with the loss of so many senior officers in the early stages and *Vindictive*'s unintentional berth almost a quarter of a mile west of its planned position, contrived to disrupt the marines' assault. In the rapid reorganisation that followed *Vindictive*'s dash to the mole, Major Bernard Weller DSC, C Company commander, took charge of the battalion and the men of Edward Bamford's B Company, having been spared the worst of the shelling, suddenly found themselves leading the attack.

No. 5 platoon, commanded by Lieutenant T.F.V. Cooke, was first off, led ashore by Bamford, with the battalion's adjutant, Captain Arthur Chater, and Sergeant-Major Charles Thatcher in close attendance. With no way down on to the mole and uncertain of their bearings, they turned right along the parapet. A splutter of rifle fire burst from the darkness and, while Chater and Thatcher searched for ropes and scaling ladders to reach the mole, Bamford set about securing their position. In an account that was a model of brevity and understatement, he wrote:

> With Lt Cooke's platoon I moved along the upper promenade of the mole, to quiet some snipers who were disturbing the landing of the remainder. We came abreast the spot where the *Iris* was trying to get alongside, and hailed her. She replied with loud cheers, but it was clear she would never get close enough to the mole to land her men, and when I last saw her she had shoved off and was being badly shelled with tracer shell. Lt Cooke was shot in the head at my side, just before 12.15am, when the submarine blew up the shore end of the mole [most accounts say this took place about five minutes later]. The blockships could now be seen stealing across the harbour towards the canal entrance, and did not appear to be receiving much attention from the Huns. I climbed down the scaling ladders abreast *Vindictive*, having withdrawn the men from the right, and crossing the mole collected men of the 7th and 8th Platoons, and with a few of the 5th started an assault against the batteries at the seaward end of the mole. This was interrupted by the general recall (Ks on the siren), and we returned to the ship, crossing the mole in small parties, so as not to clog the ladders, which were under heavy fire from the shore batteries.

Bamford's matter-of-fact record hardly did justice to his attempts to bring some order to the dislocated assault. So heavy were the losses during *Vindictive*'s approach that some platoons were reduced to barely a dozen men. Many of those who did get ashore were disoriented. Platoons became mixed, control difficult and, such was the strength of opposition, there might have been an understandable urge to seek what shelter there was. That so many did not do so was, in no small measure, due to Bamford's calm authority and inspiring example. According to Chater, his 'totally unperturbed manner had the most reassuring effect on all who came in contact with him that night'.

As the leader of the only nearly complete company of marines to land, much depended on him and his response to the many problems encountered. Fortunately for Keyes and the 4th Royal Marines, he was not found wanting. Displaying the same kind of contempt for danger he had shown on *Chester*'s shell-torn decks, Bamford appeared oblivious to the hazards confronting him. Originally charged with securing a large portion of the mole on the shoreward side, he amended his plans, settling instead for a far more limited advance towards the shore, before turning his attention to the gun batteries at the seaward end.

With the right secure, he headed back along the parapet to where Sgt Maj. Thatcher had placed a row of ladders leading on to the mole. Descending one of these, he was followed by two marines from 7 Platoon, including James Feeney, who later wrote:

> There was a group of bodies at the foot of the ladders – all Germans – who tried to knock the ladders, and amongst them three men in white ducks. The light ... was wonderful. I don't believe there was ever such a firework display. The German star shells, that light up the sea and land for miles, were terrible in their effective grandeur. I ran across to the dump-house [No. 3 Shed] opposite the ship, and took cover by lying on the ground. The ground floor of the dump-house was raised about 2½ft over the roadway, and had a pathway like as if carts were loaded there, like at a railway goods store. We had a grand chance of chucking bombs in the doors of this dump-house, as we had splendid cover ...

Bamford was joined at this point by Chater, who had been working tirelessly and at considerable personal risk to maintain communications. Chater recalled:

> Together we discussed the situation. Our battalion plan had been based on the assumption that *Vindictive* would be put alongside some 400yd from the end of the mole. All those men who belonged to units which were to have attacked the fortified zone,

therefore, now found themselves at No. 3 shed. No attack on the fortified zone had yet been made. As this was our principle objective, we decided to organise an attack ... along the mole. This entailed attacking a prepared position across some 200yd of flat pavement devoid of any form of cover ...

Although it had never been part of his remit, Bamford, as senior officer, took it upon himself to lead a charge from which he must have known he would be lucky to return. The mole had become a vast shooting gallery bathed in light. As shells tore great chunks of steel out of *Vindictive*'s ragged funnels and bullets sprayed the bare concrete breakwater, Bamford gathered his men for the assault. Marine Feeney recorded:

Captain Bamford came up, and said, quite cool, 'Fall in, B Company.' I fell in with McDowell, and Sgt Brady took charge of us. There were only sixteen there, and Capt. Bamford was leading us along, when he looked back to see how many he had, and apparently he thought we were insufficient, as he told the sergeant to retire to the ship ...

On this last point Feeney was mistaken. Weak in numbers though they were, this was not the reason why Bamford abandoned the attack. Chater, who had watched them go until 'they were well out in the open', wrote that Bamford ordered a withdrawal only after *Vindictive*'s siren was heard 'making what was taken to be the emergency recall signal'. Getting back was no easy task, especially for Bamford's party caught in the open. According to Feeney, it was a case of 'running the gauntlet over that fire-swept zone'. Feeney reached the ladders, scrambled up and, having almost fallen back over the railings, took a leap at one of the heaving gangways and landed on board, 'nervous and funky from looking at the dead and listening to the dying'. He was followed on board by Bamford, who was miraculously unscathed.

Safely aboard *Vindictive*, the night's action barely over, he discussed the operation with Chater who later observed:

We had failed to gain any of the objectives which had been laid down in our orders. We felt that our part of the operation had been a complete failure. We had lost many good men with what seemed to us no result. We felt extremely despondent. We did not then know that, although our part of the operation had not gone according to plan, the attack on the mole had created the necessary diversion to enable the blockships to enter the canal.

And that, of course, was all that mattered. For all the sound and fury of the struggle along the mole, it was of secondary importance to the passage of the three blockships into the canal entrance. The overall success of the operation hinged entirely on them. To achieve maximum effect, it was necessary for them to be manoeuvred into position as squarely across the channel as their length would allow. Only then were their bottoms to be blown out, releasing tons of concrete, thus sealing off the harbour for weeks, if not months. All this was to be carried out within point-blank range of the mole extension guns and numerous machine-guns. As if that were not enough, the crews' only hope of rescue rested with four thinly protected motor launches and their volunteer crews. It was an operation so obviously fraught with hazard that Keyes 'regarded the chances of escape from any of the blocking ships as very slender'.

The plan was for *Thetis*, *Intrepid* and *Iphigenia* to be guided into the harbour by calcium buoys carried in a launch. But before reaching the entrance, the launch was wrecked by shellfire. The three cruisers, weighed down by their concrete cargoes, ploughed on as *Vindictive*, lit by searchlights and bracketed by fire, consumed the enemy's attention. Twenty minutes after Carpenter went alongside the mole, the blockships appeared out of the smoke off the lighthouse, where their unhindered approach was seen by Edward Bamford. *Thetis*, tasked to ram the lock-gates provided no misfortune had befallen her consorts, led the way, followed in turn by *Intrepid* and *Iphigenia*. Ahead lay a barge boom with a gap at the southern end beyond which the harbour entrance could just be made out. At that moment, the mole extension guns, having failed to stop *Vindictive*, opened fire at less than 100yd range. *Thetis* was rocked by the weight of shells poured at her. Like *Vindictive*, the slow-moving cruiser was practically a sitting duck, but where Carpenter's assault ship had escaped damage to her essentials *Thetis* was not so fortunate. Holed along the waterline, with pipes ruptured and her engines labouring against the strong tide, she missed the gap in the net defences and blundered through the steel mesh which wrapped itself round the stricken vessel's propellers. Dragged to port, she ran aground 300yd short of the canal mouth, a green light shining through the curtain of smoke to guide her followers safely past.

Intrepid, having been shielded by *Thetis*, steamed smoothly into the harbour entrance, where her captain, Lieutenant Stuart Bonham-Carter, coolly manoeuvred her into position. Following through the pall of smoke that hid *Intrepid* came *Iphigenia*. She had already been hit twice, one shell severing the siren pipes to leave the fo'c'stle enveloped in a cloud of steam. Steering blindly into the smoke-masked canal, she narrowly missed colliding with the western pier, forced her way between a dredger and barge, and carried on, the smashed barge temporarily locked to her bows. Her 22-year-old captain, Lieutenant Edward Billyard-Leake, reported: 'As soon as I was clear of the barge I went ahead on both engines and sighted the *Intrepid* aground on the western bank with the gap between her bows and the eastern bank. I endeavoured to close this gap but collided with the port bow of *Intrepid* while turning.' The collision almost shoved *Intrepid* off the silt bar, forcing Bonham-Carter to blow his charges immediately. He was just in time to prevent his ship sliding completely out of position. Billyard-Leake did his level best to repair the damage. Despite intense fire, he backed away, hauling the bows out of the silt, and then went ahead again. Machine-guns were spraying the decks as Billyard-Leake edged the battered *Iphigenia* to her final resting place. Grounding on the eastern bank, he gave orders to abandon ship, before firing the scuttling charges. As the crew tumbled into the only serviceable cutter, it was as though they had exchanged the 'frying pan' for the 'fire'.

The narrow stretch of water was whipped into a witch's cauldron by a torrent of machine-gun fire and shrapnel bursts. Their chances of survival appeared minimal. The rescue force had already been halved, with one boat destroyed, another broken down and a third crowded with men taken from the sunken *Thetis*, leaving the fate of more than one hundred men in the hands of a single, feebly armed launch. Her commander was a 40-year-old RNVR lieutenant, who had been rejected by the Army as unfit. The next sixty minutes were to be the finest hour in Percy Dean's life.

ML282 had followed close behind the blockships, near enough, in fact, for Dean to see *Iphigenia* 'swinging across the canal'. No sooner had she settled than ML282 motored alongside. As she closed, 'right under the stern', a storm of shells and machine-gun bullets continued to pelt the stranded hulk. Her approach was seen by Billyard-Leake, just as *Iphigenia*'s cutter began to pull clear. It was a timely meeting. The overcrowded boat was already dangerously low in the water and had sustained a number of casualties. Despite the danger from machine-guns and pom-poms sited only feet away, Dean stopped engines.'The majority of the crew managed to get into the motor launch, which then went astern,' wrote Billyard-Leake. 'The remainder ... pulled round the stern and the ML came up and picked them up. I was the last to leave the cutter and to the best of my knowledge only three hands were left in her, one of whom was killed.'

At the same time, on the opposite bow, a skiff filled with men from *Intrepid* bumped alongside, the majority of the crew having already escaped out of the harbour aboard two cutters. In no time at all the motor-launch's foredeck was crammed with more than a hundred men, whose combined weight threatened to do what no enemy gunners had succeeded in doing. Only the intervention of an officer, who ordered the men to spread out across the decks, prevented the launch from capsizing. Then, with the oily water almost lapping over ML282's bows, the survivors of the blockships faced another ordeal: exiting the canal at extreme slow speed under the very noses of the enemy with little or no protection from the hail of fire directed at them. Faced by a rising tide of casualties, Dean cut short the transfer of *Iphigenia*'s men, deciding instead to secure the cutter to the launch's stem. ML282's engines then throbbed into life and she made her way astern, back towards the harbour mouth.

As the only vessel still moving along the narrow waterway, she was the focus for every gun. Bullets peppered her packed decks, taking their toll of rescuers and rescued alike. Three steersmen in succession were hit alongside Dean and two succumbed to their wounds; among the injured was Dean's second-in-command, Lieutenant Keith Wright. Then, all of a sudden, the fire briefly died. Behind them, towards the seaward side of the sunken *Iphigenia*, a flash of brilliant white light illuminated the canal, momentarily distracting the enemy gunners. The light came from a flare, accidentally ignited, on a Carley float, aboard which were the last survivors of *Intrepid*: her captain, first lieutenant, navigating officer and four petty officers. As a storm of fire erupted around them, they were compelled to take to the oil-covered water, where their chances seemed barely worth calculating. But, incredibly, the luck that had been with them all the way into the canal stayed with them as they attempted to swim out. In the midst of the maelstrom they were spotted by Dean, just as ML282 was preparing to pass through the canal entrance. Despite being already overburdened with the crews of two blockships and on the brink of escape, he headed back.

Once more he slowed to pick up the survivors, making the launch a target for every gun within range. Eventually, believing they were all safely aboard, Dean went astern again. However, Bonham-Carter, lagging behind the others, had been missed. He just managed to grab a rope and was dragged through the water for some distance before being noticed by one of the launch's crew. By then *Intrepid*'s skipper was exhausted and he let go the rope. With ML282 slowly disappearing in the distance, his plight seemed hopeless – until a star shell burst over the canal, lighting the scene sufficiently for Dean to see Bonham-Carter's head. For a third time ML282 headed into the canal, offering the German gun positions yet another opportunity which they failed to exploit. Finally, with Bonham-Carter added to the ranks of survivors, Dean withdrew towards the canal entrance.

The launch's decks were awash with dead and wounded. Of a crew of eight, Dean had lost two killed and two seriously wounded, the place of his leading deckhand being taken by Leading Seaman Potter, who had steered *Iphigenia* into the canal. His turn at the wheel was short-lived. No sooner had the launch cleared the entrance than the steering gear jammed. Faced with this latest crisis, Dean remained unruffled, merely noting in his post-raid report that: 'I was obliged to work my boat out under the engines.' Then, to circumvent the mole defences, he made for the curving breakwater, steering so close that the guns in the batteries could not be depressed sufficiently to fire on him. Several years later, he recalled looking up and seeing the guns and their frustrated crews just above him. As the launch drew steadily past, he claimed to have fired off half a dozen revolvers in their general direction. ML282 was still trailing *Iphigenia*'s empty cutter. Quite why is unclear. Perhaps Dean felt it might have been useful had his launch been stopped or sunk. Whatever the reasons, it was only when he cleared the mole that he finally cut the boat adrift out of concern for the safety of the men on board.

Even then, the danger had not yet passed. As Dean shaped for the pre-arranged course home, concerns were expressed about his launch's chances of making it back. Quite apart from the burden of her human cargo, there were worries about damage caused by a fire in the smoke canisters. The flames had eaten through the stern deck, 'gassing' a number of officers and men, including Billyard-Leake and Lieutenant Cory-Wright, both of whom had been instrumental in bringing the fire under control. Given the state of the launch and the number of seriously wounded men on board, some officers suggested the safest course was to run into Flushing, in neutral Holland. But having come so far, Dean was not prepared to accept internment. He decided to press on. However, the launch had hardly started its homeward passage when a burst of cheering signalled the approach of HMS *Warwick*, flying Keyes's over-sized battle banner.

Keyes could scarcely believe his eyes. Packed as tight as sardines on board ML282 were 101 men of the *Intrepid* and *Iphigenia*. Thanks to the determination of a few men under the inspired leadership of a middle-aged 'amateur' sailor, 'an apparently forlorn hope' as Keyes put it, had been converted 'into a most successful accomplishment'. Transferring the survivors and his own wounded to *Warwick*, Dean continued his charmed progress back to Dover. Alone of the launch's deck crew, he had come through uninjured after a gruelling twenty-one hours without rest. Of all the glorious deeds performed that night, few had equalled and none surpassed Dean's sustained bravery in the face of prolonged fire at point-blank range. Billyard-Leake could not speak too highly of him, while Bonham-Carter called his conduct 'simply magnificent'.

ML282 took her place in Dover harbour close by the battle-torn *Vindictive*. She had been brought out of the holocaust of Zeebrugge by Alfred Carpenter in the same masterly manner as he had taken her in, yet even so her escape was no less miraculous than his own. Twice in the space of a few minutes as *Vindictive* was preparing to draw clear from the mole, Carpenter had come within an ace of being killed. On the first occasion a shell landed among the boxes of Stokes bombs, starting a fire which was promptly and bravely stamped out by his chief quartermaster. And then, shortly afterwards, while Carpenter was standing outside the conning tower, a shell exploded behind him, giving him a deep flesh wound in the left shoulder which he described as 'very slight'. Other narrow escapes were revealed by the jagged holes torn in his cap and binoculars case. Four times fragments had torn through his clothing without hitting him. Alfred Carpenter had, indeed, been lucky.

Of all the heroic actions performed at Zeebrugge, none was considered more influential to the outcome of the mission than the calm leadership displayed by the captain of *Vindictive*, Alfred Carpenter. Keyes acknowledged his debt to him in his first despatch when he wrote: 'His great bravery ... did much to encourage similar behaviour on the part of the crew, and thereby contributed greatly to the success of the operation.'

Alfred Francis Blakeney Carpenter was born at Byfield Cottage, Barnes, Surrey, on 17 September 1881, the only son of Lieutenant (later Captain) Alfred Carpenter RN and his first wife, Henrietta Maude (née Shadwell). He boasted a notable naval pedigree. His grandfather, Commander Charles Carpenter, assisted in the capture after a long chase of the American privateer *Rattlesnake* in 1814, while his father's service had been marked by much gallantry. Among the first naval officers to be awarded the DSO in 1887, he had earlier been presented with the Albert Medal, then the highest peace-time award for bravery, for rescuing a man who fell overboard at night off the Falkland Islands in 1876.

Brought up in the traditions of the navy, Carpenter left his prep school in 1896 to begin officer training in *Britannia*. Although 'somewhat conventional in outlook', he possessed an inventive mind and a calm authority that was soon tested in combat. As a midshipman and then sub-lieutenant, he saw action in Crete in 1898, when Britain intervened with ships and troops to halt the massacres which took place there, and two years later in China, where naval brigades helped crush the Boxer Rising.

Following promotion to lieutenant in 1903, he specialised in navigation. His next step came in 1911, with promotion to lieutenant-commander. Two years later, in a remarkable echo of his father's gallantry, Carpenter was awarded the Bronze Medal of the Royal Humane Society for saving life at sea. That same year his career took a new direction when he passed a staff course that ensured much of his war-time service would be spent in essential but unexciting administrative posts.

From July 1914 to November 1915 he was on the staff of Sir John Jellicoe in the battleship *Iron Duke*, before being promoted and appointed to the *Emperor of India* as navigating commander. After two years in that post he was called to the Admiralty to take up another desk job, serving under the Director of Planning, Roger Keyes, who had been Carpenter's captain in *Venus* almost a decade earlier. There he was engaged in the secret plans which eventually grew into the attempt to block the harbours at Zeebrugge and Ostend. Having secured Carpenter's release to join him, they worked energetically to turn the theory into reality. Keyes later admitted: 'Cdr Carpenter's gift for going into the minutest details with the most meticulous care greatly assisted me in preparing a detailed plan, and orders, which embodied the work of several officers.'

In eventually acceding to Carpenter's plea to take charge of *Vindictive* during the operation, Keyes knew he was selecting a man who was not only familiar with the smallest detail of every phase of the plan but also possessed the vital navigational skills needed to ensure the landing force was delivered safe and on time. Although Carpenter ultimately missed his intended objective, an error he initially admitted but later sought to justify, his composure under the hottest fire and his skill as a ship handler were crucial to the operation's partial success and to the evacuation of so many men.

As the senior surviving officer, Carpenter was asked by Keyes to make recommendations for conspicuous gallantry, but he declined to do so, insisting that it would be invidious to select individuals where everyone had acted so splendidly. Furthermore, he refused to take part in the ballot which was then arranged to select an officer and a rating for the VC. However, that did not prevent his fellow officers in the *Vindictive* and among the naval landing force voting for him. In the event he won the ballot, and the VC, by a single vote from Lieutenant Harold Campbell, captain of the *Daffodil*, who received the DSO.

The Cross was duly announced, together with the majority of the Zeebrugge and Ostend awards, on 23 July. His gallant leadership was further recognised by the French who made him an officer of the Legion of Honour and presented him with the Croix de Guerre with Palm, all in the space of five weeks during the summer of 1918. Shortly afterwards Carpenter, who had been confirmed in his promotion to captain by Keyes, departed on a lecture tour of Canada and the United States. This venture, which stretched beyond the Armistice into 1919, provided him with the basis for what was to become, at least until the late 1950s, the most authoritative work on the operation. *The Blocking of Zeebrugge*, published in 1921 with an introduction by Admiral Earl Beatty and appreciations by Marshal Foch and Rear Admiral Sims USN, was directed at 'the man-in-the-street' and proved a best seller, running to many editions. While underplaying his own role, Carpenter heaped generous praise on his fellow officers and concluded that, contrary to enemy propaganda, the canal at Zeebrugge had been 'well and truly blocked' by an operation which he felt had done much to revive national morale and belief in the 'certainty of ultimate victory'.

Following his American tour Carpenter returned, briefly, to desk duties in the naval intelligence department, before taking charge of a war course at Cambridge for officers in the autumn of 1919. Two years later he returned to sea as captain of the light cruiser *Carysfort*. From then until his retirement, as a vice-admiral, in 1934, he would alternate seagoing commands with staff and administrative duties, running a senior officers' technical course and, from 1924 to 1926, serving as captain of the dockyard, deputy superintendent and King's harbour master at Chatham. A short spell on special attachment to the Admiralty was followed by command of the *Benbow* in August 1927 and the *Marlborough* in May 1928. He was promoted rear admiral on 3 August 1929.

The following year, Carpenter's thoughts turned again to his involvement in the raid that had gained for him worldwide renown. Unhappy with a draft of the Official History, he had suggested changes and additions with regard to his placing the *Vindictive* alongside the mole, some 340yd adrift of her goal. In his original report, he had candidly admitted his mistake, but now he claimed he had deliberately steered away from his intended berth at the request of senior marine officers in order to enfilade an enemy trench considered dangerous to the landing parties.

His comments, however, did not go down well with his former chief. To Keyes, they smacked of trying to rewrite history. He accused him of being 'unscrupulous' and dismissed the majority of his claims as being a spurious mixture of exaggeration and 'sheer invention'. While in no way denigrating Carpenter's courageous conduct, Keyes took the 'greatest possible exception' to his suggestions, 'which are obviously designed to cover and explain away Captain Carpenter's failure to place the *Vindictive* in the position I selected, with the consequent failure of the primary object of the assault on the Mole, ie, the capture of the guns at the end of the Mole in time to allow the Blockships to go past unscathed'. What prompted Carpenter's action is unclear, but as Keyes's bellicose correspondence with the official historian makes clear, it stirred painful memories of an earlier spat between the two men. The conflict dated back to May 1919 and Keyes's revision of his original Zeebrugge dispatch, about which Carpenter took umbrage. According to Keyes, it was only after a postwar visit to the Mole and a 'reconstruction' of the attack by surviving officers that he was able to appreciate 'the full extent of the reason for the failure of the assault'. Writing to Carpenter, he added:

> Your action in laying the *Vindictive* alongside the Mole and bringing her away will live for ever in Naval history, but you can't have it both ways and the failure of the assault was due to the position in which the *Vindictive* was berthed and not, as you suggested to me, to the inelasticity of the Marines' disposition.

Nothing Carpenter could say or do would ever alter Keyes's mind on this issue. Based on postwar evidence, he concluded that Carpenter had been deflected from his true course by the guns on the Mole extension opening fire during the final approach. This, he felt, had prompted him to increase speed, thus overrunning his assigned position and 'dooming' the assault's primary objective and the ability of the leading blockship to reach her goal. In a further dig at what he described as Carpenter's 'weakness for modest self-advertisement' – a reference to his lecture tour – Keyes pointedly stressed his determination to ensure his final dispatch was 'a plain statement of fact, free from risk of controversy and free from the boastful and exaggerated claims which were made in the first instance and in the press on the strength of unauthorised statements and interviews'.

Carpenter retired to St Briavels, in the Forest of Dean, where he took an active role in community affairs, becoming a JP in 1936. As a director of the South American Saint Line, he took a great interest in the training of junior officers and cadets for the Merchant Navy. The ex-admiral, who had received commendations for a variety of inventions more than two decades earlier, conceived the idea of a training ship, named *St Briavels* after his home village, in which practical ship-handling experience could be acquired. During the Second World War he donned khaki, as commander of the 17th Gloucestershire (Wye Valley) Battalion of the Home Guard, from 1940 to its disbandment in 1944. One of the few retired naval officers to hold such a command, Carpenter ended his second war career as Director of Shipping at the Admiralty.

He married twice, first in 1903 to Maud Tordiffe, who died in 1923 and by whom he had a daughter, and, secondly, in 1927, to Hilda Margaret Alison Smith. Alfred Carpenter, who was second only to Roger Keyes as the dominating figure behind the most spectacular naval operation of the war, died at his home, Chanterslure, in St Briavels, on 27 December 1955. His body was cremated and later a slate plaque was placed in St Mary's Church, St Briavels, as a lasting memorial.

Described as 'lean and ascetic', Carpenter was the rarest of men. Equally at home in command of a ship or in charge of a headquarters ashore, he was both brave and intelligent, though Keyes ultimately considered him a bit too clever for his own good. And while his reputation was undoubtedly tarnished by his ill-conceived attempt to alter his version of events at Zeebrugge, there were plenty who echoed the sentiments expressed by the contributor to *The Dictionary of National Biography* who observed that he possessed 'many of the highest qualities of the best type of naval officer'.

Albert Edward McKenzie was born on 23 October 1898 at 10 Alice Street, Bermondsey, south-east London, the youngest son of Alexander McKenzie and Eliza (née Marks). His father, a photographer, died while Albert was an infant and most of his childhood was spent at 1 Shorncliffe Road, Old Kent Road, with his widowed mother and her large brood. He was educated at London County Council schools in Webb Street, Bermondsey, and Mina Road, Southwark, and attended St Mark's Sunday School in Camberwell.

This south London parish would supply 4,286 men for the country's armed forces, the largest number of any London parish, and McKenzie was to become the most distinguished member of what became known as 'St Mark's Little Army', as well as one of more than five hundred men to lose their lives before the war's end.

Albert McKenzie joined the Royal Navy training ship *Arethusa* at Greenhithe in 1913. A fine athlete despite being only 5ft 2in tall, he excelled at football and boxing, for which he gained the first of an array of medals and trophies. Having left *Arethusa* as a Boy Second Class on 20 June 1914, he advanced one step in rank to Boy First Class a week before Christmas. Rated able seaman on St George's Day 1916, he served in minesweepers, patrol boats and in convoy escorts before being transferred to the battleship *Neptune*, part of the Grand Fleet based at Scapa Flow. While serving in her, he continued to display his talent for boxing, taking the title of lightweight champion of the 4th Battle Squadron, as well as a number of lesser prizes. One of fifty men from *Neptune* who answered the call for volunteers for special services, McKenzie had just spent seven days in the ship's cells for an unknown misdemeanour. He was one of eight '*Arethusa* Lads' to embark in *Vindictive*. All were to be decorated for bravery, seven of them receiving DSMs to set alongside McKenzie's VC.

So serious were his injuries received during the raid, he was ferried straight from the docks at Dover to the Royal Naval Hospital at Chatham. He was still recovering from his injuries when it was announced in the *London Gazette* of 23 July 1918 that he had been selected by the seamen of *Vindictive*, *Iris II*, *Daffodil* and the naval assaulting force to receive the Victoria Cross. With his mother and sister Mary, he attended, on crutches, the investiture in the quadrangle of Buckingham Palace eight days later, a newsreel camera capturing for posterity his proudest moment.

After the ceremony he returned to his mother's house in Shorncliffe Road where he was fêted all over again. Amid much civic pomp, with flags and bunting decorating the street, thronged with well-wishers, the young hero was greeted by the Mayor of Southwark, who delighted the crowd by holding aloft McKenzie's blood-stained uniform and smashed watch. His mother, who had already lost one son to the war, received a gift of War Bonds and an illuminated address from 'his many friends in the Parish of St Mark's'.

By the autumn of 1918 the young seaman was still being treated in Chatham Naval Hospital, where his wounded foot had developed septic poisoning. But just as he appeared to be making a good recovery, he fell victim to the influenza pandemic. In his weakened state the 'flu soon developed into pneumonia from which he died on 3 November, eight days before the Armistice silenced the guns in Europe.

His body was brought back to London and on 9 November, following a funeral service attended by the Rt Hon. T.J. Macnamara MP, Financial Secretary to the Admiralty, and Captain Carpenter VC, he was buried in Camberwell Old Cemetery. The manner of his death, exposing the vulnerability of even the bravest spirits to the influenza scourge, appeared to touch a raw nerve. A message from the king and queen was read to mourners: 'In the special circumstances of Able Seaman Albert Edward McKenzie's lamentable death and the fact of his being a VC and the first London sailor to receive that most honourable reward, you are authorised to express at the public funeral at St Mark's Camberwell the sympathy of their majesties with the widowed mother and family. Their majesties were grieved to hear of his untimely death and to think that he had been spared so short a time to wear the proud decoration which he so nobly won.'

To this rare gesture from royalty to one of its most humble subjects was added a tribute from McKenzie's commander aboard *Vindictive*, Captain Carpenter, who told his mother: 'The splendid example which your boy set at Zeebrugge will be accorded a high place of honour in the naval records of the British Empire.' It was the politician T.J. Macnamara, however, who found the words that caught the mood and captured the headlines. 'Mrs McKenzie has lost a son,' he said in closing his oration, 'but the nation has found a hero.'

Almost a year later, on 4 October 1919, a headstone was placed at the foot of his grave by the Mayor of Southwark with the words, 'Albert McKenzie died nobly; we perpetuate his name; God bless him!'

Arthur Leyland Harrison was born at Torquay on 3 February 1886, the son of Lieutenant-Colonel Arthur J. Harrison of the Royal Fusiliers and Adelaide Ellen Harrison. Educated at Dover College, he joined the navy as a cadet in September 1902. He was promoted lieutenant on 1 October 1908, and that same year gained his first command, Torpedo-Boat No. 16. Strong and athletic, Harrison was an outstanding sportsman who excelled on the rugby field. A tireless forward, he played for the navy, United Services and England, gaining two caps, against France and Ireland, in the winter and spring of 1914. That season, the last before the war, was generally regarded as his best and there was no doubt that the conflict robbed him of many more caps. There was nothing sophisticated about his style of play. According to one English rugby chronicler, 'his game was the sturdy, bustling type', though he was also 'quite a good place-kicker'. In March 1914 he turned out for the navy against the army at Queen's, a match regarded as the finest ever played between the two sides. He served aboard HMS *Lion*, Admiral Beatty's flagship, at the battles of Heligoland Bight in August 1914 and the Dogger Bank the following January. A shipmate and fellow gun commander of Francis Harvey VC, Harrison received a mention in despatches for the 'splendid manner' in which he took charge of A turret during the fighting at Jutland when *Lion* sustained heavy damage. He was one of three turret commanders cited by *Lion*'s captain in his post-battle report:

> All these three excellent officers led the turrets' crews with courage and great ability, enabling, owing to their efficiency, fire to be maintained over the prolonged period the action lasted.
>
> The loading and firing of 321 rounds by three turrets, with but one fault in the drill, and a minimum of machinery failures, reflects the greatest credit on these turret officers, their hydraulic and armourer staffs.
>
> I would therefore ask that special notification in their favour for future reference may be made to the Admiralty.

Promoted lieutenant-commander in October, Harrison continued to serve in the Grand Fleet, but found time on leave to play rugby in scratch games at the Old Deer Park, Richmond. Still supremely fit for his age, he was, according to one account, always 'well to the fore'. Towards the end of 1917 Harrison was among those who answered the call for volunteers to perform 'hazardous services', the euphemism by which Keyes recruited for Zeebrugge. Joining the staff at Dover, Harrison, the athlete and team player, was the obvious choice to organise and train the seamen landing parties who would storm the mole. It was a task he revelled in, creating in a short time an enviable *esprit de corps*.

Arthur Harrison was not on the original list of men recommended for the Victoria Cross. Instead, like George Bradford, his name appeared in a list of 'gallant souls who did not live to see the success of their endeavours'. According to Lt Cdr Adams, 'he behaved with great coolness and bravery, directing the advance of the various storming parties' before being killed shortly before the recall was sounded.

Given that two of the six VCs awarded for the Zeebrugge operation had been 'elected' awards specifically granted in recognition of the navy's heroic part in the assault on the mole, it might have been assumed that nothing more could be done for Harrison. Keyes, however, thought differently. On 23 February 1919, ten months to the day after the raid, he recommended to the Admiralty that Harrison and Bradford be given posthumous VCs. 'Both these officers were killed ... after displaying courage and devotion to duty of the highest order,' wrote Keyes, who then added the curious note: 'Had they survived the action both would have been strongly recommended for this coveted decoration.' The suggestion was that Keyes believed, wrongly, that their deaths precluded such awards being made, though quite why he waited so long to act is unclear. Certainly nothing else had changed about the nature or knowledge of the two actions, though the original paragraphs covering their deeds were expanded.

Though surprised by the arrival of recommendations for an additional two VCs for an operation which had already resulted in six such awards, the navy was not adverse to them. 'It always struck me as curious that no recommendations for the posthumous award of the Victoria Cross were forwarded for any of the officers who were killed in the early stages of the landing on the mole at Zeebrugge,' wrote one senior figure at the Admiralty. 'In spite of the generous number of awards already made ... the awards now proposed seem well merited.'

Both VCs were duly gazetted on 17 March 1919. Two months later Arthur Harrison's mother made the short journey from Wadden Cottage, Durham Road in Wimbledon to Buckingham Palace to receive her son's Cross. A further tribute followed fifteen years later when a Belgian ex-soldiers' organisation, the Union des Fraternelles de l'Armée de Campagne, decided to name a room after him in a new club in Ghent.

Arthur Leyland Harrison has no known grave. His name appears on the Zeebrugge Memorial in Belgium, on the Roehampton War Memorial in south-west London and on a plaque in St Mary's Church, Wimbledon. His VC was donated to the Britannia Royal Naval College, Dartmouth, by his surviving relatives in 1967. More recently, on the 82nd anniversary of his fatal charge along the mole at Zeebrugge, the Torbay branch of the Royal Naval Association unveiled an impressive limestone and granite memorial at Roundham Head, Paignton, in tribute to the navy's England international rugby player who died as he had lived, leading from the front.

'I can truly say a more honourable, straight, and gallant English gentleman never lived ...' With those words the captain of *Orion* sought to sum up the character of George Bradford, an officer 'beloved by all', who had been specially selected from the whole of the 2nd Battle Squadron to command its force of volunteers at Zeebrugge.

George Nicholson Bradford was born on 23 April 1887 at Witton Park, Durham, the second son of George Bradford and Amy Marion (née Andrews). One of four brothers, and with a sister fourteen years his junior, he enjoyed the privileges of a prosperous, long-established northern family which claimed descent from fighting 'Border stock'. His father was a mining engineer, a forceful, independent man who had risen by merit to become colliery manager, mine owner and, eventually, chairman of a group of collieries in South Wales and a steel company in Darlington, where his family lived. A stern disciplinarian who ruled his sons with the rod, George Bradford sr combined a strong work ethic with immense physical strength.

From an early age the Bradford boys – Thomas, George, James and Roland – were imbued with a love of sport and inspired by tales of derring-do. A belief in fair play, personal gallantry and the nobility of self-sacrifice became so ingrained in them that they came to adopt as the Bradford motto Bayard's famous phrase: 'Chevalier sans peur.'

George attended Darlington Grammar School, the Royal Naval School, Eltham, and Eastmans, before joining *Britannia* as a cadet in 1902. Although it was said that he worked harder than any of his brothers, his work as a scholar was overshadowed by his sporting prowess. A superb athlete, he was a fine cricketer and an outstanding boxer, having been coached as a boy by his maternal grandfather, a former bare-knuckle fighter who had challenged the likes of Tom Sayers and Jem Mace. In the course of his naval career, Bradford became officers' welterweight champion and twice reached the finals of the army and navy officers' championships. An orthodox amateur who was an enthusiastic follower of the professional sport, he boxed with grace, agility and, above all, courage. His ring craft was later celebrated in print by the naval writer Bartimeus, who based one of his stories on a memorable exhibition contest staged during the war between Bradford and a former professional boxer, then serving in the Grand Fleet as a seaman. Though given the fictional name of Lieutenant Adams, the physical description matched Bradford: 'Deep-chested, lean-flanked, perfectly proportioned ...'

A leader by example, George Bradford was a gifted trainer, capable of inspiring great loyalty and unit pride. By nature modest, he thought little of personal ambition, which probably explains why his career was marked by steady rather than rapid advancement. His last promotion, to lieutenant-commander in July 1917, followed eight years as a lieutenant.

As a midshipman he served in the battleships *Revenge* and *Exmouth* of the Channel Fleet from 1904 to 1907, and thereafter he alternated between destroyer and big ship appointments. In January 1908, as a sub-lieutenant of eight months' standing, he joined the destroyer *Chelmer*, serving under another future VC, William Loftus Jones. The following year, while acting as first lieutenant, he gave an example of his selfless courage when, following a collision between a destroyer and a trawler in the early hours of 3 March, he led the efforts to save crew-men trapped aboard the fishing boat. Having successfully brought off three men, Bradford learned that a youngster was still on board the rapidly sinking trawler. Without hesitation, he returned, 'sprang on board, rushed to the fore peak, now inky black, and as the trawler gave a lurch, appeared with the unconscious boy in his arms'. Just as he jumped into *Chelmer*'s whaler, the trawler up-ended and sank. Promoted lieutenant for his actions, Bradford joined the battleship *Vanguard* on her com-missioning in March 1910. After almost two years in her, he returned to destroyers as first lieutenant of *Amazon* from January 1912 until January 1914, when he was appointed to *Orion*.

The reluctance of the enemy to confront the might of the Grand Fleet restricted his opportunities to gain distinction. The fighting at Jutland was a rare moment of drama in an otherwise unspectacular war. Yet through all the years of frustration and inactivity his morale appeared never to flag. To his sister he once wrote: 'I think the war is going well and the prospects excellent, don't allow anyone with a long face to say otherwise ...' And in November 1917 he prophetically observed: 'I think the Huns will have had all they want by this time next year.' His letters were always signed, 'Your affect. brother G.N. Bradford', lead-ing him to comment: 'Curious thing, I have never written George in my life. A quaint family i' faith, pukka Dickens' characters.' Formal sig-nature apart, his correspondence was invariably cheery and optimistic and reflected the pride felt in his brothers' exploits. The record of their achievements and sacrifice was an extraordinary one: Tommie, later Sir Thomas, was awarded the DSO in January 1916; Jimmy, a subaltern in the 18th DLI, died of wounds in May 1917, two months after earning an MC; and, most outstanding of all, Roland collected an MC in 1915 and a VC on the Somme a year later, and became at 25 the youngest brigadier in the British army before his death in action on 30 November 1917. Of his heroic brother, George wrote: 'Poor old Roland will live in history, a marvellous leader of men and died a glorious death.'

Within five months, he too had gone, the last of three Bradford brothers consumed by the conflict, and those same words might equally have been used to describe his own sacrifice. Admiral Viscount Jellicoe, who knew him personally, wrote of his action: 'He died, as one would have expected him to die, under circumstances of the greatest gallantry.' Many senior officers wrote in similar vein and yet the war closed with no sign of recognition beyond a paltry mention in despatches. Four months later Amy Bradford, George's widowed mother, received the great news that a second son was to be awarded the country's highest martial honour. Written by Admiral Keyes on 14 March, three days before the VC was officially announced, the letter stated:

> I knew he would eventually get it, because although many actions were performed on that night by officers and men who survived, and by others who gave their lives, amongst the latter your son's act of glorious self-sacrifice stood out, I thought, alone ...

Two weeks later, on 3 April, Mrs Bradford went to Buckingham Palace to receive the Cross from the king. It was only the third instance of brothers earning the distinction, with the awards to Roland and George Bradford being the only example of the kind during the First World War.

Unlike Arthur Harrison, who was 'selected' with him, in Keyes's phrase, 'to represent the gallant throng who did not survive', Bradford has a marked grave. Having fallen to his death between the *Iris II* and the mole, his body was washed ashore a few days later, some 3 miles down the coast at Blankenberge, and was buried by the Germans in the communal cemetery there.

For years after, his sacrifice was remembered every St George's Day by an *in memoriam* notice in *The Times*. It was placed there every year until her death by Mrs Bradford, who used to take part in Armistice Day services wearing the two VCs and two MCs of her dead sons. Later, when she was too frail to attend, her place was taken by her daughter, who in April 1918 had received one of the last letters George wrote before his death. In it, he cheerily applauded her school success and looked forward to her birthday – which he would not live to see – before closing with the line that might have served as his own epitaph:

'Au revoir, don't forget the Chevalier Bayard, sans reproche, etc. Best love, your affec. brother, G.N. Bradford.'

Like Harrison, Bradford and McKenzie, Edward Bamford was a fine athlete, with a particular penchant for golf, hockey and tennis, and an enthusiasm for fishing and sailing. He was born at 34 Langdon Park Road, Highgate, London, on 28 May 1887, the second of three sons to the Revd Robert and Blanche Edith Bamford, of Elmtree, St Marychurch, Torquay. Educated at Sherborne School and Malvern House in Kearnsey, near Dover, he entered the Royal Marines on 1 September 1905 as second lieutenant and attended the Royal Naval College, Greenwich, before joining the Portsmouth Division, Royal Marine Light Infantry, on 1 July 1907. A noteworthy student, he shared in the award of the King George Prize Scholarship and was promoted lieutenant on 1 July 1906. It would be another ten years before his next promotion, during which time his appointments were mostly sea-going posts in either the Home or Grand Fleets.

His first ship was HMS *Bulwark* of the Channel Squadron, which he joined on 5 December 1908. Having passed a course in physical training, he later moved to HMS *Magnificent* on 18 March 1910, before joining HMS *Britannia*, after a few months on shore duty, on 5 September 1911. He served in this ship until the end of November 1915, and was aboard her when she ran aground near Inch Keith, on her way to support Beatty's battlecruisers in the action fought off the Dogger Bank the previous January. Returning to the Portsmouth Division, Bamford attended a musketry course at Hythe in January 1916, gaining a first class instructor's certificate, and was posted to the Western Front, on brief attachment to the Guards Brigade, then manning the lines in the Ypres salient. Having endured his baptism of fire during minor operations in April, Bamford promptly found himself posted back to sea. Promoted temporary captain on 2 May, he was appointed to the newly commissioned light cruiser HMS *Chester*, as officer commanding the Royal Marine contingent. After almost two years on the fringes of the action, he was quickly in the thick of things, especially during *Chester*'s running battle at Jutland in which she narrowly escaped destruction in her first fight.

As related in an earlier chapter, Bamford had displayed unflinching heroism while commanding two guns manned by his marines. Wounded and slightly burned about the face when his after-control station was 'blown to pieces' by a shell burst, he nevertheless 'assisted to work one gun with a much reduced crew, and controlled another gun'. Later, despite his injuries, he helped to extinguish a cordite fire and, in the words of Jellicoe's despatch, 'showed great coolness, power of command, judgement, and courage, when exposed to a very heavy fire'. His gallantry in an action he was fortunate to survive resulted in the award of the Distinguished Service Order (*LG*, 15 September 1916) and the Order of St Anne, 3rd Class (with Swords), which was conferred by the Russian Government 'for distinguished services in the Battle of Jutland' (*LG*, 5 June 1917).

Bamford's injuries healed quickly. After a spell in HMS *Chatham*, he returned to *Chester*, her battle damage repaired, and was a witness in August to the torpedoing of HMS *Falmouth* off Flamborough Head. Two weeks later, on 1 September, he was promoted captain. He remained with *Chester* until February 1918, when he was appointed to command a company of the specially formed 4th Royal Marines for the duration of the Zeebrugge operations.

What was left of the battalion returned to Deal on 23 April, where orders were received to disperse on 27 April. The day before doing so, the survivors were paraded and informed that they were to elect a representative to receive the VC. Small pieces of paper were issued and the men of the battalion were ordered to break off, with half an hour to make their choice. The CO and adjutant withdrew, leaving Edward Bamford as senior company commander to supervise the collection and counting of the voting slips. 'An hour or so later,' wrote Arthur Chater, the adjutant, 'Capt. Bamford came into the office looking very embarrassed and handed to the CO the paper … It was straightaway reported to the Vice-Admiral's Office at Dover that Capt. Bamford had been elected to receive the VC.'

The citation originally submitted, however, gave little indication of his inspiring leadership, and prompted some concern at the Admiralty. A senior officer noted: 'It is not revealed why Capt. Bamford was chosen for the VC but it would seem desirable that something more than has appeared in the despatch should appear in the *Gazette* in order to exalt the honour of the VC.' With that, the citation was promptly redrafted in suitable terms.

As one of the six original VCs, his award was gazetted on 23 July 1918 and presented to him eight days later by the king at a Buckingham Palace investiture attended by his fellow recipients, Carpenter, Dean, Finch, McKenzie and Sandford. His gallantry was further marked by promotion to brevet major and the subsequent award of the French Legion of Honour (*LG*, 23 May 1919). On 26 August 1918 he resumed his association with the Grand Fleet, joining the battleship HMS *Royal Sovereign*, in which ship he witnessed the surrender of the High Seas Fleet in the Firth of Forth ten days after the Armistice was signed.

Bamford left *Royal Sovereign* in March 1919. His next ship was HMS *Highflyer*, which he joined the following September, bound for the East Indies. Returning to his division in May 1921, he spent three months at the Deal Depot, during which time he was engaged in ceremonial duties, attached to the entourage of the Crown Prince of Japan, then on a state visit to England. In recognition of his services, Bamford was awarded the Japanese Order of the Rising Sun (4th Class) in August. The following month he attended the war staff course at the RN College, a necessary precursor to achieving senior rank, qualifying in July 1922. His varied service continued in September with his appointment to the 11th Battalion, Royal Marines, part of the Inter-Allied Mission sent to Thrace to keep the peace between Greece and Turkey. Attached for a month to the Mission's staff, he further enhanced his reputation, his name being brought to the Admiralty's notice 'for tact and energy'. A year spent in the Eastern Mediterranean was followed by home appointments until, in September 1924, he embarked on what would prove his last sea-going appointment, in HMS *Curacoa*, operating in the Atlantic. Two years later, after a short spell with the Plymouth Division, he set off for the Far East to take up an appointment as small arms instructor in Hong Kong. He was promoted major on 1 March 1928, but in September, during a stay at Wei Hai Wei, a naval base on the northern coast of China, he contracted a mysterious illness. In urgent need of hospital treatment, he was taken aboard HMS *Cumberland* on 28 September, bound for Hong Kong. A marine officer serving in *Cumberland* later recorded:

> Major Bamford occupied an officer's cabin and was supplied with a Marine orderly to look after his personal wants on the voyage. We felt very honoured at having such a passenger on board, and everything was done for him so that he would be as comfortable as possible. However, on the following day his condition grew worse ... A WT message was sent to the C.-in-C., asking whether we could make for the nearest port at all speed

as his condition was rapidly becoming worse. I do not know what the reply was, but soon afterwards we altered course and all boilers were brought into use. By midnight on the 29th we were ploughing through a moderately heavy swell at high speed – our only hope, now, of saving his life. WT messages were continuously made to Shanghai, our objective, and everything was arranged for his quick transport to hospital.

We reached Woosung Flats, about 10 miles from Shanghai, at 3.30am on the 30th, but Major Bamford quietly passed away at about 3.35. We dropped anchor, and awaited orders from England re the disposal of the body.

Later that day, as the tug *Nan Yang* came alongside, *Cumberland*'s marine detachment formed up on the quarterdeck, with the rest of the ship's company lining the guard-rail, bare-headed, while Bamford's body, draped in a Union Jack, was carried on the shoulders of six marine bearers to the strains of Chopin's funeral march. Then the band fell silent as the body was lowered gently over the side on to the tug. The marine Guard of Honour remained at the 'present' until *Nan Yang* passed out of sight on its way into Shanghai. The impressive little ceremony made a deep impact on *Cumberland*'s crew. 'It was a very sad day for us,' wrote one marine officer, 'hardly a word was spoken above a whisper on the usually noisy mess-deck all day.' *Cumberland* remained at Woosung until sunset, her ensign lowered to half-mast.

Edward Bamford was buried in the Bubbling Well Road (English) Cemetery, Shanghai. A headstone with the globe and laurel badge marked his grave until the cemetery was levelled to make way for a shopping development. Tributes to his distinguished service in peace and war take the form of a memorial in the Depot Church at Deal and a house named after him at the Royal Marine Barracks, Eastney. Bamford never married. He was wedded instead to the Marines, a force to whom he devoted more than half his life and to which, appropriately, his many distinctions were eventually presented.

Norman Augustus Finch was born at 42 Ninevah Road, Handsworth, Birmingham, on Boxing Day 1890, the son of John Finch, a postman, and his wife Emma Amelia. He attended Benson Road Board School and Norton Street Council School and worked as a tool machinist for the Birmingham firm H.W. Ward & Co., before joining the Royal Marine Artillery on 15 January 1908. He was described on his papers

as standing 5ft 11½in, with brown hair, blue eyes and a fresh complexion.

Finch, who later forfeited 346 days' service towards his engagement and pension for being under age, trained at Eastney and embarked in the cruiser *Diadem*, his first ship, on 17 June 1909. The following year he left the Home Fleet and, as gunner second class, joined HMS *Minotaur* for a two-year stint on the China Station. A short time at Eastney separated spells in the Portsmouth training cruiser HMS *Spartiate* and the Chatham cruiser HMS *Antrim*, which he joined on 3 December 1912. He served in her for more than three years, being successively promoted bombardier (1 June 1913) and corporal (2 January 1915), before returning once more to Eastney on 19 August 1916. During this time *Antrim* operated out of Rosyth with the Third Cruiser Squadron as Rear-Admiral William Pakenham's flagship. *Antrim* had narrowly evaded a U-boat attack on 9 October 1914, and a report, subsequently published in the *Birmingham Mail*, stated that Finch had been given a shore job after 'his nerves gave way'.

He quickly found a niche as a trainer. Promoted sergeant on 15 March 1917, he became a temporary instructor for gunnery at sea in November. Finch went back to sea in the battlecruiser *Inflexible*, part of the Grand Fleet, in the following January, but shortly afterwards was recalled as preparations began for the raid on Zeebrugge.

Finch was still recovering in hospital from shrapnel wounds to his right hand and right leg when he learned that he had been chosen to receive the Victoria Cross. Officially it was stated that he was elected for the honour by the non-commissioned officers and other ranks of the 4th Royal Marines. But this was not the case. The battalion's adjutant has recorded that the unit only discovered it should select a second VC on the day after the original election was held. The news was brought to them personally by Vice-Admiral Keyes. 'The CO and Adjutant withdrew and after a brief talk told the Admiral that the second VC should go to Sergeant Finch,' wrote Arthur Chater. Although 'most irregular and certainly not in accordance with the Royal Warrant', Chater said the award proved 'completely acceptable' to all ranks.

No one was more surprised than Finch himself. 'Seems to me if one has the VC, the whole lot ought to have it,' he told Second Lieutenant J. Keble Bell, who was writing a semi-official publication about the raid. Finch made as little of his injuries as he did of his actions. To Keble Bell, he said: 'I didn't want to come here. I wanted to go back to barracks with my pal. I never noticed I was hurt ... All I know is I'm dreading this business that's coming.' The 'business' was a euphemism for the flag-waving pomp he knew was sure to follow. 'He had visions', wrote Keble Bell, 'of impetuous and quite strange ladies flinging their arms about his modest neck.'

After his investiture at Buckingham Palace on 31 July, Finch returned to Eastney barracks in style, with a band leading the way and his flag-bedecked car being drawn by a party of marines to the parade ground, where, amid loud cheering, he was received by the Commandant, RMA.

He married Elizabeth Jane Ross on 3 April 1919 in Birmingham, and five days later took up a new appointment as Instructor of Coast Defence Gunnery. The following August, Finch, who had been paid a war gratuity of £32 with £14 from the Naval Prize fund, was promoted colour sergeant. He signed on for a further engagement on 8 January 1921, and in July joined the 10th RM Battalion, his service with this unit being broken by two months in HMS *Crescent*. In September 1922 he went to the 11th Battalion which, with the Corps' other Zeebrugge VC, Edward Bamford, among its officers, was deployed in the Eastern Mediterranean for a year.

On 27 January 1924 Finch received a Long Service and Good Conduct medal. Promoted barrack quartermaster sergeant on 23 December 1925, he eventually retired in 1929 on his 39th birthday, with three good conduct badges to his name and a recommendation for the Meritorious Service Medal, which he duly received.

Settling in Southsea with his wife and son, who later served in the RAF, Finch became a postman and then, a bank messenger in Portsmouth's North End. On New Year's Day 1931 he was made a Yeoman of the Guard. Mobilised briefly during the Munich crisis of 1938, Finch returned to his old job as quartermaster sergeant in the Portsmouth Division in October 1939. He served in Corps home establishments throughout the war, being promoted temporary lieutenant (quartermaster) on 25 February 1943. Released from service on 16 August 1945, he returned to his job as a bank messenger and ceremonial duties with HM Bodyguard of the Yeoman of the Guard, in which he became only the second marine to hold the rank of divisional sergeant major. His last award was the Royal Victorian Medal (silver) which he added to his 1935 Jubilee Medal and 1937 and 1953 Coronation Medals.

Following the death of his wife from cancer, Finch, then in his 60s, moved to a small flat. He lived there alone until, after suffering a heart attack, he was persuaded to move in with a friend, another ex-marine, and his family. Finch spent the last two years of his life with the Shaws, whose children nicknamed him 'Flump' on account of his expansive girth. Ruth Shaw remembered him as a jolly figure, determined and optimistic, who still bore the scars of his gallant action. 'He was a lovely character, humorous, funny and very kind,' she said. 'Children loved him. In order to get my children through university, I took students in and they loved him too. He used to play cards with them.'

Norman Finch died in St Mary's Hospital, Milton, Portsmouth, on 15 March 1966 and was cremated at Portchester six days later. His impressive collection of medals was bequeathed to the Corps he had served so faithfully. As an enthusiastic member of the Zeebrugge Association, he had participated in many pilgrimages back to Belgium, including the ceremony to unveil the memorial there in 1925. And thoughout his life he felt he was merely the temporary custodian of the VC on behalf of his fellow marines. As Ruth Shaw remembered:

> He once gave a talk on the radio in which he emphasised he was holding the VC for other marines. That was the way he saw it. He never boasted about the award or even mentioned it. I think my husband was prouder of it than Norman!

Richard Douglas Sandford was born at 15 The Beacon, Exmouth, on 11 May 1891, the seventh son of the Ven. Ernest Grey Sandford, Archdeacon of Exeter, and Ethel (née Poole). Like his elder brother Francis, Richard was educated at Clifton College before going on to HMS *Britannia* at Dartmouth en route to a career in the Royal Navy. He became a midshipman on 15 September 1908, serving on the battleship HMS *Hibernia* and then, from January 1910 until April 1911, on the torpedo-boat destroyer HMS *Arab*. During the following three years his career oscillated between 'big ship' duties and destroyers. After *Arab*, he went to the battle-ship *Formidable* and then, in December 1911, as a sub-lieutenant, to the destroyer HMS *Mohawk*, before joining the cruiser *Duke of Edinburgh* as an additional officer in February 1913.

What had been an orthodox career path was broken in January 1914 when he joined HMS *Dolphin* (2nd Submarine Flotilla) for submarine training. This service, still in its first flush of youth, evidently suited him, and the remainder of his naval career was spent as a submariner. On completion of the course, he moved to HMS *Onyx* (1st Submarine Flotilla) at Devonport in May, as a spare officer.

His first boat was the Armstrong-Laubeuf type *W1*, which he joined as second-in-command while she was under construction at Newcastle in November 1914. On her completion he moved with her to Portsmouth for trials, before transferring to the 10th Submarine Flotilla at Immingham in May 1915. Based on a French design, the W-class boats were unsuitable for North Sea work and were later sold to the Italian government. After an uneventful seven months Dick Sandford transferred to the 11th Submarine Flotilla at Blyth, where his new sub-marine, the overseas boat *G6*, was being built. By coincidence, his first lieutenant on *C3*, John Howell-Price, would later also serve in *G6* as navigation officer. Sandford's time in *G6*, however, was unusually brief. In August 1916, two months after her completion, he transferred to *C34*, a smaller, coastal boat, part of the Dover Patrol's 4th Flotilla. *C34* later fell victim to a German U-boat, but by then the much-travelled Sandford had long since departed for yet another new boat which was under construction. This was *K6*, a huge, steam-driven boat that belonged to the most ill-starred submarine class ever built for the Royal Navy. In the space of little more than a year, four K-boats were lost, all through accidents, leading one officer to comment: 'The only good thing about K-boats was that they never engaged the enemy.' Sandford spent two months waiting for his boat's completion, eventually joining her as first lieutenant in February 1917. Designed to operate with the Grand Fleet, these cruiser submarines, with the speed of a destroyer and the turning circle of a battlecruiser, were initially regarded as pres-tige boats. Their shortcomings, however, quickly became apparent and their work was restricted to exercises and anti-submarine patrols. To counter the boredom, *K6*'s captain encouraged his crew to start a garden! The dull routine, however, was to be dramatically interrupted on a night in January 1918, destined to be remembered as the most calamitous in submarine history.

On 31 January the ships in the Firth of Forth were ordered out on a full-scale Grand Fleet exercise. The Rosyth contingent included the 5th Battle Squadron and the 2nd Cruiser Squadron, together with the 1st, 3rd and 4th Light Cruiser Squadrons, numerous destroyers and two

K-class flotillas, sailing on the surface behind their light cruiser leaders. The night was pitch black with patches of mist and the nine submarines were sandwiched between forces of darkened cruisers. That was bad enough, given their difficulties in station-keeping but, unfortunately, across their path, near May Island, lay a group of minesweepers, totally oblivious of the Fleet manoeuvres. In the tragic chaos that ensued, *K14* was struck by *K22*, which in turn was rammed by the cruiser *Inflexible*. Miraculously both boats struggled back to Rosyth, but worse was to follow. Led by their flotilla cruiser, the remaining three boats turned back to try to help, but succeeded only in adding to the confusion and loss. For in steering to avoid one vessel, they blundered into the path of the light cruiser *Fearless*, leading the four K-boats of the 12th Flotilla. *Fearless* was unable to avoid a collision with *K17*, which sank with the loss of all but nine men, and as *K4* veered away, *K6*, which was third in line, followed and rammed her amidships. The officer on watch on *K6* was Dick Sandford and the crew included a 17-year-old midshipman by the name of Lord Louis Mountbatten. Moments earlier, Sandford had taken avoiding action to miss *K12*, one of the inbound 13th Flotilla, but in doing so he lost sight of *K3* ahead of him. Mistaking a light ahead of him for *K3*, he steered towards it only to discover too late that it belonged to *K4* which had gone off course and stopped, broadside on to *K6*. Too close to avoid the collision, *K6*, with Sandford a helpless observer on the bridge, smashed into *K4*, almost slicing her in half. For thirty seconds the two submarines remained locked together, and as *K4* began to sink it seemed that *K6* would be dragged down with her. Finally, she broke clear and, having been narrowly missed by *K7*, limped back to Rosyth, with six inches or so of water slopping around in her flooded fore compartment. Of *K4* and her crew nothing was ever seen again.

Following an inquiry into what became known as the Battle of May Island, there were a number of changes in personnel. Among those who left Rosyth was Dick Sandford, though in his case it was a matter of leaving one 'Suicide Club', as the K-boat men called them-selves, for another, in the shape of a one-way ticket into Zeebrugge as part of Vice-Admiral Keyes's audacious plan to block the Belgian port. Following the catastrophic events of 31 January, Sandford had attended the 'perisher course' for potential submarine commanders at HMS *Dolphin* and was put in temporary command of *K2*. But when his elder brother Francis, who was serving as demolitions officer on Keyes's staff, approached him with the offer of commanding *C3* on its mission to blow up the viaduct, he seized the opportunity to transform his fortunes and rescue an otherwise undistinguished career.

Of all the VCs awarded for the operations at Zeebrugge and Ostend, Dick Sandford's was perhaps the most universally approved. When his Cross was gazetted on 23 July 1918, it was said to have 'snowed telegrams' on his family. One simply read: 'Well done, Uncle Baldy!' Sandford, typically, made light of it, insisting to one journalist: 'We only got there because every bally thing went wrong.' Eight days after the announcement, Sandford, his wounds sufficiently healed, went to Buckingham Palace to receive his VC from the king. To this, the French added their Legion of Honour (Knight), which was gazetted on 28 August.

By then, Sandford had returned to duty in command of the 6th Flotilla's *C30*. His stay was short. In October he was transferred to the 10th Flotilla, based on Teesside, where he became relief CO and then CO of the *G11*. Shortly afterwards, however, he contracted typhoid fever and went into Cleveland House Naval Hospital, Grangetown, where he died on 23 November 1918. The cause of death was given as: typhoid fever, nineteen days, and perforation of ulcer of intestine, two days. It was the cruellest of ironies. Having miraculously survived an exploit many thought would end in certain death, he had succumbed to a bacterial disease. He was 27 and had been afforded little time to bask in the glory of his richly merited rewards.

Dick Sandford was buried in Eston Cemetery, near Middlesbrough, and is remembered on a number of memorials, including one in the Submarine Museum, which features a carved portrait and was originally displayed in Cleveland House. Sandford Avenue, Gosport, is also named after him, while Exeter Cathedral, a place he knew well as a child, bears mute testimony to the heroic services of Dick Sandford and his brother Francis, whose honours included a DSO won in the Dardanelles and a French Croix de Guerre with Palm awarded for his part in the Zeebrugge operation. Francis died in 1926. On a plaque which stands not far from similar memorials to three other VC holders – Sir Redvers Buller, Howard Elphinstone and Garth Walford – the inscription reads: 'To the glorious memory of two brothers ... who in a dark hour of peril on St George's Day 1918 together maintained the highest traditions of the Navy.'

Percy Thompson Dean, at 40 the oldest of all the Zeebrugge VCs, was born on 20 July 1877, at Witton Bank, Witton, Blackburn, in Lancashire, the son of John Dean and Ellen (née Thompson). The Deans were a prominent middle-class family with strong economic and political associations

in the neighbourhood. Both his paternal grandfather and his maternal uncle were former mayors of Blackburn, while the family's wealth was founded on successful slate merchant and cotton spinning businesses.

Educated at King Edward's School, Bromsgrove, from 1890 to 1895, Percy was an undistinguished scholar with little evidence of any sporting prowess beyond the fives' court. Given his background, academic achievement was of little consequence. Convention dictated that Percy would follow in his father's commercial footsteps, and this he duly did, to marked success, reviving the slate business which had fallen into decline since his father's death. In doing so, he gained a reputation as a 'model employer' and soon acquired most of the trappings of prosperous provincial life: a wife, Mabel Ratcliffe, whom he married in 1906, and a son. It was the first of his three marriages. Following his first wife's sudden death in 1907, he married Jeanne Marie Klein in 1908, by whom he had a daughter. They were divorced in 1921 and in 1927 he married Mrs M.R. Hardicker, the widow of Lieutenant-General J.O. Hardicker.

Having been 'nurtured on politics and reared in the orthodoxy of Conservatism', it was perhaps inevitable that he should eventually enter public life. Indeed, it was surprising that he waited so long. It was not until 1911 that he was appointed chairman of the Young Unionist League in Blackburn, even though he was then in his mid-30s. His rise thereafter was rapid. In 1913 he became a town councillor, wresting a seat from the Labour Party, and two years later he was selected as chairman of the local Conservative Party.

By then, Britain was at war and political office seemed to offer the only means of serving his country. An attempt to join the army was rejected because of a bizarre injury suffered during a Christmas vacation in 1912. While staying at a hotel in Blackpool, he was washing his feet in a bathroom basin when it broke, severing a tendon at the back of his leg. Despite surgery, the damage was never entirely repaired and he was left with a slight limp for the rest of his life.

Refusing to be put off, Dean then turned his attentions to the navy. In so doing he was motivated by the conviction that his skill as a yachtsman outweighed any disadvantage caused by his minor disability. Sailing had, in fact, been his main recreation for some time. He was a popular member of the West Lancashire Yacht Club at Hoylake, and a friend later recalled how for many years before the war 'all his spare time from Easter to September ... was spent in racing or cruising in small boats, mostly in Liverpool Bay and the Menai Straits, with a cruise to the Irish and Scottish coasts in his summer holiday'. During these ventures, which sometimes took him as far as the Hebrides and the Baltic, he proved himself an accomplished seaman as well as a leader. 'If sail had to be reefed in a seaway, head sails changed, or some lumber aloft cleared, as rope jammed or fouled, the owner or owners did the job,' wrote a colleague. 'No paid hand was carried in his early days, and the little ship always made its port in seamanlike style, the finest training this for self-reliance and future service.'

His efforts paid off. In June 1916 he was commissioned as a temporary sub-lieutenant in the RNVR. Although at 38 he was considerably older than most men of similar rank, the tall, fair-haired amateur sailor retained a youthful thirst for adventure. Joining the Dover Patrol in July, he fitted in well, and in April 1917 played a supporting role in the celebrated destroyer action which resulted in an enemy ship being rammed and a boarding party repelled. Promoted lieutenant in June, he was commanding a motor-launch when the call went out for volunteers to take part in the blocking operation against Zeebrugge.

Having come through the raid miraculously unscathed, he returned home on leave, where a journalist found him 'bronzed and fit' and buoyed by a raid he described as 'absolutely successful'. 'I know this is so,' he declared, 'because I was up against the stern of the block-ships for some considerable time and saw them sunk.' His VC, one of only two non-elected awards in the original list, was gazetted on 23 July 1918 and presented to him at Buckingham Palace eight days later. His skill and daring were further recognised by promotion to lieutenant-commander, back-dated to 23 April.

Dean had been hailed a hero in his home town long before he received any official recognition, and local politicians were quick to take advantage of his celebrity. On 3 July 1918, almost three weeks before his VC was announced, he accepted the nomination to stand as Blackburn's Conservative candidate at the first post-war election. Five months later the naval hero was a MP, having trounced the eminent Labour politician Philip (later Viscount) Snowden. His parliamentary career, however, was short and undistinguished, and in 1922 he stood down.

As managing director of Messrs John Dean Ltd, Messrs Forrest & Crabtree Ltd, and the Moelferna and Deeside Slate and Slab Quarries, and chairman of Messrs Dean, Waddington & Co., he had much to occupy him. But politics continued to exert a pull. In 1930 he was appointed for a second time chairman of the Blackburn Conservative and Unionist Association. He held the post for three years, until the pressure of his business interests in London brought about his resignation. The remainder of his life was spent mostly in the capital, where he occasionally gave lectures on his war-time experiences. His last public appearance in Blackburn was as a guest speaker at the Old Contemptibles' annual dinner in November 1938. By then his health was beginning to fail. Early the following year he became seriously ill and in an attempt to recover embarked on a cruise to the West Indies. It was all to no avail. On 20 March 1939, with war clouds gathering again, Percy Dean died at his north-west London home.

Among the mourners at his funeral at Golders Green Crematorium were many political figures and former naval colleagues, including another motor-launch VC commander, Geoffrey Drummond, and one of the men who accompanied him on his most famous mission, his second-in-command aboard ML282, Keith Wright. Nor did Blackburn forget one of its most distinguished sons. Flags were flown at half-mast over civic buildings and a memorial service in the town's St Silas' Church was timed to coincide with the funeral in London. A plaque on the Old Town Hall, a place he came to know so well in his political life, was a fitting tribute to Blackburn's greatest amateur seaman. Writing in *The Times*, an anonymous obituarist observed: 'the seas have lost some of their savour with his passing. We shall not see his like again in the little ships that sail the narrow seas.'

G.H. DRUMMOND
R.R.L. BOURKE
AND V.A.C. CRUTCHLEY

Ostend, 9–10 May 1918

If Zeebrugge could be counted a partial success, rendered glorious by skilful propaganda, nothing could disguise the abject failure of the attempt to seal Ostend. Almost everything that could go wrong had conspired to do so. Marker buoys upon which the blockships depended for their pre-determined course were moved at the last minute. The wind had changed direction, throwing smokescreens offshore and the attack into confusion. Off course and blinded by the smoke that was supposed to protect them, the blockships blundered through a storm of fire on to a sandbar as the operation turned into a fiasco with first *Brilliant* and then *Sirius* running aground. Realising the hopelessness of the situation, *Brilliant*'s captain, Commander Alfred Godsal, ordered the charges blown. *Sirius*, already badly hit and close to sinking, followed suit, and both ships settled on the sand 1½ miles east of their objective.

Calamitous as it was, the operation might have been even worse but for the courageous efforts of the supporting motor-launches which braved heavy fire to bring off the crews. Notable among these was ML276 commanded by Lieutenant Rowley Bourke, a 32-year-old Canadian. Four times he ran alongside the stranded *Brilliant* as she was pelted by shore batteries and machine-guns. On his third trip, he took off *Brilliant*'s redoubtable, red-bearded first lieutenant, Victor Crutchley, whose first words were to request them not to leave without his captain, whom he called a 'jolly sort'. Godsal departed only after making sure no one was left aboard. Bourke eventually made Dunkirk at 6.30 a.m. with an additional thirty-eight officers and men on board, having had a crippled launch in tow for much of the way back. By then, he had been on the bridge for twelve hours without a break.

No sooner were Godsal and Crutchley ashore than they began plotting a second attempt. Despite their disappointment, both were convinced the canal could be reached and blocked. Together with Lieutenant-Commander Henry Hardy, captain of *Sirius*, they begged Commodore Hubert Lynes, the Ostend force commander, to be given another chance. Keyes needed no such urging. Already of the same mind, it took him only a few hours to lay down the principles for the next attempt. Discussing the matter with Lynes, Godsal and Hardy, he made a two-hour inspection of the battered *Vindictive* and then wired the Admiralty with his intention of fitting her out for one last mission: to block Ostend.

Work started immediately. While electrical staff worked flat out to rewire the shattered communications, dockyard engineers replaced the tattered funnel casings. At the same time the holes torn in her side, some of them 5ft across, were patched and all unnecessary fittings removed. As specialists installed a new compass, men from the Dover Garrison filled the after magazines and bunkers with 200 tons of concrete and rubble. Within forty-eight hours *Vindictive* was ready, but by then the weather had broken and it was a case of waiting for the right conditions.

Executive command again went to Lynes, with Godsal given command of *Vindictive*. All of *Brilliant*'s officers volunteered for the second effort, but Keyes insisted on taking the fewest possible crew in order to minimise the number of casualties. As a result, Godsal selected only Crutchley, his shipmate from *Centurion*, to act as first lieutenant, Sub-Lieutenant Angus MacLachlan and Petty Officer Joseph Reed, senior petty officer aboard the *Brilliant*, who had impressed him by his coolness during the first attempt. They were joined by Engineer Lieutenant-Commander William Bury, *Vindictive*'s engineer at Zeebrugge, and Lieutenant Sir John Alleyne, a navigating officer expert in the workings of the ship's new compass and knowledgeable about Belgian coastal waters. Bury brought with him some of his engine-room team, while the remainder of the forty-eight ratings were selected from three times as many volunteers.

Difficulties arose at Dunkirk in selecting a rescue launch to accompany *Vindictive*. Rowley Bourke had demanded the job as soon as he heard of Godsal's involvement, but his crew had no desire to push their luck a second time. In any case, his launch was still being repaired after the first attempt. So the task was given to another volunteer, Lieutenant Geoffrey Drummond, commander of ML254. Like Bourke, Drummond had taken part in the first operation, where his experiences were typical of the operation as a whole. In charge of one of the force's smoke units, he spent much of the night 'drifting helplessly' after a fault in the smoking apparatus choked his engines. Given a tow, he eventually regained power just in time to screen the blockships as their crews were being taken off. Shortly after the action, Drummond suffered more bad luck when a number of his crew were injured during a raid on Dunkirk. This left a number of vacancies. Among the volunteers to fill them was Rowley Bourke, who agreed to waive his command to serve as Drummond's first lieutenant.

Doughty seamen though they were, Bourke and Drummond were an unlikely choice. At first sight, neither seemed cast in the heroic mould. Frail in appearance and in health, Drummond jokingly referred to himself as a 'professional invalid', while the heavily bespectacled Bourke, who looked more like a bank clerk than the rancher he was, had been rejected by the Canadian army on account of his poor eyesight. But their keenness was never in doubt and they quickly forged a close understanding. Drummond was particularly struck by his new officer's ingenuity. Bourke, he recorded, 'was most efficient and suggested all sorts of stunts, such as removing the gun, the only thing on deck heavy enough to detonate a shell. Half emptying the acid tanks. A big fender of brass warp all round the ship. And defences of torpedo mats round the four Lewis guns and the bridge ...' Their partnership, however, did not last long. The operation having been delayed, Bourke went on leave and returned to the news that he was no longer to be Drummond's first lieutenant but was to take his own launch as a standby boat – provided he could have her ready in time. The change was prompted by Keyes's decision to add a second blockship, *Sappho*, to the operation.

Timing was critical. To have the best possible chance of success, the force needed to make the passage from Dunkirk to Ostend under cover of the darkest of nights, while the blockships needed to make their run-in at high water, with an easterly tidal stream essential to enable them to swing across the canal mouth. Rough seas having ruled out a second attempt within four days of the first, the next favourable date was 9/10 May. This gave Bourke barely a day to prepare his boat, but he was not to be denied, even if his dynamo was useless and many of the boat's fittings had been placed in ML254. 'Anyway,' he wrote, 'I got together all the gear such as rope mattresses, shrapnel helmets, Lewis guns, etc., etc., and also got the dynamo from another launch which was out of action, also a complete new volunteer crew gathered from here and there and was ready on time and crossed to Dunkirk ...' On board the bastardised ML276 were Sub-Lieutenant James Petrie, who had tried unsuccessfully to find a berth on the first raid; Chief Motor Mechanics Edgar Chivers and George Kerr; Leading Deckhands Joseph Hamshaw and Hugh Sutherland; and Deckhands William Hutchinson, Henry Jarvest and Percy Humphreys. The coxswain's post was taken by Hamshaw, a schoolteacher from Lowestoft, who had volunteered in order to get leave to visit his wife and children. Hutchinson was a last-minute addition to the crew. Bourke had offered him passage to Dunkirk, where he was due to join another ship. But when they arrived, the ship was not there, so Hutchinson agreed to complete the launch's crew.

The weather on the evening of 9 May was near perfect. A slight but steady breeze was blowing, its direction and strength perfect for smoke-laying. Beneath a lead-blue, moonless sky, faintly freckled with stars, the sea was smooth enough for the smallest craft. At approximately 10.45 p.m. the Dunkirk armada was joined by *Vindictive* and *Sappho*. In no time the two blockships had disembarked their surplus crews and taken their places alongside the escorts. Operation VS was on.

From the destroyer *Faulknor*, Commodore Lynes's flagship, the remainder of the force was visible only 'as swift silhouettes of black-ness, destroyers bulking like cruisers in the darkness, motor-launches like destroyers, and coastal motor-boats showing themselves as racing hill-ocks of foam'. Though fraught with danger, the short journey along the Belgian coast was not without humour. Drummond in ML254 recalled:

> We were much amused, as we were going along in enemy terri-tory with all lights out and complete silence ordained, to hear the squeals of the pigs (a most lucrative proposition) being moved on one of the big monitors from under the 15-inch [gun] to a place less concussionable. It was quite a relief to strained nerves …

The light relief did not last. Two minutes before midnight the force suf-fered its first setback. A manhole joint in one of *Sappho*'s boilers blew out and her speed dropped to 6 knots, forcing her to pull out of line. As she limped back to Dunkirk, Lynes had to decide whether to aban-don the operation or press ahead with *Vindictive* alone. He decided to go on, and by 1.30 a.m. all preliminary dispositions were complete, although not without some difficulty. Shortly before making her pre-determined turn inshore, Drummond had served his crew with tots of whisky ('we didn't have rum for some occult reason'):

> Then I ordered gas masks and started putting my own on, which stuck and blinded me for a few moments. During that time there was a crash and we had been rammed by another ML. I sent a hand forward to see if the fo'c'stle had been damaged. He, wish-ing to carry on, gave me a report that all was well. I don't think from after events that this can have been quite true. However, we

did; but by that time all trace of the fleet was lost. I saw a double flashing light ... and made for it. However, I very soon found by my watch that it was too far east and I turned straight inshore and was lucky enough to spot the eastern smoke unit. Knowing the bearing they were working on I was able to set a course for my proper station on the position of the Stroom Bank buoy. Just as I got there the *Vindictive* loomed up going all out. I wrenched my helm over and rang for full speed but it was all we could do to keep her in sight.

Events now moved rapidly towards their climax. At 1.35 a.m., as CMBs trailed a smokescreen between the shore and ships, a searchlight stabbed the darkness. Eight minutes later Lynes gave the signal to his monitors to open fire and for an air attack to begin. But even as the first projectiles crashed down, the weather, so benign an hour earlier, turned against them. Lynes observed that by 1.45 a.m. the sky had become completely overcast and within five minutes ships and shoreline were enveloped in a thick sea-fog. For the next hour Lynes could only keep in touch with his force by sound.

Yet his problems were as nothing compared with those facing Godsal and his attendant launches. *Sappho*'s misadventure apart, everything had gone well to this point. The torpedo-boat marking the Stroom Bank buoy was passed without incident and when speed had to be increased, it was done so without a hint of flames from the funnels. From *Vindictive*'s bridge, the smoke-laying operation seemed perfectly executed, with a clear lane showing between the eastern and western sections. Enemy fire, meanwhile, was light and apparently haphazard. But then, just as Godsal was preparing to make the final run-in, the fog came down, blotting out the harbour and every other landmark. Unable to see the entrance, Godsal altered course to the west to run parallel with the shore, reducing speed to 9 knots as eyes strained for a glimpse of any identifiable marker. Crutchley, alongside Godsal on the bridge, later reported:

As we still failed to see the entrance we altered course 16 points to starboard and returned along the shore to the eastward. We again failed to find the entrance and so altered course 16 points to starboard. All this time owing to fog and smoke the visibility was not more than 1½ cables [300yd] ...

Twice *Vindictive* steamed straight past the harbour from different directions without sighting it, offering the German batteries fleeting glimpses through the smog of what they took to be two cruisers. Finally, at the third attempt, the entrance was sighted barely 200yd on the port beam. At the same moment the shore batteries spotted *Vindictive* and almost immediately opened a heavy and accurate fire. For a second time in three weeks the gallant cruiser was peppered with shrapnel. As she ploughed doggedly on to her final berth, Crutchley passed orders to Bury to clear the stokeholds in an effort to reduce casualties. But so heavy was the destruction up top that Bury decided it was safer for them to stay below for the time being.

Having made the harbour, Godsal's plan was to turn the ship starboard side to seaward, thereby offering his men the best chance of escape via the ship's cutters, which were deliberately situated starboard. Ordering a turn to take *Vindictive* into the harbour's mouth, Godsal, who was directing the ship from the conning tower, ordered smoke laid. The last few yards were made through a frenzy of explosions. Shell after shell slammed into her superstructure and from the after steering control came the feeble message, 'All out here,' the last words heard from Sub-Lt MacLachlan. But Godsal was not to be deflected. Passing between the pier-heads, he stepped out of the conning tower to make sure of his position. He had just given the order to go hard a-starboard when a heavy shell burst either on or near the conning tower. Godsal was never seen again and the blast from the explosion momentarily knocked out everyone on the bridge. In those critical moments, *Vindictive* veered towards the eastern pier, until Crutchley, himself concussed by the blast that killed his captain, took control. He later reported:

> I ... ordered the port telegraph to full speed astern to try to swing the ship across the channel. She grounded forward on the eastern pier when at an angle of about 3 points to the pier. As the ship stopped swinging and at the time I considered that no more could be done, I ordered the ship to be abandoned ...

Vindictive, her port propeller damaged at Zeebrugge, failed to answer Crutchley's last order, and came to rest outside the main channel, the tide pushing her further away. Once again Godsal had been thwarted, and Crutchley, despite doing more than anyone could have expected in the circumstances, later blamed himself for the failure. In his report, he commented: 'I should have gone full speed astern both and tried to place her again.' It was a harsh judgement. After the shell burst, he barely had time to think, and the ship having grounded his main concern was to ensure the charges were blown and the crew given a chance to escape.

THE ATTACK ON OSTEND

To Bury fell the responsibility of setting off the main charges. First, though, he waited to make sure his engine room was cleared. He later wrote:

There was a fearful din on the upper deck. The machine-gun bullets were making a noise like pneumatic caulkers. Several of our people never got further than the escape doors, and all made for the cutters, which were just touching the water. Seeing that the ship was not slewing, and also there was a danger of the falling funnels and things cutting the electric leads, I made my way aft, to the dynamo-exploders, and fired the after mines. Several portions of the port engine shot up into the air, and the poor old ship sat down on the mud with a loud crash, at an angle of about 30 degrees to the pier, where her bows touched, and on a fairly even keel.

As *Vindictive* shuddered from the blow, Crutchley fired the forward auxiliary charges, though such was the shock from the first blast that he was uncertain whether they detonated. It hardly mattered. *Vindictive* was stuck fast, and it was time to think of self-preservation. By then the splintered decks were flayed by machine-guns, making the task of abandoning ship a desperately perilous business. Crutchley, however, had one last duty to perform. His electric torch making him a target for every enemy machine-gun, he picked his way through the wreckage of the bridge and along the port side of the upper deck in a vain attempt to find Godsal. On his solitary round, he found the after smoke canisters had not been lit, so he calmly stopped and lit them himself while bullets cracked around him. Not content with that, he searched the shattered remains of the after control for any sign of life. Only then, when he was satisfied no one was left alive, did he follow his men off. He tumbled down on to a motor-launch, her deck already crammed with survivors and her bows almost awash. It was Drummond's ML254 and her precarious presence there was in itself a minor miracle.

Since first sighting *Vindictive* through the murk, ML254 had endured a fearful mauling at the hands of the shore batteries as Drummond struggled to stay close to the blockship during her somewhat erratic manoeuvring:

All the shells that didn't hit exploded on the bottom ... On one occasion I was blown off my feet by a shell bursting alongside. The fireworks were amazing and very pretty; the star shells were red, green, blue and yellow. And then there were the 'flaming onions' as we called them (small calibre projectiles calibrated

together in groups of twenty-five on the same trajectory) ...
I got one string along my bridge. It took off the back of my right
hand-rail, broke everything there, signal lamps, switches, etc.,
but by the mercy of Providence the compass and its light and
the telegraph handles and chains were untouched. Shortly after
that, a 4-inch burst just by the mast. Number One (Lieutenant
Gordon Ross, Bourke's replacement and another Canadian) at
that moment had left his torpedo-mat fort to get some trays of
Lewis gun ammunition, which we had stacked by the mast, and
it killed him outright, also the relief coxswain standing alongside
me, chipped the coxswain's hand and I got 2½ inches of copper
driving band into the back of my left thigh ...

Still *Vindictive* had not succeeded in finding the entrance. But having
followed this far, Drummond was determined to hang on. Ignoring the
damage to his launch and pain from his own grievous injuries, he stayed
close enough to see her final difficult entry between the piers. 'She ...
was so close to them when she picked them up that she had hardly room
to turn in,' he observed. Following up, the launch came under heavy
fire. Closing the pier head, Drummond was hit again, a piece of shrapnel
lodging behind his collar-bone within a fraction of his lungs. Already
numb from loss of blood, it took a superhuman effort for him to stay
upright and keep control. Barely able to see through the clouds of smoke
and fog, he was forced to rip open the bridge's canvas roof 'and stand
on the shelf with my head and shoulders out'. In this exposed position,
working the launch's telegraphs with his feet, Drummond made it into
the harbour's mouth, only to discover more problems:

The *Vindictive* had arranged for us to go alongside her starboard side
and had all her boats slung out close to the waterline so that her crew
could slide down the falls and be on a level with us. Had she rammed
the western pier as intended, we should have been protected by her
bulk; as it was, we had to go the shore side of her in the full limelight,
with a machine-gun about 20yd away on the other pier. Doing its level
best, it gave me two in the right forearm, but they dropped out on the
way home, only having penetrated about half an inch; my theory is that
they were so close that they didn't pick up their spin and so got held up
by my duffel coat ...

Others were not so lucky. Caught in the full glare of the harbour
searchlights, the crowded launch was raked by fire. Among those
wounded was Lt Cdr Bury. Others among *Vindictive*'s crew suffered
ankle injuries after jumping off her deck. Drummond counted twenty-
six men aboard before Crutchley, the last man off, scrambled down to

tell him there was no one left. No sooner had he begun to back out, however, than a call came from the forward end that someone had seen a man in the water. 'I stopped abruptly,' Drummond wrote, 'luckily, because just then the other rescue ML came round the stern of *Vindictive* and crashed into us. As my ship appeared to be sinking (we had 2in freeboard forward instead of 2ft 6in at least) I called out to the other skipper that there was someone in the water and would he pick them up.'

The 'other skipper' was Rowley Bourke, and his journey into Ostend had been nothing if not eventful. Outside the harbour mouth, ML276 was swallowed in the 'acrid fog of chlorosulphonic acid gas' that made up the eastern smoke-screen. Invisible shore batteries were already in action, shells 'churning the sea into foam' and ricocheting across the surface to throw up 'geysers', which drenched the deckhands as they waited, 'gasping and choking', to follow *Vindictive* in. Finally, they caught a glimpse of her, 'surrounded by columns of water'. To Sub-Lieutenant Petrie, she appeared 'ghostly grey, like a strange phantom ship'. In a vivid broadcast recorded for the BBC on the sixth anniversary of the raid, Petrie transported listeners aboard ML276 during her charge into Ostend:

> We dash across to her, lose her, find [her] again, again to lose her in a maze of turnings in the patchy smoke. Crash! A grinding forward and a terrific impact throws us to the deck. We have 'rammed' the eastern arm of the pier but 50 yards from the beach. As we back out a shell explodes on our forecastle and our splendid coxswain goes west …

With Hamshaw slumped dead at the wheel, Petrie immediately took over. Moments later, he called out to Bourke, asking to 'have a bash' at the lighthouses, which were helping the shore batteries range on the attackers. Permission granted, he leapt out from the wheelhouse, slammed a tray of ammunition on the Lewis gun and shot out the eastern light. As he did so, a bullet tore the empty tray out of his hand, and a piece of shrapnel smacked into the 'mattress' in front of him. Another deckhand fell wounded as Petrie swung the gun round and swept the top of the western tower, extinguishing the other light.

As ML276 ran into the smoke-shrouded harbour, Bourke saw Drummond's ML254 slowly emerging with its deck crammed with survivors. He shouted across, asking if everyone had been picked up. Crutchley replied that they were all safe, but as luck would have it, Bourke couldn't make out what he said. And so, based on some sixth sense, he decided to press on. In a letter to his half brother in Canada, he later explained:

> I thought someone might have been overlooked so went into the harbour and turned, shouting to see if I could get a reply. We thought we heard someone but could not be sure and then, as we heard nothing, started out of the harbour, and again we thought we heard someone, so put back. We could not, however, locate where the shouting came from and thought it might be the wily Hun trying to detain us till we were quite done in, so started out again ...

In all, Bourke made three journeys back and forth into the harbour, which by then was a cauldron of fire. ML276 was hit repeatedly until she resembled a floating sieve. How Bourke escaped death or injury was a marvel. His coxswain had been killed beside him, along with last-minute volunteer William Hutchinson, and all five crewmen had suffered wounds from bullets or shrapnel that peppered the hull and wheelhouse. Not only had they contrived to miss the bespectacled skipper, but, by some miracle, they had also failed to damage any of the launch's vitals. And it was just as they were leaving the harbour for a third time that they heard a voice calling out. Returning for a fourth time, they discovered the source of the shouting. Two of *Vindictive*'s seamen and the ship's badly wounded navigator, Sir John Alleyne, were clinging to the end of an upended boat on the landward side, close by the enemy shore batteries. Under a hail of fire from pom-poms and machine guns, Bourke manoeuvred the launch alongside them while Petrie leapt down and helped haul them onto the deck. Finally, with the survivors safely aboard, Bourke headed out of the harbour at full speed with a stream of tracer chewing his wake.

The tiny launch had already survived one direct hit from a 6-inch shell, which smashed the crew's dinghy before exploding overboard. Now, as they departed, they were seriously hit again by a shell that carried away the compressed air tank and burst in the engine room. Had it happened a minute or so earlier, while the launch was stopped, Bourke was convinced their fate would have been sealed, for 'we could not have started our engines'. As it was, there was an anxious pause as the starboard engine almost stuttered to a halt before power returned and 'the exhaust burst into the roar of full speed'. Moments later, the port propeller turned over and started the second engine. Even then, as ML276 surged out of the harbour for the last time, her ordeal was not yet over. Bourke later wrote:

My port acid tank had again been pierced and as my hose had been shot away I could not sluice [the] acid overboard so that about twelve hours after leaving Ostend it had eaten its way through [the] deck into [the] after cabin and, on contact with water in bilges, started to smoke. Lieutenant Allayn [*sic*] was on [a] bed in [the] after cabin, badly wounded, so I went below to get him up before he was gassed. At this minute a monitor was reported, so I decided to go alongside and put my wounded and gassed men aboard her. I went alongside her blister and her men waded over carrying the surgeon, who superintended the removal of the wounded slung in stretchers. We then had to be towed on account of having no air to start engines again.

Drummond's escape proved even more eventful. Having backed out of the harbour, the heavily laden launch turned and headed out to sea, SOS signals flickering from her captain's electric torch. Progress was necessarily slow as the fore end was so low that every wave came over her bows, but given her parlous state it was amazing she was afloat at all. Drummond later wrote:

The forecastle was full up to the top rung of the ladder. The wardroom was burning merrily aft, a pom-pom having landed in one of the bunks, and although we only had about 150 gallons of petrol instead of 2,000, it was right aft, only separated by a bit of galvanised iron from the fire.

Not for the first time that night, Victor Crutchley proved, in Drummond's words, 'a tower of strength'. Organising parties of men to bale out the flooded fo'c'stle, he led a team aft to subdue the fire before it ignited the launch's fuel tanks, and then helped with the wounded, applying a tourniquet to Drummond's leg which by then was 'quite numb'. He also produced a signalman with a lamp (Drummond's being broken) who managed to contact the waiting *Warwick*. It was just as well he did, for by the time the launch bumped alongside she was so waterlogged as to be almost unsteerable.

Looking down on the heroic company, Admiral Keyes saw Drummond 'huddled up near the wheel' and the tall figure of Crutchley with other unwounded men in the fore part of the launch, 'up to their waists in water, baling hard and trying to keep the water under control'. Contrary to many accounts, including the subsequent citation accompanying Crutchley's well-deserved Victoria Cross, Drummond had never for a moment relinquished his command, even though, as he later wrote, 'I must have bled the best part of a gallon and a half', leaving 'a puddle on the deck 6ft across'. It was a remarkable display of willpower, but Drummond's ordeal was not quite finished yet.

While he was talking to Keyes's flag officer, Commander Osborne, about the *Vindictive*'s position between the Ostend piers, there was a sudden, tremendous explosion, which shattered the lights and threw Drummond out of his armchair. At almost the same moment, Crutchley had been discussing the night's events with Keyes in the chartroom. He had just taken off his lifebelt, which was smeared with the blood of the men he had helped carry from the *Vindictive* on to the launch, when the crash came. 'Victor,' said Keyes, 'you had better put it on again.' Down below, Drummond, who had been feeling drowsy moments before the explosion, found himself being seized by his injured arm ('which woke me properly') and led out of the wardroom by Osborne. He later recalled: 'I staggered after him, dropping one leg down the ammunition hatch, which woke me further, and crawled up the ladder on deck.'

Warwick had struck a mine and was in serious danger of sinking. Keyes ordered the rescued crewmen from *Vindictive* and ML254, including Drummond, to be transferred to the destroyer *Velox*, which was lashed alongside. All climbed aboard, with the exception of Victor Crutchley who, having tied his lifebelt once again around his waist, 'thought he might be useful to act as First Lieutenant'. *Warwick*, under tow from a destroyer and with tugs standing by, eventually reached Dover at 4.30 p.m.

Across the Channel at Dunkirk, Rowley Bourke had spent the early part of the morning examining his launch. Altogether, he found more than fifty-five holes, no fewer than sixteen of them through the wheelhouse. After breakfast, he spent the rest of the morning helping the commodore prepare his report. 'It hardly seemed worthwhile to go to bed then,' he wrote, 'so I did not turn in till the evening, after a strenuous 48 hours without sleep.' Shortly afterwards, Bourke, who had delayed putting in for leave because of the impending operations against Zeebrugge and Ostend, reapplied and had it granted, although Keyes hinted he might be up for a decoration and expressed surprise at him wishing to go. But Bourke's mind was made up. 'I told him I did not wish to wait for a decoration, but would stop if they had anything else to put into Ostend!'

Bourke spent five weeks in Canada, a period he described as the happiest of his life. In the course of his leave, he became engaged to Linda Barnett, 'a very old friend' whom he had known for years. A few hours after he left Nelson on his way back, a cable arrived with the news he had been given a DSO (*LG*, 23 July 1918) for his part in the first Ostend raid, and no sooner had he reached England than it was announced that he had been awarded the Victoria Cross for his rescue efforts during the second operation. There was also a Distinguished Service Cross for Petrie, Distinguished Service Medals for the injured mechanics Chivers and Kerr and mentions in dispatches for the rest of the crew.

The same *London Gazette* of 28 August 1918 also carried news of two more VCs for the heroes of Operation VS. They went to Geoffrey Drummond, for his courage in bringing away two officers and thirty-seven men from *Vindictive* despite being seriously wounded, and Victor Crutchley, whose earlier exploits aboard *Brilliant* had been recognised by the award of a DSC. All three VC recipients were among around three hundred officers and men decorated by the king at Buckingham Palace four months and a day after their near-miraculous escape from the jaws of death at Ostend.

While Drummond was recovering from his wounds in the hospital ship *Liberty*, moored in Dover harbour, a rumour spread among the injured of another attempt to block Ostend. Such was the spirit among the men that 'the doctors had a lot of trouble,' according to Drummond, 'to keep some of the patients from volunteering ...'

Geoffrey Heneage Drummond was born on 25 January 1886 at 13 St James' Place, London, the third of seven sons to Captain Algernon Heneage Drummond of the Rifle Brigade and Margaret Elizabeth (née Benson), who also had two daughters. The Drummonds, who were part of the banking dynasty that founded the Royal Bank of Scotland, divided their time between Cornwall Gardens, London, and Maltman's Green, a house in Gerrards Cross, which was the setting for many lively summer gatherings when the guests often included their cousins, the Bowes-Lyon girls.

Geoffrey attended Evelyn's preparatory school, Eton, but from the age of 9 his education was seriously curtailed when he fell down a flight of stone steps and dislocated his neck. Thereafter, he suffered from severe headaches and was able to spend only a few terms at Evelyn's, at Christchurch College, Oxford, and Wye Agricultural College. For a long period in his childhood, he lived with a doctor in Lichfield, and taught himself to play the piano.

His disability did not prevent him working as a land agent in Staffordshire and in the Australian Outback. Nor did it stop him enjoying his favourite recreation, yachting. In the years before the First World War he did a great deal of sailing around the south coast and on the continent. Anxious to serve his country, he underwent further treatment on his injured neck and, as a result of manipulation by a Swedish doctor, it was sufficiently improved for him to join the RNVR in December 1915.

He joined HMS *Resourceful* at Southampton on 2 January for a month's intensive training. This was followed by a spell at Poole, ferrying messages to the drifter patrol. Following courses in navigation at Greenwich and gunnery at Whale Island, he was ordered to commission 'one of these strange and wonderful motor boats' at a Gosport boatyard. Joining her as second-in-command, he was posted to Dover in September 1916, only to have his orders changed at the last moment. He was told, instead, to proceed to Scapa Flow and take command of another ML. His job was to patrol the approaches to Pentland Firth, two days on and two days off, from an hour before dawn to an hour after sunset. The dull routine ended after three months when he suffered a severe bout of sciatica. 'After being lifted out of bed by my crew and literally hauled on deck for about a week I had to give it up and go to hospital,' he later wrote.

Drummond, now a sub-lieutenant, spent two weeks in Chatham Hospital, and after a spell of sick leave he was recalled to Portsmouth where he took charge of a new ML with a crew of mainly Londoners, only one of whom had ever been anywhere near tidal waters. Much of 1917 was spent at Portsmouth, Dover and Dunkirk, with the latter becoming his permanent base from January 1918 until the dramatic events of May. Following an enemy raid on the drifter barrage, the MLs were largely employed on long night patrols. The longest and most depressing of these was in the Zuidicote Pass towards Nieuport on the Belgian coast. 'Our small vessel was all alone with nothing between us and the enemy, and listening to the mournful groans of the Whistle buoy,' wrote Drummond. In the event of sighting an enemy vessel, his job was to fire Very lights 'and try to pile up on a bank inshore to avoid our barrage'. Due to the shortage of MLs caused by preparations for the Zeebrugge operation, Drummond completed thirty-two successive night patrols, 'coming back as a rule just in time for the morning air raid' which was a feature of life at Dunkirk.

Following his gallant action at Ostend, Drummond, whose injuries included a bullet through his shoulder and the near loss of his left leg, spent three weeks in Chatham Naval Hospital, before being discharged on 'unemployed time'. During this period he married Maude Aylmer Tindal Bosanquet and enjoyed what he called a 'perfectly good honeymoon lasting about ten months', finishing up at Cannes on the French Riviera. It was not until a year after the Ostend operation that Geoffrey Drummond returned to duty at Dover, in command of an ML attached to minesweepers engaged in clearing the Channel. During this time he attended the reopening of the port of Ostend and marched in the 'peace procession' through London, which he thought 'not much fun' given that he was as 'lame as a tree'. Transferred to Queenstown in Ireland, he was engaged in more mine clearance work and night patrols aimed at preventing the flow of arms to the IRA.

Demobilised in 1919, he teamed up with an RNVR friend, Hugh Littleton DSO, who commanded one of the MLs at Zeebrugge, driving and repairing a small fleet of lorries from a base near Waterloo station. For a while business, much of it generated by the Wembley Exhibition, was good, but declining orders and the physical strain eventually proved too much for Drummond. A partnership in a firm of builders' merchants was hardly enough to sustain his family and by the late 1920s he was living off his pension and touring the country in search of work. 'Having the VC does not make any difference,' he told one journalist.

In 1928 he left England for Australia, with the intention of developing a holiday resort on the west coast, about 30 miles north of Perth. He was accompanied by his wife, 9-year-old daughter and 7-year-old son. His 2-year-old daughter was to follow when they were settled. But the plan was still-born; there was no proper road, only a track, and very few people came, so the project was abandoned.

Returning to England Drummond was given a job at ICI's Millbank head office by the chairman, Lord Melchett, who was a personal friend. Although fairly mundane, the post in the staff and establishment department was better than nothing, and he remained there until war broke out again in 1939.

Despite his fragile health, Drummond tried to re-enlist in the RNVR. Rejected as too old and unfit, he immediately joined the River Emergency Service on the Thames and subsequently transferred to the Royal Naval Patrol Service as a second hand (equivalent in rank to an able seaman) in July 1940. His friends Sir Roger Keyes and Captain Hamilton Benn lobbied to get him a commission in the RNVR, but their efforts were overtaken by tragedy. In April 1941, while carrying a heavy sack of coal, his left leg, weakened by the effects of his injuries twenty-three years before, gave way and he fell, hitting his head on the deck housing. He suffered severe concussion and died in St Olave's Hospital, Rotherhithe, on 21 April. The most distinguished second hand in the navy was buried in Chalfont St Peter Cemetery, Buckinghamshire.

Mortimer Drummond, who had joined the navy in 1938 and served throughout the Second World War, wrote of his father:

> He was a man of great charm and humour and he had a great many friends. He had a strong religious belief and a strict sense of honour and duty to his country and his family. He never hesitated to do what he felt was right.

Keyes, who knew courage when he saw it, described Rowley Bourke as 'the bravest of all holders of the Victoria Cross'. He was also something of a contradiction: a man who revelled in action and yet who would be remembered by his friends as a quiet, mild-mannered gentleman whose favourite pastime was a game of bridge.

Rowland Richard Louis Bourke was born on 28 November 1885 in Redcliffe Square, London, the son of Isidore McWilliam Bourke MD, a retired surgeon major of the 72nd (Seaforth) Highlanders, of Curraleegh, County Mayo, Ireland, and his Italian second wife, Marianna (née Carozzi). Isidore's first wife, by whom he had three sons, had succumbed to cholera during his service in India. He had four children by his second marriage, Rowley being the only boy among them, and two adopted nephews, and he settled in London, where he had a medical practice.

Around 1898, at the time of the gold rush in the Klondike, Isidore Bourke joined the flood of emigrants seeking their fortune out west. He went to Dawson, in the Yukon territory of north-west Canada, where he established the city's first hospital. Rowley, who was educated by a number of Roman Catholic Orders in England, followed him to Canada in 1902 to try his luck in the goldfields.

The Bourkes were an unlucky family. In addition to his first wife's early death, Isidore lost a brother, who was shot and killed in Ireland, and had a son murdered in Siam. Tragedy also followed them to Canada. Not only was their house in Dawson destroyed by fire, but also one of Rowley's adopted cousins, Cecil, was accidentally killed around 1907 by the premature explosion of a dynamite charge while he was clearing tree stumps at their ranch at Crescent Bay, Nelson. Nearly blinded by the same blast, Rowley was severely injured and left with permanently damaged eyesight. Such was the shattering impact of the tragedy that the family, including Rowley, uprooted and immigrated to New Zealand. Rowley, however, returned and was farming a property at Nine Mile when war broke out.

His attempts to enlist in all three services each met with rejection on account of his poor eyesight. To help the war effort, he donated a waterfront lot from his land to be raffled off, with proceeds going to a local Patriotic Fund supporting the families of serving soldiers. It was not enough. Still determined to 'do his bit', he left Nelson and paid his own passage back to England, where, on 7 January 1916, he finally succeeded in securing a commission as a sub-lieutenant in the Royal Naval Volunteer Reserve. After undergoing courses at Greenwich and Southampton, he was posted to Larne, on the north-east coast of Ireland, where he took command of ML341. For the next year, he toiled at the dull routine of anti-submarine patrols. 'Although the work was useful as a preventative, we had only negative results ... to show for our labours [sic],' he wrote. Frustrated by the lack of action, he asked to be transferred to a more active command. Eventually, after what he described as a 'considerable delay on the part of Dover', his wish was granted, and in November 1917, he exchanged command of ML341 for ML276. Rowley joined Dover Patrol, or Harry Tate's Navy, as it was more popularly known, at an auspicious moment in its history. Barely a month earlier, Roger Keyes, a man after Rowley's own heart, had taken over command with the intention of going on the offensive.

By then a lieutenant, Rowley found life at Dover and its sister port Dunkirk much more to his taste. Once, during an enemy raid on the French port, a colleague recalled seeing him striding along the quay, rubbing his hands with glee as shells crashed about them and shouting: 'This is splendid, this is war!' Nevertheless when word reached him that all Canadians were entitled to a spell of home leave, he decided to apply. The following February, having heard nothing about his application and with his launch undergoing repairs, he asked again, only to be told that 'important operations' were expected soon. Later, hearing that volunteers were wanted for 'special dangerous work, the nature of which was not specified', he immediately volunteered, only to be turned down. 'I was very cut up when I heard this,' he later wrote, 'especially after postponing my Canadian leave and working hard to be ready on time.' On confronting his commanding officer, he was told 'it was on account of my sight'. Refusing to be put off, Bourke badgered his CO until he finally relented and agreed to appoint ML276 as a standby rescue launch. The next six weeks were the most dramatic period of his life. As well as earning a VC and a DSO, he was appointed a Knight of the Legion of Honour by the French government (*LG*, 12 December 1918), mentioned in despatches and promoted to lieutenant-commander, with seniority back-dated to 23 April 1918.

By October, however, he was growing bored again. 'I ... hope the war will end soon,' he wrote to his half-brother. 'I am fed up with the monotony and no signs of excitement.' A month to the day after writing those words his hope was fulfilled. Back home in Canada in 1919 he married Rosalind (Linda) Barnet, an accomplished musician originally from Sydney, Australia, to whom he had become engaged after the Ostend operations and whom he had promised to marry 'as soon as the war is over'.

Demobilised the following year, he returned to the Kootenays and his North Shore farm, but by 1931 his eyesight had deteriorated to the extent that he feared he might be going blind. He decided to quit farming and, with his wife, moved in 1932 to Victoria, taking a Federal Civil Service post on the staff of the Royal Canadian Naval Dockyards at Esquimalt. Shortly before the Second World War Rowley Bourke helped organise the Fishermen's Naval Reserve, a west coast patrol operation. At the outbreak of war he joined the RCN Volunteer Reserve, serving variously as a recruiting officer and an extended defence officer, before being appointed as acting commander to HMCS *Givenchy*, a training ship, at Esquimalt and Burrard, Vancouver. After the war he returned to his civil service post and retired in 1950 as officer-in-charge of the civilian security guard at Esquimalt's naval dockyard.

Accompanied by his wife, he travelled to England in 1953 for the coronation of Queen Elizabeth II and returned three years later for the VC centenary celebrations. Almost twenty years earlier Rowley Bourke had been among the distinguished Canadians who received King George VI and Queen Elizabeth during their 1938 Dominion tour, and he fulfilled a similar role shortly before his death when Princess Margaret made a visit to Canada. But such events were more the exception than the rule. A modest man, he disliked too much attention and positively detested having his photograph taken. Judith McWilliam-Bourke, whose grandmother was his elder sister, remembered him in retirement as 'a man of short stature, with twinkling eyes behind his thick spectacles, and a gentle nature, who was devoted to his wife'.

Rowley Bourke VC, DSO, died at his home, 1253 Lyall Street, Esquimalt, on 29 August 1958. Following a requiem mass at Our Lady Queen of Peace Church, he was buried with full military honours at Royal Oak Burial Park, Victoria, a naval guard of honour firing a final salute of three volleys over his grave as the Last Post was sounded. In his will he left his medals to the National Archives in Ottawa and they have since been displayed on loan in the Maritime Museum of British Columbia and the CFB Esquimalt Naval Museum, where the exhibits also included a pair of his famously thick-lensed glasses.

Today a rocky outcrop north-west of Goose Island in the Golby Passage and a mountain south-west of Megin Lake bear the name of Canada's only naval Victoria Cross recipient of the First World War, grandiose memorials to a modest hero, described by one obituarist as a 'steady, buoyant figure of much kindness and goodwill … who left a fine memory of courage and integrity'.

The recommendation for Victor Crutchley's Victoria Cross was unusual among naval awards for mentioning his gallant actions in three different vessels during a single night's action: *Vindictive*, Drummond's ML254, which he had done so much to keep afloat, and lastly *Warwick*, after she had been mined. Crutchley was also unique among the three men awarded VCs for the Ostend operation by dint of being the only career naval officer. And what an outstanding fighting career it proved to be, spanning two world wars, in which he saw action as a lieutenant and as a rear admiral.

Victor Alexander Charles Crutchley was born on 2 November 1893 at 28 Lennox Gardens, London, the son of Percy Edward Crutchley JP and the Hon. Frederica Louisa (née Fitzroy), second daughter of the 3rd Baron Southampton.

Crutchley attended the naval colleges at Osborne and Dartmouth and joined his first ship, *Indomitable*, of the 1st Cruiser Squadron, as a midshipman in 1911. It was the beginning of a remarkable run of near-continuous sea appointments that would end only with his posting to Gibraltar as Flag Officer in 1945. He began his first war as a recently promoted sub-lieutenant, earned promotion to lieutenant on 30 September 1915, and during almost three and a half years in the battleship *Centurion*, during which he saw action at Jutland, he impressed senior officers by his seamanship. That he was a young officer of great promise was confirmed by his exceptional gallantry as a volunteer first lieutenant on both the Ostend blocking operations. In noting his bravery during the first attempt on 22–23 April, Cdr Godsal remarked on his 'great coolness under heavy fire', while to his recommendation for the VC an anonymous hand, possibly Keyes's, lauded him as an 'inspiring example to all thrown in contact with him'. For his part, Crutchley felt it invidious to select any among *Vindictive*'s company for special distinction since 'every man, without exception, behaved splendidly'.

Crutchley ended the war a lieutenant, noted for early promotion, with a VC, DSC, French Croix de Guerre and a mention in despatches, all achieved within the space of three weeks.

His last spell of action for twenty years came during operations against the Bolsheviks in the Black Sea during 1918 and 1919 and, despite Keyes's enthusiastic recommendation, he received no further promotion until 1923. By then his career had taken on a familiar peace-time pattern with occasional spells in royal yachts sprinkled among sea-going appointments of roughly two years duration. The list was nothing if not varied: *Petersfield*, on the South American Station (1919–21), Cadets' Divisional Officer in *Thunderer* (1922–24), *Queen Elizabeth*, flagship of the Mediterranean Fleet (1924–26), and *Ceres* (1926–28). In the midst of these, he served in the HM Yachts *Alexandra* (1922–23) and *Victoria & Albert* (1924). Promoted commander on 30 June 1928, he was briefly appointed training commander at the RN Barracks, Devonport, in 1929, before embarking on a long and distinguished association with the navies of Australia and New Zealand.

Loaned to the New Zealand Division of the Royal Navy as executive officer of the division's flagship, HMS *Diomede*, in August 1930, Crutchley spent the next three years in the southern Pacific, visiting many of the islands that were to feature so prominently in his Second World War service. Once again his ability to meet unexpected challenges became evident when he assumed command of *Diomede* after her captain fell ill, and during a critical period when the ship's crew gave assistance to the people of Napier after it was struck by an earthquake in 1931. His Antipodean service was also memorable for an incident which almost cut short his brilliant career at a single devastating stroke. In March 1932, while returning to Auckland from ceremonies to mark the opening of Sydney Harbour Bridge, *Diomede* was struck by a huge wave that swept one seaman to his death. Crutchley, who was almost washed overboard as well, survived only by clinging to deck fittings. Promoted captain on 31 December 1932, he remained in command of *Diomede* until 1933 when his loan period ended.

Marked out for high command, he passed the Senior Officers' War Course the following year and, after short spells as commander of the 1st Minesweeping Flotilla and the Fishery Protection and Minesweeping Flotilla, he was given the coveted appointment of captain of the battleship *Warspite*. Like her new captain, *Warspite* was a veteran of Jutland, but she had just undergone an extensive modernisation programme when Crutchley took over in the summer of 1937. He remained in command for three years, in the course of which he took part in the celebrated Second Battle of Narvik in April 1940, when *Warspite*'s heavy guns were instrumental in sinking eight German destroyers while one of her aircraft chalked up a submarine 'kill'. Shortly afterwards, Crutchley was given his first shore posting in more than a decade, although even then he remained very much in the firing-line as Commodore-in-Charge of Devonport Naval Barracks at the height of the Plymouth blitz.

Promoted rear admiral on 6 February 1942, he was lent to the Royal Australian Navy and assumed command of Task Force 44, a joint Australian and American force comprising the heavy cruisers *Australia* (his flagship), *Canberra*, *Chicago*, *Salt Lake City*, the light cruiser *Hobart* and three destroyers, at Brisbane on 13 June 1942. Within two months, however, he was plunged into controversy after his force suffered a devastating defeat at the hands of the Japanese. On the night of 8/9 August 1942, in what became known as the Battle of Savo Island, a force of Japanese cruisers surprised Crutchley's force while it was acting as a protective screen for transports involved in the landings at Guadalcanal. The enemy cruisers sank the American cruisers *Astoria*, *Quincy* and *Vincennes* and the Australian *Canberra*. Crutchley, who had been called to a conference with the American commander of the amphibious force and was absent when the attack took place, was blamed by some American critics for the disaster. Subsequent investigations, however, exonerated him, showing that his dispositions were not to blame for the débâcle. The following year, Admiral King, C.-in-C. United States Navy, commended his performance during the Solomons campaign, declaring that he had been 'in no way inefficient, much less at fault' in executing his part of the operation. Crutchley went on to command a cruiser squadron in the US Seventh Fleet during operations in New Guinea.

After the war, until his retirement in 1947, Crutchley served as flag officer, Gibraltar. By then, his uniform was ablaze with medal ribbons.

To his First World War decorations, he had added the Polish Order of Polonia Restituta, Third Class (*LG*, 22 December 1942); the United States Legion of Merit, Chief Commander (*LG*, 2 January 1945); and, from his own country, a Companion of the Order of the Bath (*LG*, 1 January 1945) and a knighthood (*LG*, 13 June 1946), all of which are now on public display in the National Museum of the Royal Navy.

Sir Victor Crutchley, who had married Joan Coryton in 1930 and by whom he had a son and a daughter, headed the naval contingent at the VC centenary parade in 1956 and enjoyed a long and active retirement in Dorset, serving as Deputy Lieutenant and High Sheriff. The last surviving naval recipient of the Victoria Cross, he died aged 92 on 24 January 1986, at Mappercombe, near Bridport, and was buried in St Mary's Churchyard, Powerstock.

In appearance the very model of a gruff, stern-faced Victorian admiral, complete with full beard, Crutchley was in fact a forward-thinking officer, who combined great personal gallantry with outstanding leadership qualities. Above all, he was, as Keyes observed back in 1918, 'a fine seaman'.

H. AUTEN

English Channel, off Prawle Point, 30 July 1918

To the naked eye it appeared no more than 'a slight disturbance' rippling an otherwise placid sea, a thousand yards or so away on the starboard beam of the armed decoy ship. But what Lieutenant Edward Grey took to be a school of dolphins stirring the surface proved, with the aid of binoculars, to be an altogether more threatening sight. Spotted at 5 p.m. on 30 July 1918, the 'slight disturbance' turned out to be a torpedo and it was streaking straight for the Q-ship *Stock Force*, on which he was standing. Instinctively ordering the helm Hard a-port, he rang the ship's rattlers. *Stock Force*'s captain, Lieutenant Harold Auten, just had time to reach the bridge before the torpedo struck. The force of the explosion lifted the ship and threw her 'bodily to port' while great baulks of timber, designed to give the ship greater buoyancy, erupted out of the forehold and crashed down on the bridge, all but wrecking it. A deluge of water followed, leaving a number of the crew feeling violently sick. The damage below was even worse. The blast had pushed one of the watertight bulkheads clean through the other side and torn a 40ft hole along almost a quarter of her length. Already the sea was gushing in. It was, to say the least, an unpromising beginning for an action that would be described by Admiral Sir Lewis Bayly as 'one of the best examples of coolness, discipline and good organisation that I have come across ...'

'The charm of Q-boat warfare,' Harold Auten once wrote, 'was its uncertainty.' An unusual sentiment perhaps, but there was no doubting his sincerity, based as it was on years of experience in one of the navy's most exacting and hazardous roles. As one of those who formed the nucleus of Bayly's original decoy force at Queenstown, Auten had seen more Q-ship service than almost anyone else afloat. Like many decoy officers, he revelled in the freedom the work offered him. Never afraid to voice an opinion, he had pressed for a smaller collier of the type being regularly attacked off the Irish coast to be fitted out as a Q-ship – and much to his surprise he had been promptly sent to find such a vessel. His quest ended in Cardiff with *Stock Force*, a 361-ton collier. With a 29ft beam, capable of mounting one or two 4-inch guns without the need to alter her appearance, she seemed, as Auten put it, 'made for the job'. His selection endorsed, Auten stayed on to supervise the conversion. 'Bulkheads were put in, guns were got into position, and, bearing in mind the necessity of having the timber well stowed, I had it done by the crew,' he wrote. 'It was three months of long, hard work; but the result was good. The ship looked exactly as she had before ... and we had put into her all we knew and had learned from previous experience.' As added camouflage, Auten hit upon the idea of supplementing his crew with a black seaman, his choice falling on a man who had already survived three sinkings. 'These little touches,' he wrote, 'were what made the thing realistic.'

Hidden from sight were two 4-inch guns, two 12-pounders, one 3-pounder and two 14-inch torpedo tubes. As a final deception, Auten issued bogus sailing orders and gave the collier a temporary new look designed to confuse watching enemy agents. The ruse worked. *Stock Force* made a safe exit from harbour and by March 1918 was ready to embark on her first mission. Her early forays were uneventful and for a time, instead of hunting U-boats, she was employed against Sinn Fein gun-runners. Returning to her intended role, she nearly succumbed to her first submarine encounter when, in rough seas, a torpedo passed beneath her. The submarine chased *Stock Force*, close enough for Auten to smell the 'burnt petrol' fumes emanating from her exhaust, but the collier, having evaded a second attack, made it safely back to port. Her crew's next encounter would tax their resolution even further. On 30 July *Stock Force* was steaming through a mist-shrouded English Channel. In a display of innocence, the ship's single black rating was leaning over the rail, a pipe clenched in the corner of his mouth. 'Nothing was anywhere visible, and everything seemed peaceful and quiet,' wrote Auten. 'There was hardly a ripple on the water, and somewhere about 8am the island of Guernsey became visible through the morning mist. A little later the sun's rays played on the many glass-houses of the island.'

Shortly afterwards Auten received a signal informing him that a submarine had been seen, operating 'roughly on the line between Cascquets to 20 miles south of Start Point'. Delighted by what seemed a promising opportunity, Auten altered course to pass 5 miles south of Lizard Point. Around 10 a.m., however, he received unwelcome attention from two French seaplanes. Ignorant of *Stock Force*'s true intentions, they buzzed the small vessel in a theatrical display intended to warn him off. For almost two hours, to Auten's intense annoyance, the seaplanes flew about, dropping messages warning of a submarine and even dropping a few bombs on an oil slick, before one splashed down a short distance away only to take off again and head towards the French coast.

Relieved of her unwanted escorts, *Stock Force* set about her task of inviting attack. Hours passed with no sign of anything, until around 4.45 p.m. Auten's patience was finally rewarded by Grey's report. Auten recalled:

> At this moment the majority of those on board were having tea, the officers being seated in the saloon discussing the events of the morning … I reached the bridge just in time to see the torpedo, then about 50yd off, coming direct for the ship. She was coming very slowly in the end, having been fired at a long range and appearing to have very nearly run her distance. It looked to everybody on the bridge as if the torpedo would pass ahead; but suddenly, to my amazement, it took a turn in towards the ship and struck us abreast of no. 1 hatch.

The damage was immense. The foredeck was twisted and derricks were blown overboard. 'Everyone on the bridge', recorded Grey, 'was thrown down and the next thing planks and other stuff from the forehold of the ship came down on top of us, some on the bridge and some back in the fore part of the ship again … I don't know how any of us lived.' Everyone on the bridge was wounded with the exception of Auten. 'All I recollected,' he wrote, 'was going up in the air, and coming down to find myself underneath the chart table.' Barely had the shock subsided than they were drenched by water. Auten 'felt immediately very sick'. To one man it appeared as though 'the end of the world had come'. Auten, too, feared the worst, but as he scrambled clear he found, much to his surprise, that nobody had been killed. While some wounded were carried below for treatment, there was no immediate relief for the ship's most seriously injured man. Officers' steward Reginald Starling, his head gashed, his jaw smashed and one arm sprained, lay trapped beneath a pile of wreckage near the forward gun. To free him risked not only unmasking the gun, but taking men away from important duties. With the ship settling by the head, Auten took the difficult decision to leave him.

Despite the devastation wrought by the torpedo, the Q-ship's crew, some of them wounded and many of them in a state of shock, had taken up their action stations. Auten ordered the 'abandon ship party', who had been carrying out their 'theatrical performance', to shove off, and then made his way to the after gun house, the fore control and bridge communications having been knocked out. Fortunately, both the after 4-inch guns were still functioning, although the roof shielding the foremost no. 2 post was on the point of collapse. Lt Grey, who had been wounded in the head, found water pouring over the gun's telescopic sights and the cordite. Reacting quickly, he ordered some men to prop the roof up with boat oars and detailed others to hold it up as soon as the covering flaps were released. Then, having examined the cordite, he loaded the gun and ordered his men to lie flat. 'No one', he wrote, 'was to speak a word, and the man at the voice pipe was just to whisper ...'

It was the beginning of a tense waiting game. There was already almost 3ft of water in the forward magazine and the area between decks where the wounded were sheltering. The only question was: could the submarine be tempted to the surface before *Stock Force* sank? Auten had his doubts. The fo'c'stle was practically submerged. 'At one time,' he later admitted, 'I felt she would not last much longer.'

From his position in the after gun house, Auten could see almost all around except right ahead, and it was there that *Stock Force*'s 'abandon ship' party saw the U-boat surface, half a mile away. Shortly after, two men were seen to emerge from the conning tower, whence they surveyed their victim for fifteen minutes. Apparently satisfied that it was not a trap, the submarine approached, its gun unmanned. Taking their cue, the 'panic party' pulled slowly down *Stock Force*'s port side in an attempt to lure the U-boat into the ship's gun-sights. The submarine swallowed the bait, cautiously following the boat, until she came into Auten's field of vision. By then, she was no more than 400yd away, but Auten held his fire in the hope she might come within range of both guns. He recalled:

> Everybody on board lay absolutely quiet and hardly daring to breathe. The submarine came on slowly, awfully slowly. It seemed ages before she got on the beam where both the 4-inch guns could bear. Time after time the after-gunner and myself peeped through the little crack we were using as an observation position ... At last she reached the fatal spot. Submarine bearing, red 90, range 300yd, 'stand by' I whispered through the voice-pipes; then a second or so later, 'Let go'.

As the flaps fell away, the U-boat was right in front of the after gun, where Auten was directing operations alongside the gun's captain,

Assistant Paymaster Athol Davis. 'We opened fire and our first shot seemed to skim the conning tower and carry away several small things on top but it didn't explode,' recorded Davis. 'I saw it strike the water beyond the submarine. The second shot went right into the centre of the conning tower and burst, breaking the tower, and throwing up a lot of splinters. The third shot was observed to hit the submarine in the centre and this appeared to make the conning tower crumble in front … '

In the meantime Grey's gun had joined in, although not before a moment of near farce had contrived to disrupt their participation. For as the trainer hurriedly wheeled the gun round, a pool of water which had formed on the buckled roof sloshed over, knocking him off his feet. Grey immediately took over, and while still training round saw the first shot from the after gun carry away the U-boat's periscope and what looked like a wireless mast, and the second hit the conning tower, hurling one man, believed to be the captain, into the air:

> The next shot I fired myself, or rather my gunlayer fired it, and that hit her just where the conning tower had been but right down at the water's edge, and that seemed to rent a big hole in her. A lot of blue smoke came out of her and her bow went up in the air a bit, making a better target than ever. She remained then absolutely stationary. We continued to fire, putting shells in as hard as ever … until the submarine was finally smashed up and disappeared.

All told, Auten reckoned his crew scored twenty direct hits. Seven of these were credited to the after-gun, whose commander had no doubt that the submarine was destroyed. Her engines appeared to have stopped, and according to Auten, she 'sank in a very short time' to leave the sea stained with debris. Grey reported seeing the top of a table and what he 'imagined' to be dead bodies floating amid the wreckage. Auten, however, was too busy trying to save his ship to investigate further. Had he done so, he would have been disappointed.

Contrary to Grey's impression, there were no bodies, and the submarine involved, the *UB-80*, had not been sunk, though she had been damaged and was fortunate to escape the trap that had been set for her. According to her experienced commander, Kapitanleutnant Max Viebeg, she had been struck twice at close range and had suffered no casualties. Indeed, the Pour le Mérite holder's report of the engagement with what he described as a tanker five times the size of *Stock Force* told a very different story to the British version. Having scored a hit with his first torpedo, fired from a range of 1,200m, Viebeg claimed that his suspicions were immediately aroused by the fact that his victim was so slow to sink. He estimated it took some fifteen minutes before he saw signs of her going down by the bow, and his next act was almost his last. His staccato report continued:

> Surfaced at about 400 metres distant. The steamer opened fire with several concealed guns. Crash-dive. During the dive, the boat took two hits. Went to 11 metres depth, fired a second torpedo despite inability to raise either periscope. Remained submerged until dusk. Surfaced. One shot had penetrated the bridge shield and the periscope support. Both periscopes had broken lenses, were filled with seawater and useless …

While Viebeg took stock before plotting a new course home 'round the north of England' made necessary by the destruction of his periscopes, Auten faced an even greater struggle. *Stock Force* was steadily sinking and, having recovered his 'panic party', Auten immediately ordered full speed in a desperate attempt to beach her.

Around 6.30 p.m. two trawlers, drawn to the scene by the sound of gunfire, were sighted. By then *Stock Force* was practically awash forward, with most of the starboard side under water. Transferring his wounded and half his men to the trawlers, Auten remained on board with a volunteer party in a last-ditch attempt to save his vessel. But it was hopeless. The engine room was already making water and by 9.15 p.m. it was clear she was beyond salvation. Auten sent the remainder of his crew away and, five minutes later, he and Grey followed them into a dinghy and paddled across to a waiting torpedo-boat. At 9.25 p.m., more than four and a half hours after she had been struck by a torpedo and a little under four hours since she had exacted her revenge, *Stock Force* slipped beneath the waves, 8 miles from land.

In his official report, compiled that first day back on land, Auten heaped praise on his crew: 'Although many were suffering with wounds and all from the tremendous shock sustained through a torpedo striking so small a ship and the apparent imminence of her foundering, everyone went about their duties, which included lying doggo for a full 40 minutes on the part of the guns' crews and later stoking in a stokehold fast filling with water, as though they were exercising at quarters.'

The humble *Stock Force* was showered with honours. In all, twenty-three out of the crew of forty-four were decorated or received mentions in despatches. Grey and Davis were among five officers to receive DSCs, the same award also going to Lieutenant Louis Workman, who had joined *Stock Force* three days before sailing and took charge of the 'abandon ship' party. Officer's Steward Starling, who had remained trapped beneath debris throughout the action, lived to receive the CGM, as did Able Seaman Samuel Livingstone, who twice dived overboard to recover the ship's logbooks which were blown overboard. The list was headed by the award of the Victoria Cross to Lt Harold Auten DSC. Gazetted on 14 September 1918, it was the last Q-ship VC of the war.

Recognition was given in spite of the fact that the Admiralty was already aware of the suspect nature of the claimed success. As early as 18 August, Admiral Sir William Hall, director of Naval Intelligence, had reported his doubts. However, noting the 'striking parallel' with the similarly indecisive encounter between HMS *Prize* and *U-93*, he stressed: 'This, of course, in no way detracts from the extreme gallantry of the action.'

Harold Auten was born at The Shrubberies, Leatherhead, Surrey, on 22 August 1891, the son of William Blee Auten, a retired navy paymaster, and Edith Fanny (née Ross). He was educated at Wilson's Grammar School, Camberwell, and joined the P&O Line as a 17-year-old cadet.

In 1910 he joined the Royal Naval Reserve and was made sub-lieutenant two months before the outbreak of war. The summer of 1915 found him on the staff of the Captain of Devonport Dockyard, as junior assistant to a commander charged with fitting out trawlers for patrol work. His mundane duties were interrupted, however, in September by orders telling him to report to the *Zylpha*, a 'mysterious' vessel about which no one seemed to know anything. It proved to be Auten's introduction to the Q-ships. The *Zylpha*, described by Auten as a 'dirty old tramp', was one of three ex-colliers which formed Admiral Bayly's original decoy force, and Auten was among a special list of six chosen officers, who included Gordon Campbell, transferred to the Queenstown command in southern Ireland.

With his fertile imagination, the tall, dashing Auten found himself well suited to his new role. Forever coming up with new ideas and tactics, he would later claim credit for having suggested packing the decoys' holds with timber to give them extra buoyancy if they were torpedoed. It was he also who came up with the idea of setting light to a tubful of dried seaweed during a U-boat encounter to give the enemy gunners a false impression of the range and their accuracy.

Auten served aboard *Zylpha* for about eighteen months, engaged on an endless round of patrols, most of which proved uneventful. Submarine encounters were rare. Once, during a three-month spell in

West Indian waters in 1916, *Zylpha* was dispatched into the Gulf of Mexico to hunt for a U-boat reportedly seen operating there. It later emerged that the submarine belonged to an enterprising film maker who was engaged in 'shooting' realistic scenes of attacks on merchantmen. Auten later commented: 'I often wonder what really would have happened if the Q-boat had come across this submarine, especially at a time when a famous American film actress and party were on board giving a special show.' The closest *Zylpha* came to a genuine success was in April 1917. Having narrowly escaped a torpedo attack, she was heavily bombarded (some fifty-three shells were counted) yet managed to score a hit on her attacker before she made off.

This action was Auten's last aboard *Zylpha*. On 22 April he was appointed to command the Q-sloop *Heather* (Q-16), whose previous captain had been killed in an unsuccessful engagement with a U-boat. Although glad of the opportunity, Auten had little faith in *Heather*, considering her usefulness as a decoy to have been compromised by her recent encounter. Five months spent vainly attempting to tempt U-boats into close-quarter action in the Irish Sea served only to confirm him in this view. Eventually, in September, he was given permission to find and fit out a small coastal collier: a decision that led him to *Stock Force* and the VC action the following summer.

Auten, who was awarded the Distinguished Service Cross on 6 April 1918, went to Buckingham Palace on 18 September to receive his VC from King George V. As he marched forward to be decorated the band struck up 'Hush, Hush, Here Comes the Bogeyman,' and an amused Auten would cheerfully refer to himself by that nickname for the rest of his life. At the time Auten was engaged in commissioning the ex-collier *Suffolk Coast*, his fourth Q-ship. On 10 November she sailed out of Queenstown for gunnery trials. The following day, bad weather forced her to put into Milford Haven, where he was greeted by a chorus of ships' hooters signalling the signing of the Armistice. Instead of fighting U-boats, *Suffolk Coast* became a 'show ship' touring home ports to raise money for naval charities.

In 1919 Auten published his memoirs, *Q Boat Adventures*. This book, the first to be written by a decoy commander, ran to several editions and helped inspire the silent movie 'Q-Ships, Vampires of the Deep', on which Auten acted as technical adviser. Perhaps encouraged by his new-found success, Auten abandoned any thoughts of resuming his Merchant Navy career and from 1922 made his way in the film business. It proved a sound decision. He rose to become executive vice-president of the Rank Organisation in New York and later became the American representative for the Australian-based Greater

Union Theatres. He also held a post with United Artists for a number of years. For almost thirty years he lived in Bushkill, Pennsylvania, a small village about 95 miles from New York. From there he variously ran a small antiques business and the extensive Bushkill Manor motel complex, as well as the local playhouse, both of which he owned.

Remembered by his secretary Shirley Shinaman as 'a tall, heavy set man', not unlike Alfred Hitchcock whom he knew, Auten had the stern, gruff manner of an old sea captain. He smoked heavily and walked with a noticeable limp, thought to have been the legacy of an attack of polio, but it did not stop him serving his country again during the Second World War. Auten, who remained in the RNR between the wars, had been promoted commander just five days before Britain's declaration of war. He held a senior post in the port of New York, where his efforts in organising convoys bound for Europe were later recognised by the awards of the United States Legion of Merit and the Dutch Order of Orange Nassau.

Harold Auten was twice married, first to Margaret, by whom he had two children, and then to Dagmar, who had worked as his secretary in New York. Both marriages ended in divorce.

Although not a particularly religious man, in 1948 Auten undertook to build a Catholic church in Bushkill, apparently in gratitude for the care given to him by nuns while he was growing up in England. His benevolence, however, proved a severe drain on his finances. By the early 1960s his business, which had suffered various setbacks, including a serious flood, was in trouble, although he continued to live in and operate the motel complex. When Harold Auten died of lung cancer in Monroe County Hospital on 3 October 1964, he left only debts.

'Penniless', he was buried in his secretary's family plot at Sandhill Cemetery, Bushkill, his name commemorated in the Church of St John that he built. (It is now a visitor centre.) He left no will and his medals were sent to his old school in London before being presented to the Royal Naval Museum, Portsmouth, where they are now held.

In a life rich in character and incident, Auten had proved himself a fearless and occasionally fearsome figure, as a fighting seaman, movie executive and entrepreneur. 'He was difficult to work for, but I got along fine with him,' said Mrs Shinaman. 'I think it was his voice that frightened people. It was the voice of a ship's captain. He gave orders and he expected you to follow him.'

Almost forty years after his death, his former secretary remembered him as a man who strove for the highest standards in all he did, but ultimately over-reached himself. 'Everything he did was top notch,' she recalled. 'Everything had to be A1 or nothing.'

SOURCES

The following collections have been consulted in the course of my research: The Lummis VC files at the National Army Museum, London; RN Submarine Museum, Gosport; Royal Marines Museum, Southsea; The Public Record Office, Kew, Surrey; *The London Gazette* 1914–20 (HMSO).

Published Works

Anon, *Brig-Gen. R.B. Bradford VC, MC and his Brothers*, 1919
Anon, *From Dartmouth to the Dardanelles*, Wm Heinemann, 1916
Anon, *Jack Cornwell*, Hodder & Stoughton, 1917
Anon, *Register of the Victoria Cross*, This England, 1981
Auten, H., *Q-Boat Adventures*, Herbert Jenkins, 1919
Bell, 2nd Lt J. Keble, *The Glory of Zeebrugge and the Vindictive*, Chatto & Windus, 1918
Bingham, Cdr the Hon B., VC, *Falklands, Jutland and the Bight*, John Murray, 1919
Bishop, A., *Our Bravest and Our Best*, McGraw-Hill Ryerson, 1995
Boyle, W.H.D., *Gallant Deeds*, Gieves, 1919
Bridgland, A., *Sea Killers in Disguise*, Leo Cooper, 1999
Brodie, C.G., *Forlorn Hope 1915*, Frederick Books, 1956
Campbell, Rear Adm. G., *My Mystery Ships*, Hodder & Stoughton, 1928
——, *Number Thirteen*, Hodder & Stoughton, 1932
Carpenter, Capt. A.F.B., VC, *The Blocking of Zeebrugge*, Herbert Jenkins, 1922
Cato, C. (C. Cox), *The Navy in Mesopotamia 1914 to 1917*, Constable, 1918
Charlewood, C.J., OBE, DSC, RD, RNR, *Channels, Cloves and Coconuts, The Western Press,* nd

Chatterton, E.K., *Q-Ships and their Story*, Conway Maritime Press, 1972

Corbett, Sir J.S., *Naval Operations: Official History*, Vols I–V

Creagh, Sir O'Moore & Humphris, E.M., *The VC and DSO*, Standard Art Book Company, 1924

Crook, M.J., *The Evolution of the Victoria Cross*, Midas Books, 1975

Halpern, P.G., *The Battle of the Otranto Straits*, Indiana University Press, 2004

Halpern, P.G. (ed.), *The Keyes Papers 1914–1918*, Vol 1, Navy Records Society, 1972

Harvey, D., *Monuments to Courage*, Kevin and Kay Patience, 1999

Holloway, S.M., *From Trench and Turret*, Royal Marines Museum, nd

——, *The Three Old Portmuthian VCs*, Portsmouth Grammar School Monographs No. 2, 1998

Howard, G., *'Gunner Billy'*, The Navy Museum, Devonport, Auckland, 2007

Jameson, W., *Submariners VC*, Davies, 1962

Kendall, P., *The Zeebrugge Raid 1918: 'The Finest Feat of Arms'*, Spellmount, 2008

Kirby, H.L. & Walsh, R.R., *The Four Blackburn VCs*, THCL Books, 1986

Lake, D., *Smoke and Mirrors: Q-Ships against the U-boats in the First World War*, Sutton Publishing, 2006.

——, *The Zeebrugge and Ostend Raids 1918*, Pen & Sword, 2002.

Lindsay, S., *Merseyside Heroes: A Collection of Biographical Notes*, privately published, 1988

Little, M., *The Royal Marines Victoria Crosses*, Royal Marines Museum, 1986

Masters, D., *ID: New Tales of the Submarine War*, Eyre & Spottiswoode, 1935

Nunn, Vice-Adm. W., *Tigris Gunboats*, Melrose, 1932

Pillinger, D. & Staunton, A., *Victoria Cross Locator*, revised & updated 2nd edn, 1997

——, *Victoria Cross Presentations and Locations*, privately published, 2000

Pitt, B., *Zeebrugge: St George's Day, 1918*, Cassell, 1958

Ritchie, C., *Q-Ships*, Terence Dalton, 1985

Rudenno, V., *Gallipoli: Attack from the Sea*, Yale University Press, 2008

Satterthwaite, S., *Bonner VC*, SR Print Management, 2008

Shankland, P. & Hunter, A., *Dardanelles Patrol*, Collins, 1964

Thomas, L., *Raiders of the Deep*, Doubleday, Doran & Co., 1928

Tisdall, Sub Lt A.W. St C., VC, *Verses, Letters and Remembrances*, Sidgwick & Jackson, 1916

Walter, J., *The Kaiser's Pirates*, Arms & Armour, 1994

Warner, P., *The Zeebrugge Raid*, William Kimber, 1978

Wester Wemyss, Lady, *The Life and Letters of Lord Wester Wemyss, Admiral of the Fleet*, Eyre & Spottiswoode, 1935

Wester Wemyss, Lord, *The Navy in the Dardanelles Campaign*, Hodder & Stoughton, 1924

Williams, W.A., *The VCs of Wales and the Welsh Regiments*, Bridge Books, 1984

Willis, C.J. & Rogers, D.F., *For Valour: HMS Conway & HMS Worcester*, Conway Club & Assn of Old Worcesters, 1984

Wilson, M. & Kemp, P., *Mediterranean Submarines*, Crecy, 1997

Winton, J., *The Victoria Cross at Sea*, Michael Joseph, 1979

Yuyama-Knippel, M., *John Travers Cornwell VC, 1900–1916*, privately published, nd

Articles & Periodicals

Together with numerous newspaper reports, the following have been particularly useful:

Captain B.H. Smith, 'Dardanelles Details', *Naval Review 24*, 1936

John Marshall, 'The Otaki Shield', nd

'Major F.J.W. Harvey VC, RMLI', *Globe and Laurel*, April 1973

'George Samson's Adventures with Midshipman Drewry VC', George Samson, *Sunday Post* special series of articles, September 1915

Albert McKenzie VC, website, by Colin McKenzie, with much information on Zeebrugge, http://www.mckenzie.uk.com

The *Sunday Graphic and Sunday News* ran an informative series of articles in 1935:

'Holbrook VC – The Man who Scared the Turkish Navy', Boatswain T. Davey DSM, 19 May; 'Sandford VC – The Man Who Blew Up Zeebrugge Mole', Petty Officer W.G. Cleaver CGM, DSM, 26 May; 'Peel Ritchie Won His VC in the "Abode of Peace"', Petty Officer T.J. Clark CGM, 2 June; 'Auten VC and his Gallant Q-Ship', Petty Officer T.R. Cunningham DSM, 9 June; 'Loftus Jones VC – A Hero of Jutland', Petty Officer W.C.R. Griffin DSM, 16 June

Unpublished Papers

H.P. Ritchie: W. Westall (letter via W. Westall); N.D. Holbrook: Report
of Proceedings of Submarine B11 (PRO), G. Holbrook (family papers
via R. Matthews), W.C. Mortimer DSM (letter via D. Mortimer); E.G.
Robinson: P. Millen and S. Clayton (family papers); E. Unwin: Captain
H.C. Lockyer (letters, IWM), Vice-Adm. R.E. Wemyss (reports, IWM);
G.L. Drewry: G.L. Drewry (letters, IWM), H. Thorne (family papers);
W. St A. Malleson: H. St A. Malleson (correspondence), J.P. Macintyre
(family papers); G. McK. Samson: C. MacDonald, N.S. Kogut and M.S.
Robertson (family papers); W.C. Williams: Chepstow Museum (various
papers via A. Rainsbury); A.W. St C. Tisdall: J.C. Wedgwood (letters,
PRO); D. Heald (research notes); E.C. Boyle: Report of Proceedings
of Submarine E14, 27.4.15–18.5.15 (RN Submarine Museum),
J.T. Haskins DSM (diary, IWM); E.G. Stanley DSC (Passage of the
Dardanelles by E14, RN Submarine Museum); M.E. Nasmith: M.E.
Nasmith (Some Recollections of Submarine Work in the Sea of Marmora
in 1915, IWM), Report of Proceedings of Submarine E11, 19.5.15–
7.6.15 (IWM), E. Lohden DSM (diary, RN Submarine Museum),
H. Plowman DSM (diary, RN Submarine Museum), A. Jordan (bio-
graphical notes and references); F.D. Parslow: M. Finlay and A. Walker
(family papers), P.M.B. Barber (research notes); F.J.W. Harvey: R. More
(family papers), H. Willons (Reminiscences of Q Turret, HMS *Lion*,
National Maritime Museum); E.B.S. Bingham: North Down Heritage
Centre (various papers via I. Wilson); J.T. Cornwell: N. Lawson (Captain
R. Lawson letters), M. Yuyama-Knippel (correspondence), R.A. Strong
(research notes), Stratford Library and archives (various papers via R.
Durack), The Scout Association archives (various papers via P. Styles);
L.W. Jones: J. Walker (family papers); R.N. Stuart: I. Stuart (family
papers and recollections), C. Buchanan (research notes), Canadian
Pacific Archives (various papers via S. Lyons); W. Williams: K. Williams
(research notes), T. Roberts (recollections); E. Pitcher: P. Strickland
and G. Willey (family details); A.B. Smith: Robert Gordon's College
(various papers), J. Thoirs (research notes), A. Park (research notes),
N. Newlands (family papers), Kapitanleutnant Hermann A.K. Jung
(diary extracts via Brian Lockhart); S. Rabson (P&O archives); W.E.
Sanders: T. McRae (family papers); J. Watt: G. Macdonald (F. Lamb
details), Fraserburgh Library (various papers), J.M. Cameron (research
notes); T. Crisp: T.W. Crisp (unpublished memoir), D. Hague (family
papers), Chambers Chronicle, Suffolk Record Office (various papers),
J. Blackman (recollections); J.H. Carless: Walsall library archives (various papers via L. Purchase); G.S. White: R. Perkins DSM (letter), RN

Submarine Museum (biographical notes); A.F.B. Carpenter: Wyedean School (Victoria Cross Trail), Gloucester Library (various papers), M. Burns (research notes); E. Bamford: RM Museum (various biographical papers), Maj. Gen. A.R. Chater (private papers), C. Lamplough (Zeebrugge narrative), Old Shirburnian Society (school records); N. Finch: R.E. Shaw (various papers and recollections), RM Museum (various biographical papers); G.N. Bradford: H. Moses (research notes), J. Cremer (family details); A.L. Harrison: Museum of Rugby, Twickenham (biographical notes and rugby career details), Old Dovorian Club (obituary), Wimbledon Library (various papers); A.E. McKenzie: C. McKenzie (various papers), Shaftesbury Homes & Arethusa (1918–19 annual report); R.D. Sandford: M. Wood and E. Sandford (family details), RN Submarine Museum (biographical notes); P.T. Dean: Blackburn Library (various papers via N. Monks); R.L. Bourke: J. McWilliam-Bourke (family papers and recollections), P.T. Maule (research notes); G.H. Drummond: M. Drummond (family papers and recollections); H. Auten: S. Shinaman (various papers and recollections).

INDEX